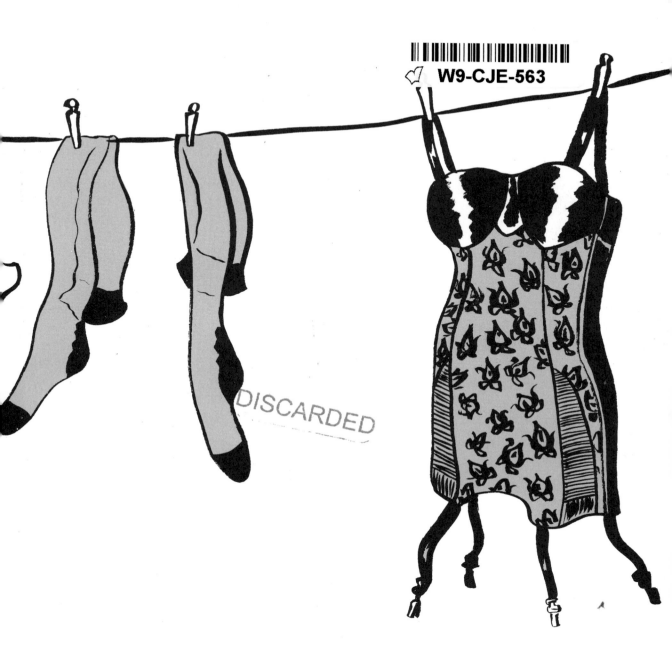

UNTERZAKHN

UNTERZAKHN
Leela Corman

Schocken Books, New York

This is a work of fiction. Names, characters, places, and incidents either are the product of the author's imagination or are used fictitiously. Any resemblance to actual persons, living or dead, events, or locales is entirely coincidental.

 Published in the United States by Schocken Books, a division of Random House, Inc., New York, and in Canada by Random House of Canada Limited, Toronto.

Schocken Books and colophon are registered trademarks of Random House, Inc.

Portions of this work were previously published in different form in the Forward and Lilith.

Library of Congress Cataloging-in-Publication Data

Corman, Leela.
Unterzakhn / Leela Corman.
p. cm.
ISBN 978-0-8052-4259-1
1. Twin sisters—Comic books, strips, etc. 2. Immigrants—New York (State)—New York—Comic books, strips, etc.
3. Lower East Side (New York, N.Y.)—Comic books, strips, etc. I. Title.
PN6727.C67U58 2012 741.5'973—dc23 2011043769

www.schocken.com

Jacket design by Leela Corman and Brian Barth

Printed in the United States of America

First Edition

2 4 6 8 9 7 5 3 1

For New York

1909

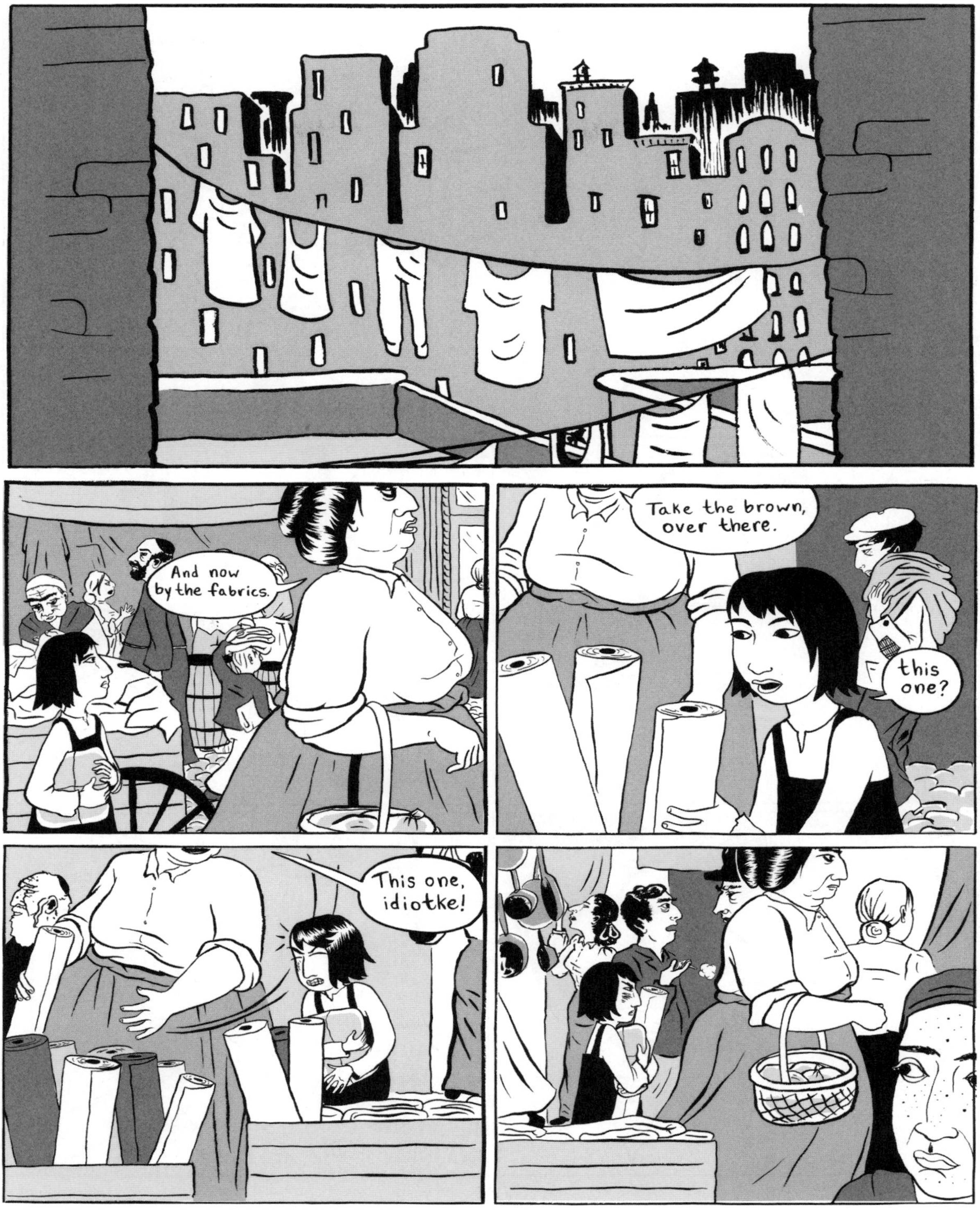
And now by the fabrics.
Take the brown, over there.
this one?
This one, idiotke!

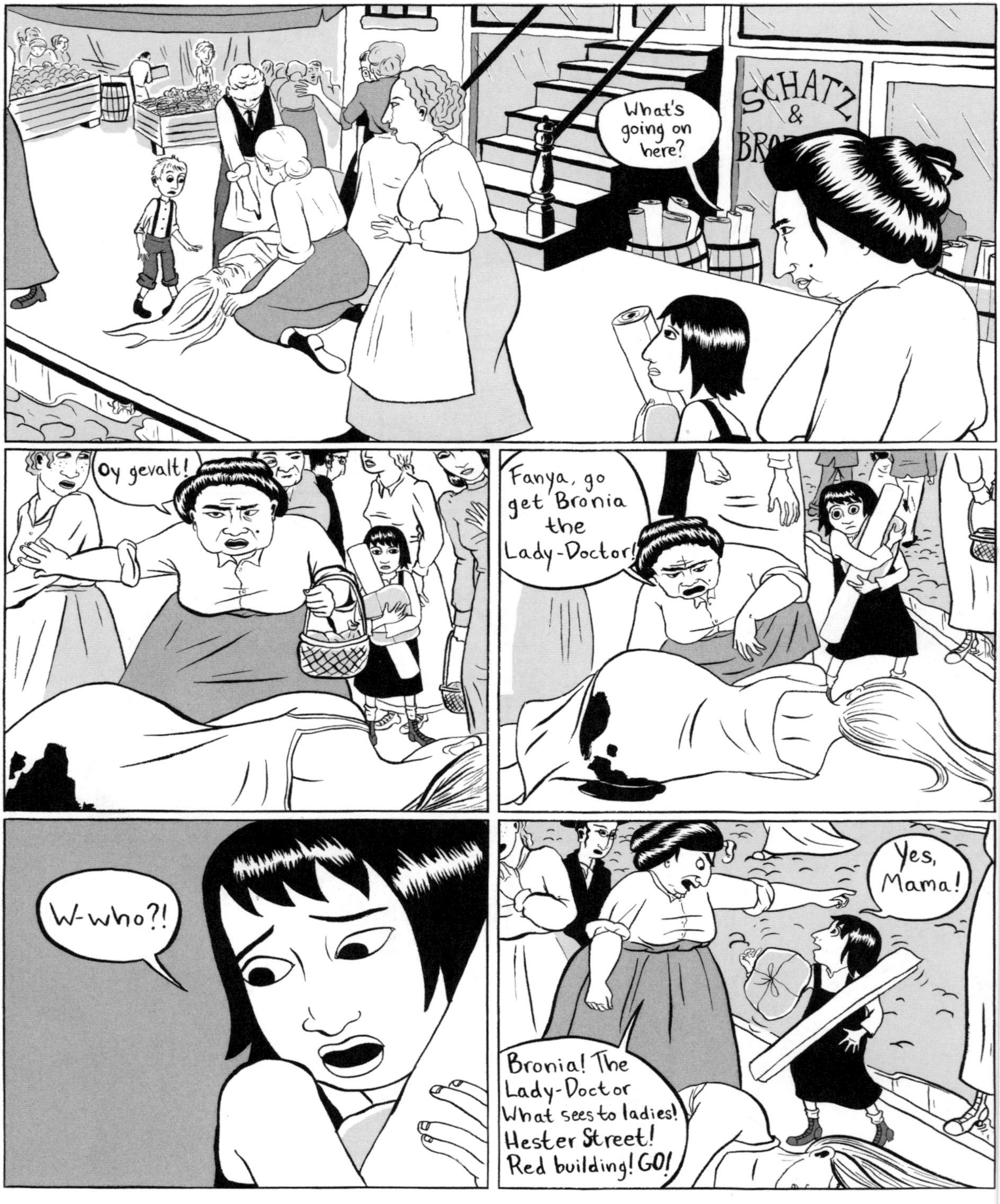
SCHATZ & BRO
What's going on here?
Oy gevalt!
Fanya, go get Bronia the Lady-Doctor!
W-who?!
Bronia! The Lady-Doctor What sees to ladies! Hester Street! Red building! GO!
Yes, Mama!

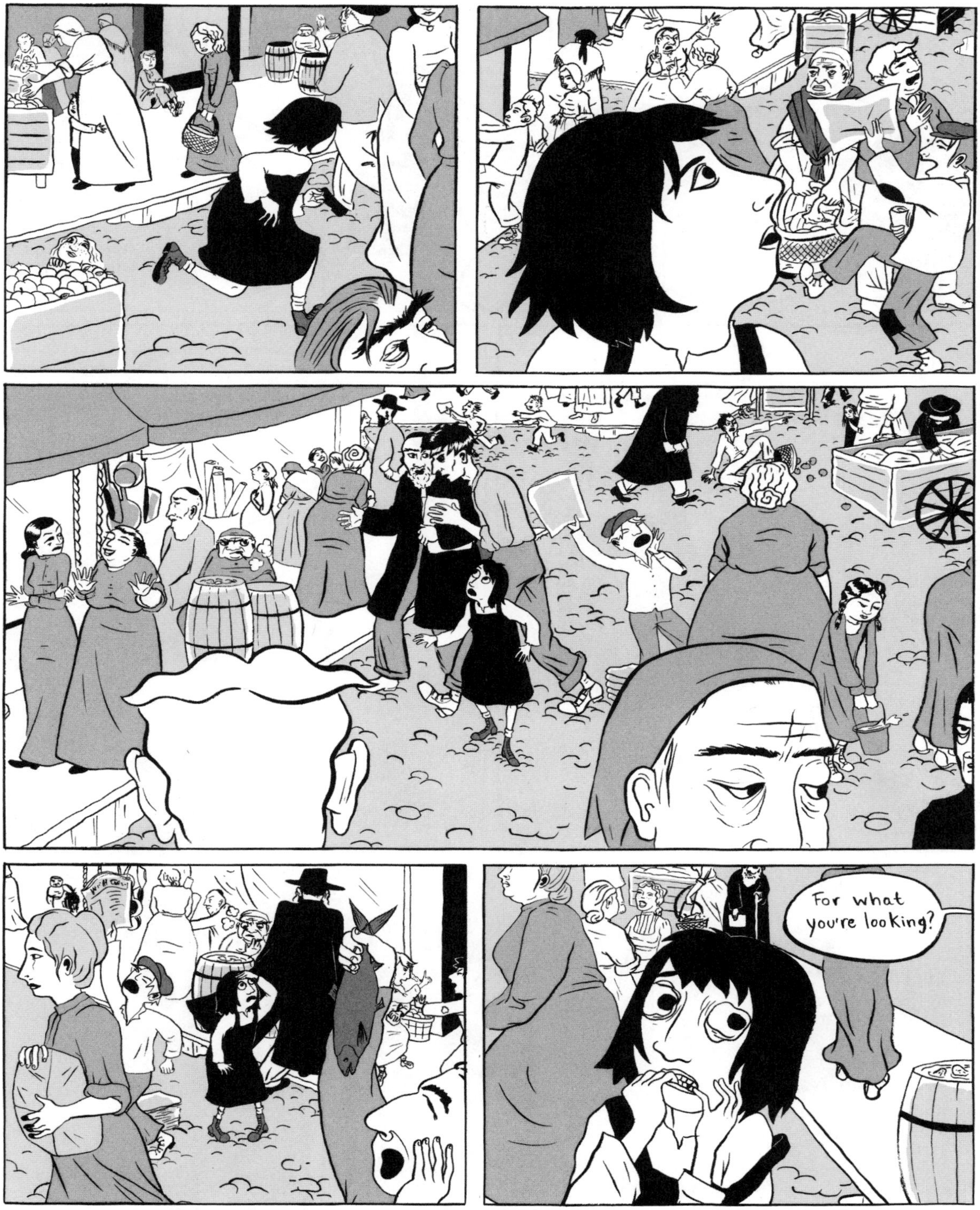
For what you're looking?

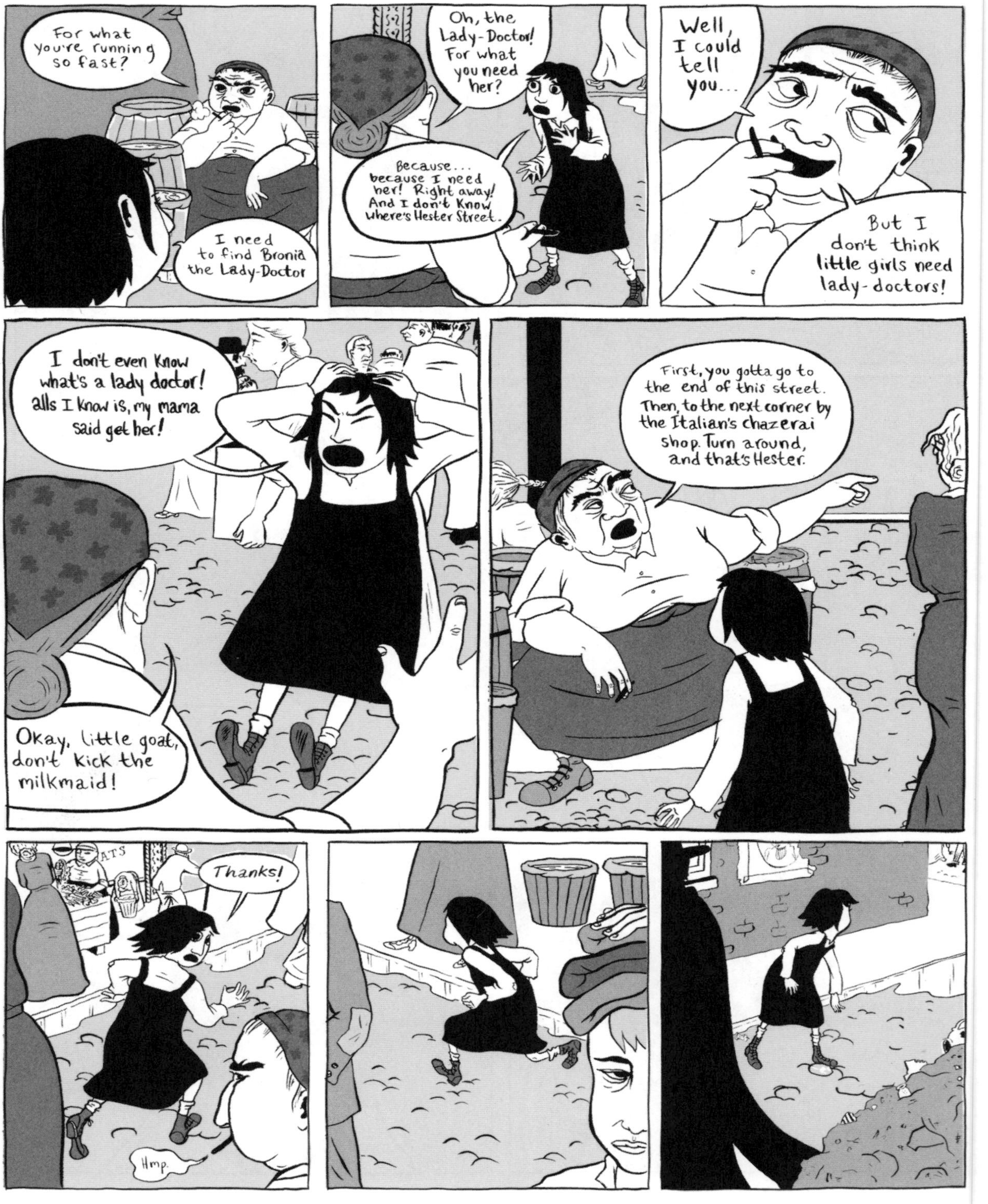
For what you're running so fast?
I need to find Bronia the Lady-Doctor
Oh, the Lady-Doctor! For what you need her?
Because... because I need her! Right away! And I don't Know where's Hester Street.
Well, I could tell you...
But I don't think little girls need lady-doctors!
I don't even Know what's a lady doctor! alls I Know is, my mama said get her!
Okay, little goat, don't kick the milkmaid!
First, you gotta go to the end of this street. Then, to the next corner by the Italian's chazerai shop. Turn around, and that's Hester.
Thanks!
Hmp.

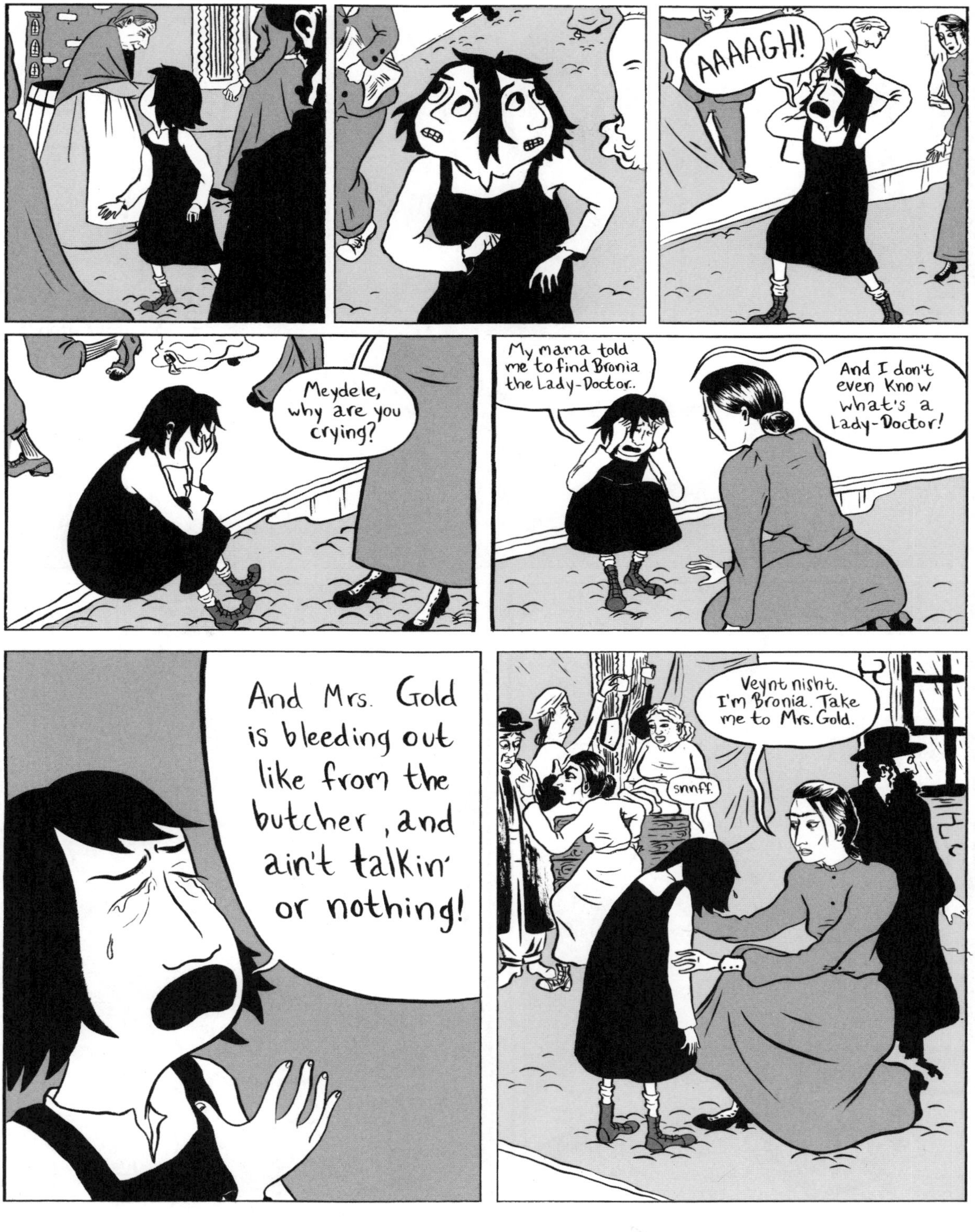
AAAAGH!
Meydele, why are you crying?
My mama told me to find Bronia the Lady-Doctor..
And I don't even Know what's a Lady-Doctor!
And Mrs. Gold is bleeding out like from the butcher, and ain't talkin' or nothing!
Veynt nisht. I'm Bronia. Take me to Mrs. Gold.
snnff.

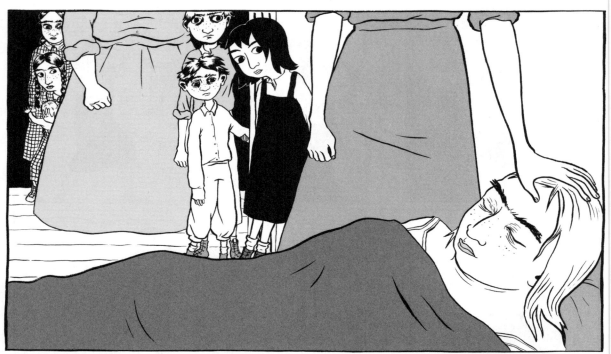

Children, your mama needs to rest for a bit. Could you go to Mrs. Feinberg's for a little while?

Minna, I think it's best if you keep the little ones with you for now, and send Fanya to fetch Mr. Gold.

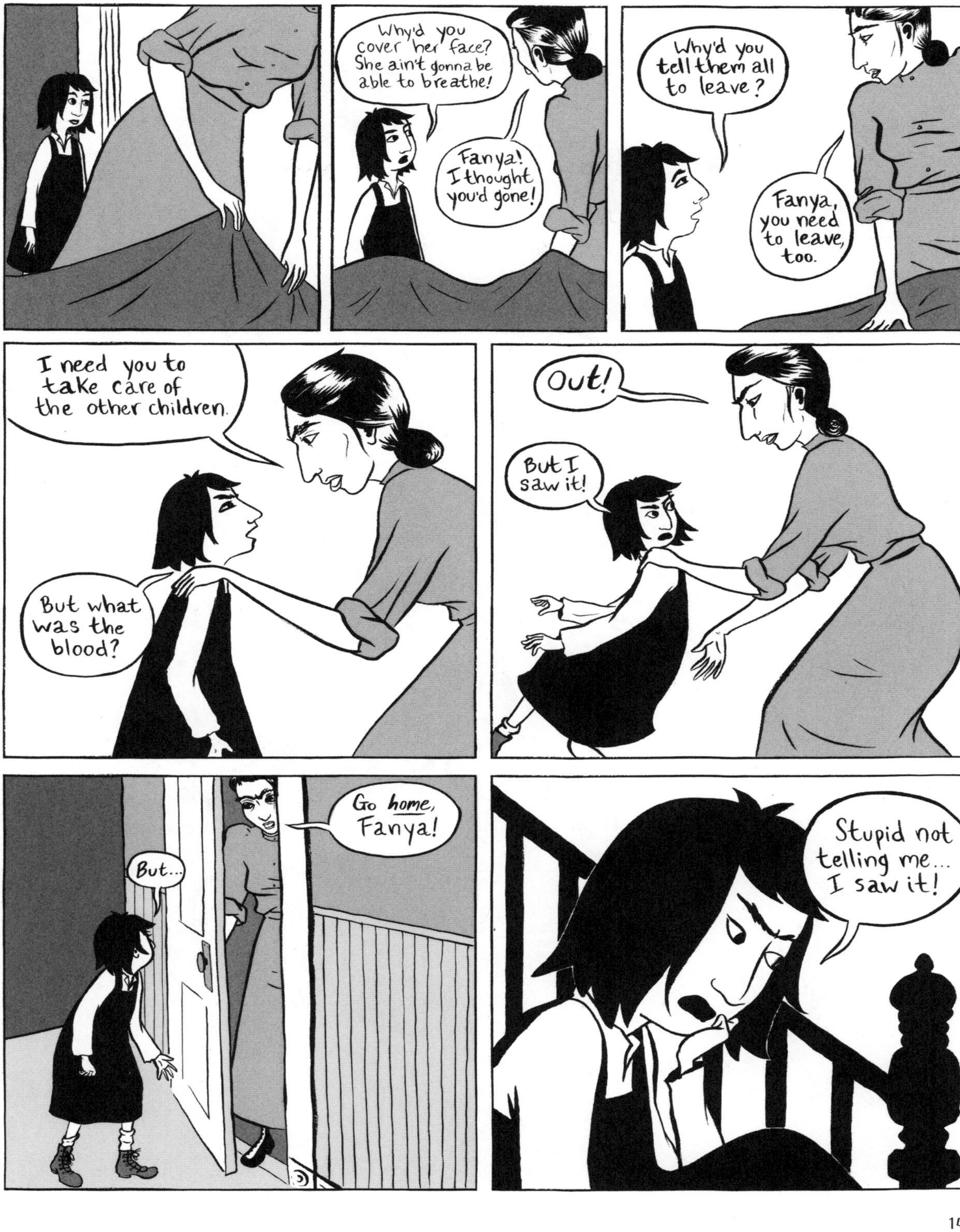
Why'd you cover her face? She ain't gonna be able to breathe!
Fanya! I thought you'd gone!
Why'd you tell them all to leave?
Fanya, you need to leave, too.
I need you to take care of the other children.
But what was the blood?
Out!
But I saw it!
But...
Go home, Fanya!
Stupid not telling me... I saw it!

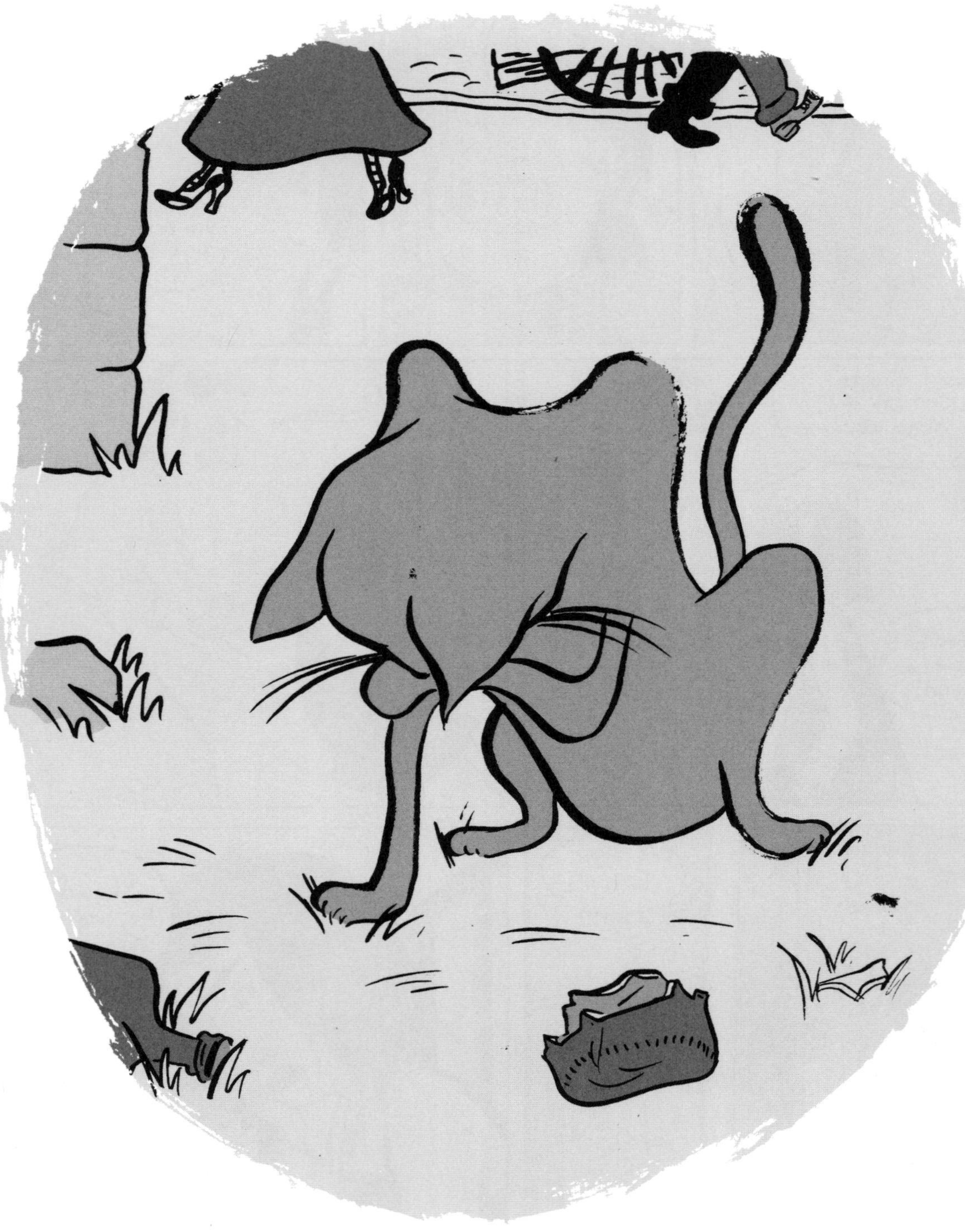

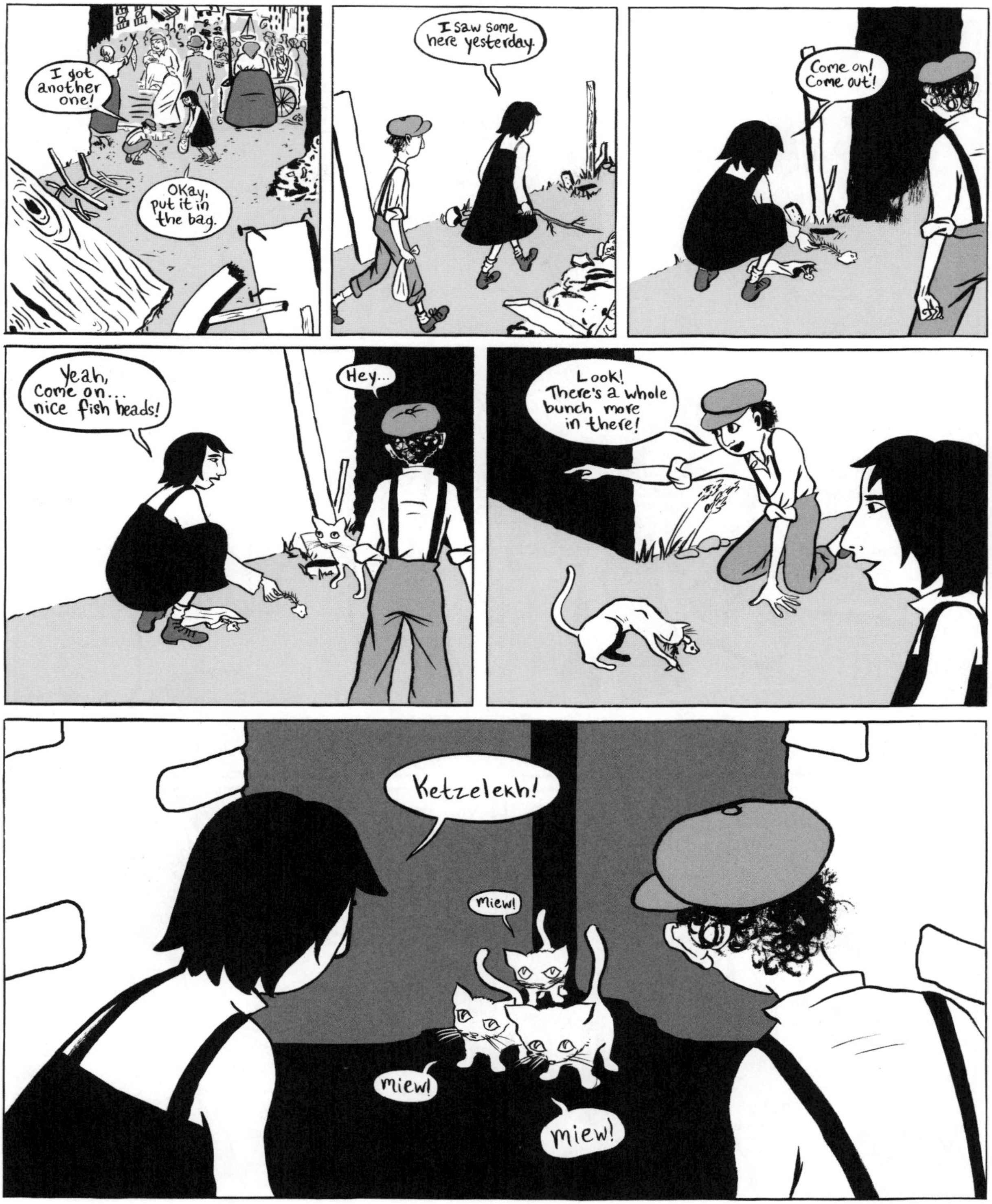
I got another one!
OKay, put it in the bag.
I saw some here yesterday.
Come on! Come out!
Yeah, come on... nice fish heads!
Hey...
Look! There's a whole bunch more in there!
Ketzelekh!
miew!
miew!
miew!

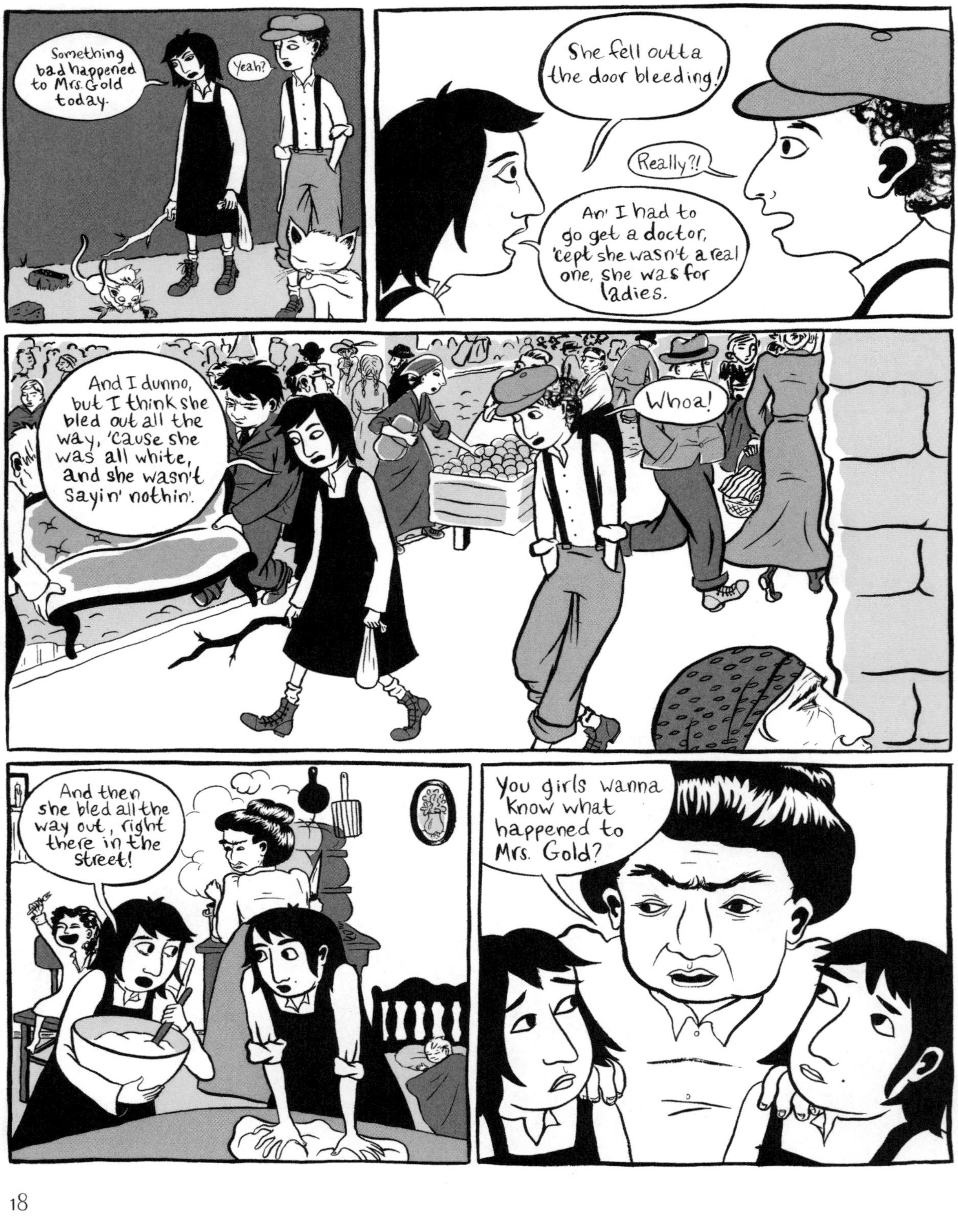
Something bad happened to Mrs. Gold today.
Yeah?
She fell outta the door bleeding!
Really?!
An' I had to go get a doctor, 'cept she wasn't a real one, she was for ladies.
And I dunno, but I think she bled out all the way, 'cause she was all white, and she wasn't sayin' nothin'.
Whoa!
And then she bled all the way out, right there in the street!
You girls wanna know what happened to Mrs. Gold?

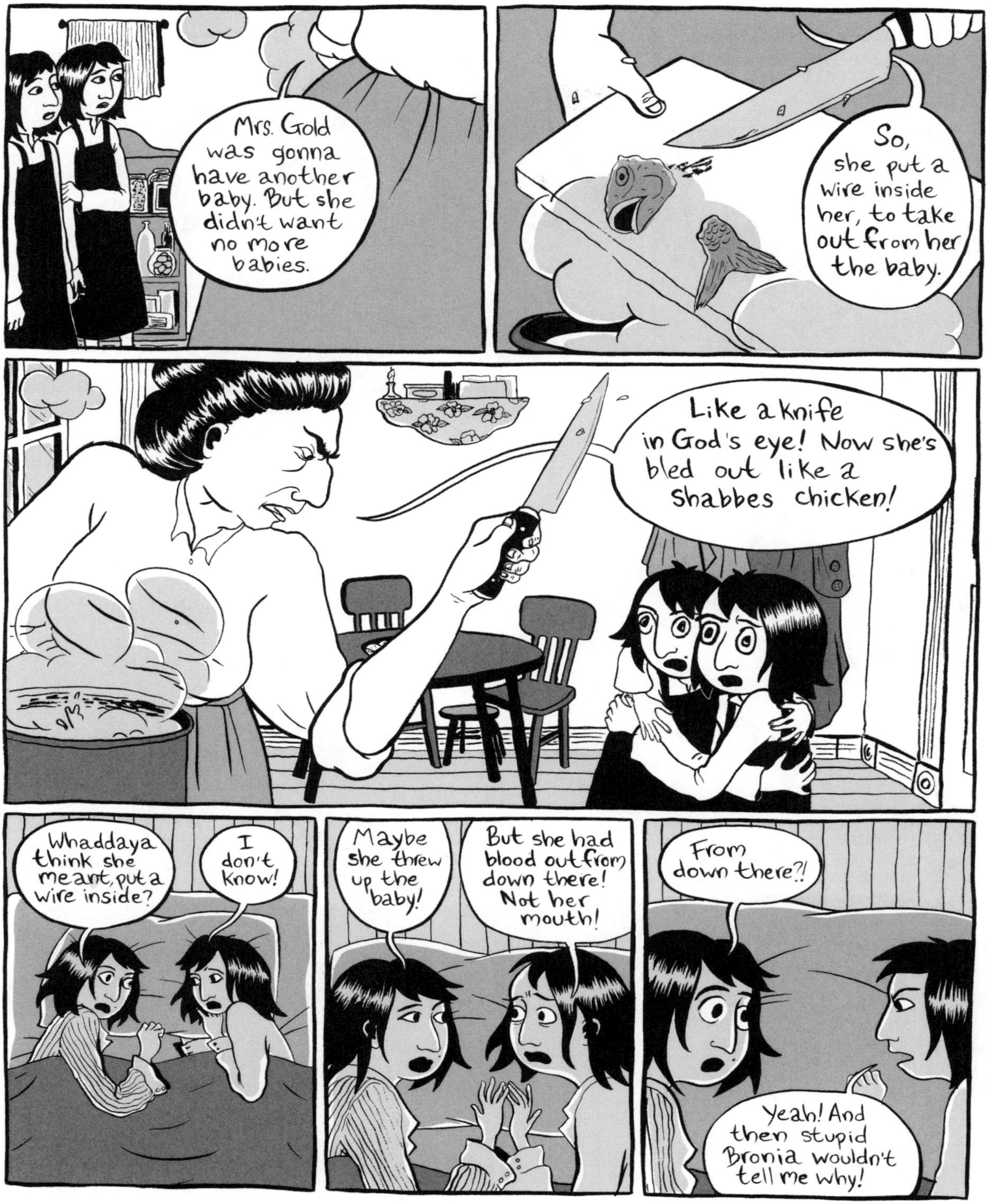

Mrs. Gold was gonna have another baby. But she didn't want no more babies.
So, she put a wire inside her, to take out from her the baby.
Like a knife in God's eye! Now she's bled out like a Shabbes chicken!
Whaddaya think she meant, put a wire inside?
I don't know!
Maybe she threw up the baby!
But she had blood out from down there! Not her mouth!
From down there?!
Yeah! And then stupid Bronia wouldn't tell me why!

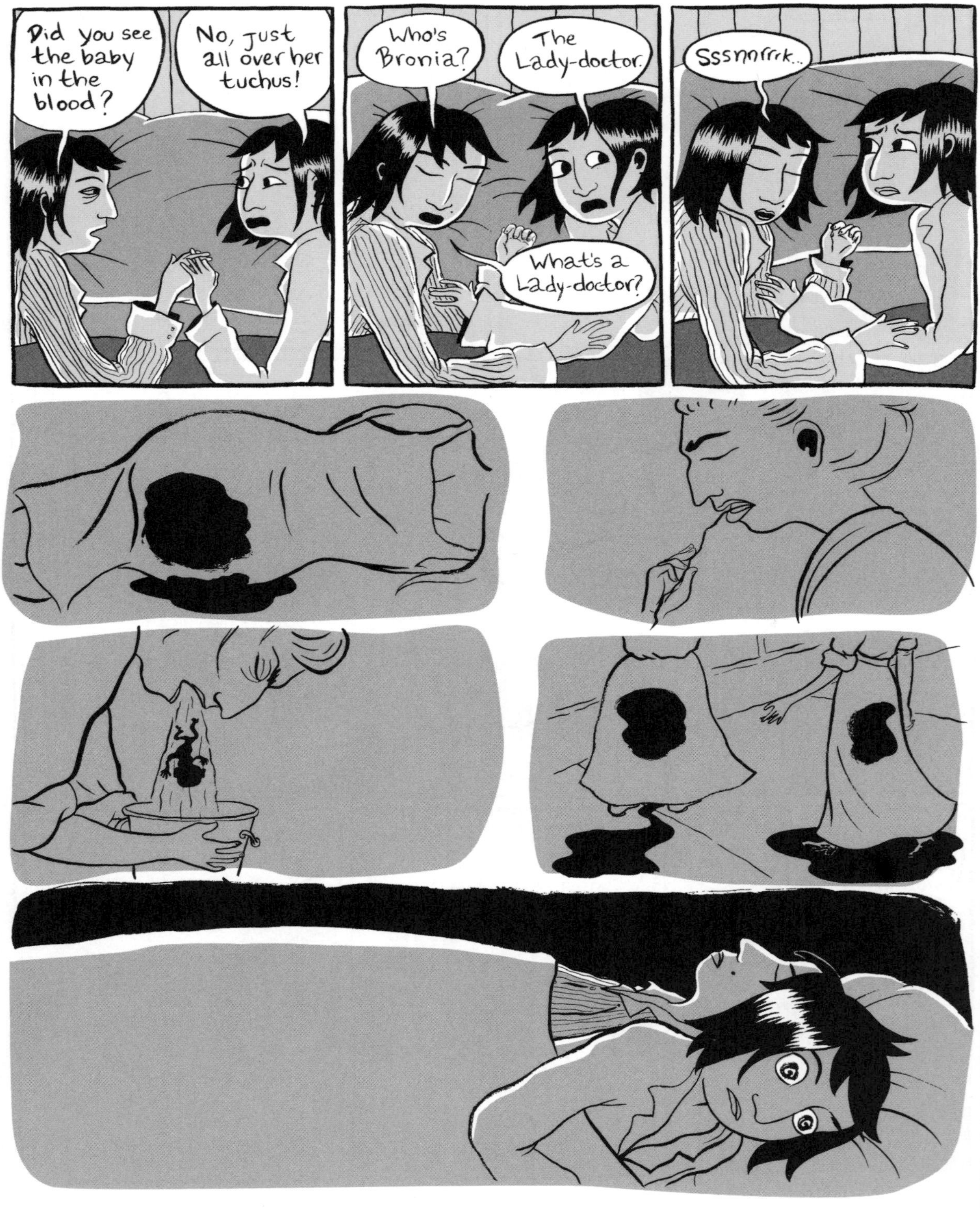
Did you see the baby in the blood?
No, just all over her tuchus!
Who's Bronia?
The Lady-doctor.
What's a Lady-doctor?
Sssnnrrrk...

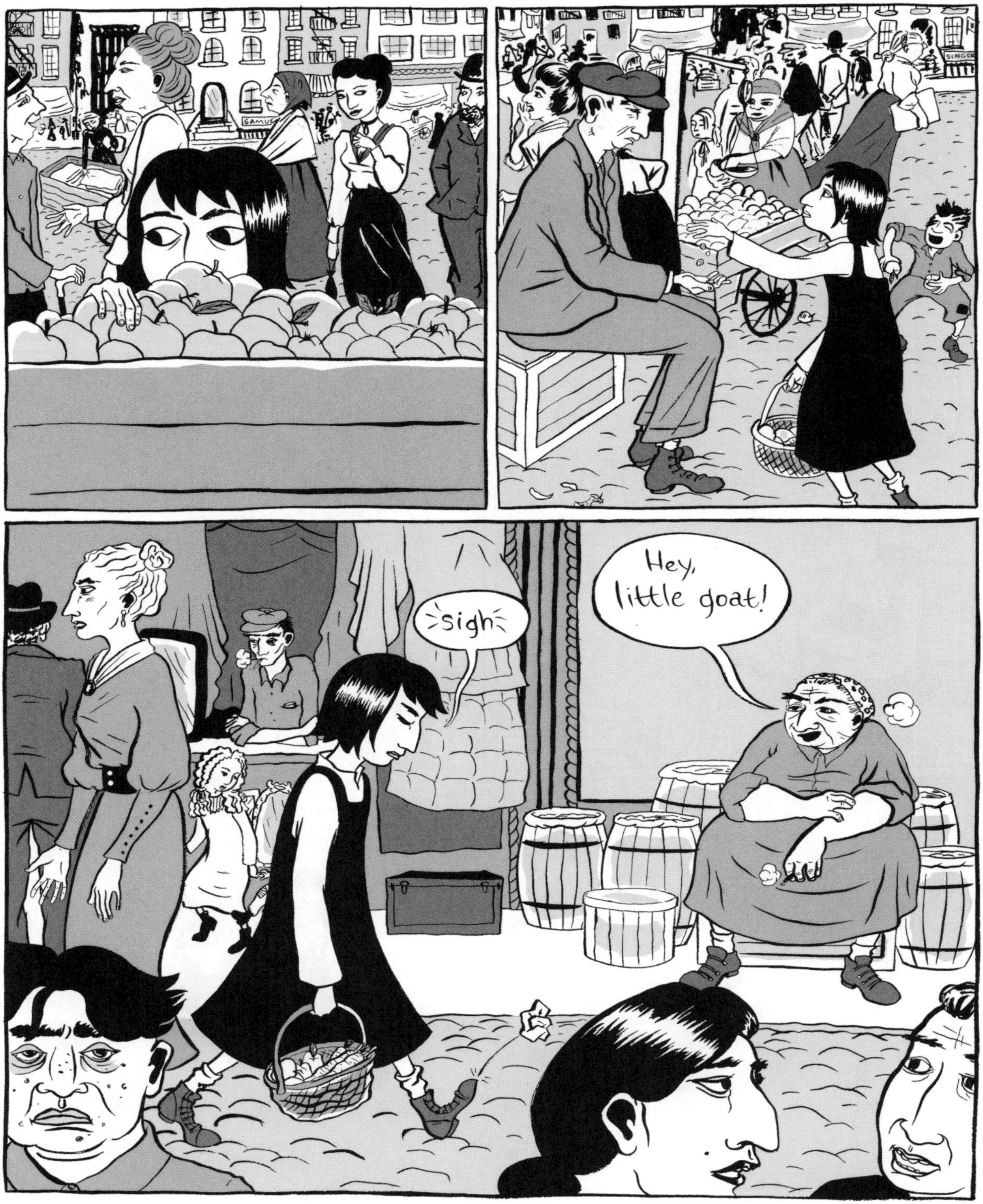
sigh
Hey, little goat!

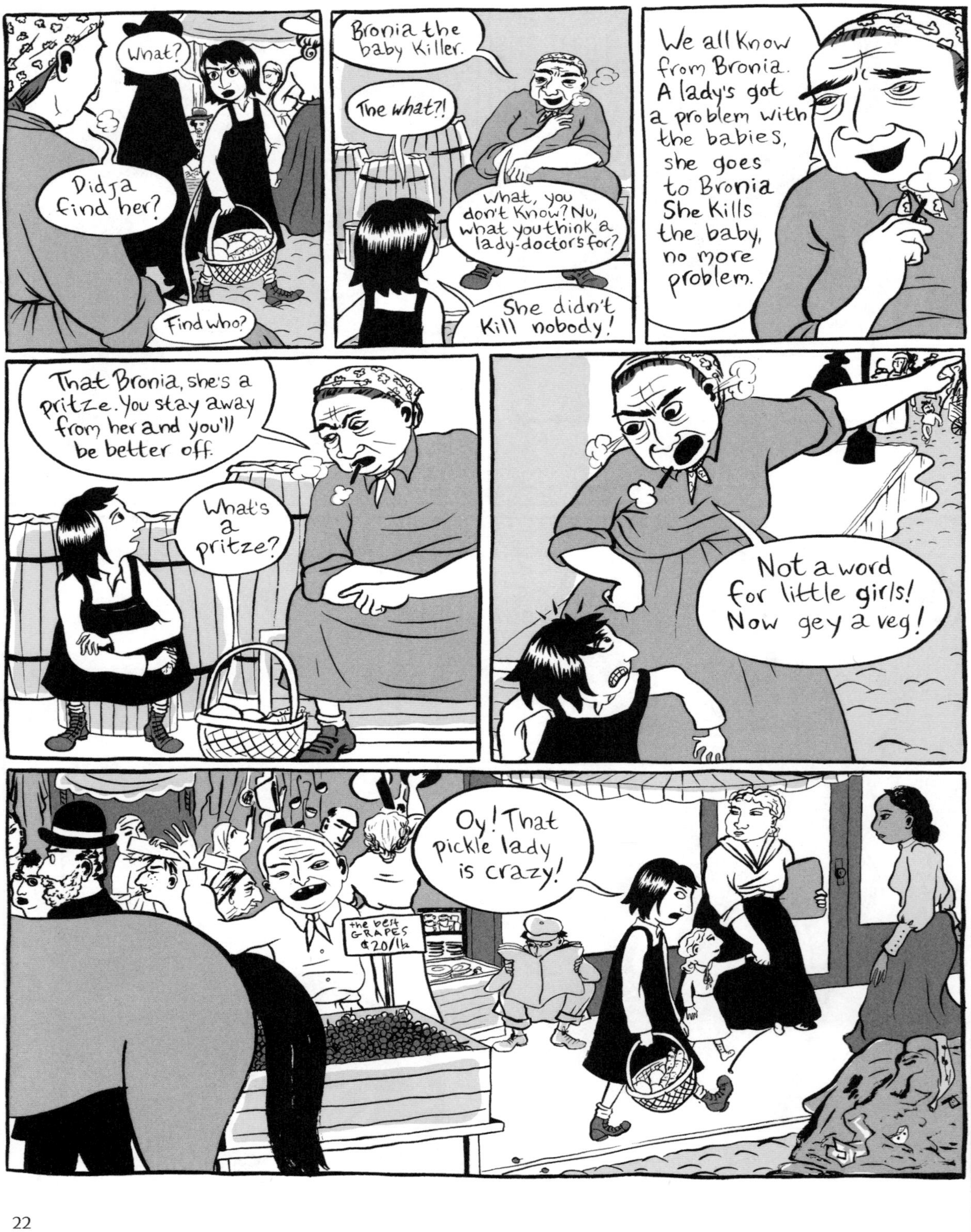
What?
Didja find her?
Find who?
Bronia the baby Killer.
The what?!
What, you don't Know? Nu, what you think a lady-doctor's for?
She didn't Kill nobody!
We all Know from Bronia. A lady's got a problem with the babies, she goes to Bronia She Kills the baby, no more problem.
That Bronia, she's a pritze. You stay away from her and you'll be better off.
What's a pritze?
Not a word for little girls! Now gey a veg!
Oy! That pickle lady is crazy!
the best GRAPES ¢20/lb

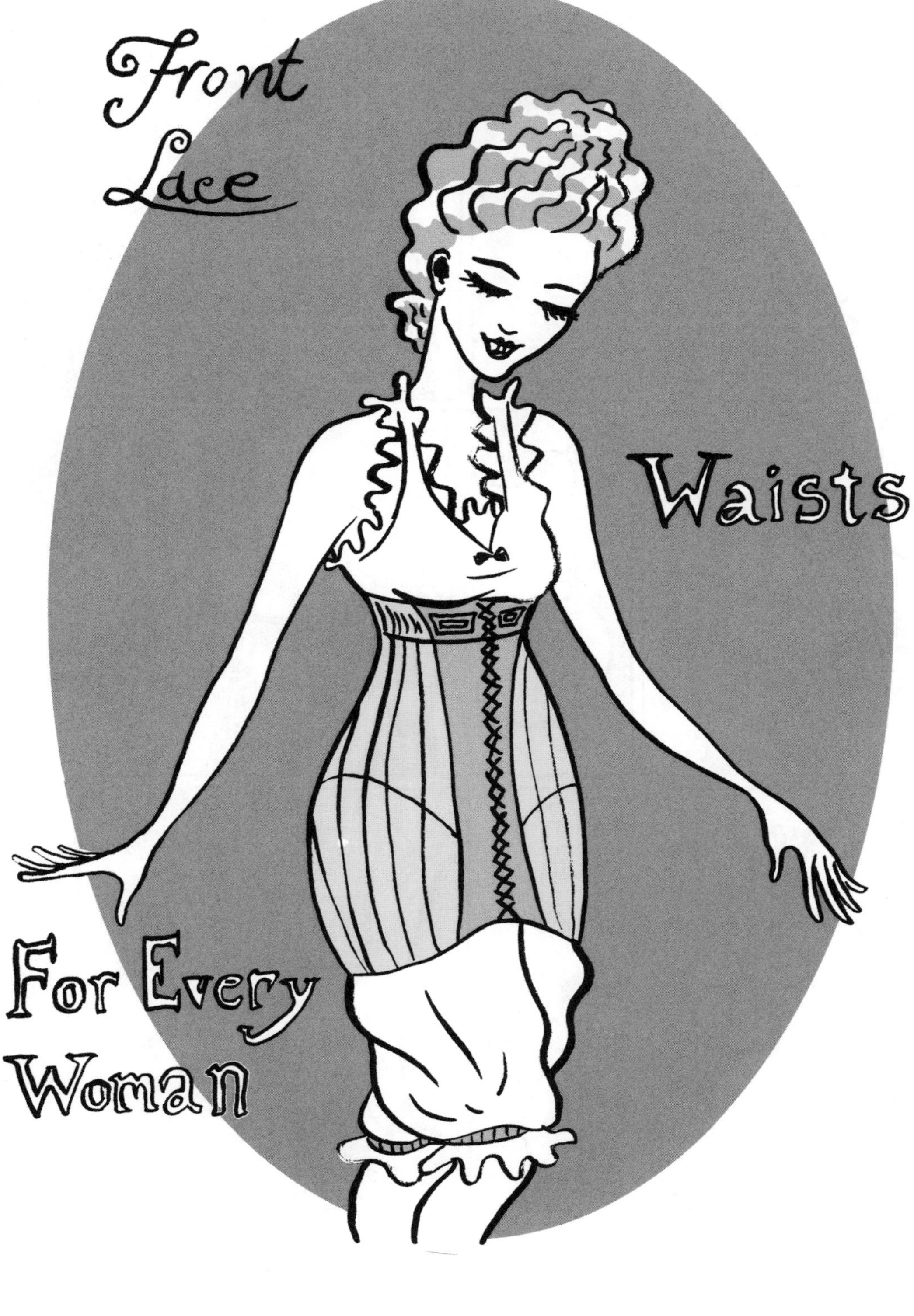
Front Lace
Waists
For Every Woman

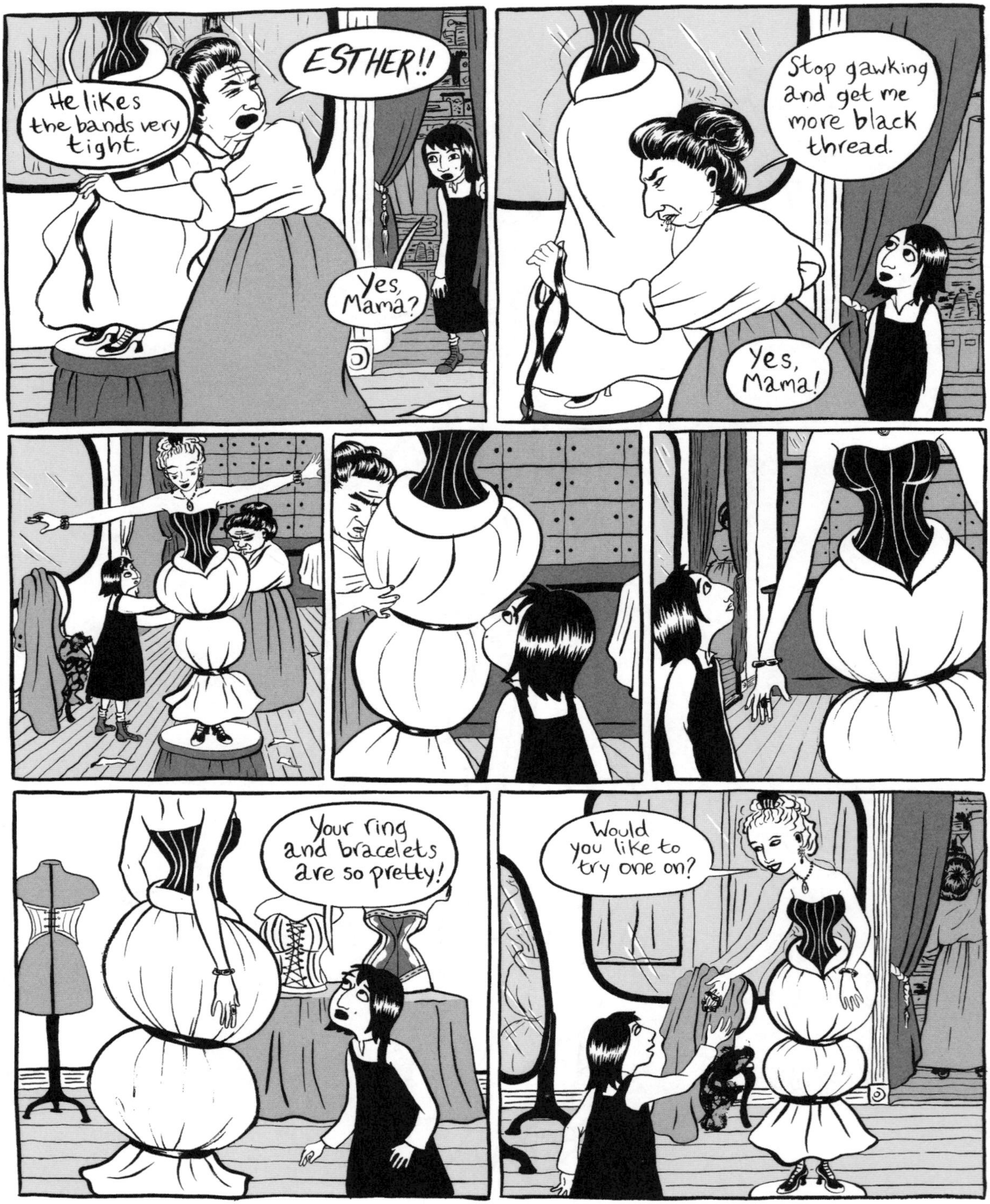
He likes the bands very tight.
ESTHER!!
Yes, Mama?
Stop gawking and get me more black thread.
Yes, Mama!
Your ring and bracelets are so pretty!
Would you like to try one on?

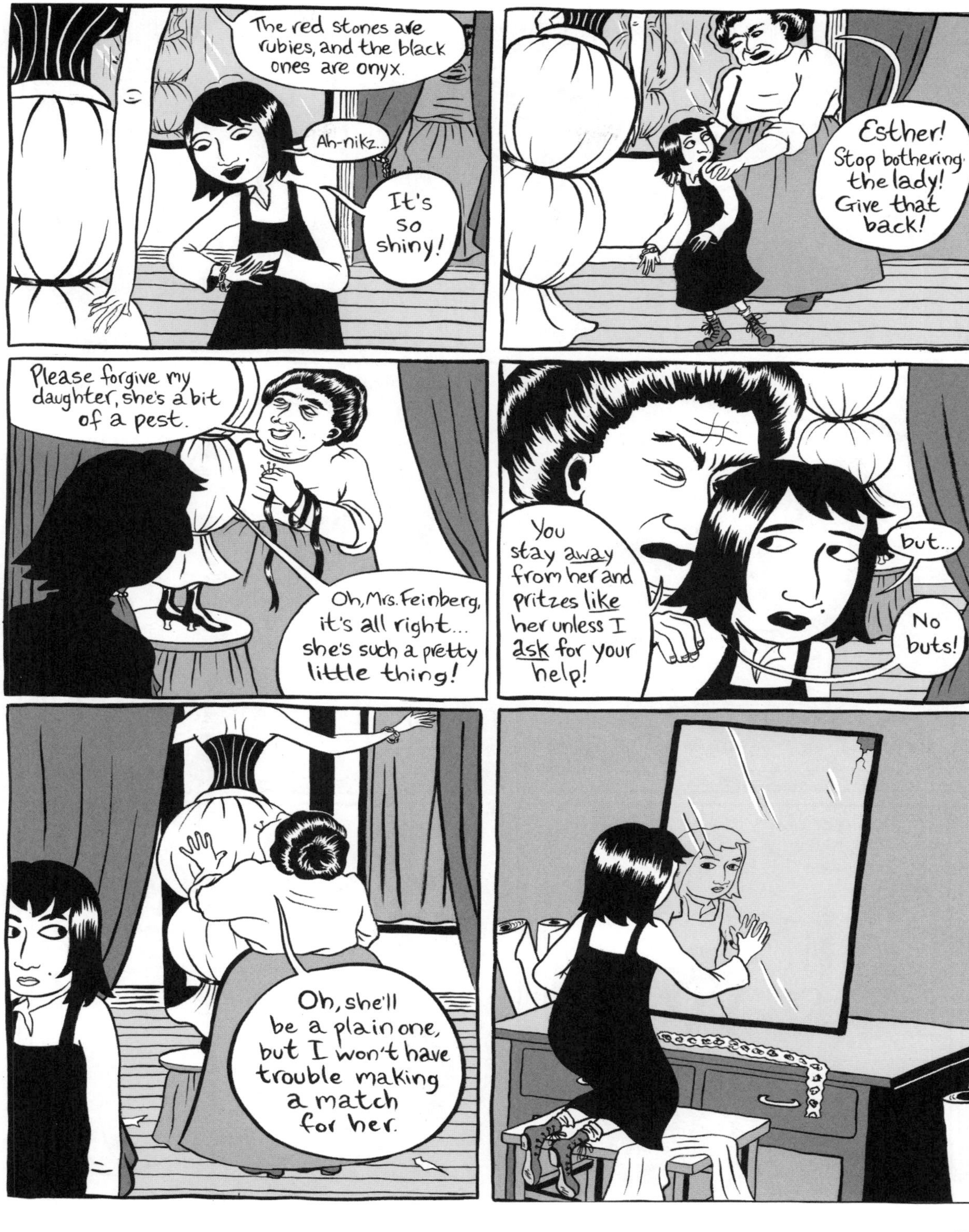
The red stones are rubies, and the black ones are onyx.
Ah-nikz...
It's so shiny!
Esther! Stop bothering the lady! Give that back!
Please forgive my daughter, she's a bit of a pest.
Oh, Mrs. Feinberg, it's all right... she's such a pretty little thing!
You stay away from her and pritzes like her unless I ask for your help!
but...
No buts!
Oh, she'll be a plain one, but I won't have trouble making a match for her.

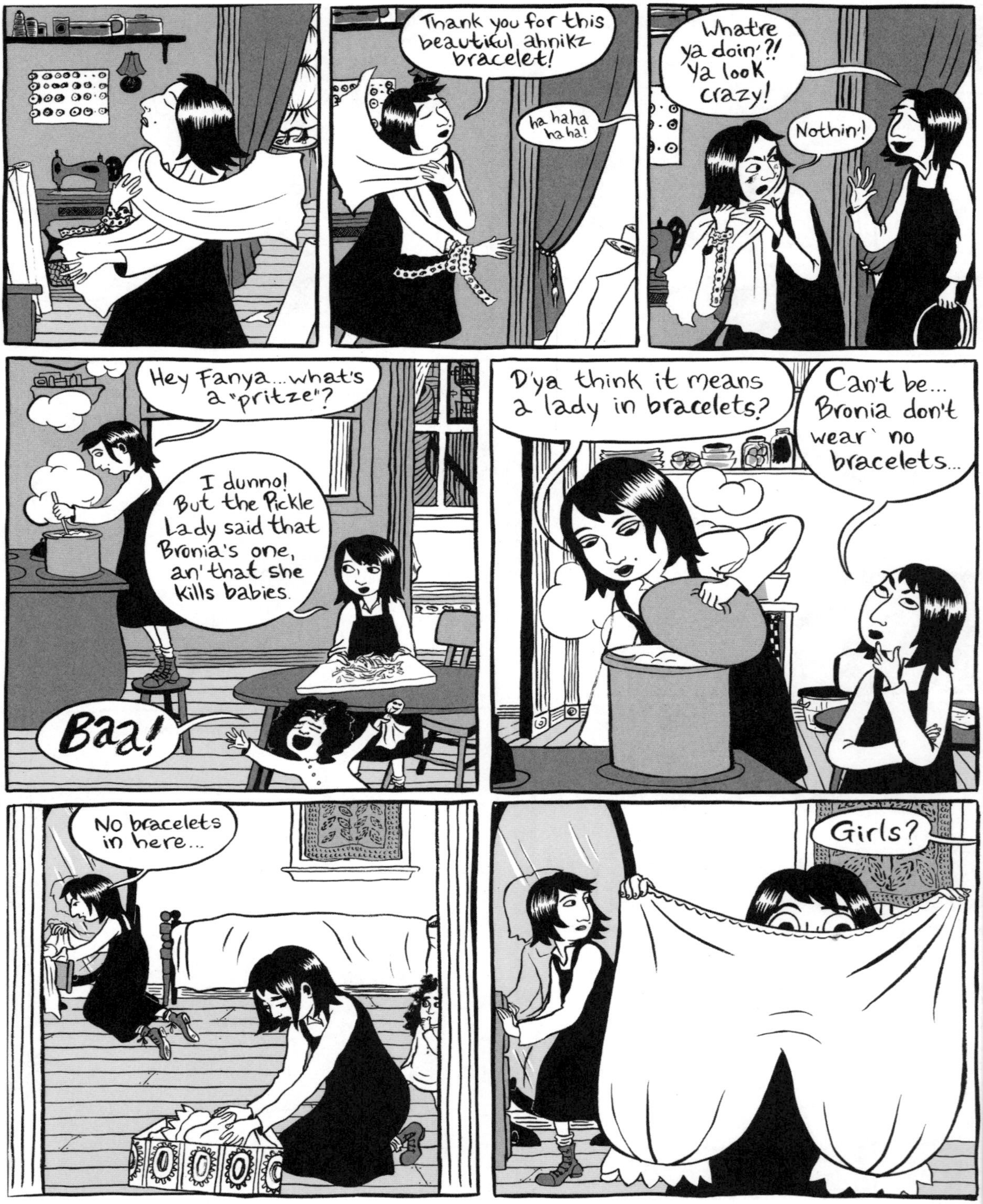

Thank you for this beautiful ahnikz bracelet!
ha ha ha ha ha!
What're ya doin'?! Ya look crazy!
Nothin'!
Hey Fanya...what's a "pritze"?
I dunno! But the Pickle Lady said that Bronia's one, an' that she kills babies.
Baa!
D'ya think it means a lady in bracelets?
Can't be... Bronia don't wear no bracelets...
No bracelets in here...
Girls?

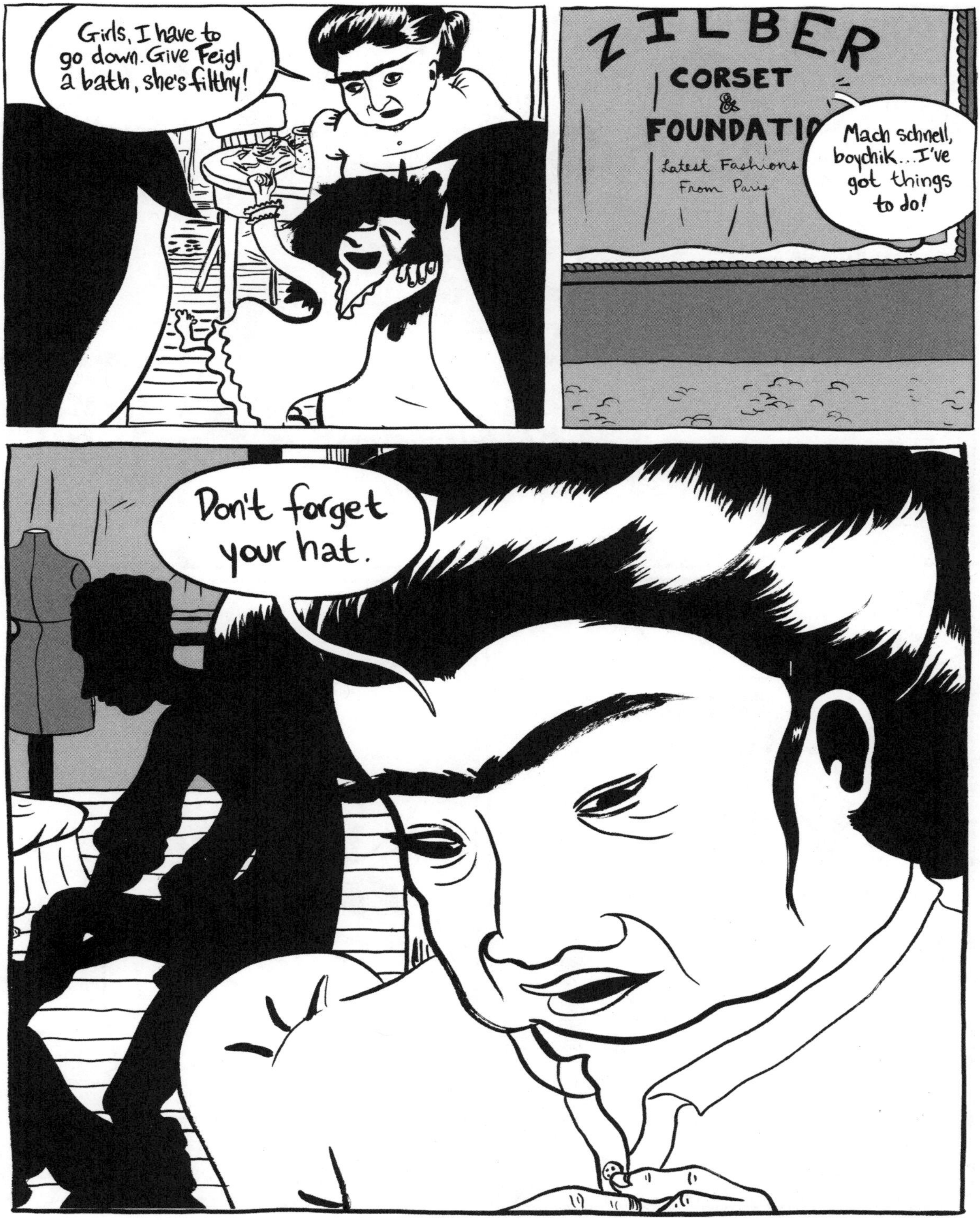
Girls, I have to go down. Give Feigl a bath, she's filthy!
ZILBER
CORSET & FOUNDATIO
Latest Fashions From Paris
Mach schnell, boychik... I've got things to do!
Don't forget your hat.

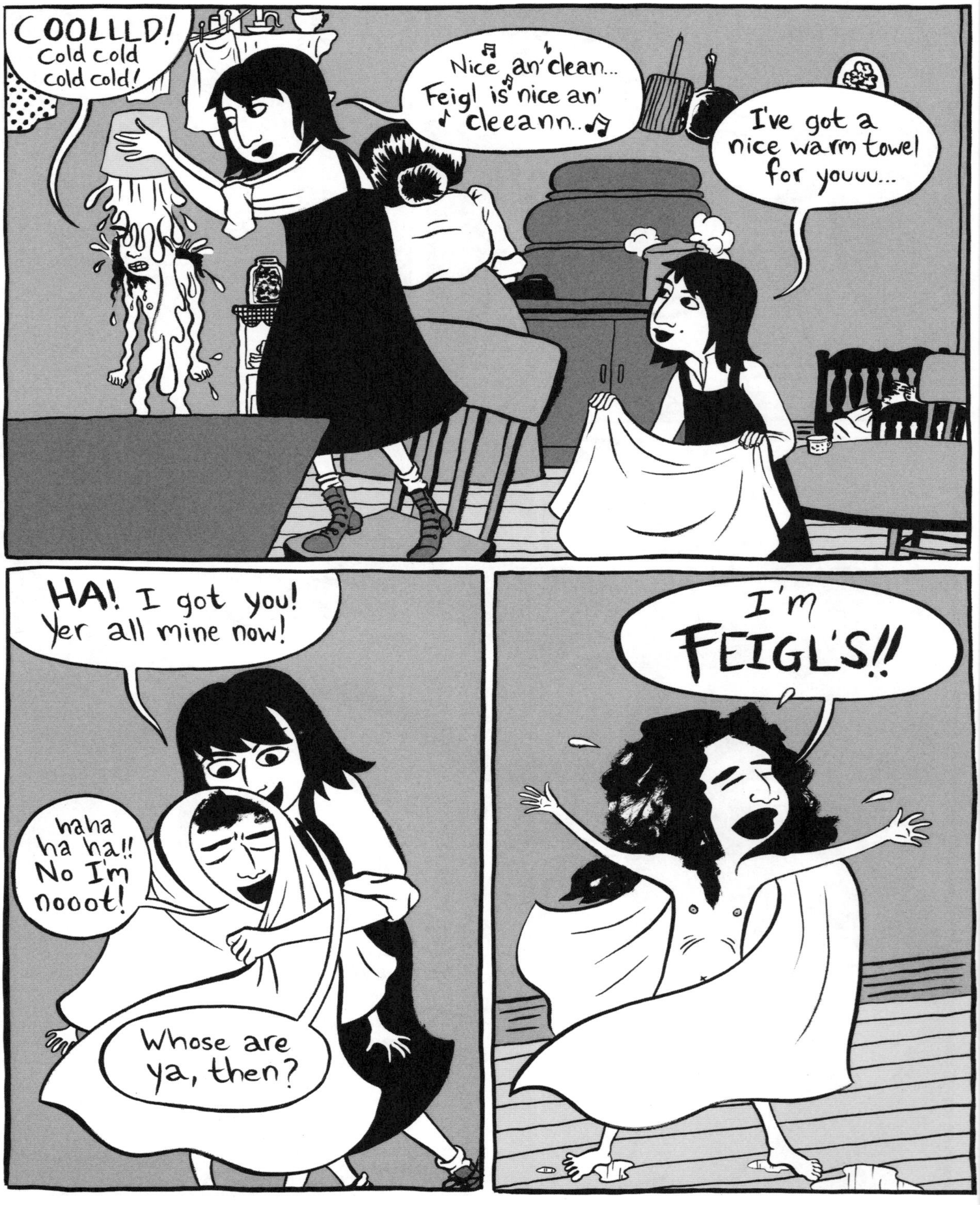
COOLLLD! Cold cold cold cold!
Nice an' clean... Feigl is nice an' cleeann...
I've got a nice warm towel for youuu...
HA! I got you! Yer all mine now!
haha ha ha!! No I'm nooot!
Whose are ya, then?
I'm FEIGL'S!!

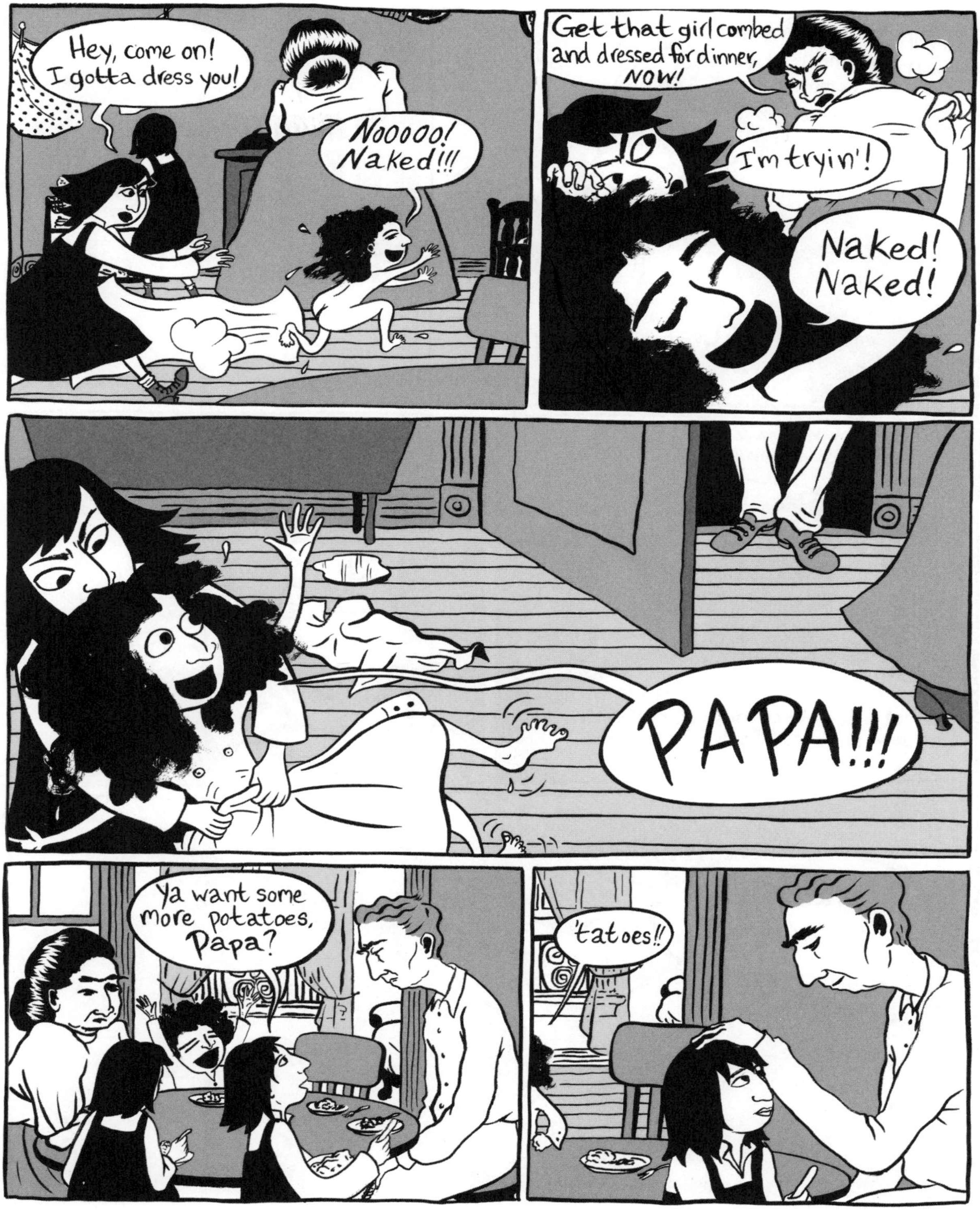
Hey, come on! I gotta dress you!
Nooooo! Naked!!!
Get that girl combed and dressed for dinner, NOW!
I'm tryin'!
Naked! Naked!
PAPA!!!
Ya want some more potatoes, Papa?
'tatoes!!

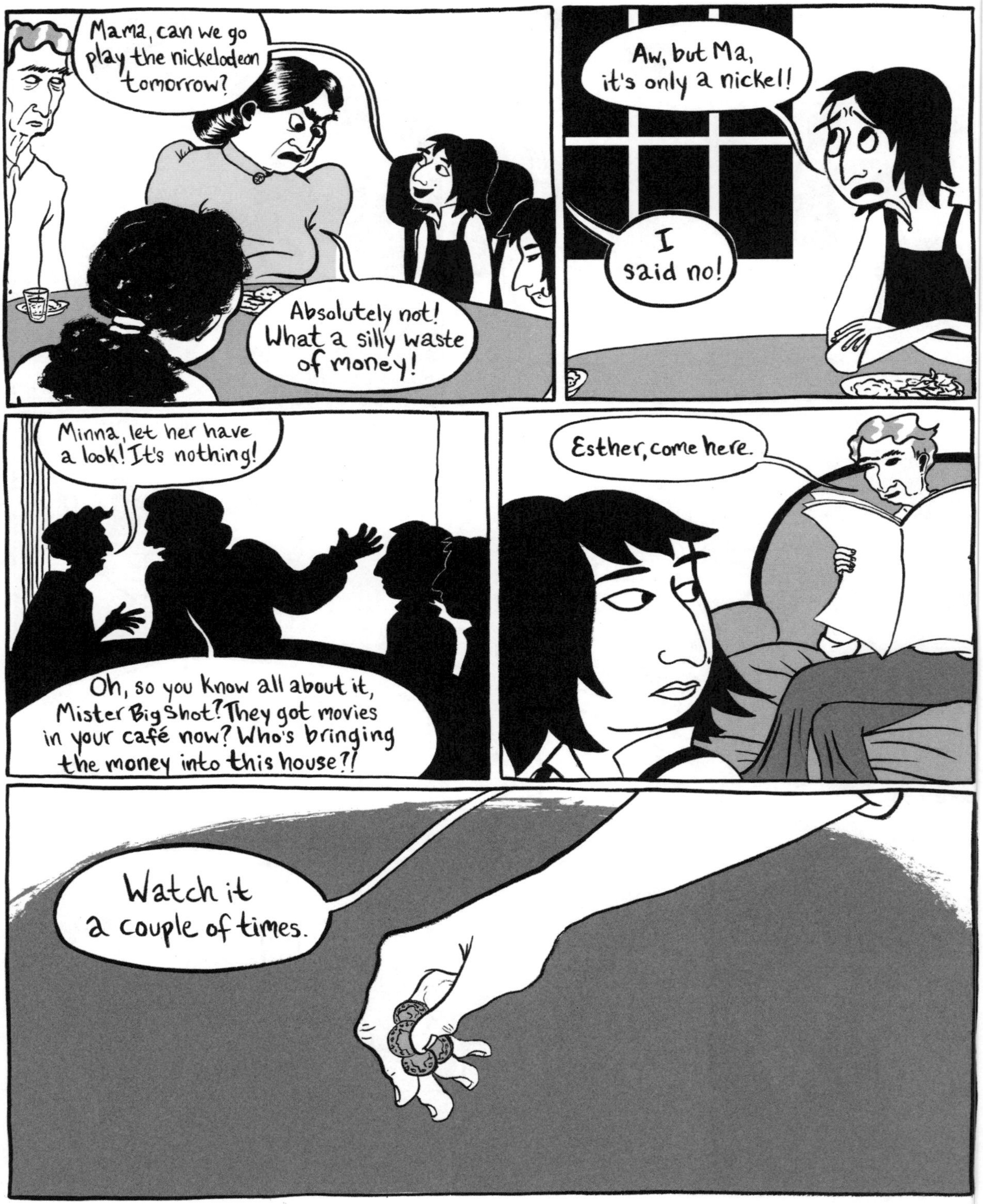
Mama, can we go play the nickelodeon tomorrow?
Absolutely not! What a silly waste of money!
Aw, but Ma, it's only a nickel!
I said no!
Minna, let her have a look! It's nothing!
Oh, so you know all about it, Mister Big Shot? They got movies in your café now? Who's bringing the money into this house?!
Esther, come here.
Watch it a couple of times.

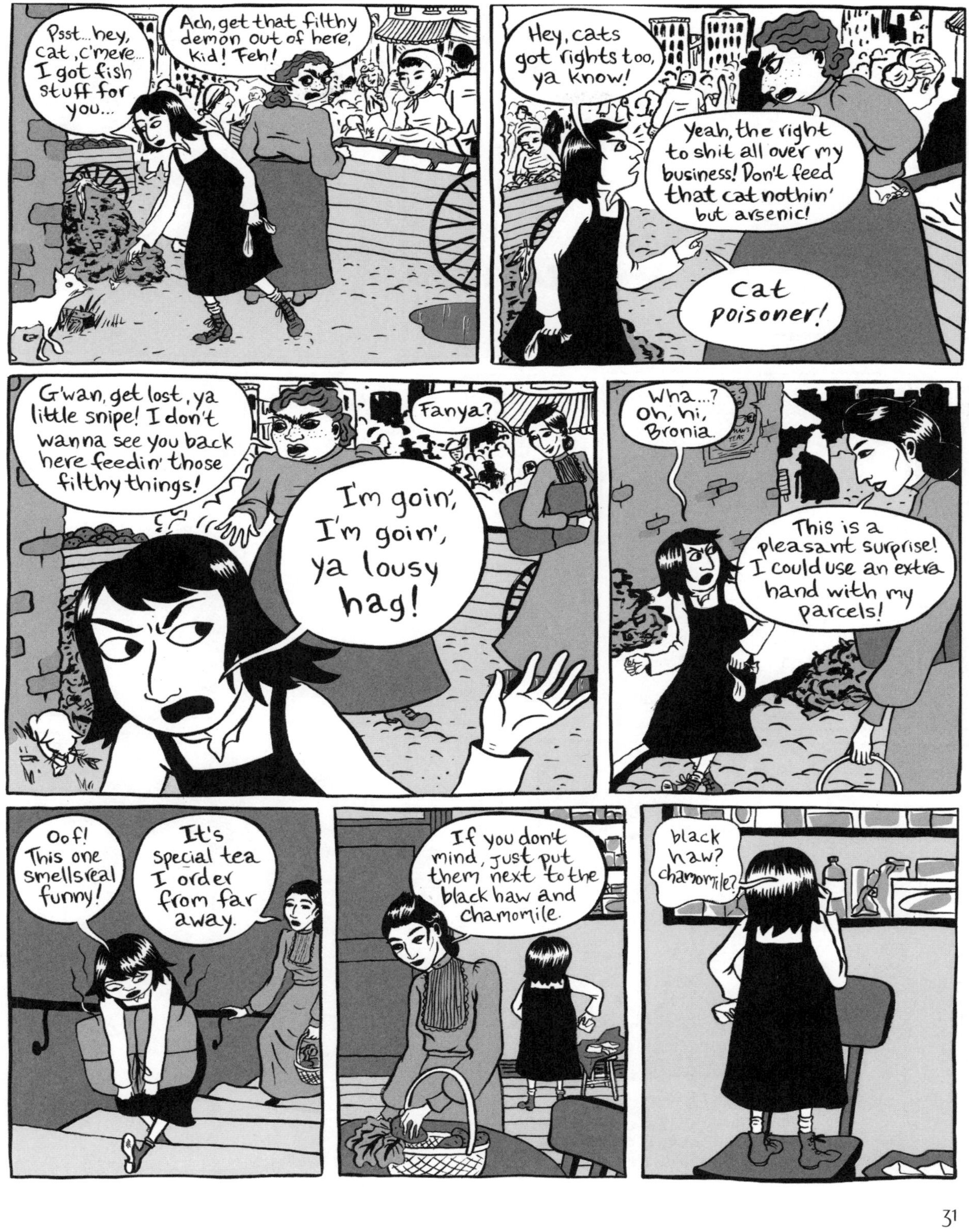

Psst... hey, cat, c'mere... I got fish stuff for you...
Ach, get that filthy demon out of here, kid! Feh!
Hey, cats got rights too, ya know!
Yeah, the right to shit all over my business! Don't feed that cat nothin' but arsenic!
Cat poisoner!
G'wan, get lost, ya little snipe! I don't wanna see you back here feedin' those filthy things!
Fanya?
I'm goin', I'm goin', ya lousy hag!
Wha...? Oh, hi, Bronia.
This is a pleasant surprise! I could use an extra hand with my parcels!
Oof! This one smells real funny!
It's special tea I order from far away.
If you don't mind, just put them next to the black haw and chamomile.
black haw? chamomile?

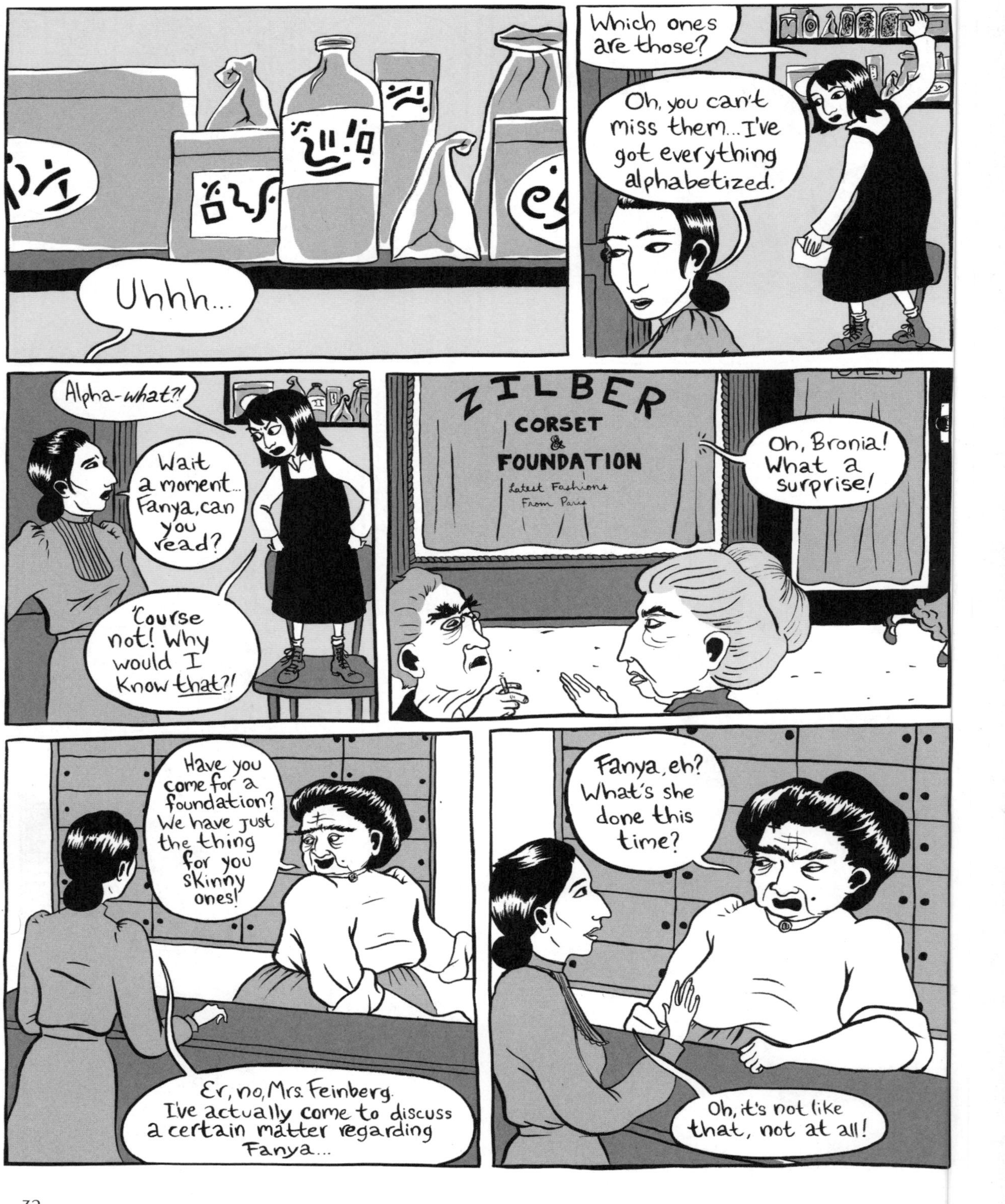

Uhhh...
Which ones are those?
Oh, you can't miss them... I've got everything alphabetized.
Alpha-*what*?!
Wait a moment... Fanya, can you read?
'Course not! Why would I Know that?!
ZILBER
CORSET & FOUNDATION
Latest Fashions From Paris
Oh, Bronia! What a surprise!
Have you come for a foundation? We have just the thing for you skinny ones!
Er, no, Mrs. Feinberg. I've actually come to discuss a certain matter regarding Fanya...
Fanya, eh? What's she done this time?
Oh, it's not like that, not at all!

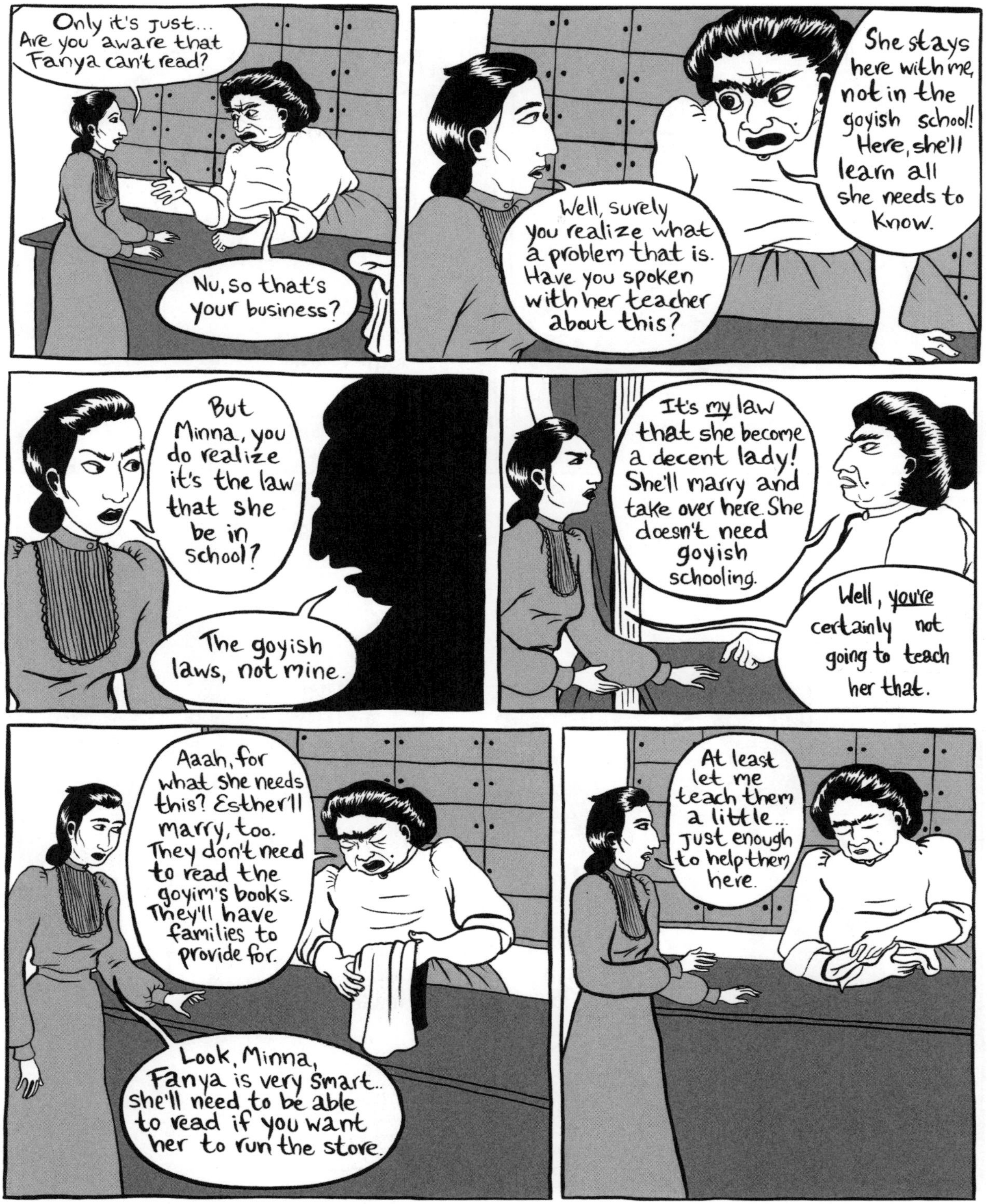
Only it's just... Are you aware that Fanya can't read?
Nu, so that's your business?
Well, surely you realize what a problem that is. Have you spoken with her teacher about this?
She stays here with me, not in the goyish school! Here, she'll learn all she needs to know.
But Minna, you do realize it's the law that she be in school?
The goyish laws, not mine.
It's my law that she become a decent lady! She'll marry and take over here. She doesn't need goyish schooling.
Well, you're certainly not going to teach her that.
Aaah, for what she needs this? Esther'll marry, too. They don't need to read the goyim's books. They'll have families to provide for.
Look, Minna, Fanya is very smart.. she'll need to be able to read if you want her to run the store.
At least let me teach them a little... Just enough to help them here.

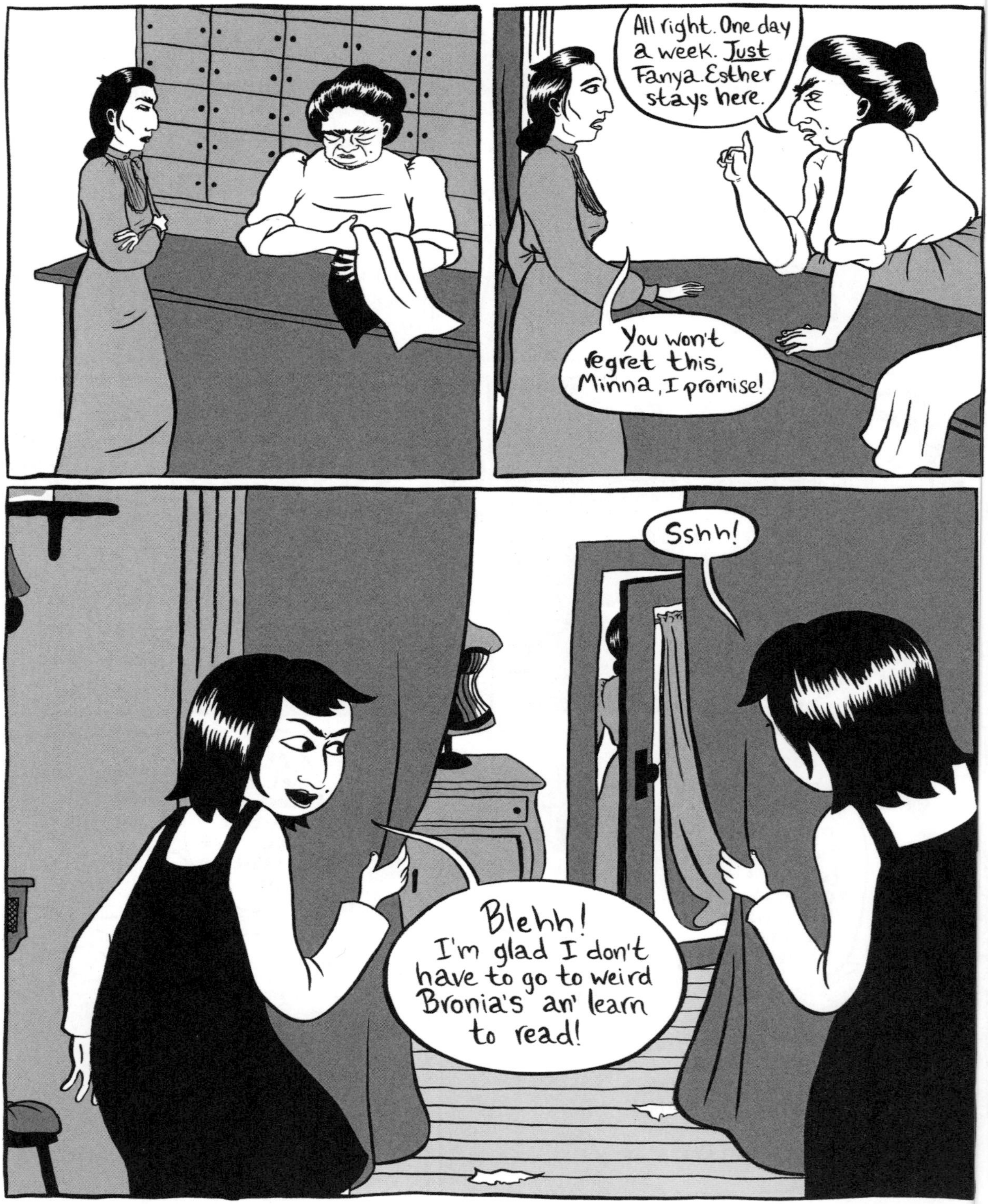
All right. One day a week. Just Fanya. Esther stays here.
You won't regret this, Minna, I promise!
Sshh!
Blehh! I'm glad I don't have to go to weird Bronia's an' learn to read!

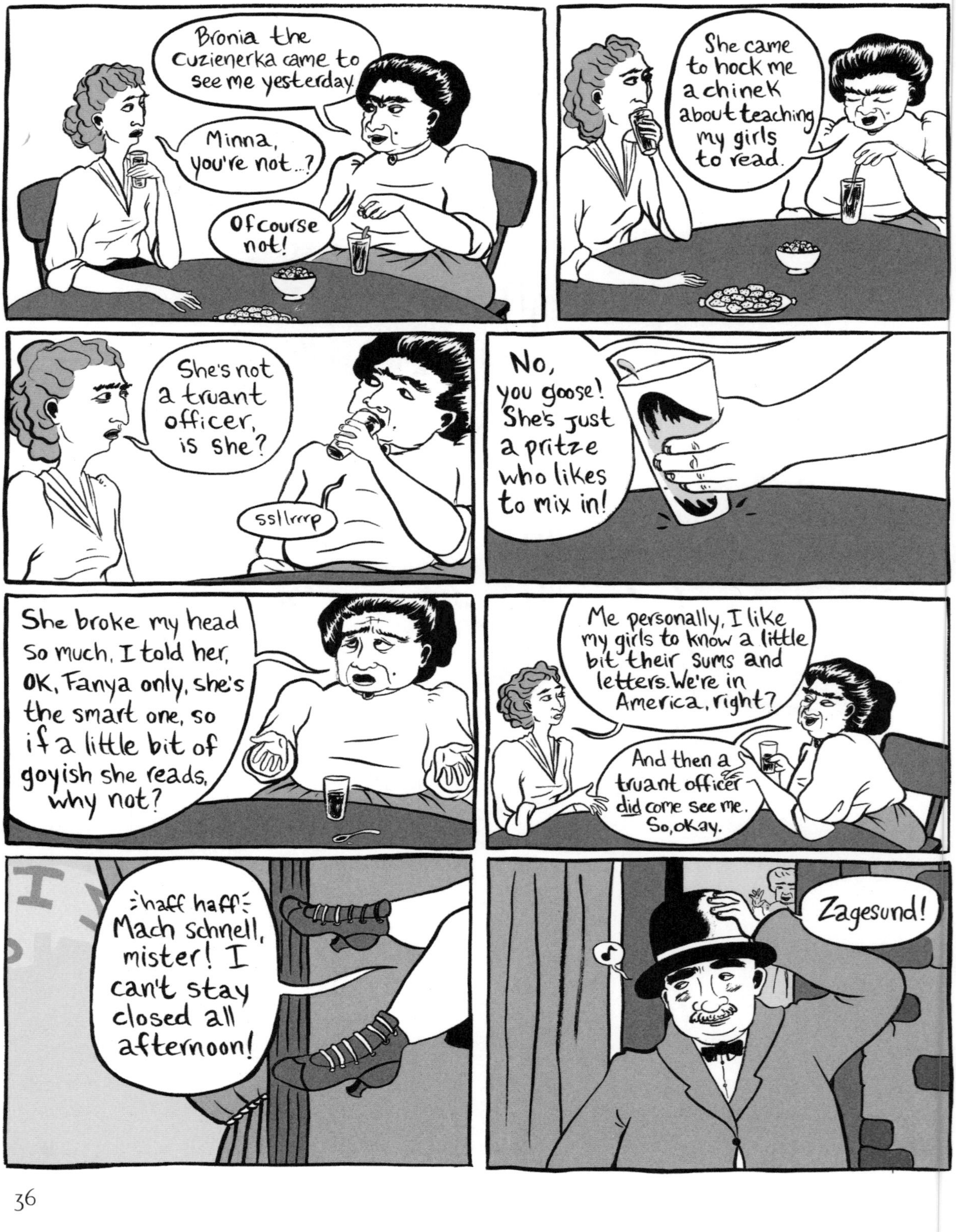
Bronia the Cuzienerka came to see me yesterday.
Minna, you're not...?
Of course not!
She came to hock me a chinek about teaching my girls to read.
She's not a truant officer, is she?
ssllrrrp
No, you goose! She's just a pritze who likes to mix in!
She broke my head so much, I told her, OK, Fanya only, she's the smart one, so if a little bit of goyish she reads, why not?
Me personally, I like my girls to know a little bit their sums and letters. We're in America, right?
And then a truant officer did come see me. So, okay.
haff haff
Mach schnell, mister! I can't stay closed all afternoon!
Zagesund!

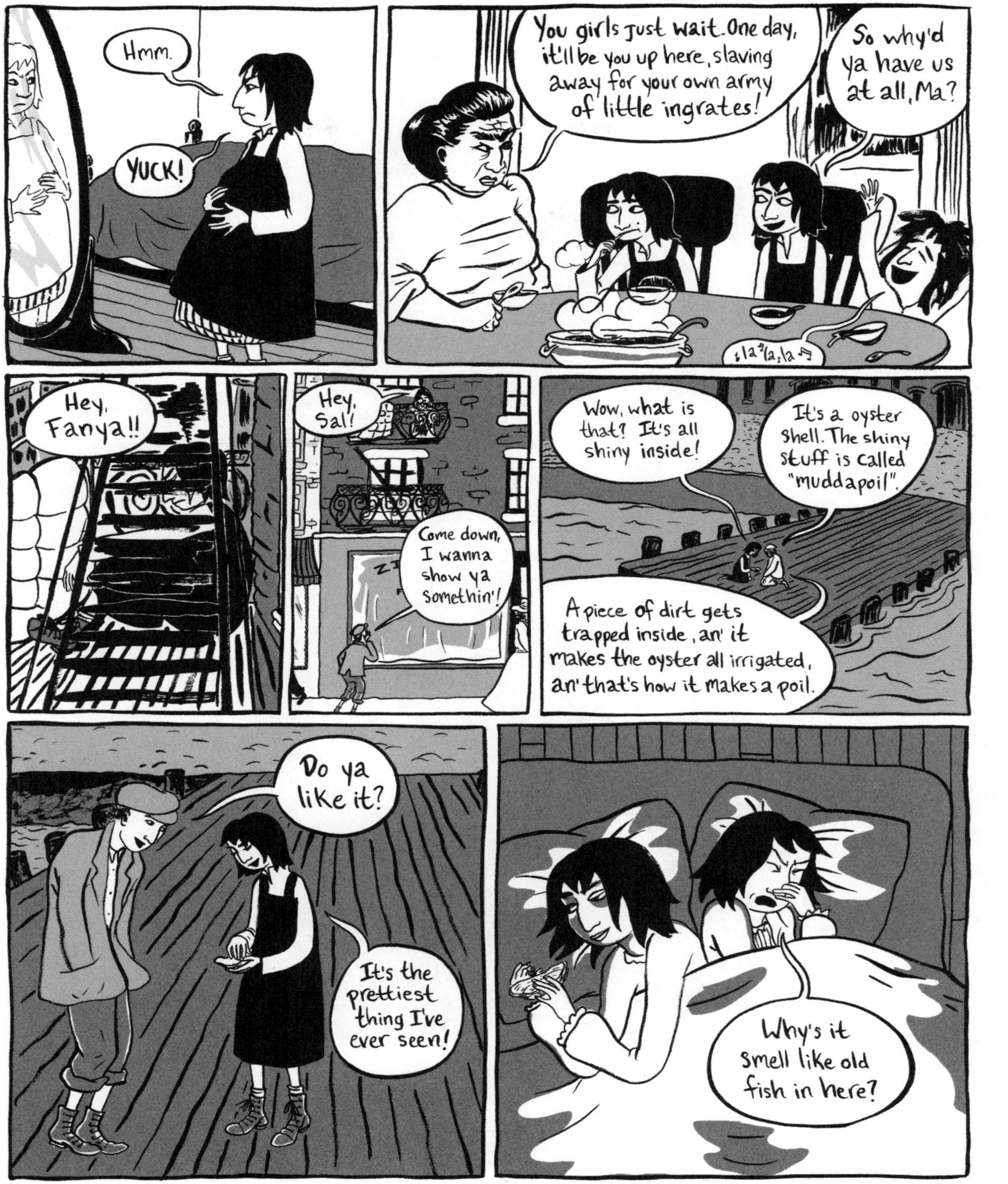
Hmm.
YUCK!
You girls just wait. One day, it'll be you up here, slaving away for your own army of little ingrates!
So why'd ya have us at all, Ma?
la la, la
Hey, Fanya!!
Hey, Sal!
Come down, I wanna show ya somethin'!
Wow, what is that? It's all shiny inside!
It's a oyster shell. The shiny stuff is called "muddapoil".
A piece of dirt gets trapped inside, an' it makes the oyster all irrigated, an' that's how it makes a poil.
Do ya like it?
It's the prettiest thing I've ever seen!
Why's it smell like old fish in here?

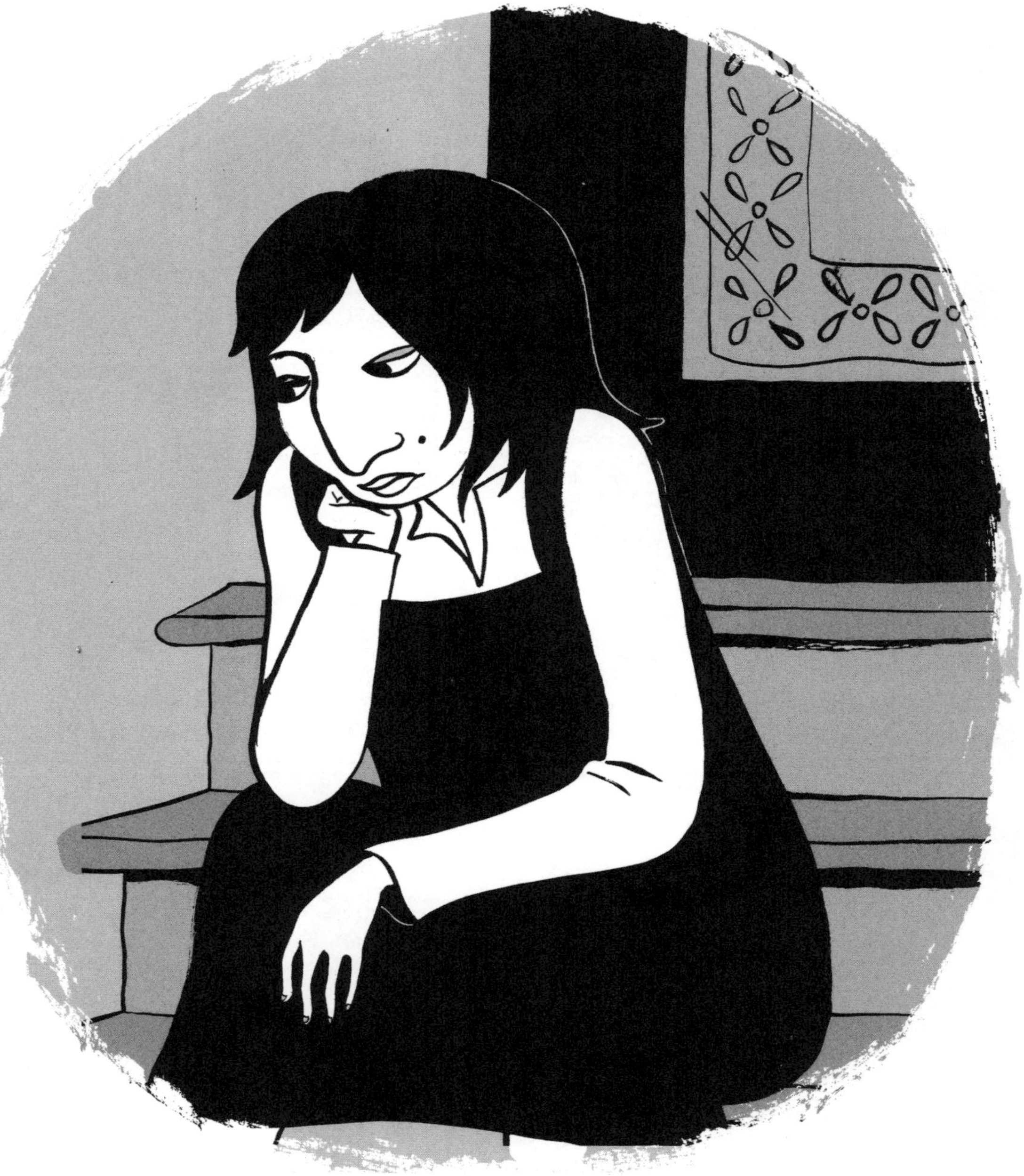

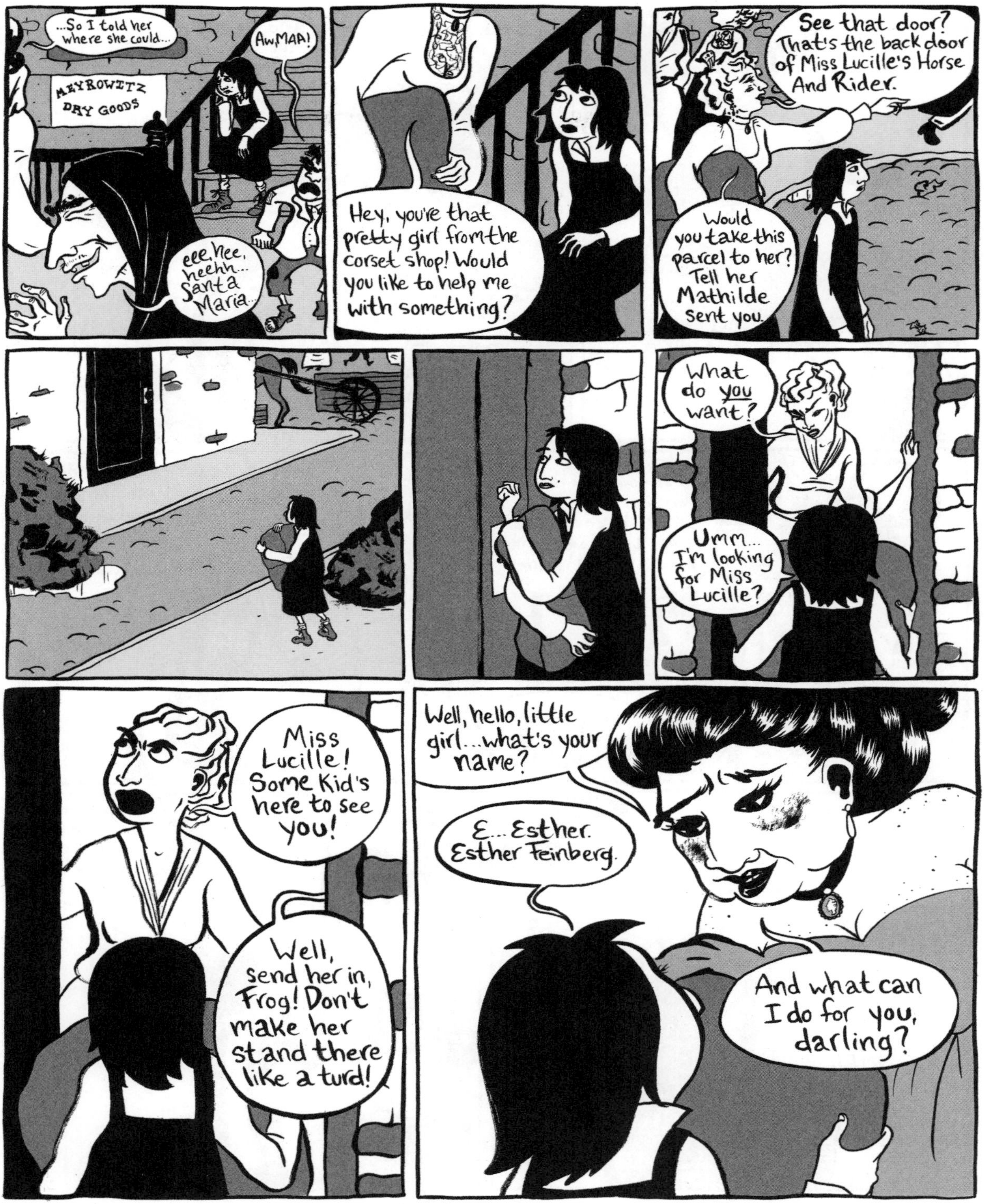
...So I told her where she could...
Aw, MAA!
MEYROWITZ DRY GOODS
eee, hee, heehh... Santa Maria...
Hey, you're that pretty girl from the corset shop! Would you like to help me with something?
See that door? That's the back door of Miss Lucille's Horse And Rider.
Would you take this parcel to her? Tell her Mathilde sent you.
What do you want?
Umm... I'm looking for Miss Lucille?
Miss Lucille! Some Kid's here to see you!
Well, send her in, Frog! Don't make her stand there like a turd!
Well, hello, little girl...what's your name?
E... Esther. Esther Feinberg.
And what can I do for you, darling?

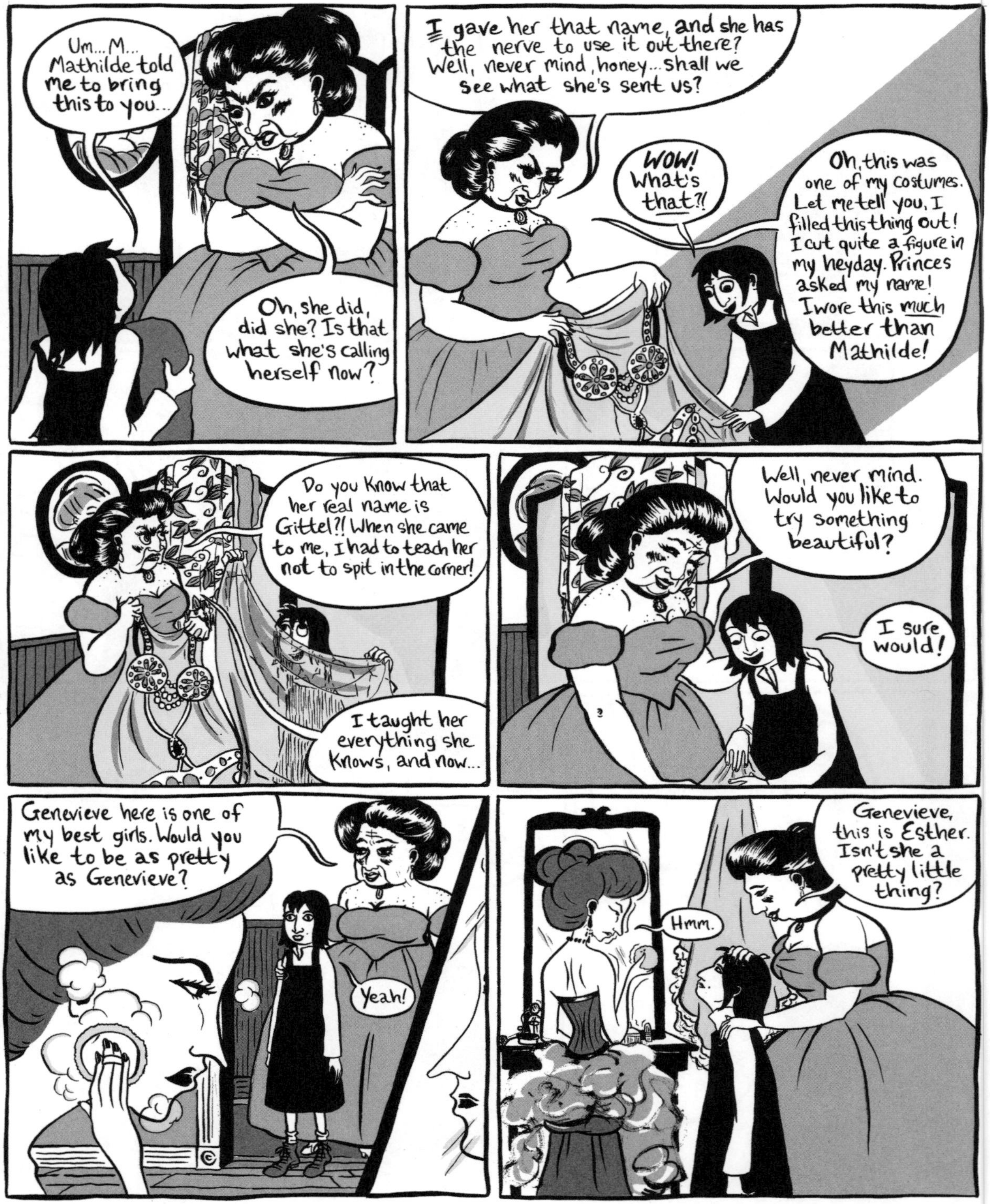

Um... M... Mathilde told me to bring this to you...
Oh, she did, did she? Is that what she's calling herself now?
I gave her that name, and she has the nerve to use it out there? Well, never mind, honey... shall we see what she's sent us?
WOW! What's that?!
Oh, this was one of my costumes. Let me tell you, I filled this thing out! I cut quite a figure in my heyday. Princes asked my name! I wore this much better than Mathilde!
Do you know that her real name is Gittel?! When she came to me, I had to teach her not to spit in the corner!
I taught her everything she knows, and now...
Well, never mind. Would you like to try something beautiful?
I sure would!
Genevieve here is one of my best girls. Would you like to be as pretty as Genevieve?
Yeah!
Genevieve, this is Esther. Isn't she a pretty little thing?
Hmm.

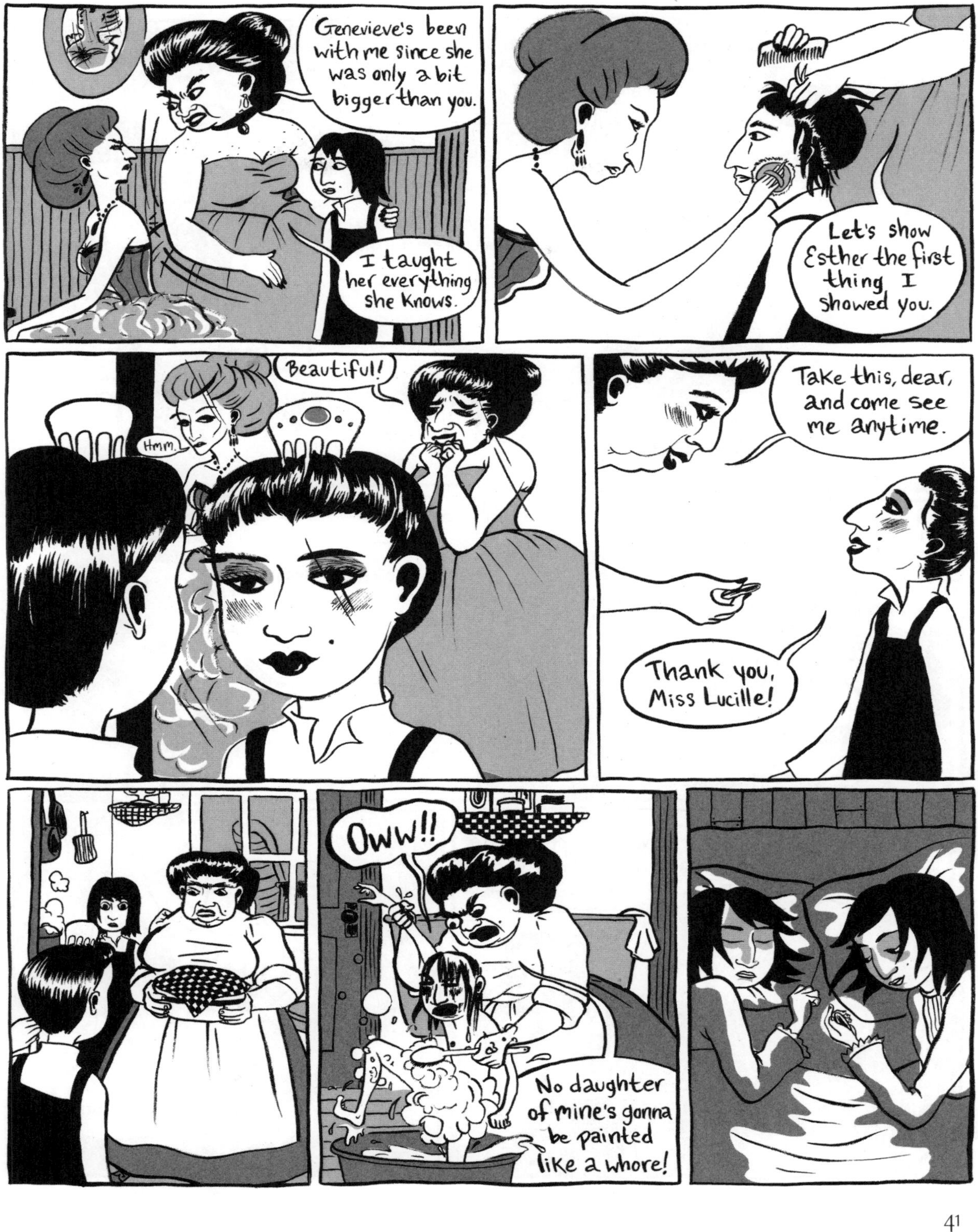
Genevieve's been with me since she was only a bit bigger than you.
I taught her everything she knows.
Let's show Esther the first thing I showed you.
Beautiful!
Hmm.
Take this, dear, and come see me anytime.
Thank you, Miss Lucille!
OWW!!
No daughter of mine's gonna be painted like a whore!

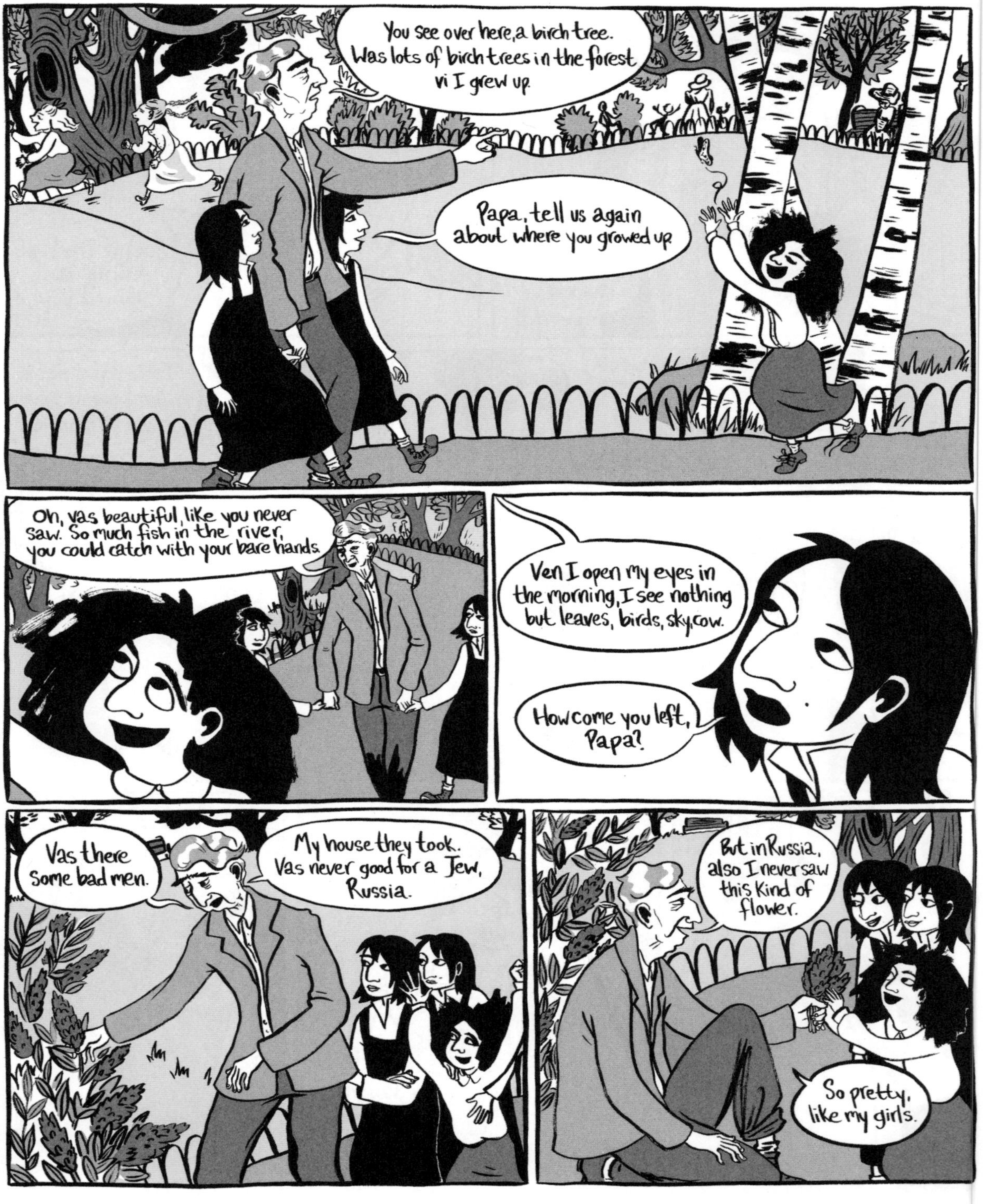
You see over here, a birch tree. Was lots of birch trees in the forest vi I grew up.
Papa, tell us again about where you growed up.
Oh, vas beautiful, like you never saw. So much fish in the river, you could catch with your bare hands.
Ven I open my eyes in the morning, I see nothing but leaves, birds, sky, cow.
How come you left, Papa?
Vas there some bad men.
My house they took. Vas never good for a Jew, Russia.
But in Russia, also I never saw this kind of flower.
So pretty, like my girls.

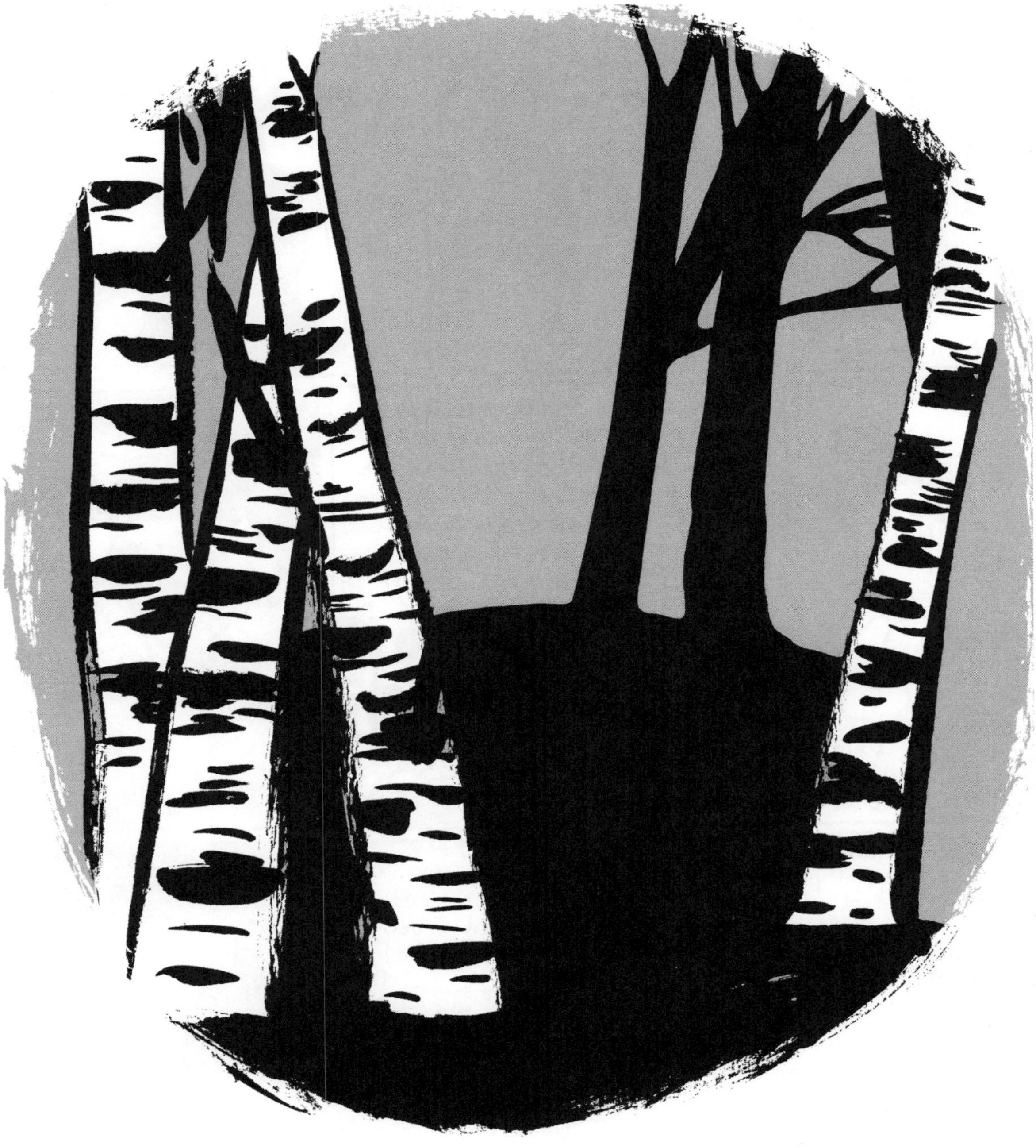

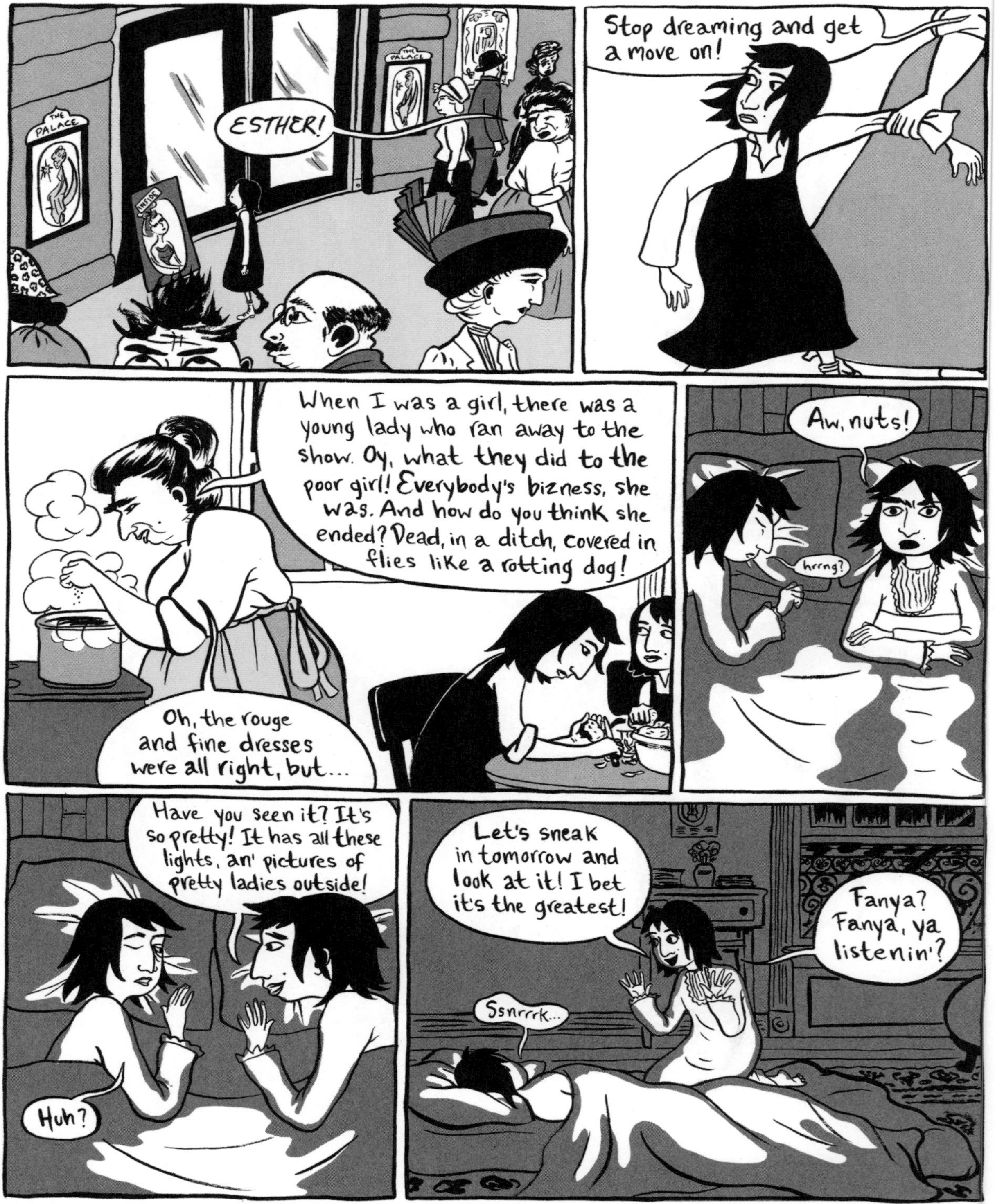
ESTHER!
Stop dreaming and get a move on!
When I was a girl, there was a young lady who ran away to the show. Oy, what they did to the poor girl! Everybody's bizness, she was. And how do you think she ended? Dead, in a ditch, covered in flies like a rotting dog!
Oh, the rouge and fine dresses were all right, but...
Aw, nuts!
hrrng?
Have you seen it? It's so pretty! It has all these lights, an' pictures of pretty ladies outside!
Huh?
Let's sneak in tomorrow and look at it! I bet it's the greatest!
Ssnrrrk...
Fanya? Fanya, ya listenin'?

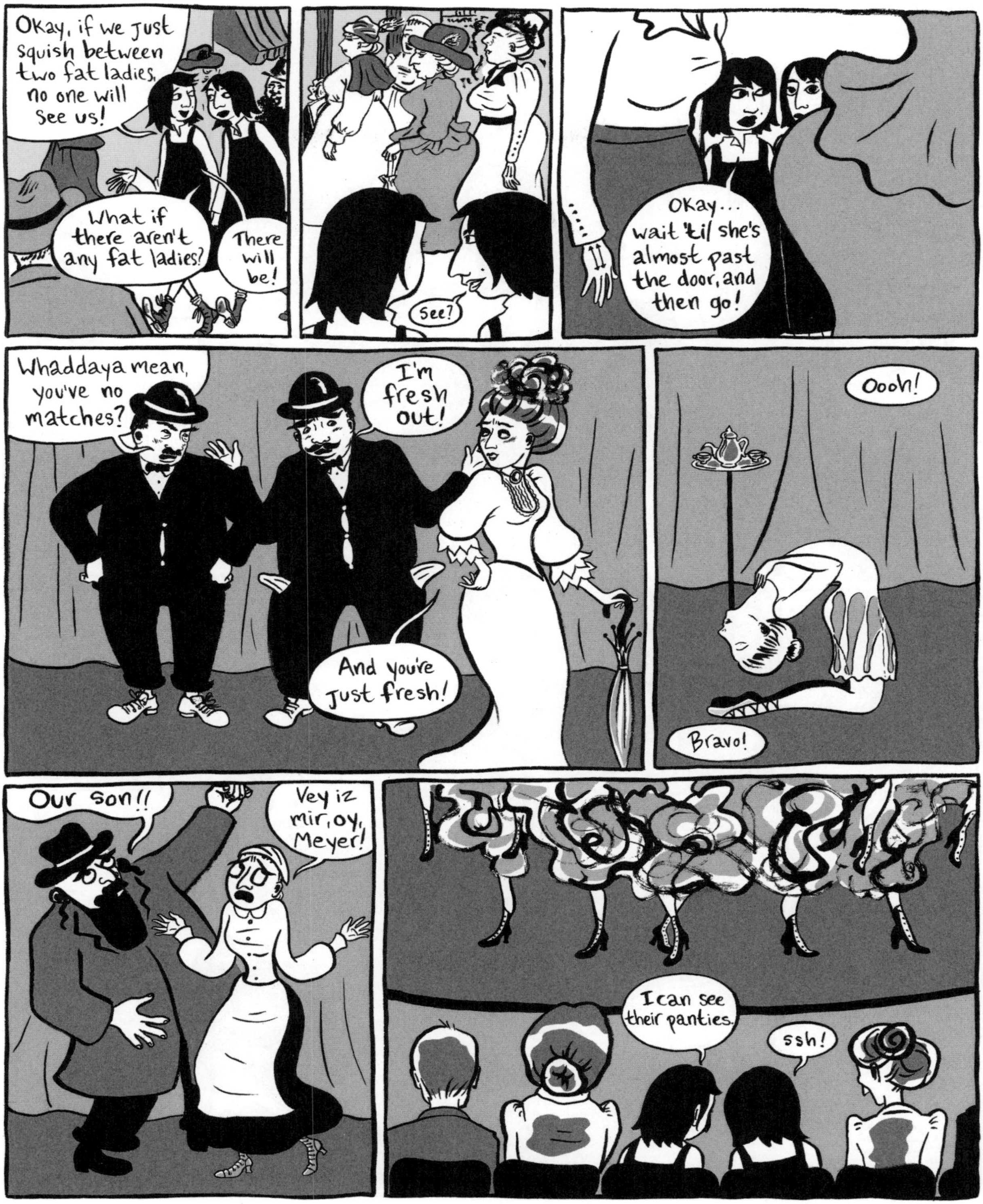
Okay, if we just squish between two fat ladies, no one will see us!
What if there aren't any fat ladies?
There will be!
See?
Okay... wait 'til she's almost past the door, and then go!
Whaddaya mean, you've no matches?
I'm fresh out!
And you're just fresh!
Oooh!
Bravo!
Our son!!
Vey iz mir, oy, Meyer!
I can see their panties.
ssh!

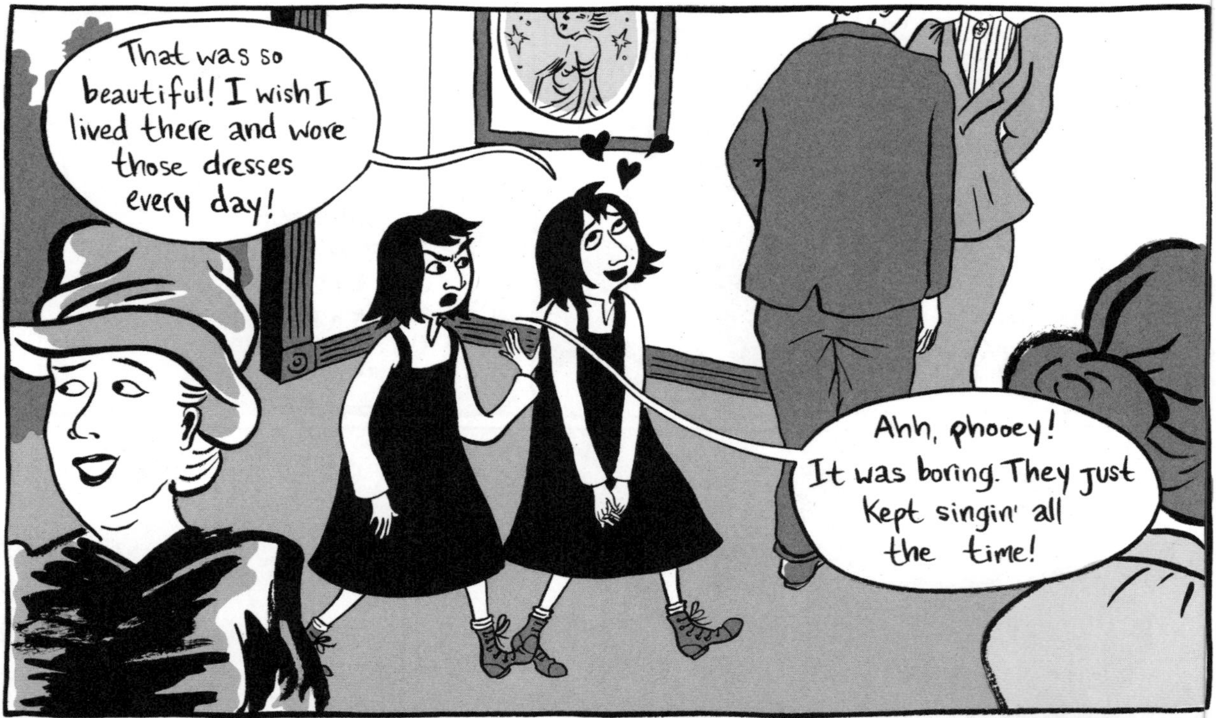
That was so beautiful! I wish I lived there and wore those dresses every day!
Ahh, phooey! It was boring. They just kept singin' all the time!

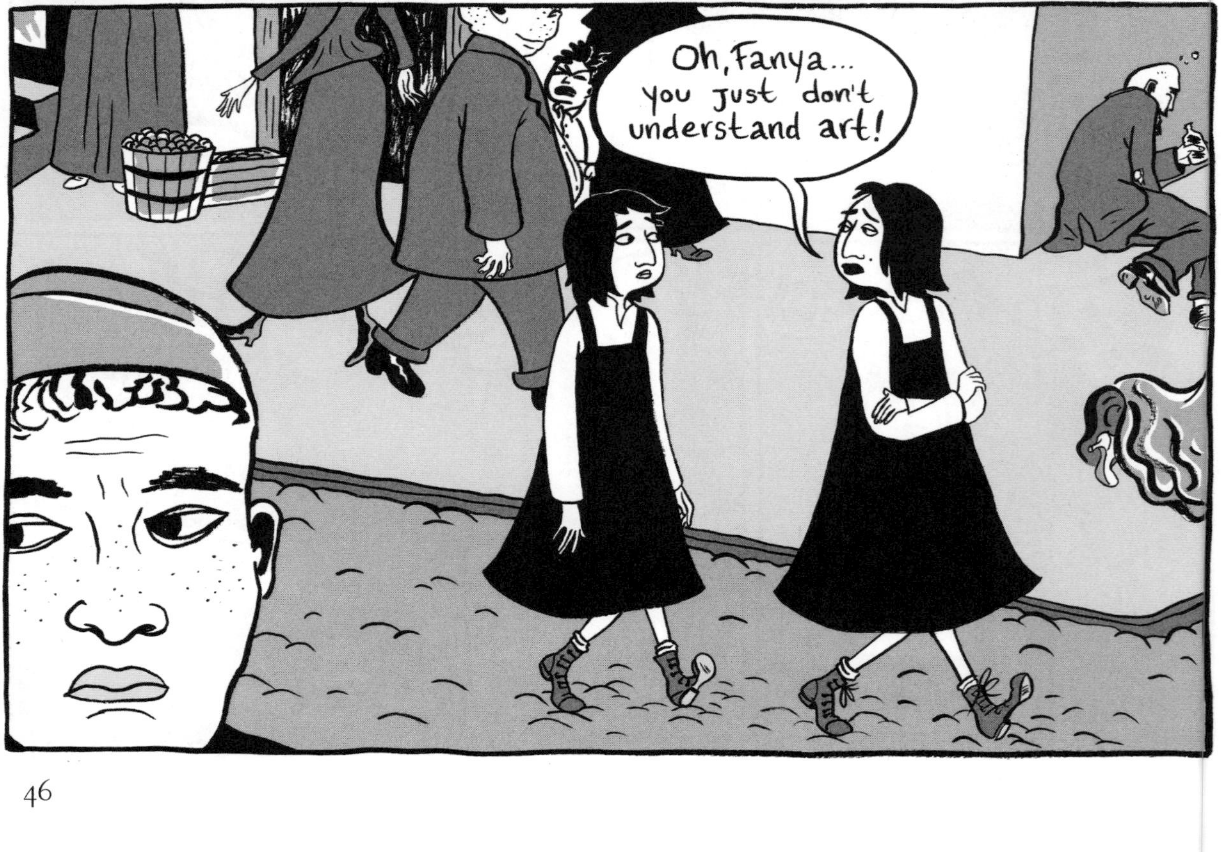
Oh, Fanya... you just don't understand art!

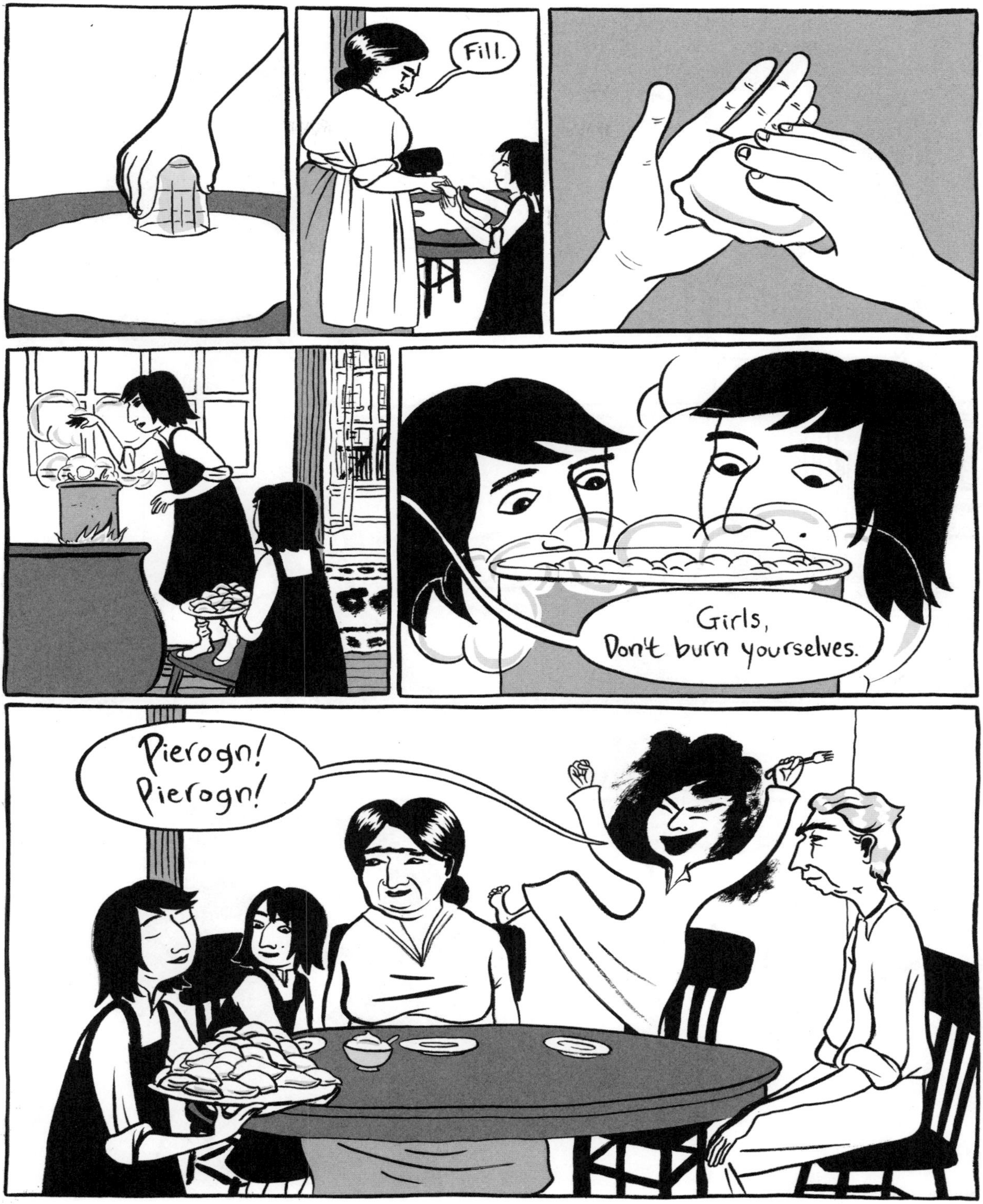
Fill.
Girls, Don't burn yourselves.
Pierogn! Pierogn!

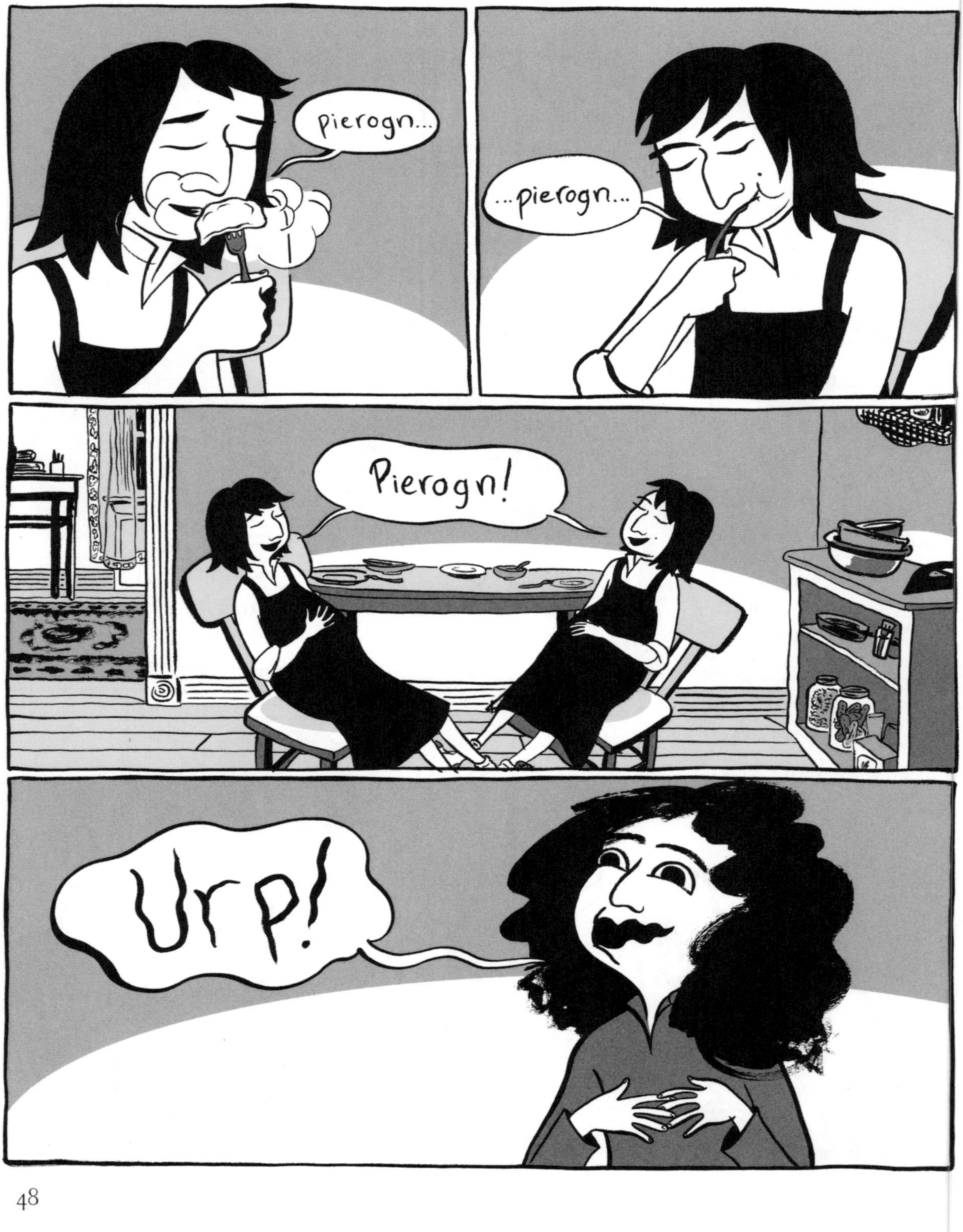
pierogn...
...pierogn...
Pierogn!
Urp!

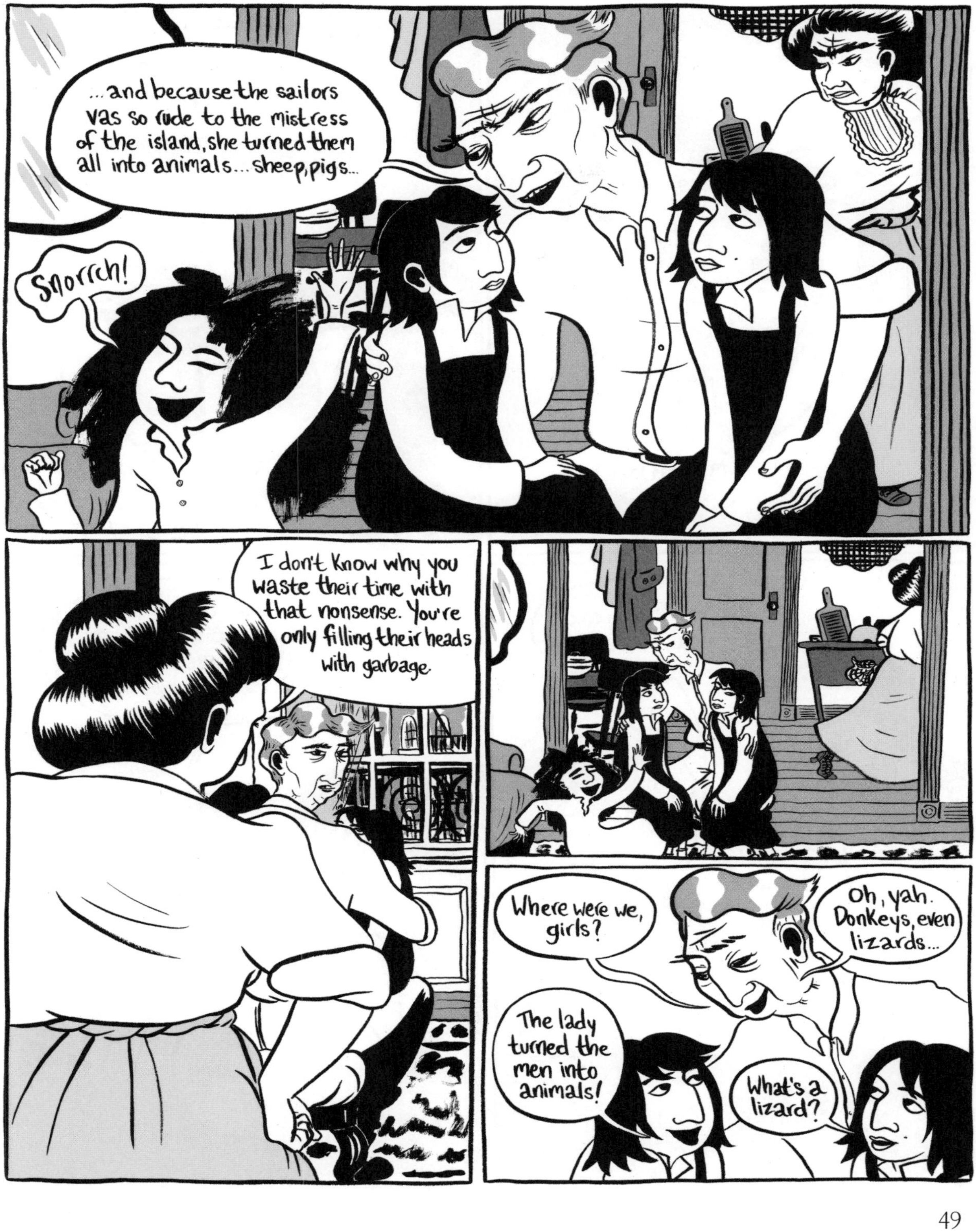
...and because the sailors vas so rude to the mistress of the island, she turned them all into animals... sheep, pigs...
Snorrch!
I don't know why you waste their time with that nonsense. You're only filling their heads with garbage.
Where were we, girls?
Oh, yah. Donkeys, even lizards...
The lady turned the men into animals!
What's a lizard?

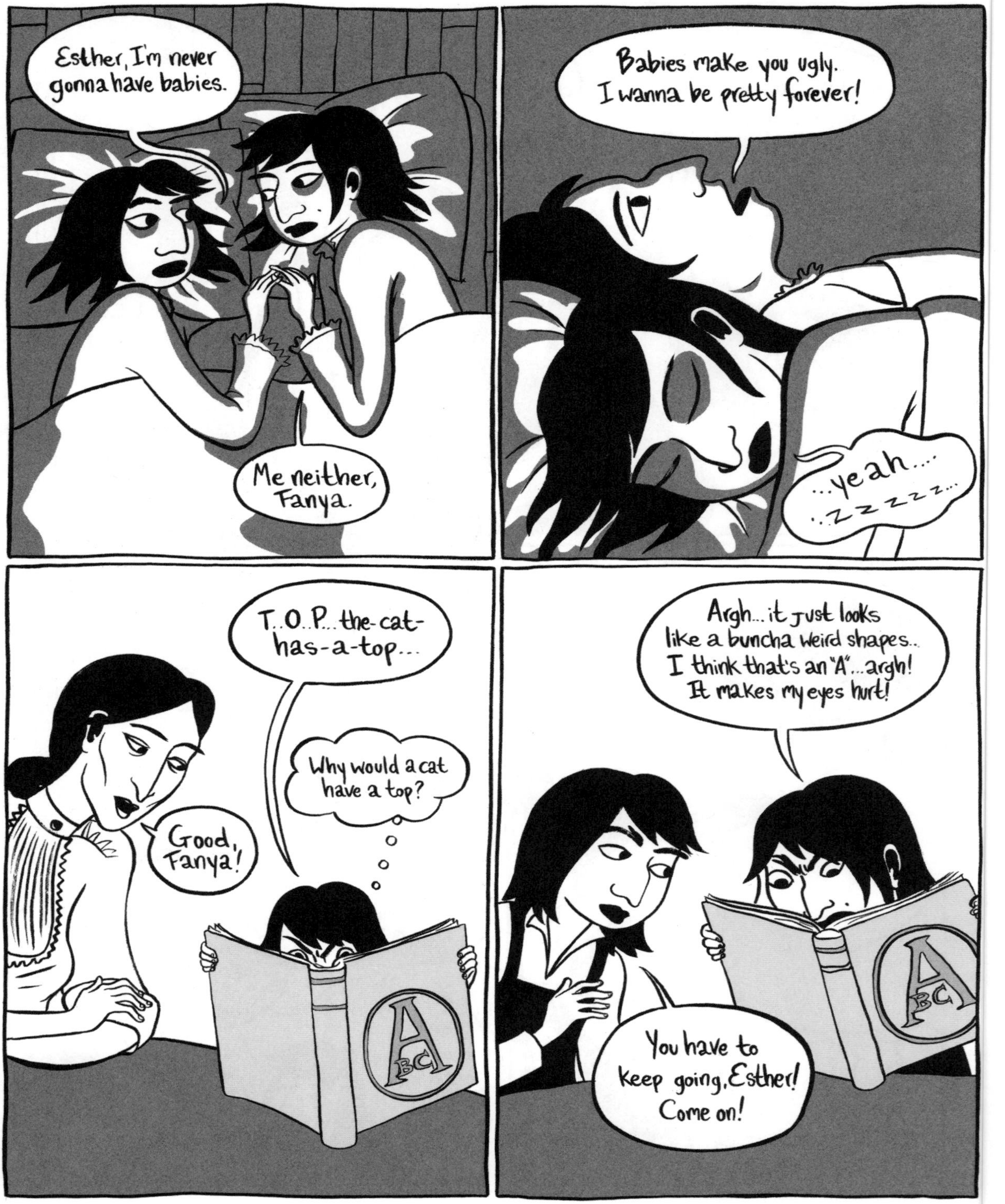
Esther, I'm never gonna have babies.
Me neither, Fanya.
Babies make you ugly. I wanna be pretty forever!
...yeah.... ..zzzzz...
T..O..P... the-cat-has-a-top...
Why would a cat have a top?
Good, Fanya!
Argh... it just looks like a buncha weird shapes.. I think that's an "A"... argh! It makes my eyes hurt!
You have to keep going, Esther! Come on!

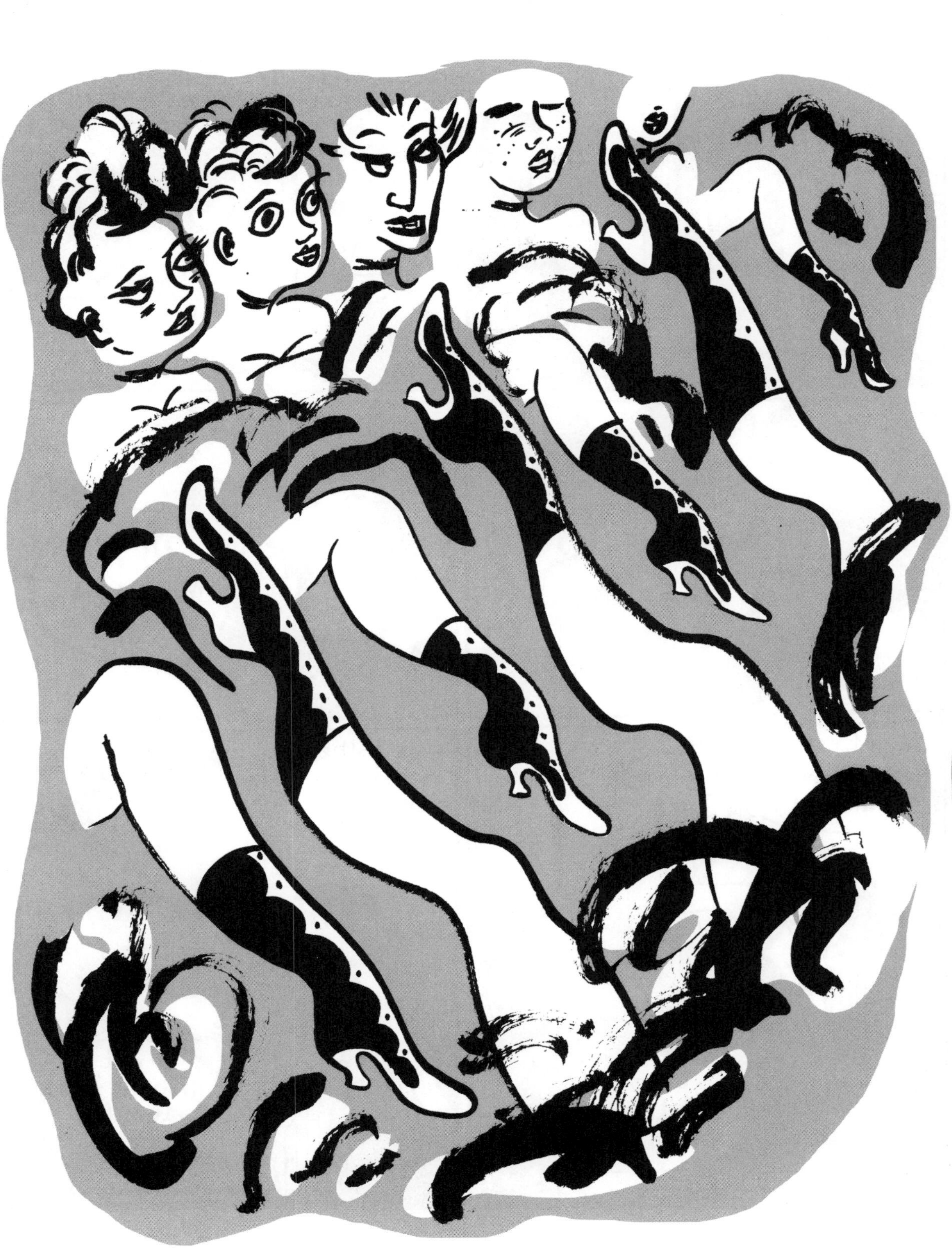

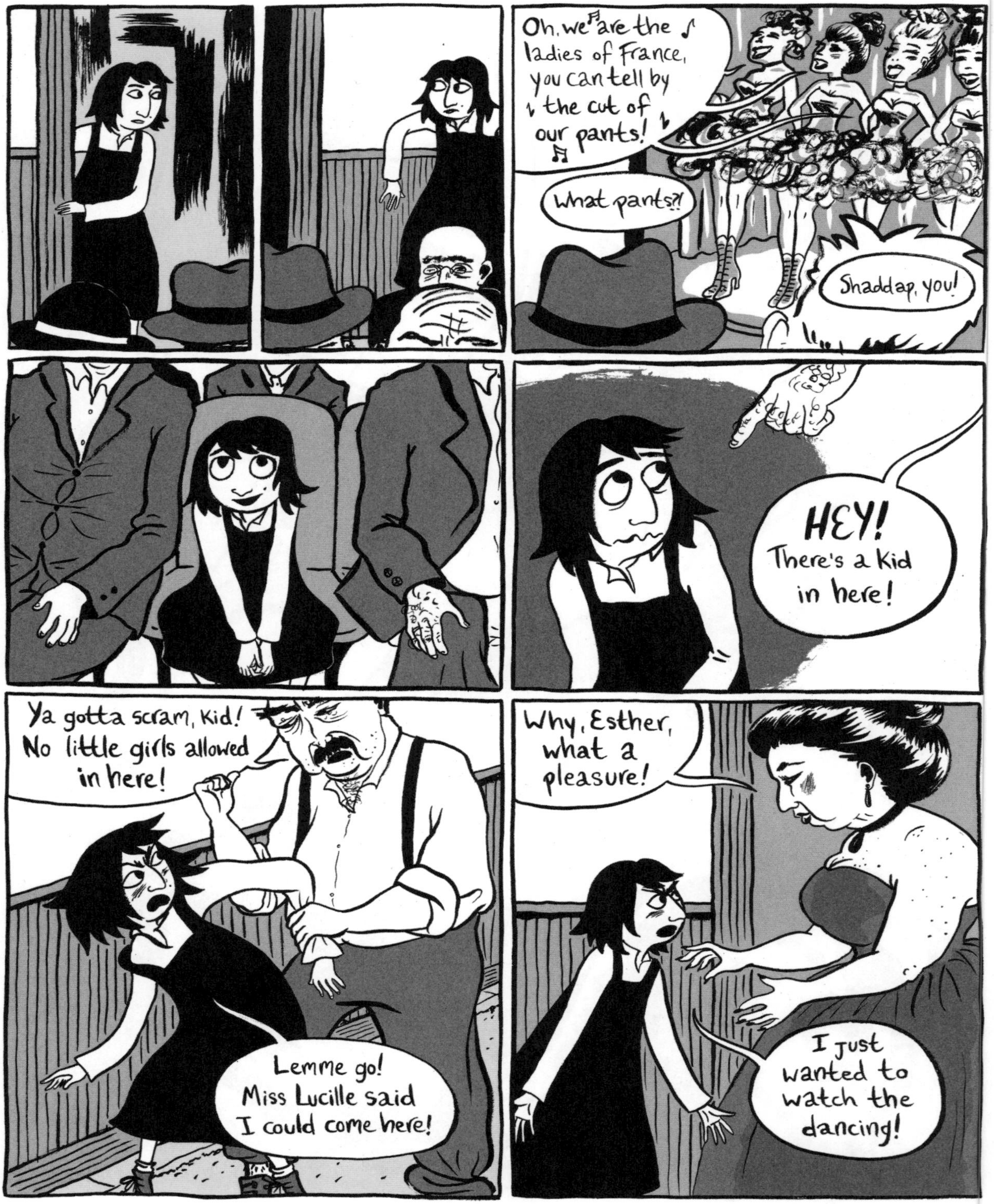
Oh, we are the ladies of France, you can tell by the cut of our pants!
What pants?!
Shaddap, you!
HEY! There's a kid in here!
Ya gotta scram, kid! No little girls allowed in here!
Lemme go! Miss Lucille said I could come here!
Why, Esther, what a pleasure!
I just wanted to watch the dancing!

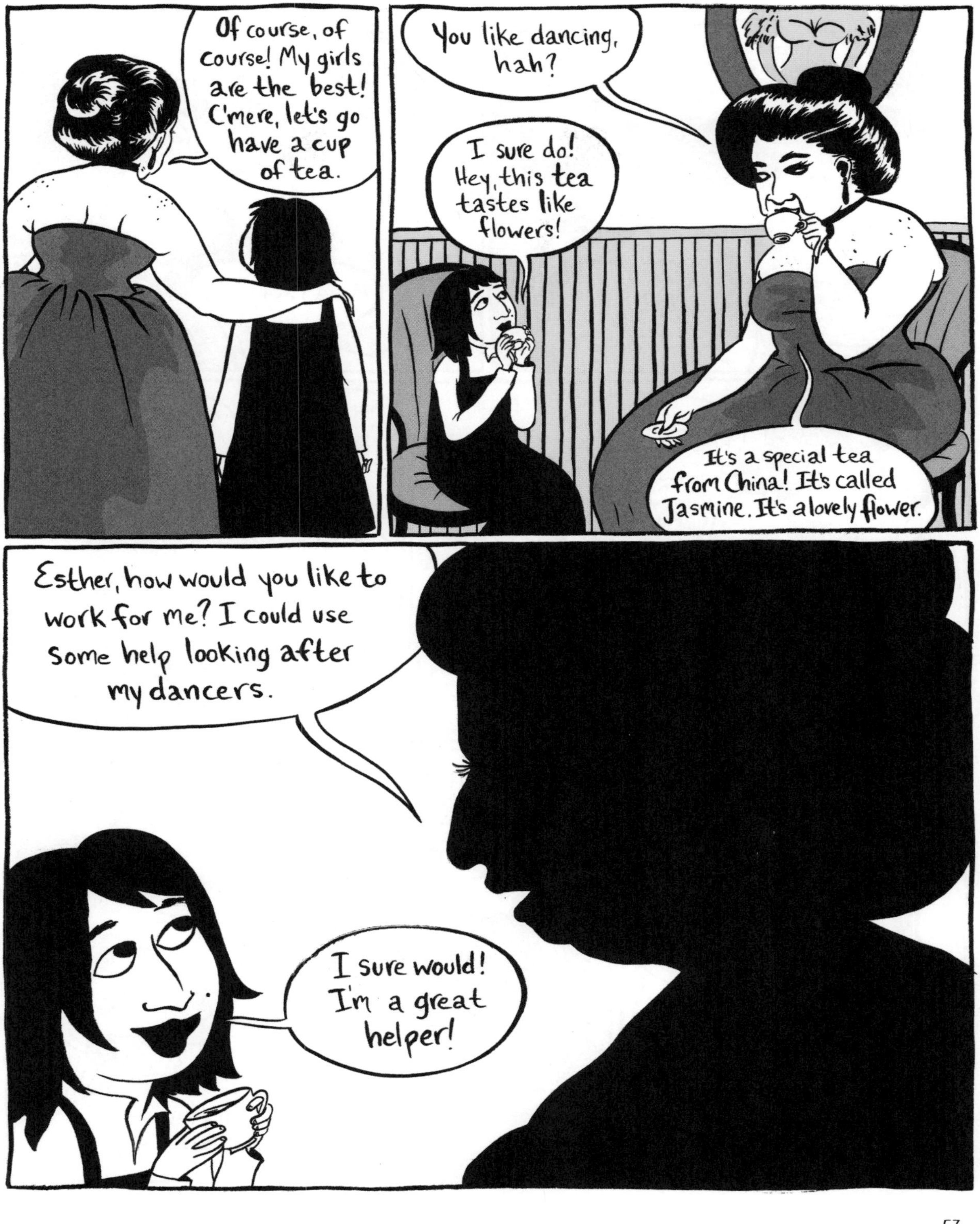
Of course, of course! My girls are the best! C'mere, let's go have a cup of tea.
You like dancing, hah?
I sure do! Hey, this tea tastes like flowers!
It's a special tea from China! It's called Jasmine. It's a lovely flower.
Esther, how would you like to work for me? I could use some help looking after my dancers.
I sure would! I'm a great helper!

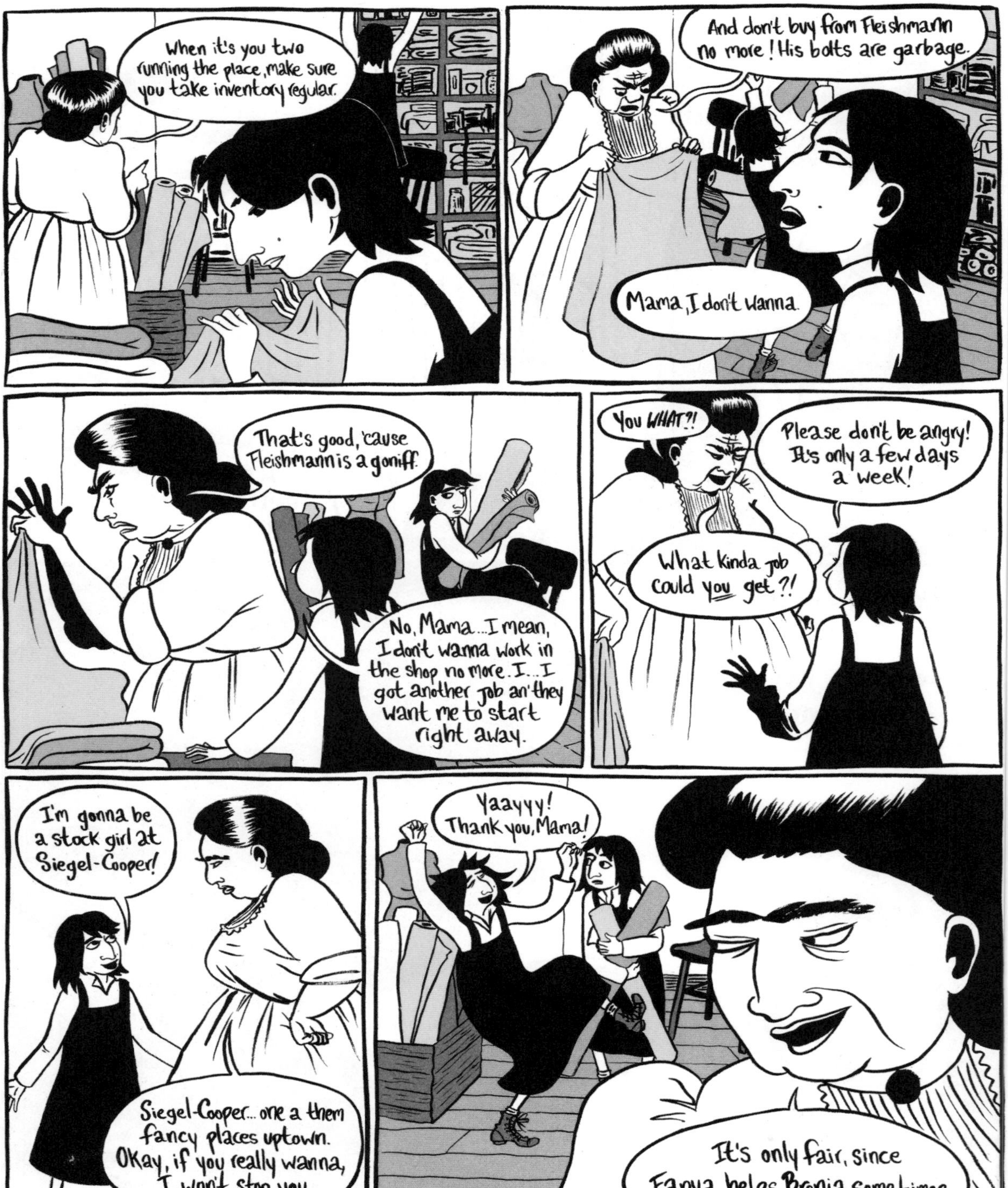
When it's you two running the place, make sure you take inventory regular.
And don't buy from Fleishmann no more! His bolts are garbage.
Mama, I don't wanna.
That's good, 'cause Fleishmann is a goniff.
No, Mama...I mean, I don't wanna work in the shop no more. I...I got another job an' they want me to start right away.
You WHAT?!
What kinda job could you get?!
Please don't be angry! It's only a few days a week!
I'm gonna be a stock girl at Siegel-Cooper!
Siegel-Cooper... one a them fancy places uptown. Okay, if you really wanna, I won't stop you.
Yaayyy! Thank you, Mama!
It's only fair, since Fanya helps Bronia sometimes.

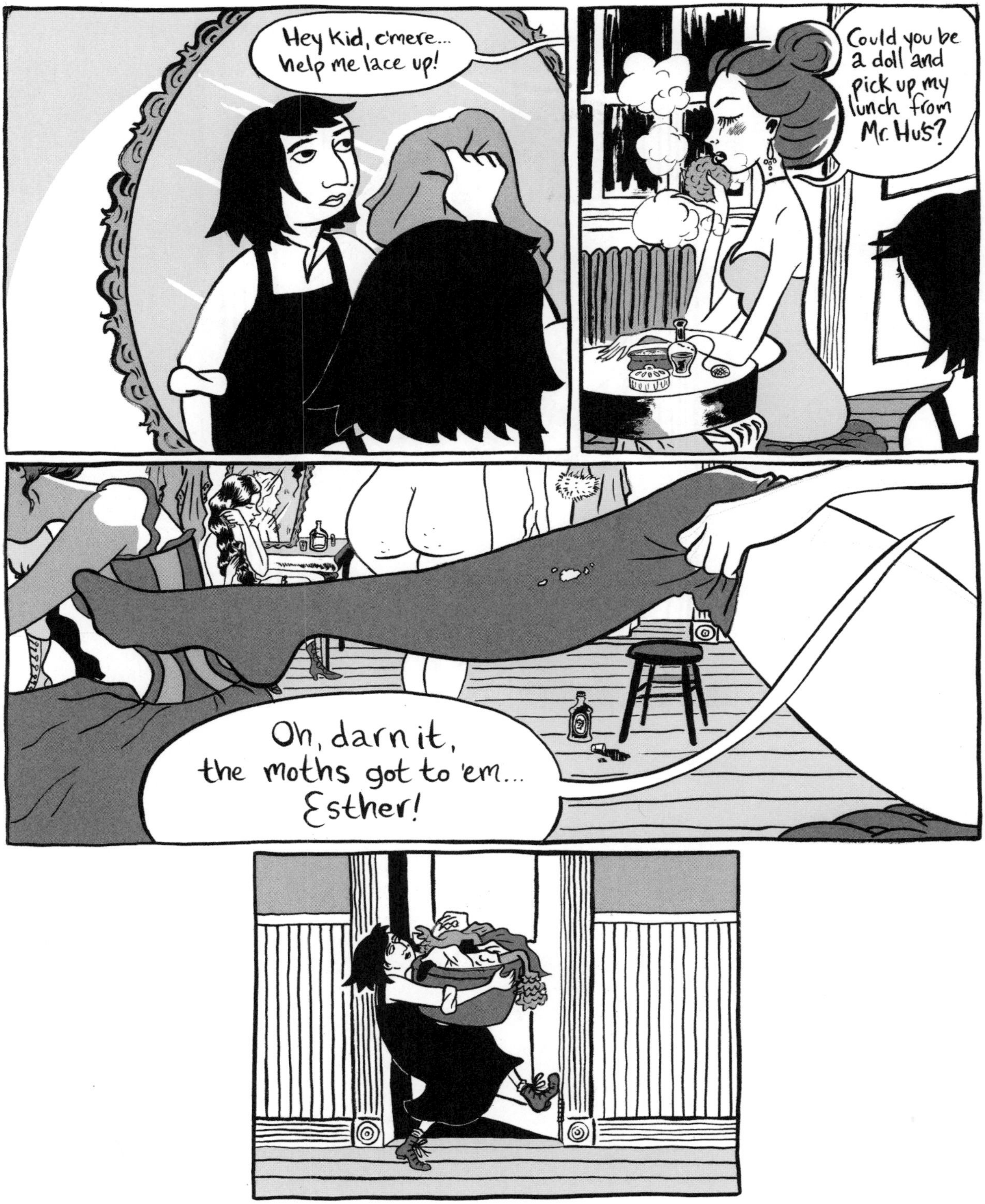
Hey kid, c'mere... help me lace up!
Could you be a doll and pick up my lunch from Mr. Hu's?
Oh, darn it, the moths got to 'em... Esther!

1912

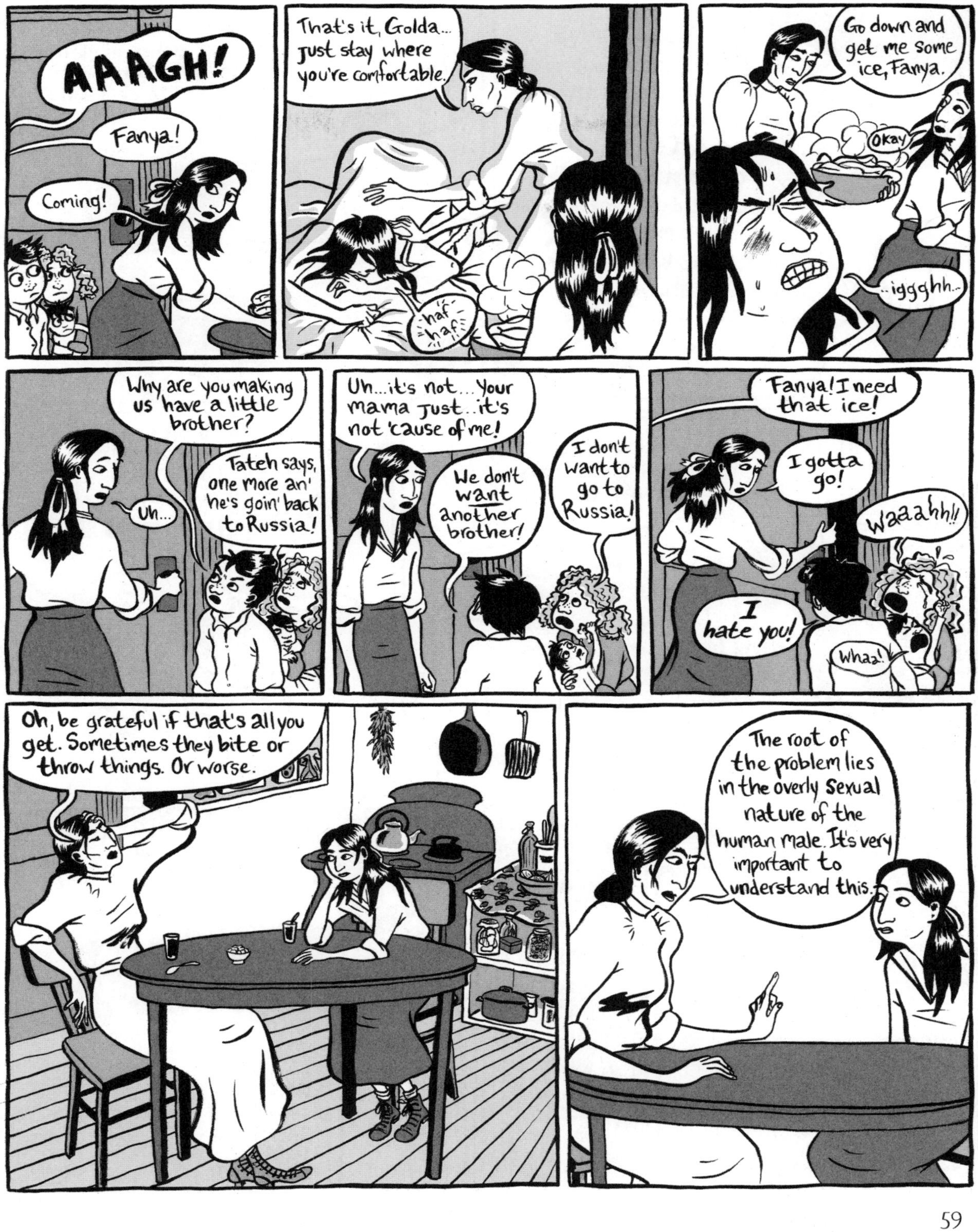
AAAGH!
Fanya!
Coming!
That's it, Golda... Just stay where you're comfortable.
haf haf
Go down and get me some ice, Fanya.
Okay
...iggghh...
Why are you making us have a little brother?
Uh...
Tateh says, one more an' he's goin' back to Russia!
Uh...it's not... Your mama Just...it's not 'cause of me!
We don't want another brother!
I don't want to go to Russia!
Fanya! I need that ice!
I gotta go!
Waaahh!!
I hate you!
Whaa!
Oh, be grateful if that's all you get. Sometimes they bite or throw things. Or worse.
The root of the problem lies in the overly sexual nature of the human male. It's very important to understand this.

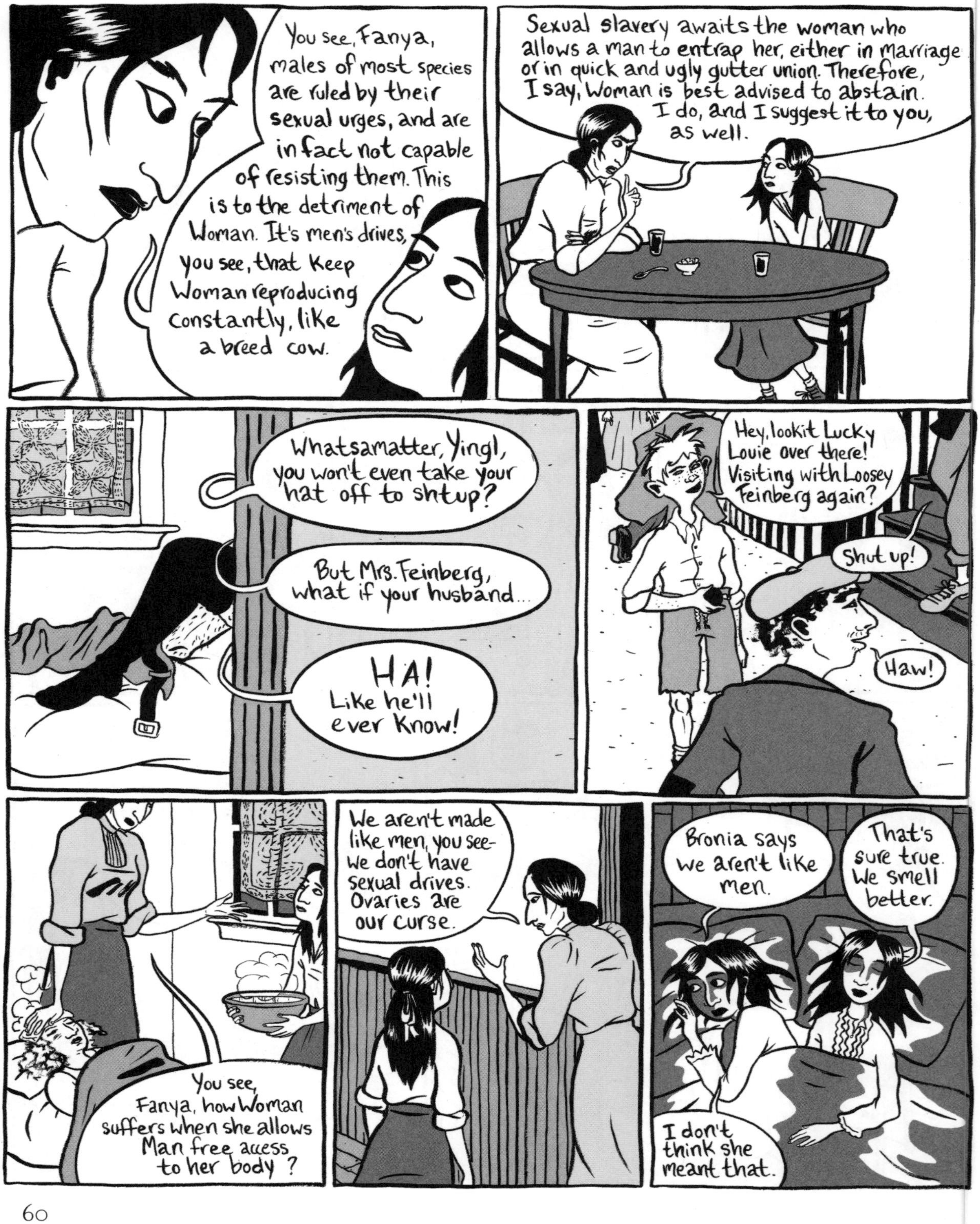
You see, Fanya, males of most species are ruled by their sexual urges, and are in fact not capable of resisting them. This is to the detriment of Woman. It's men's drives, you see, that keep Woman reproducing constantly, like a breed cow.
Sexual slavery awaits the woman who allows a man to entrap her, either in marriage or in quick and ugly gutter union. Therefore, I say, Woman is best advised to abstain. I do, and I suggest it to you, as well.
Whatsamatter, Yingl, you won't even take your hat off to shtup?
But Mrs. Feinberg, what if your husband...
HA! Like he'll ever know!
Hey, lookit Lucky Louie over there! Visiting with Loosey Feinberg again?
Shut up!
Haw!
You see, Fanya, how Woman suffers when she allows Man free access to her body?
We aren't made like men, you see- we don't have sexual drives. Ovaries are our curse.
Bronia says we aren't like men.
That's sure true. We smell better.
I don't think she meant that.

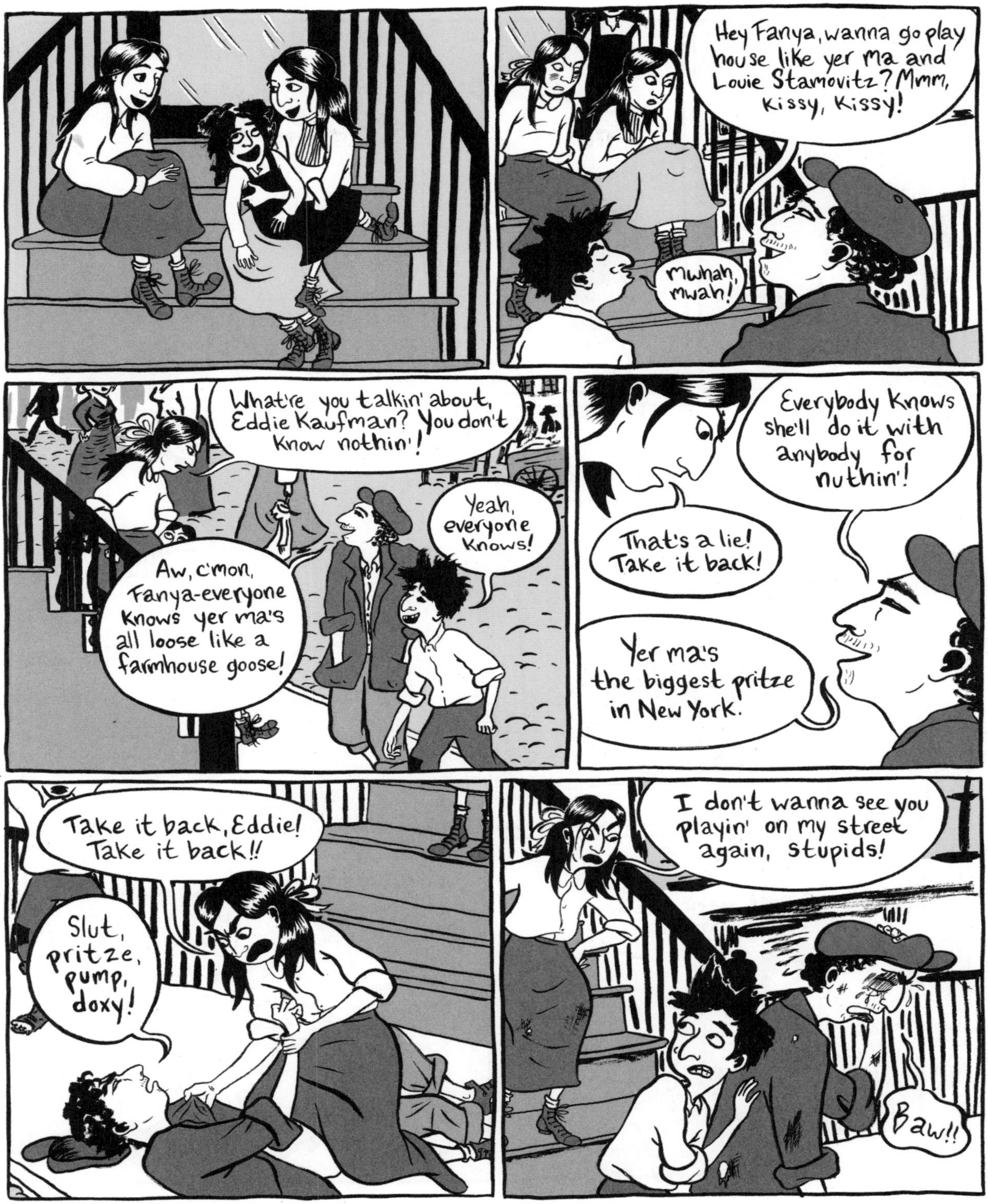

Hey Fanya, wanna go play house like yer ma and Louie Stamovitz? Mmm, Kissy, Kissy!
Mwhah, mwah!
What're you talkin' about, Eddie Kaufman? You don't Know nothin'!
Aw, c'mon, Fanya-everyone Knows yer ma's all loose like a farmhouse goose!
Yeah, everyone Knows!
Everybody Knows she'll do it with anybody for nuthin'!
That's a lie! Take it back!
Yer ma's the biggest pritze in New York.
Take it back, Eddie! Take it back!!
Slut, pritze, pump, doxy!
I don't wanna see you playin' on my street again, stupids!
Baw!!

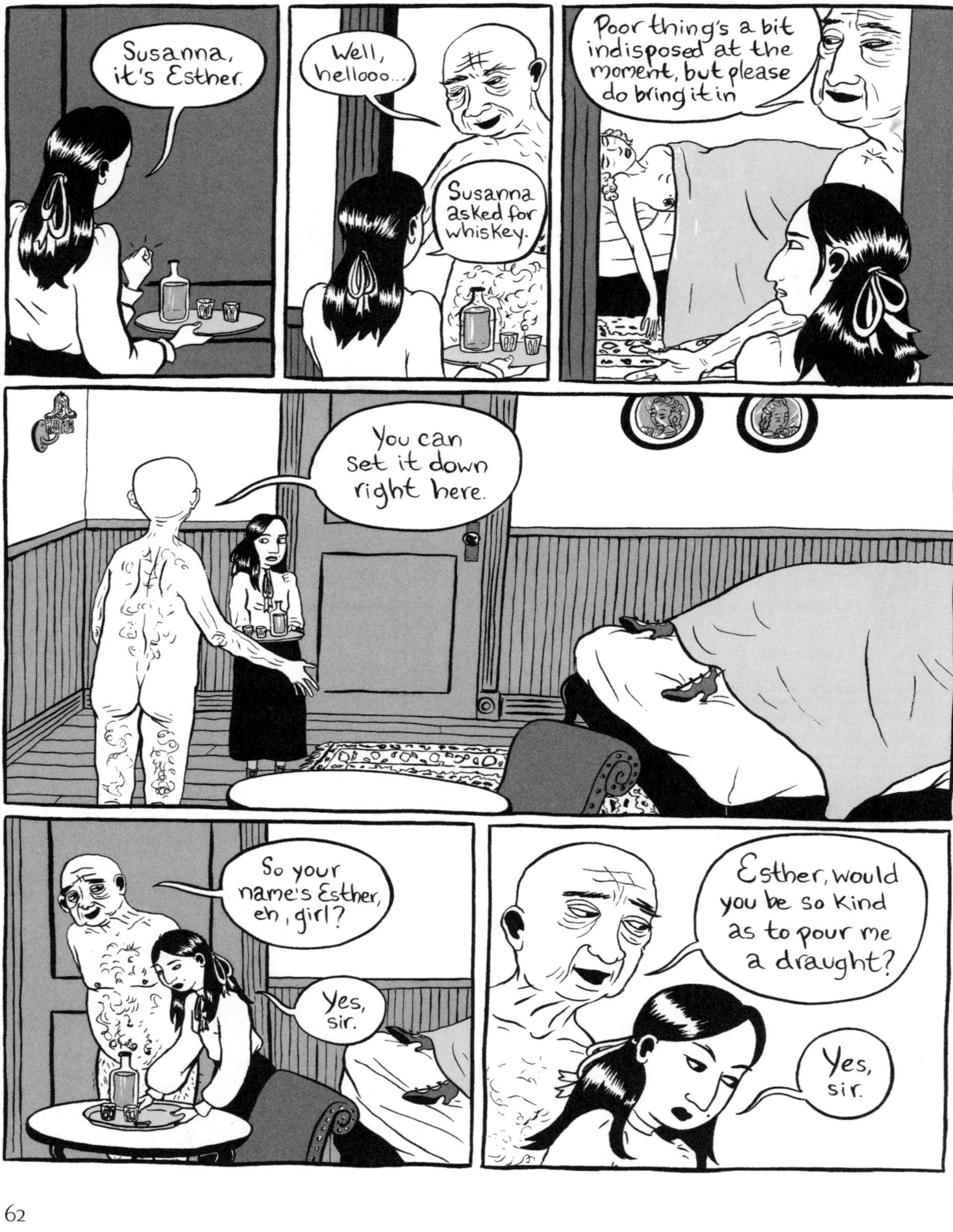
Susanna, it's Esther.
Well, hellooo...
Susanna asked for whiskey.
Poor thing's a bit indisposed at the moment, but please do bring it in
You can set it down right here.
So your name's Esther, eh, girl?
Yes, sir.
Esther, would you be so kind as to pour me a draught?
Yes, sir.

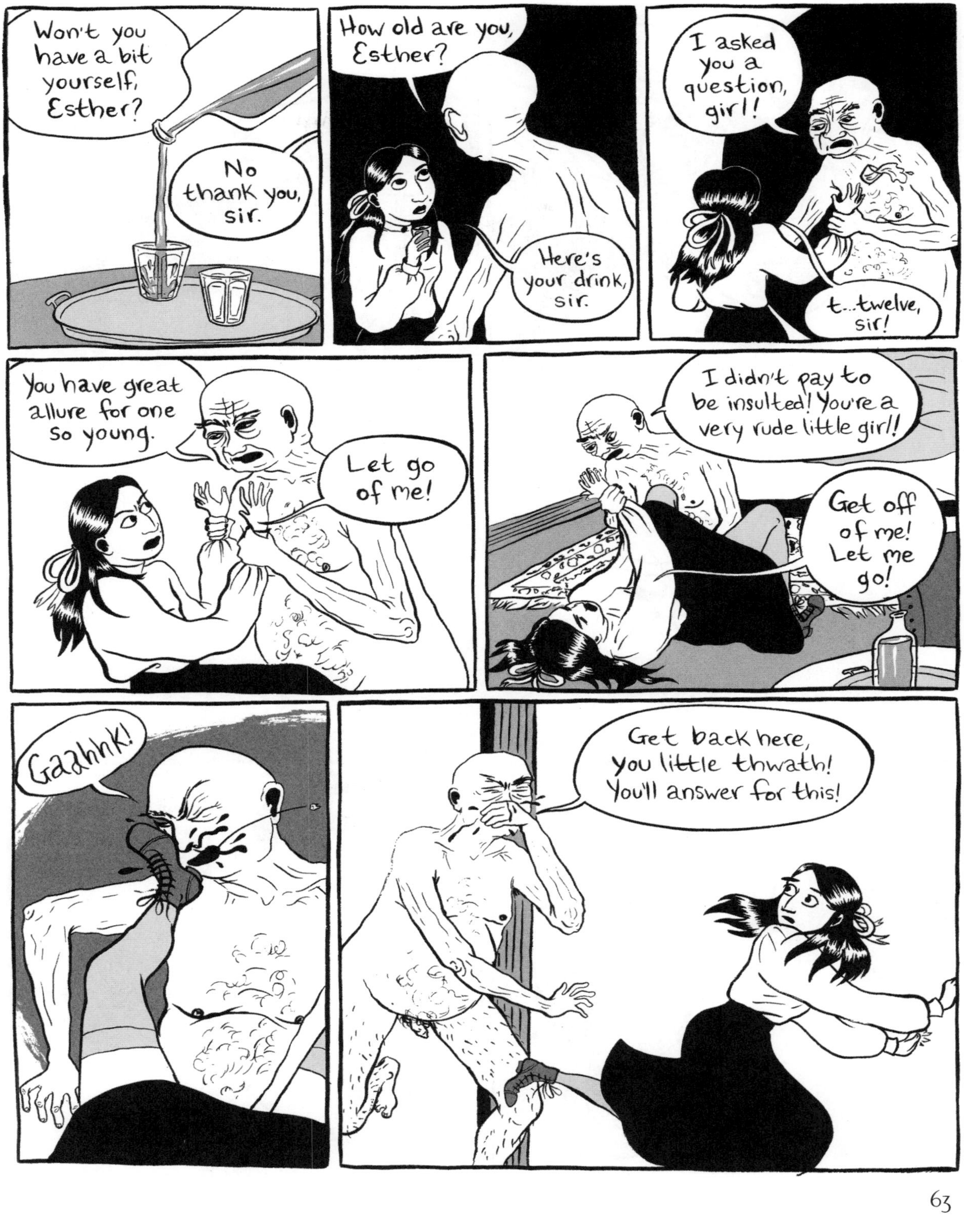
Won't you have a bit yourself, Esther?
No thank you, sir.
How old are you, Esther?
Here's your drink, sir.
I asked you a question, girl!
t...twelve, sir!
You have great allure for one so young.
Let go of me!
I didn't pay to be insulted! You're a very rude little girl!
Get off of me! Let me go!
Gaahhk!
Get back here, you little thwath! You'll answer for this!

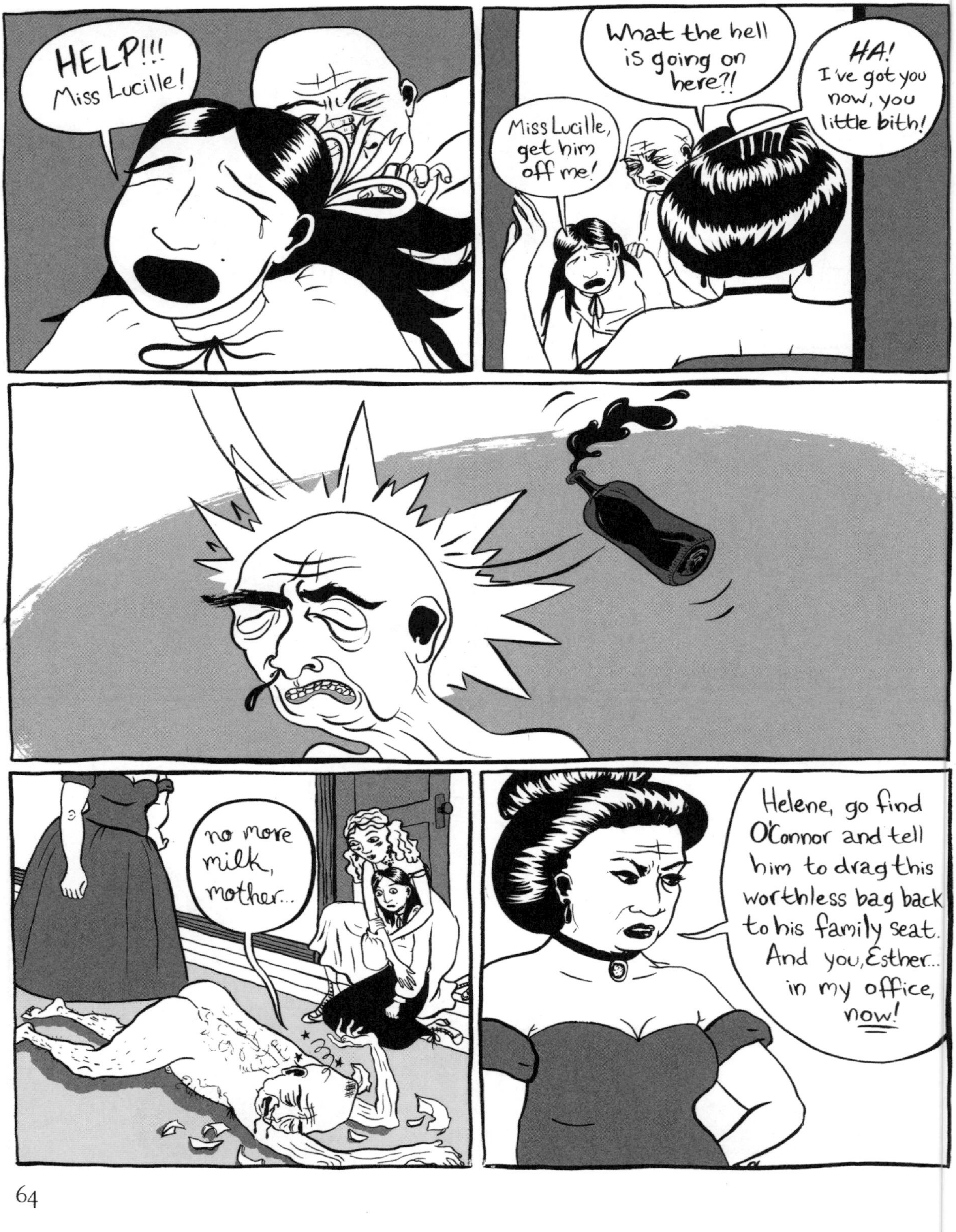
HELP!!!
Miss Lucille!
What the hell is going on here?!
HA! I've got you now, you little bith!
Miss Lucille, get him off me!
no more milk, mother...
Helene, go find O'Connor and tell him to drag this worthless bag back to his family seat. And you, Esther... in my office, now!

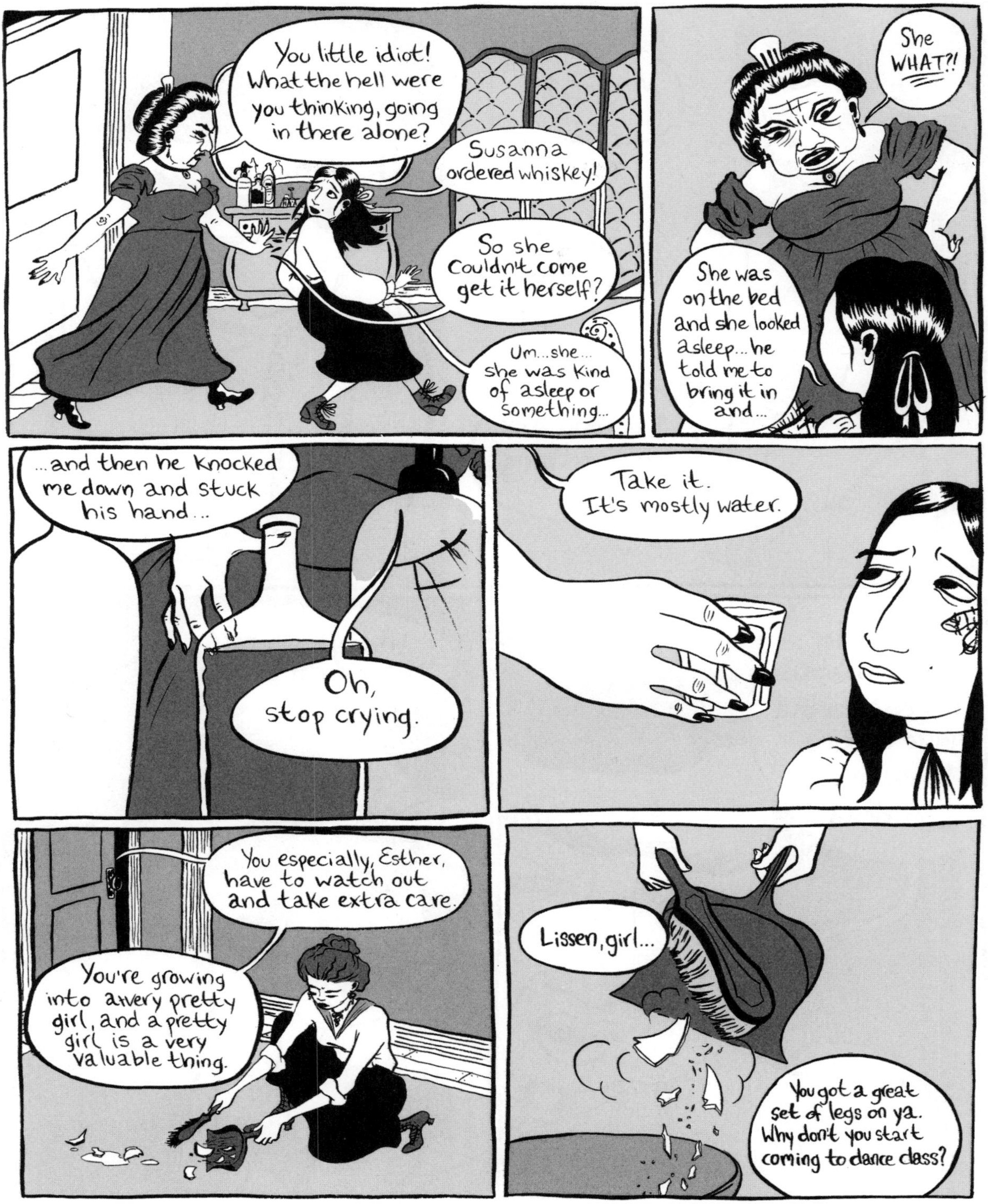
You little idiot! What the hell were you thinking, going in there alone?
Susanna ordered whiskey!
So she couldn't come get it herself?
Um...she... she was kind of asleep or something...
She WHAT?!
She was on the bed and she looked asleep... he told me to bring it in and...
...and then he knocked me down and stuck his hand...
Oh, stop crying.
Take it. It's mostly water.
You especially, Esther, have to watch out and take extra care.
You're growing into a very pretty girl, and a pretty girl is a very valuable thing.
Lissen, girl...
You got a great set of legs on ya. Why don't you start coming to dance class?

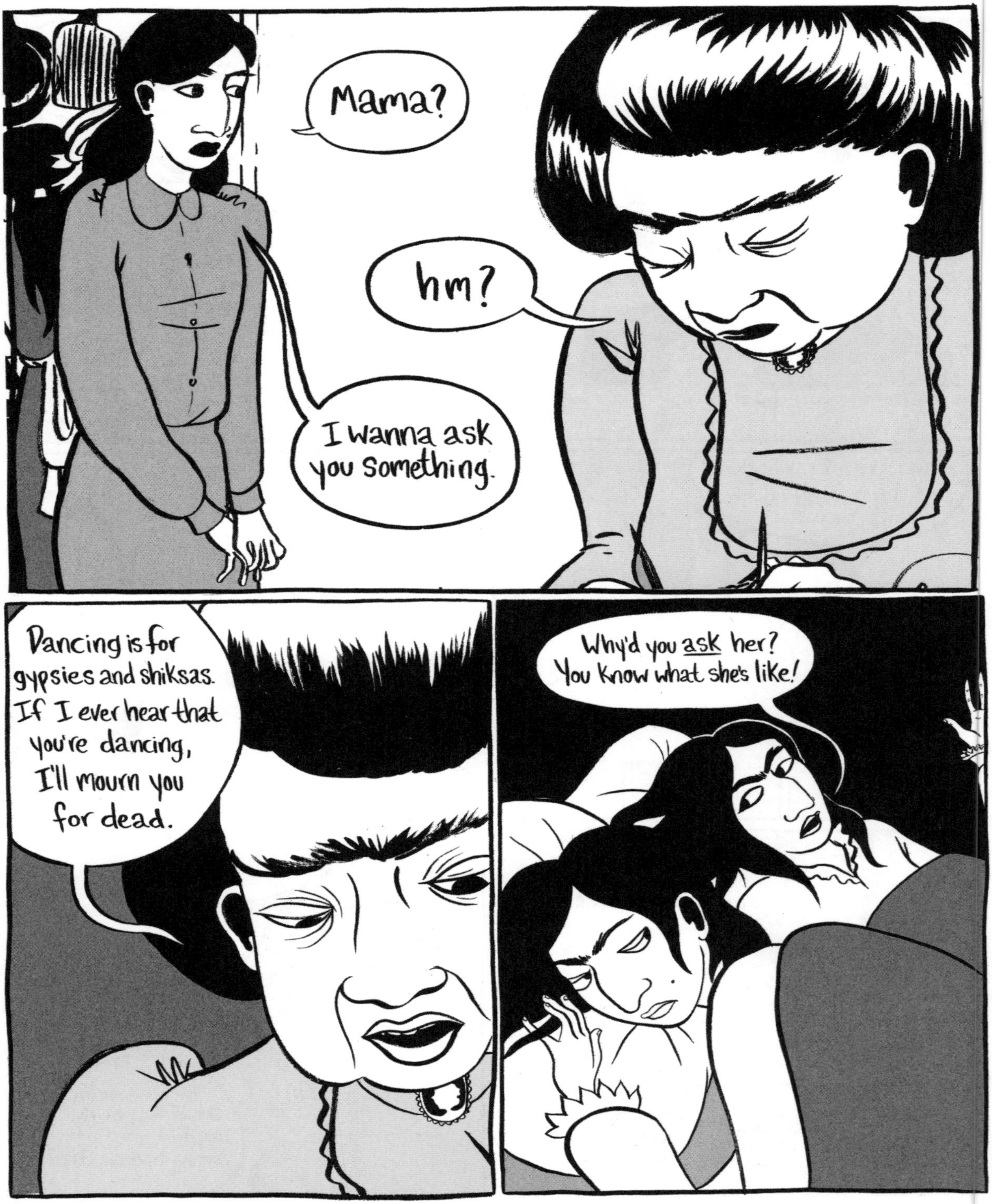
Mama?
hm?
I wanna ask you something.
Dancing is for gypsies and shiksas. If I ever hear that you're dancing, I'll mourn you for dead.
Why'd you ask her? You know what she's like!

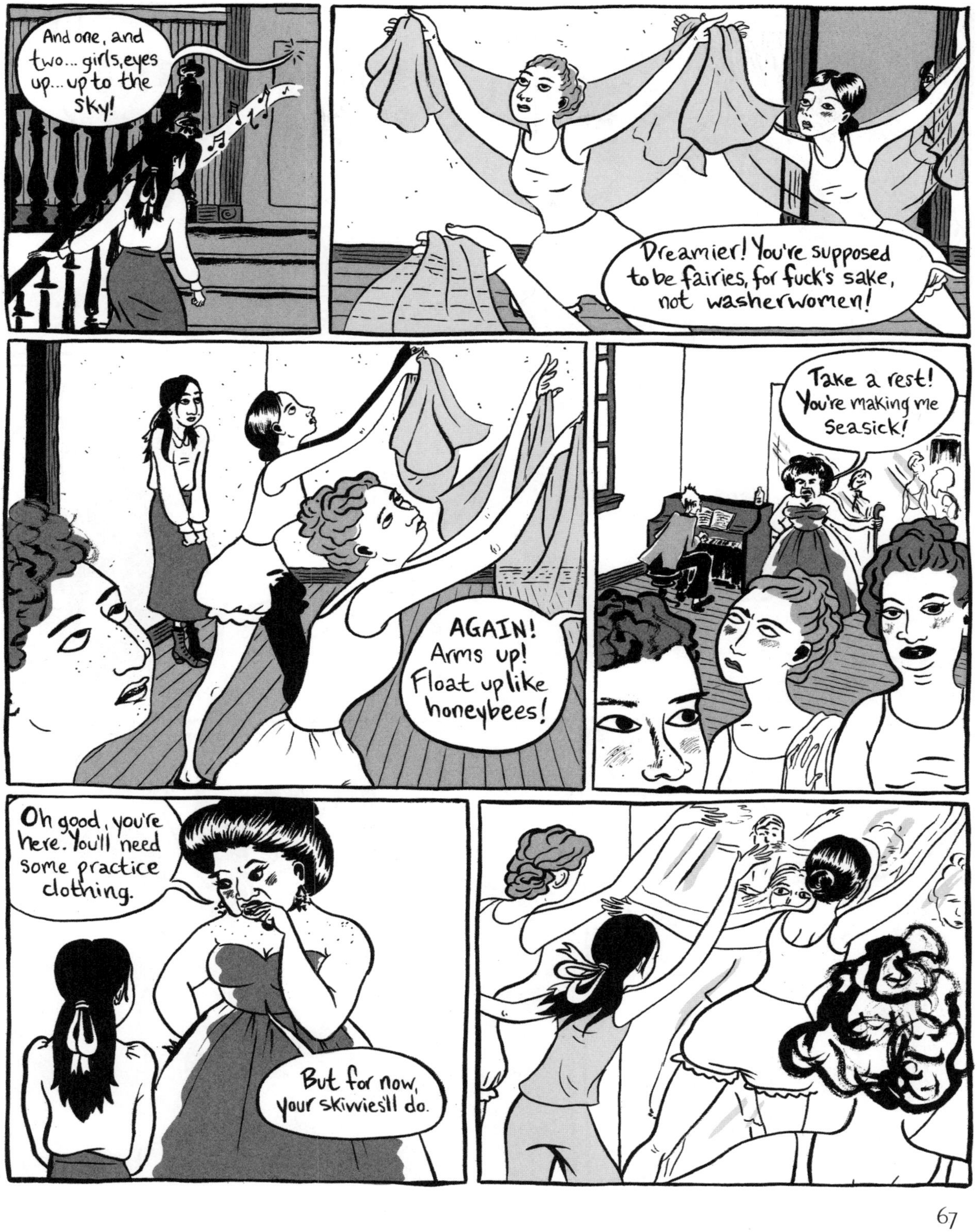
And one, and two... girls, eyes up... up to the sky!
Dreamier! You're supposed to be fairies, for fuck's sake, not washerwomen!
AGAIN! Arms up! Float up like honeybees!
Take a rest! You're making me seasick!
Oh good, you're here. You'll need some practice clothing.
But for now, your skivvies'll do.

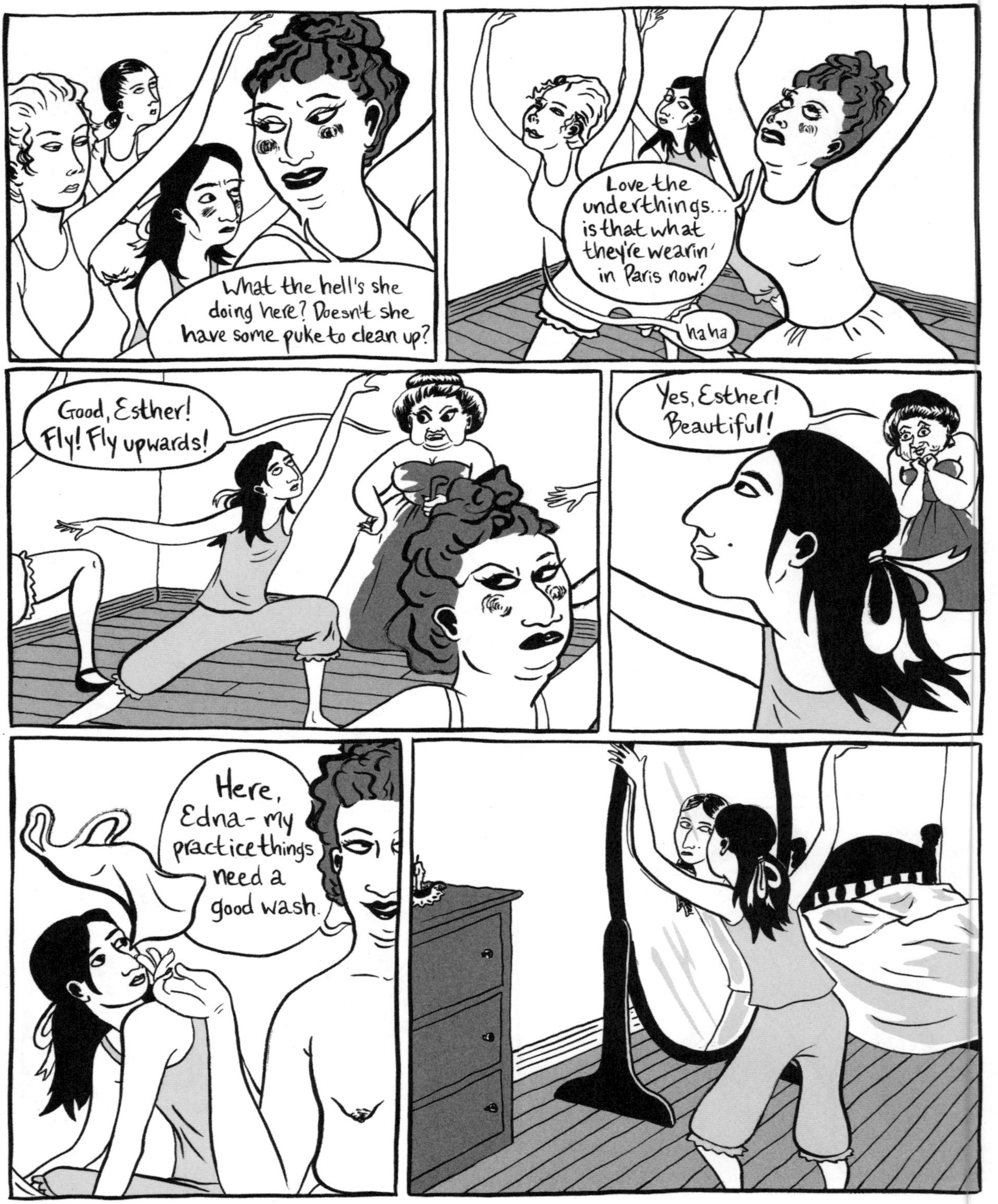
What the hell's she doing here? Doesn't she have some puke to clean up?
Love the underthings... is that what they're wearin' in Paris now?
haha
Good, Esther! Fly! Fly upwards!
Yes, Esther! Beautiful!
Here, Edna- my practice things need a good wash.

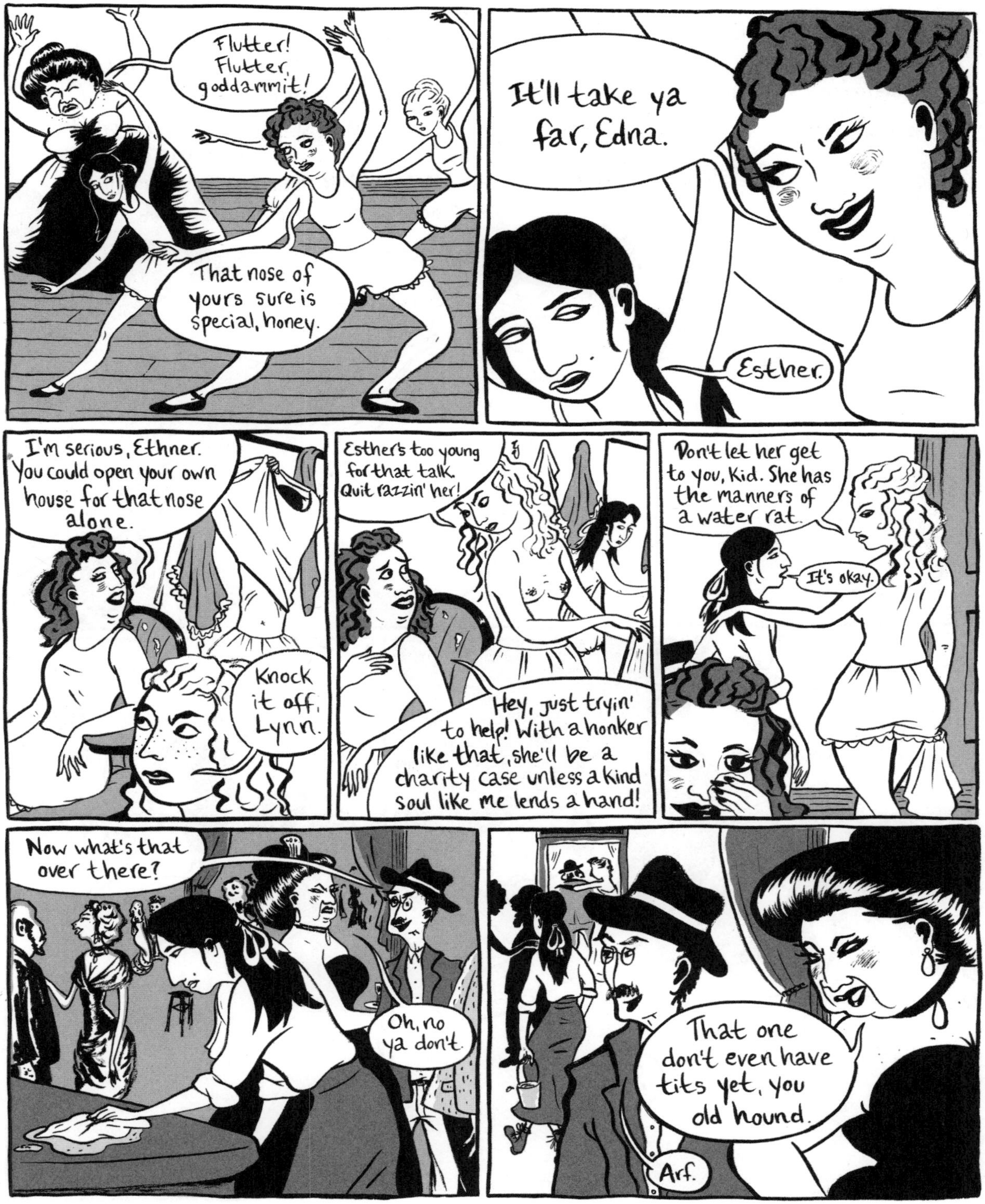

Flutter! Flutter, goddammit!
That nose of yours sure is special, honey.
It'll take ya far, Edna.
Esther.
I'm serious, Ethner. You could open your own house for that nose alone.
Knock it off, Lynn.
Esther's too young for that talk. Quit razzin' her!
Hey, just tryin' to help! With a honker like that, she'll be a charity case unless a kind soul like me lends a hand!
Don't let her get to you, Kid. She has the manners of a water rat.
It's okay.
Now what's that over there?
Oh, no ya don't.
That one don't even have tits yet, you old hound.
Arf.

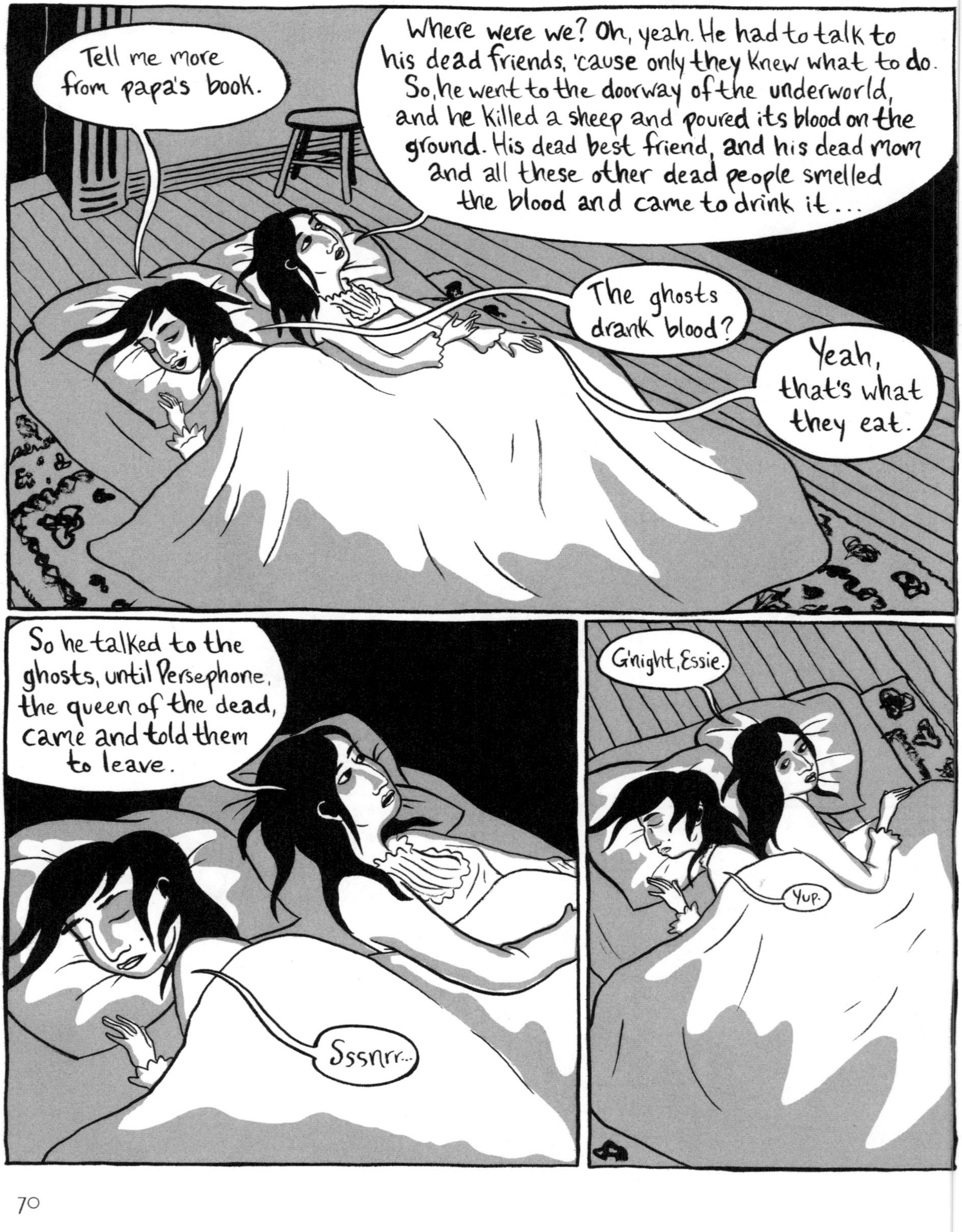
Tell me more from papa's book.
Where were we? Oh, yeah. He had to talk to his dead friends, 'cause only they knew what to do. So, he went to the doorway of the underworld, and he killed a sheep and poured its blood on the ground. His dead best friend, and his dead mom and all these other dead people smelled the blood and came to drink it . . .
The ghosts drank blood?
Yeah, that's what they eat.
So he talked to the ghosts, until Persephone, the queen of the dead, came and told them to leave.
Sssnrr...
G'night, Essie.
Yup.

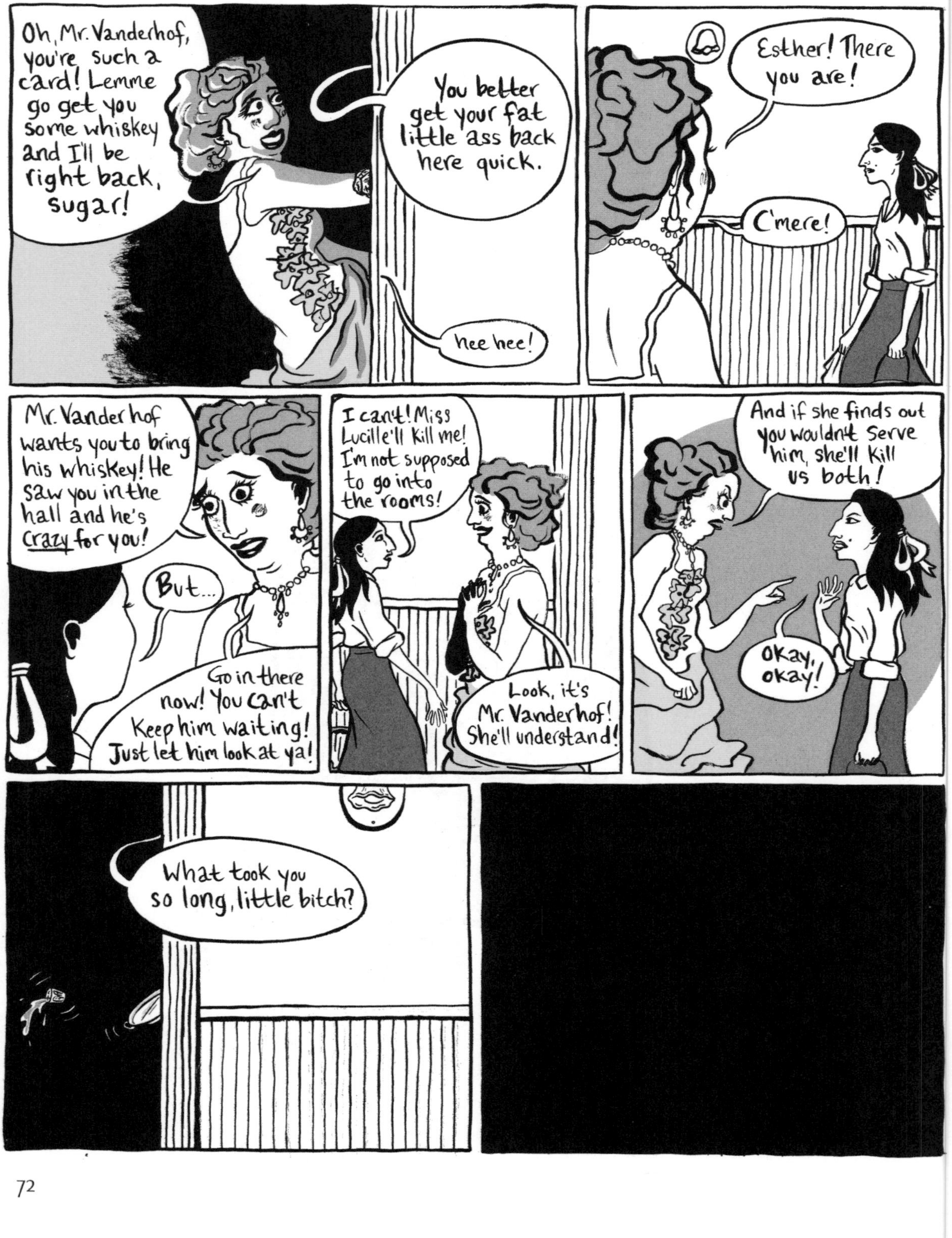
Oh, Mr. Vanderhof, you're such a card! Lemme go get you some whiskey and I'll be right back, sugar!
You better get your fat little ass back here quick.
hee hee!
Esther! There you are!
C'mere!
Mr. Vanderhof wants you to bring his whiskey! He saw you in the hall and he's crazy for you!
But...
Go in there now! You can't keep him waiting! Just let him look at ya!
I can't! Miss Lucille'll kill me! I'm not supposed to go into the rooms!
Look, it's Mr. Vanderhof! She'll understand!
And if she finds out you wouldn't serve him, she'll kill us both!
Okay, okay!
What took you so long, little bitch?

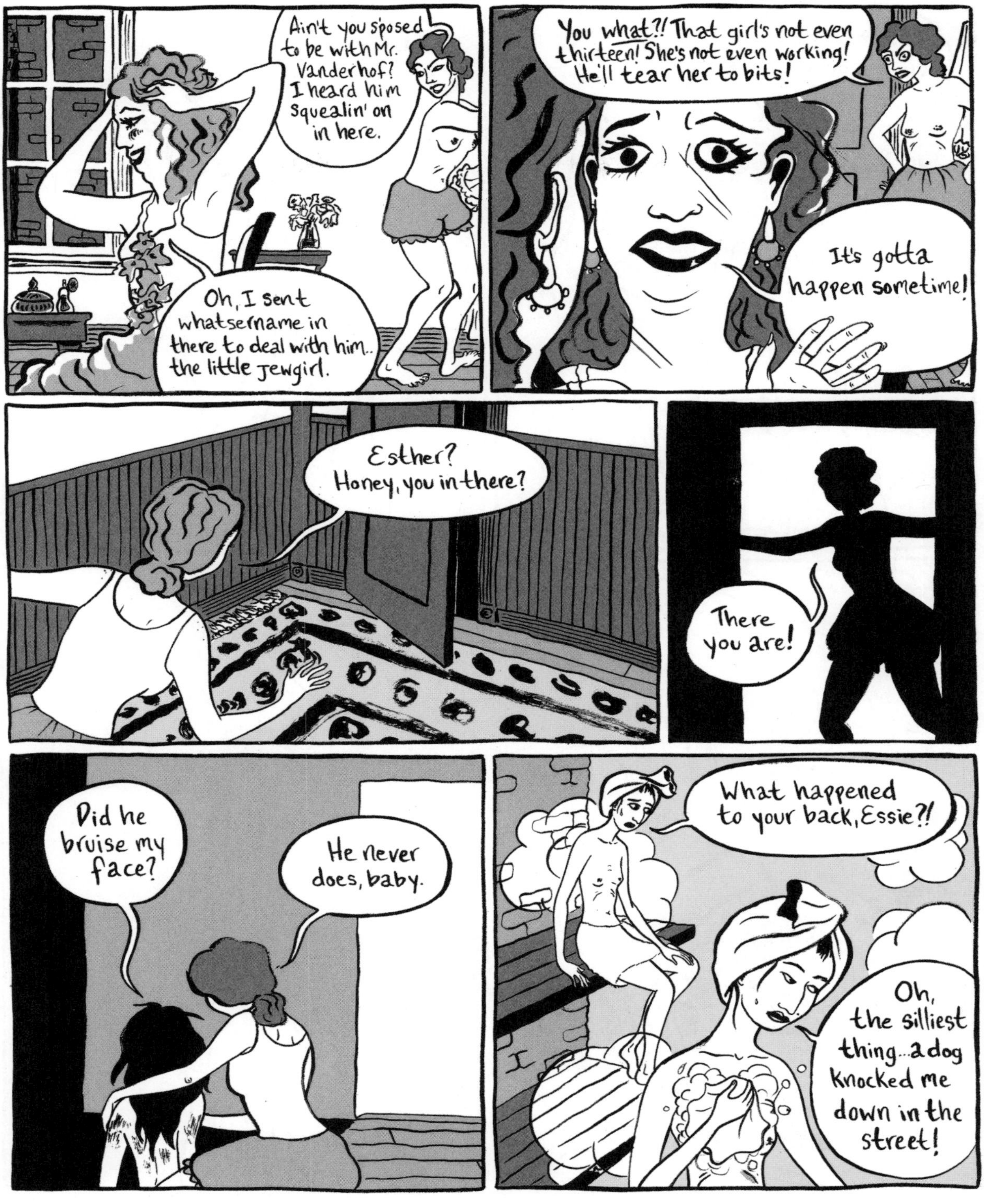

Ain't you s'posed to be with Mr. Vanderhof? I heard him squealin' on in here.
Oh, I sent whatsername in there to deal with him.. the little Jewgirl.
You what?! That girl's not even thirteen! She's not even working! He'll tear her to bits!
It's gotta happen sometime!
Esther? Honey, you in there?
There you are!
Did he bruise my face?
He never does, baby.
What happened to your back, Essie?!
Oh, the silliest thing...a dog knocked me down in the street!

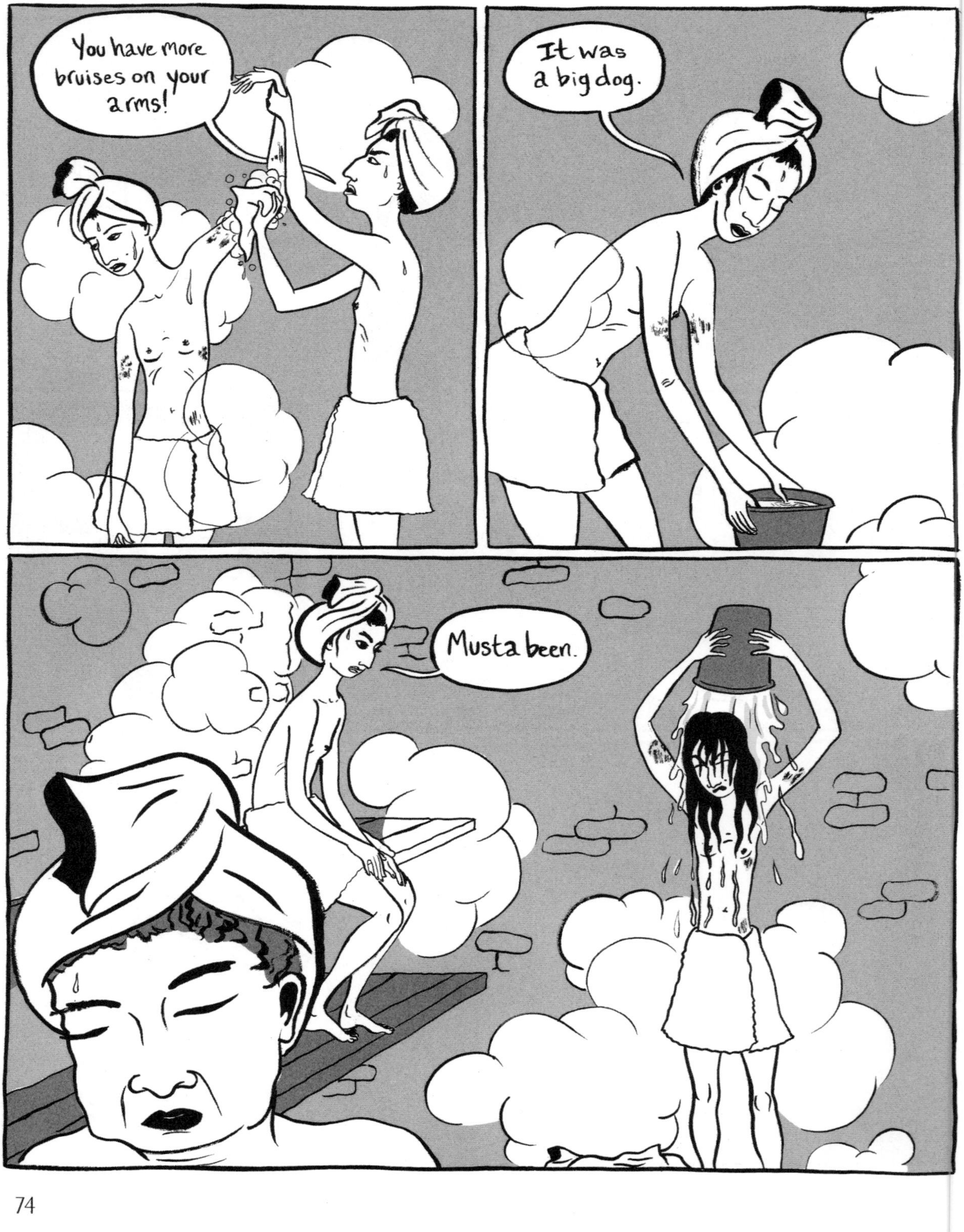
You have more bruises on your arms!
It was a big dog.
Musta been.

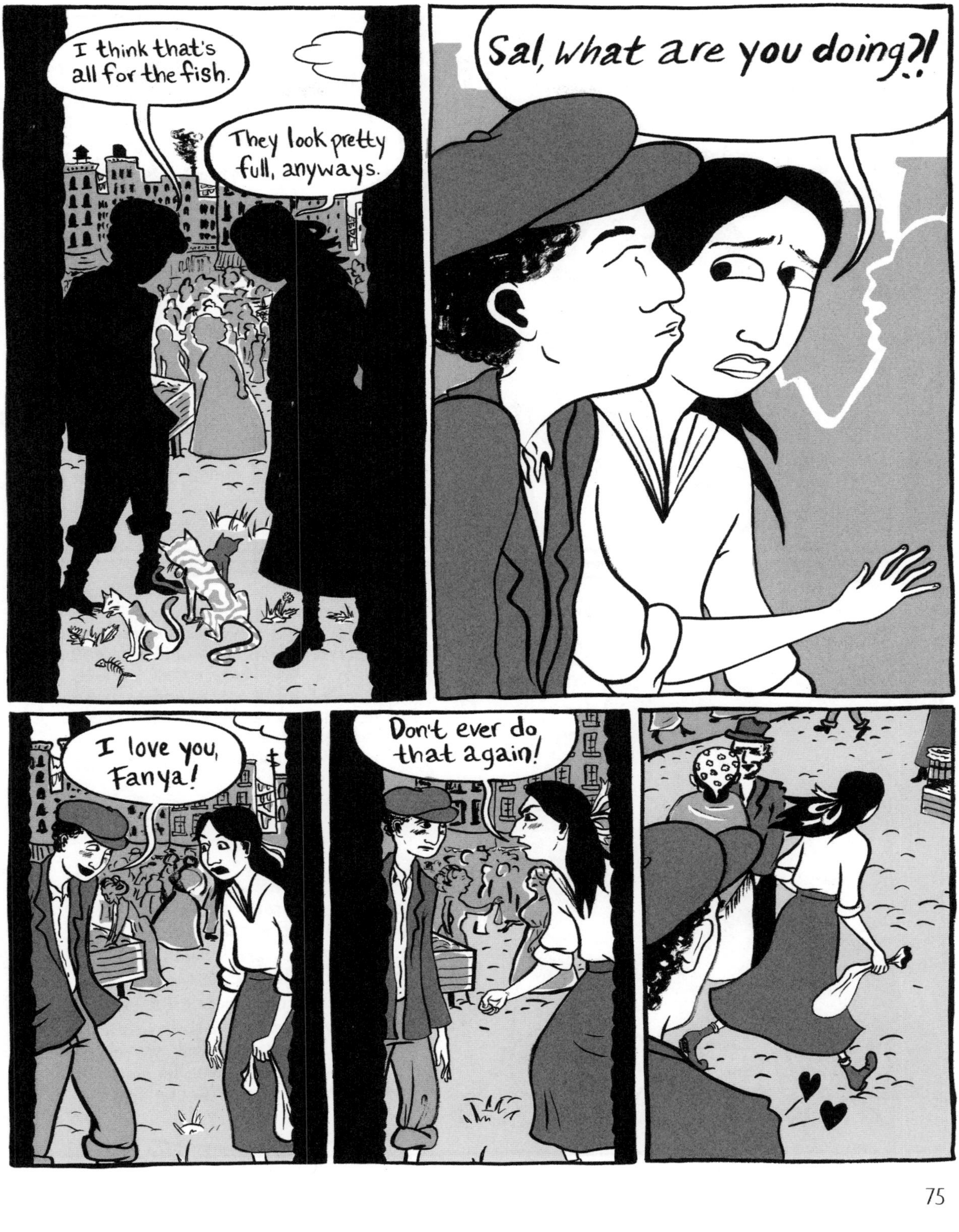
I think that's all for the fish.
They look pretty full, anyways.
Sal, what are you doing?!
I love you, Fanya!
Don't ever do that again!

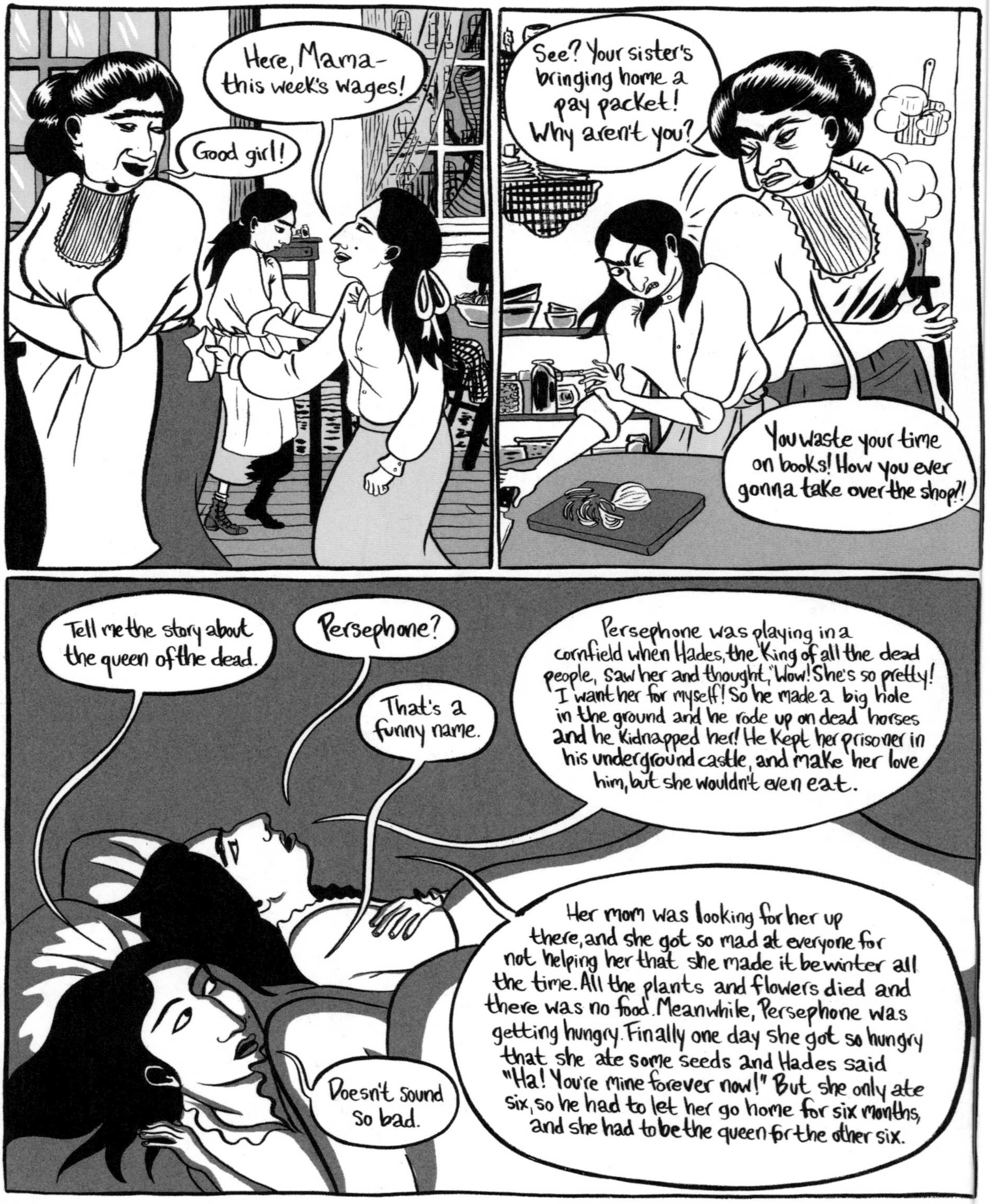
Here, Mama- this week's wages!
Good girl!
See? Your sister's bringing home a pay packet! Why aren't you?
You waste your time on books! How you ever gonna take over the shop?!
Tell me the story about the queen of the dead.
Persephone?
That's a funny name.
Persephone was playing in a cornfield when Hades, the King of all the dead people, saw her and thought, "Wow! She's so pretty! I want her for myself! So he made a big hole in the ground and he rode up on dead horses and he kidnapped her! He kept her prisoner in his underground castle, and make her love him, but she wouldn't even eat.
Her mom was looking for her up there, and she got so mad at everyone for not helping her that she made it be winter all the time. All the plants and flowers died and there was no food. Meanwhile, Persephone was getting hungry. Finally one day she got so hungry that she ate some seeds and Hades said "Ha! You're mine forever now!" But she only ate six, so he had to let her go home for six months, and she had to be the queen for the other six.
Doesn't sound so bad.

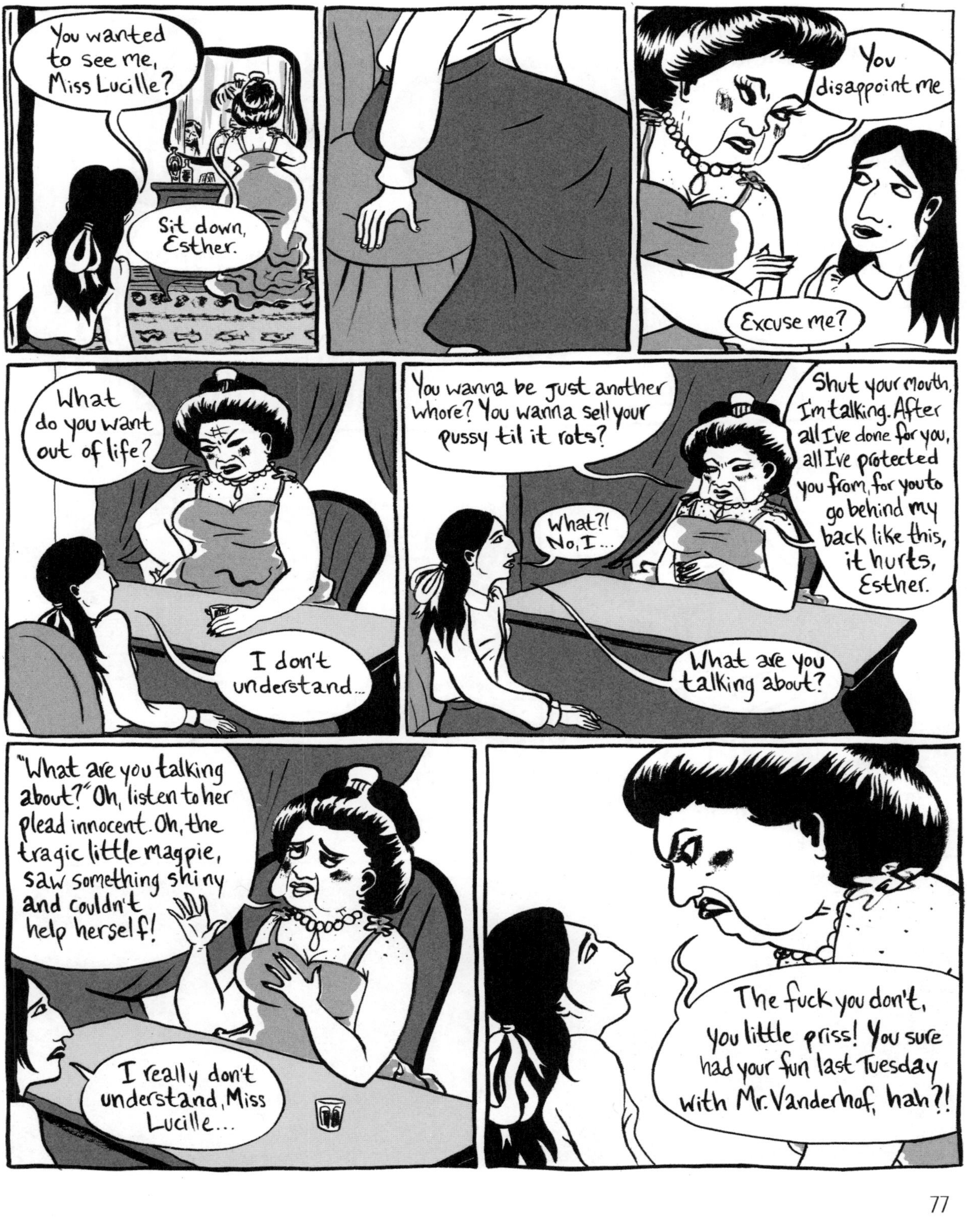
You wanted to see me, Miss Lucille?
Sit down, Esther.
You disappoint me.
Excuse me?
What do you want out of life?
I don't understand...
You wanna be just another whore? You wanna sell your pussy til it rots?
What?! No, I...
Shut your mouth, I'm talking. After all I've done for you, all I've protected you from, for you to go behind my back like this, it hurts, Esther.
What are you talking about?
"What are you talking about?" Oh, listen to her plead innocent. Oh, the tragic little magpie, saw something shiny and couldn't help herself!
I really don't understand, Miss Lucille...
The fuck you don't, you little priss! You sure had your fun last Tuesday with Mr. Vanderhof, hah?!

If you're achin' to sell it so bad that you'll do it in my house, without my permission, well, who am I to stop you? I'd been hoping to début you to one of our more... discerning clients, but since you've beaten me to it, you may as well continue.

Tomorrow you start working in the house, like the other girls. Now get your ass to dance class.

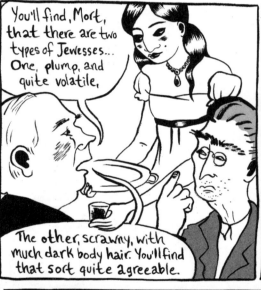

You'll find, Mort, that there are two types of Jewesses... One, plump, and quite volatile,

The other, scrawny, with much dark body hair. You'll find that sort quite agreeable.

You smell like a silly woman's perfume.

Guess I'm just a silly woman.

78

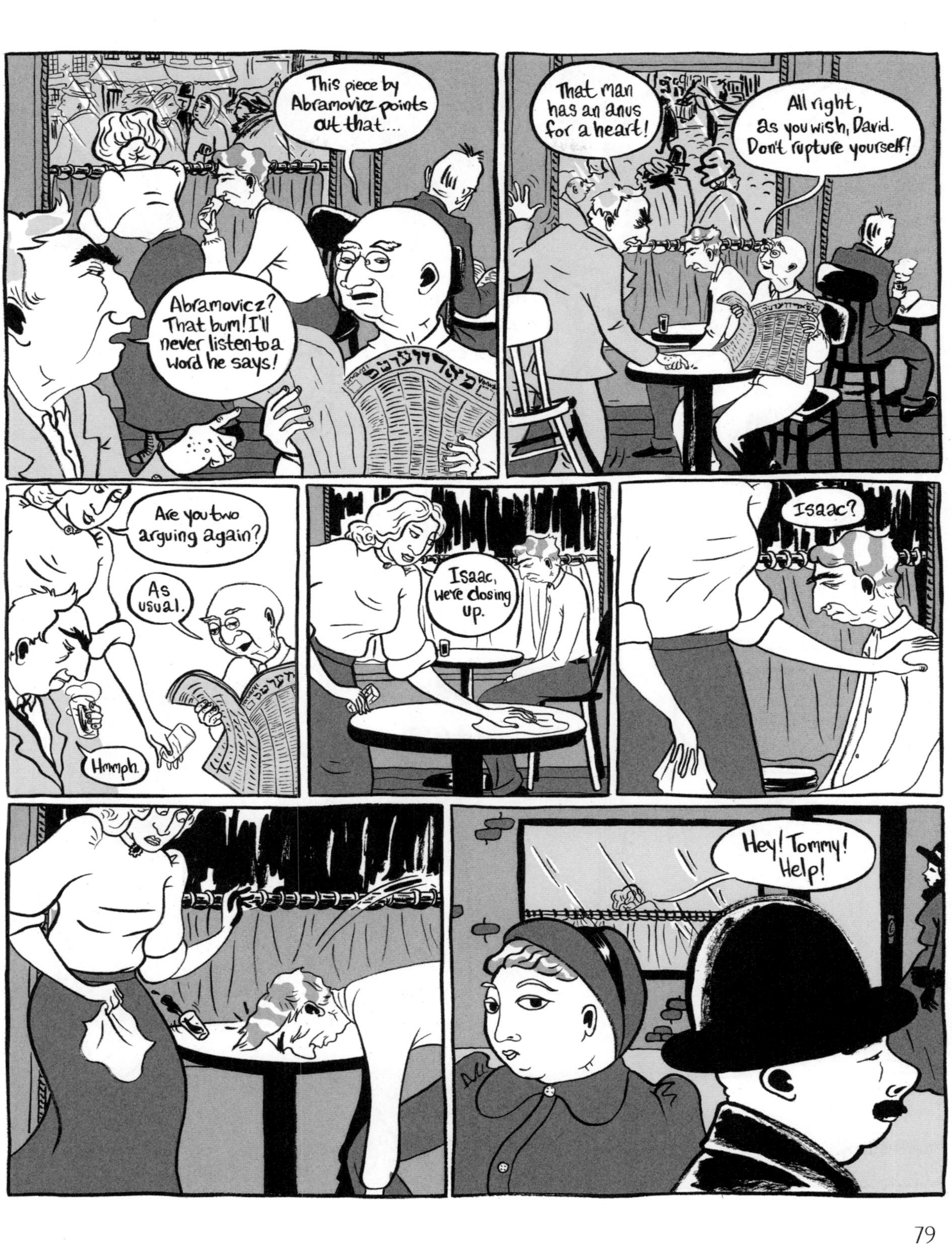
This piece by Abramovicz points out that...
Abramovicz? That bum! I'll never listen to a word he says!
That man has an anus for a heart!
All right, as you wish, David. Don't rupture yourself!
Are you two arguing again?
As usual.
Hmmph.
Isaac, we're closing up.
Isaac?
Hey! Tommy! Help!

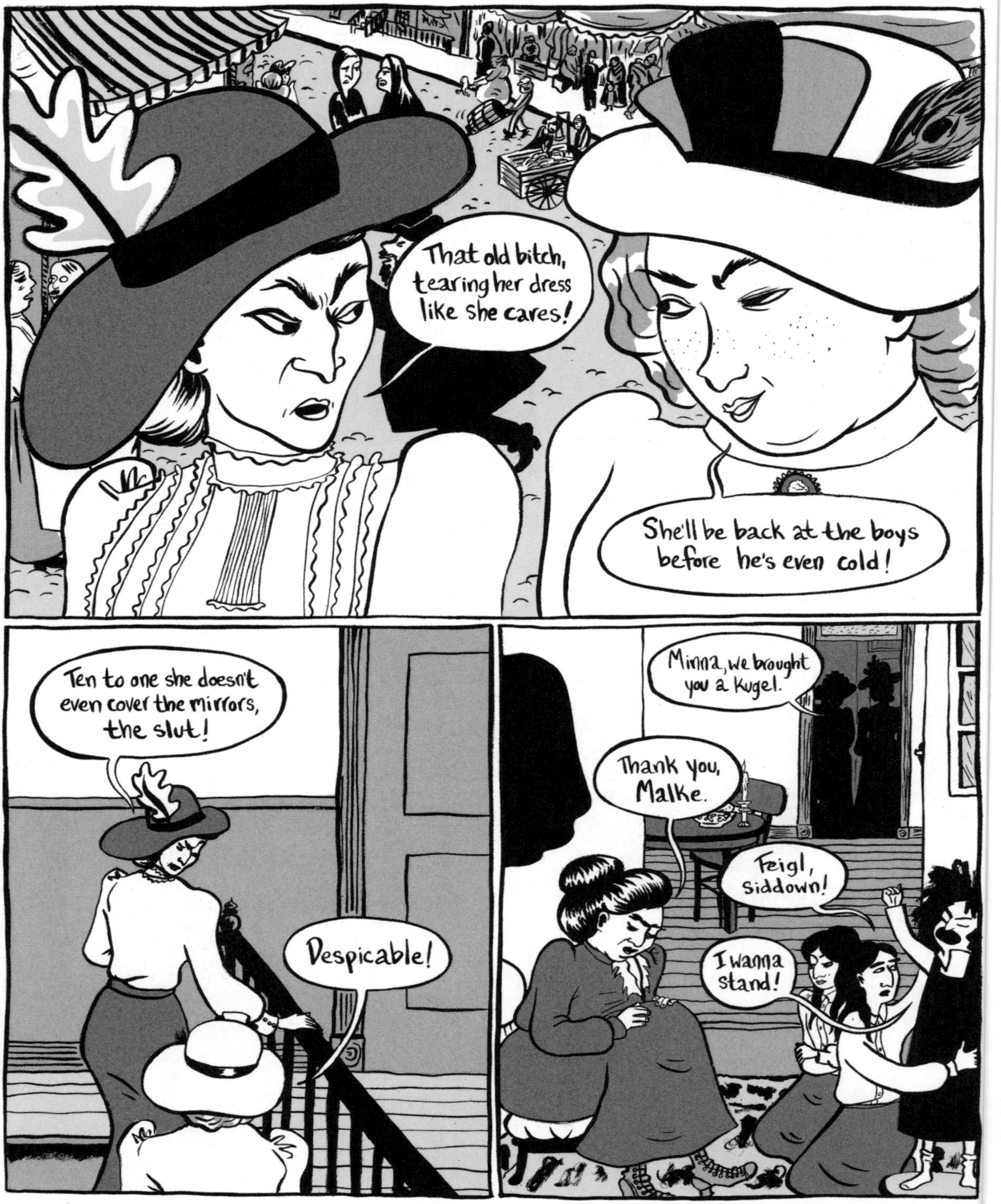
That old bitch, tearing her dress like she cares!
She'll be back at the boys before he's even cold!
Ten to one she doesn't even cover the mirrors, the slut!
Despicable!
Minna, we brought you a kugel.
Thank you, Malke.
Feigl, siddown!
I wanna stand!

1895

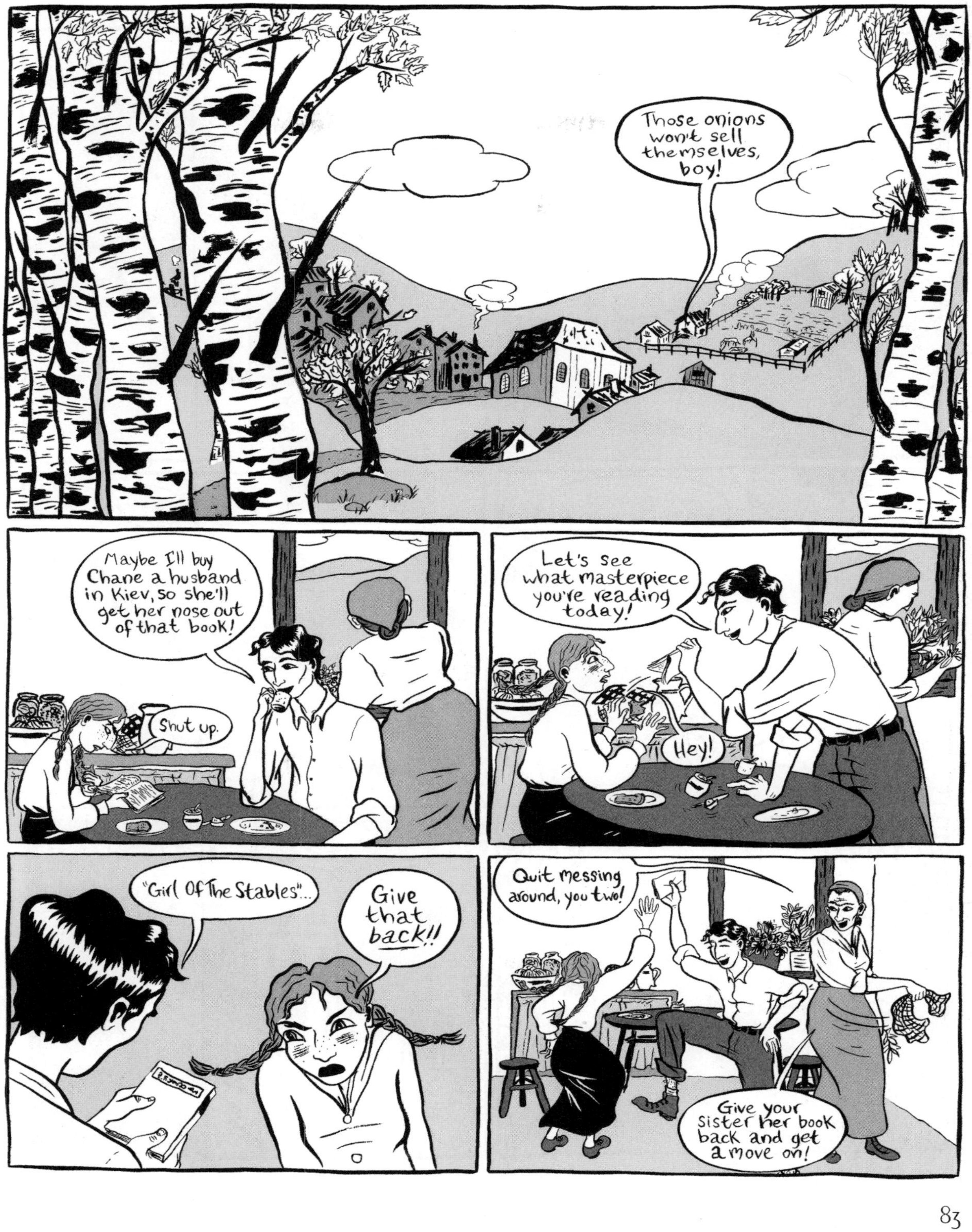
Those onions won't sell themselves, boy!
Maybe I'll buy Chane a husband in Kiev, so she'll get her nose out of that book!
Shut up.
Let's see what masterpiece you're reading today!
Hey!
"Girl Of The Stables"...
Give that back!!
Quit messing around, you two!
Give your sister her book back and get a move on!

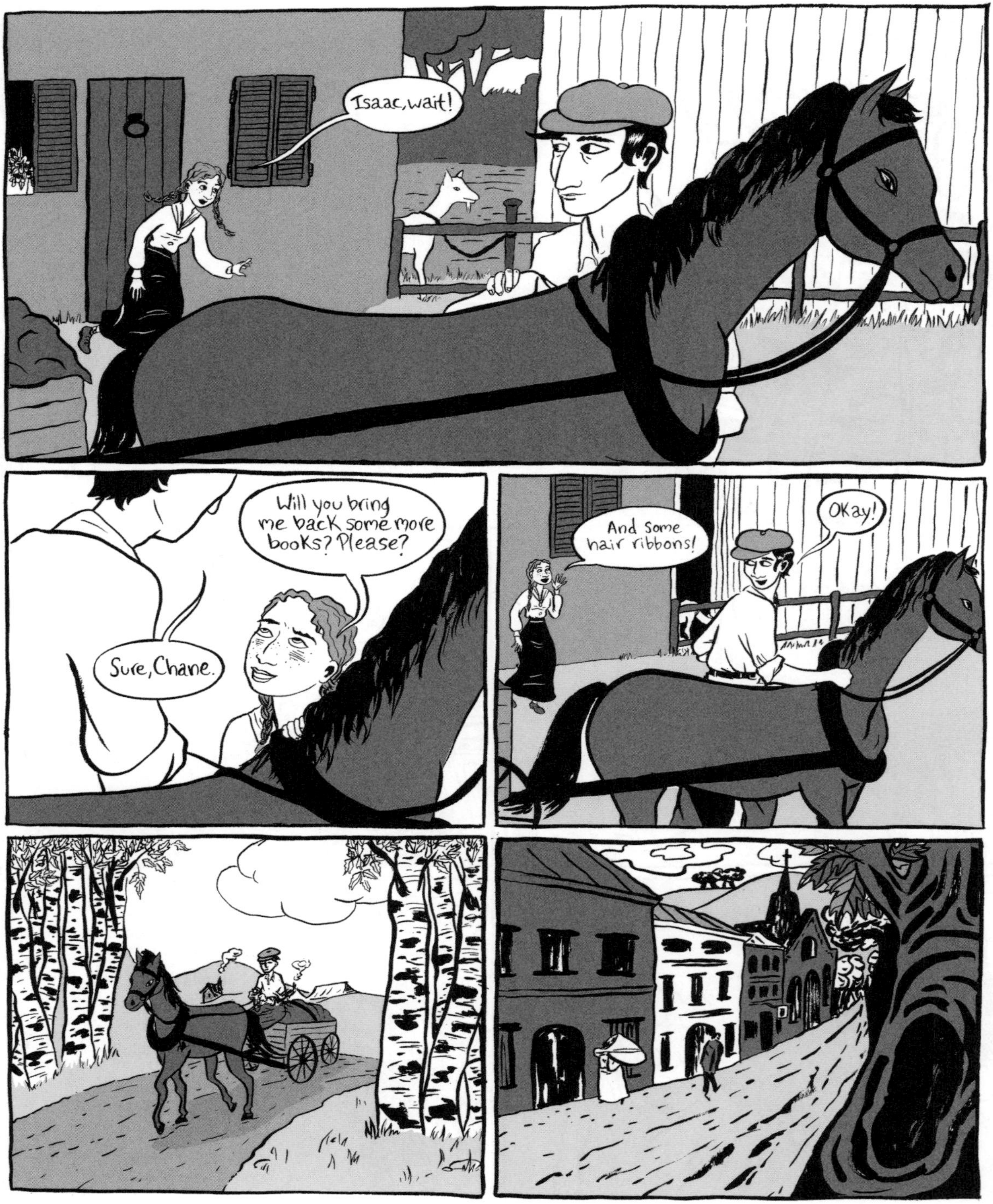
Isaac, wait!
Will you bring me back some more books? Please?
Sure, Chane.
And some hair ribbons!
Okay!

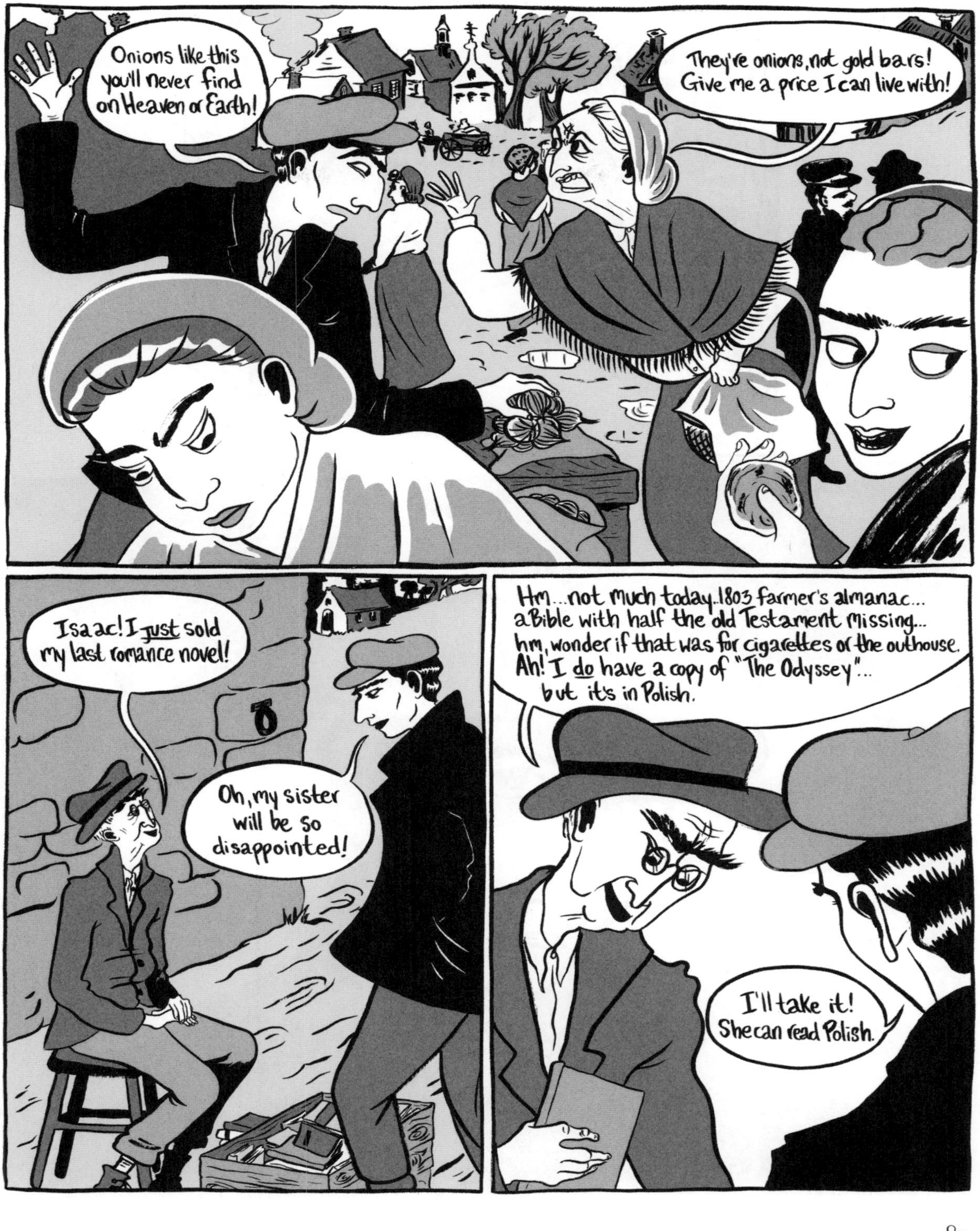
Onions like this you'll never find on Heaven or Earth!
They're onions, not gold bars! Give me a price I can live with!
Isaac! I just sold my last romance novel!
Oh, my sister will be so disappointed!
Hm...not much today..1803 farmer's almanac... a Bible with half the old Testament missing... hm, wonder if that was for cigarettes or the outhouse. Ah! I do have a copy of "The Odyssey"... but it's in Polish.
I'll take it! She can read Polish.

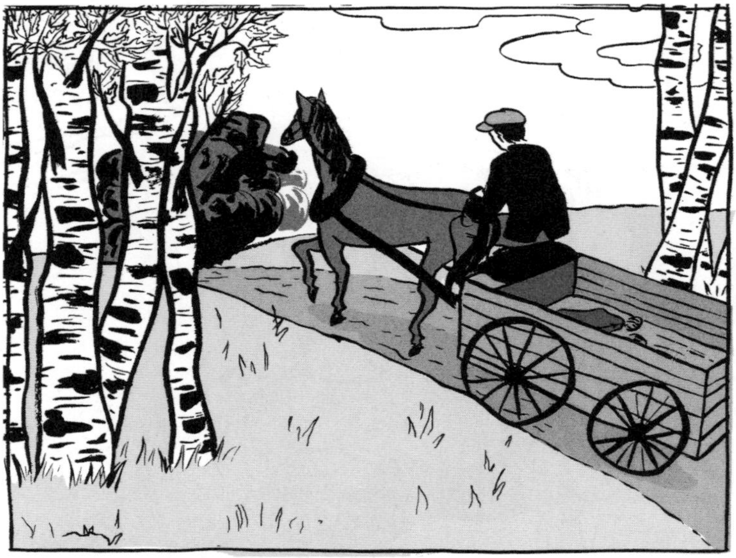

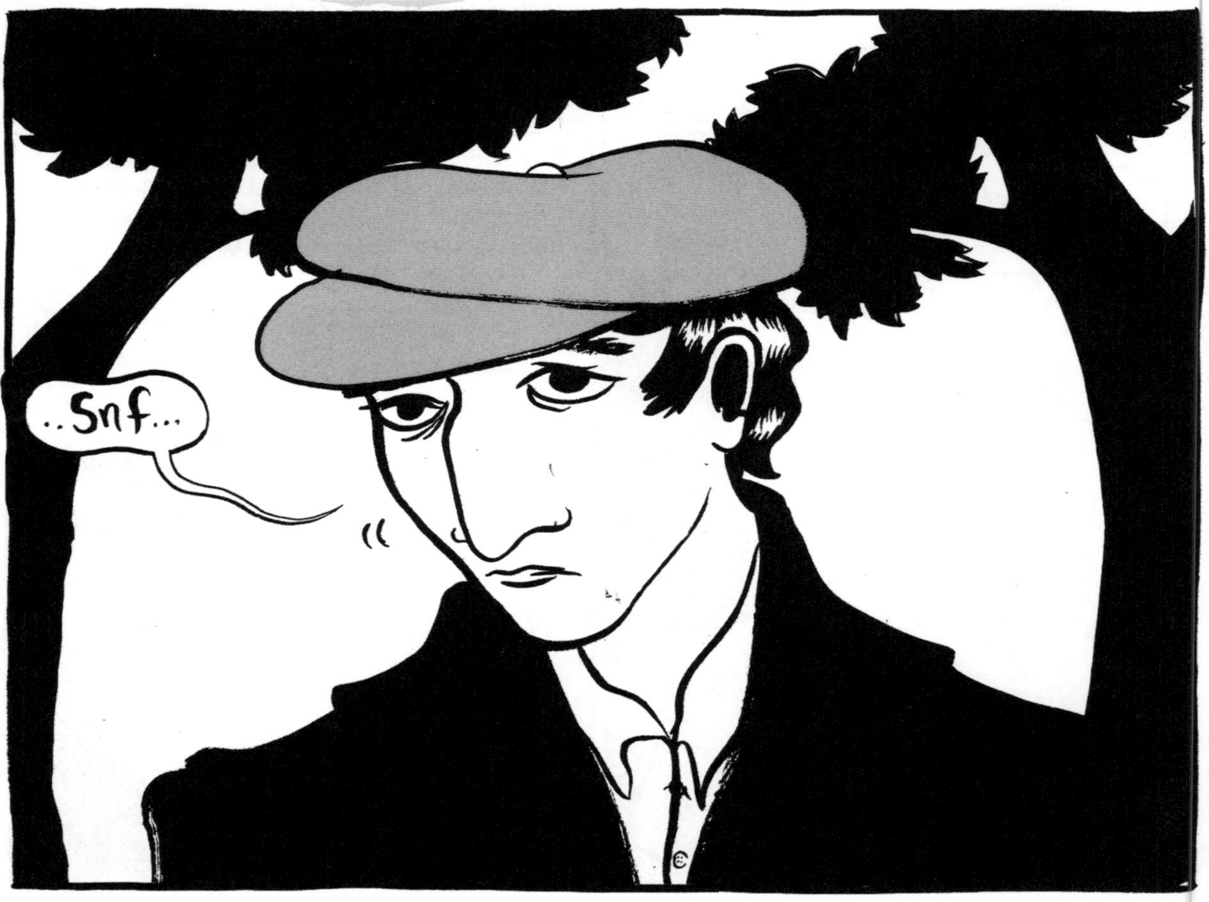
..Snf...

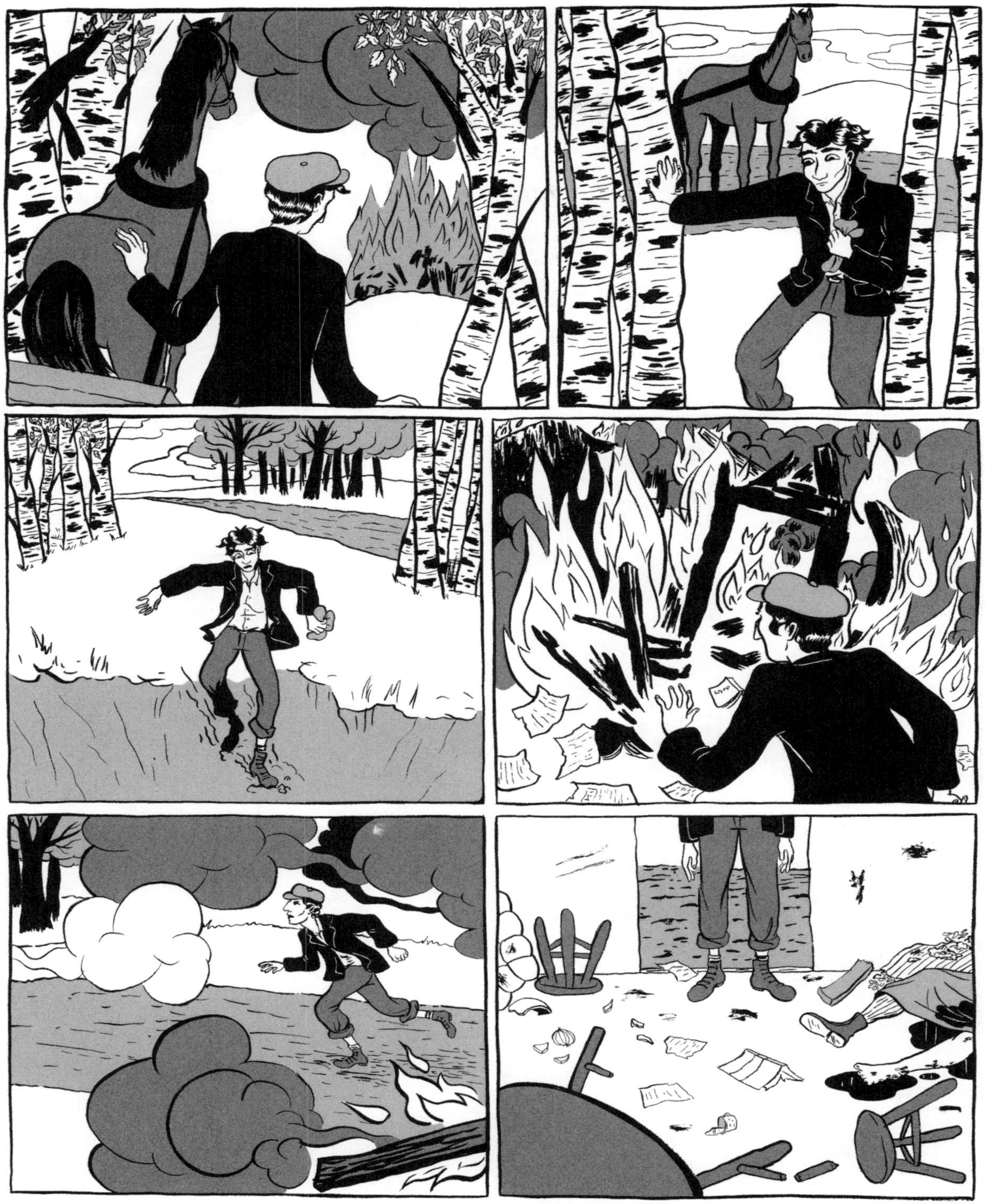

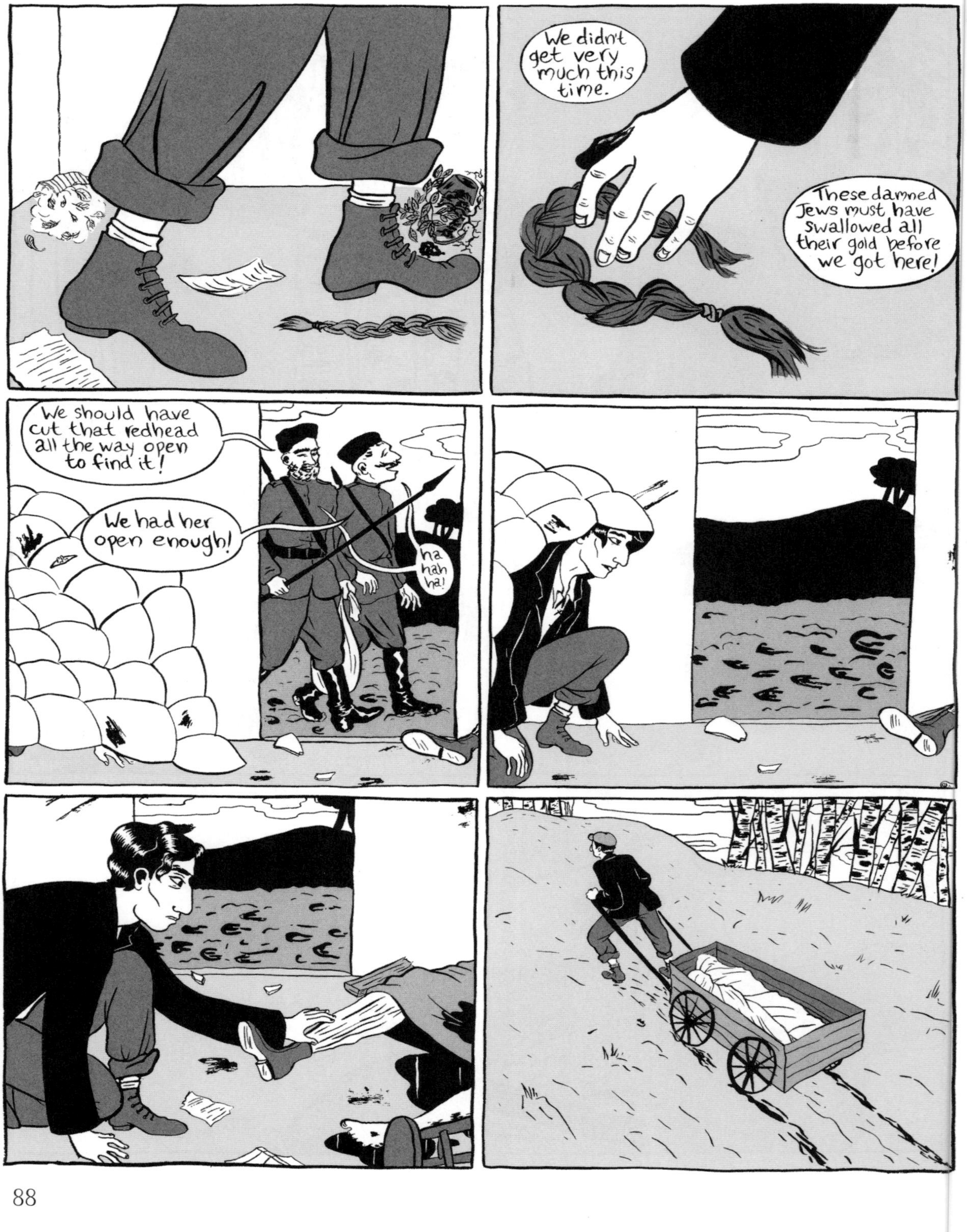
We didn't get very much this time.
These damned Jews must have swallowed all their gold before we got here!
We should have cut that redhead all the way open to find it!
We had her open enough!
ha hah ha!

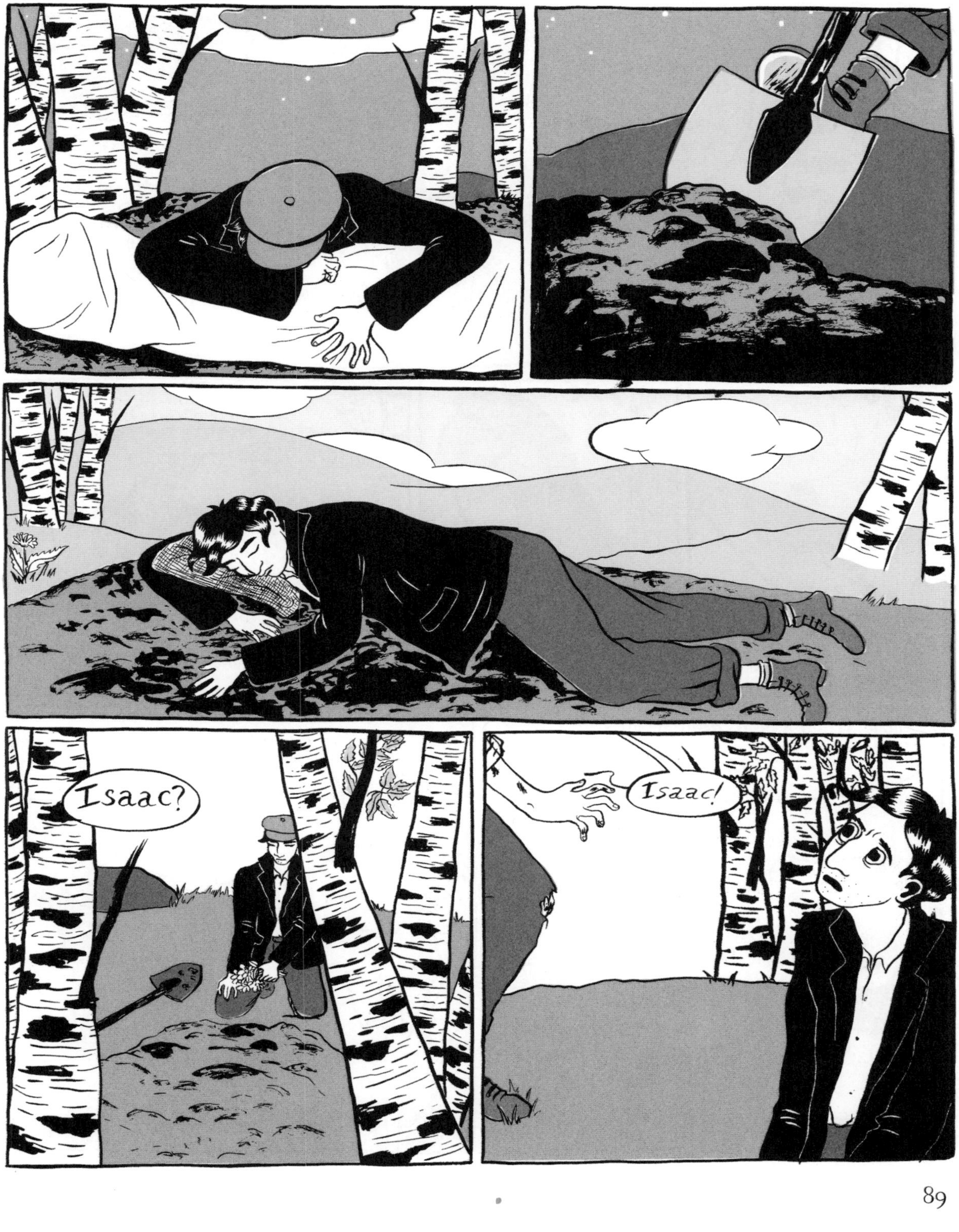
Isaac?
Isaac!

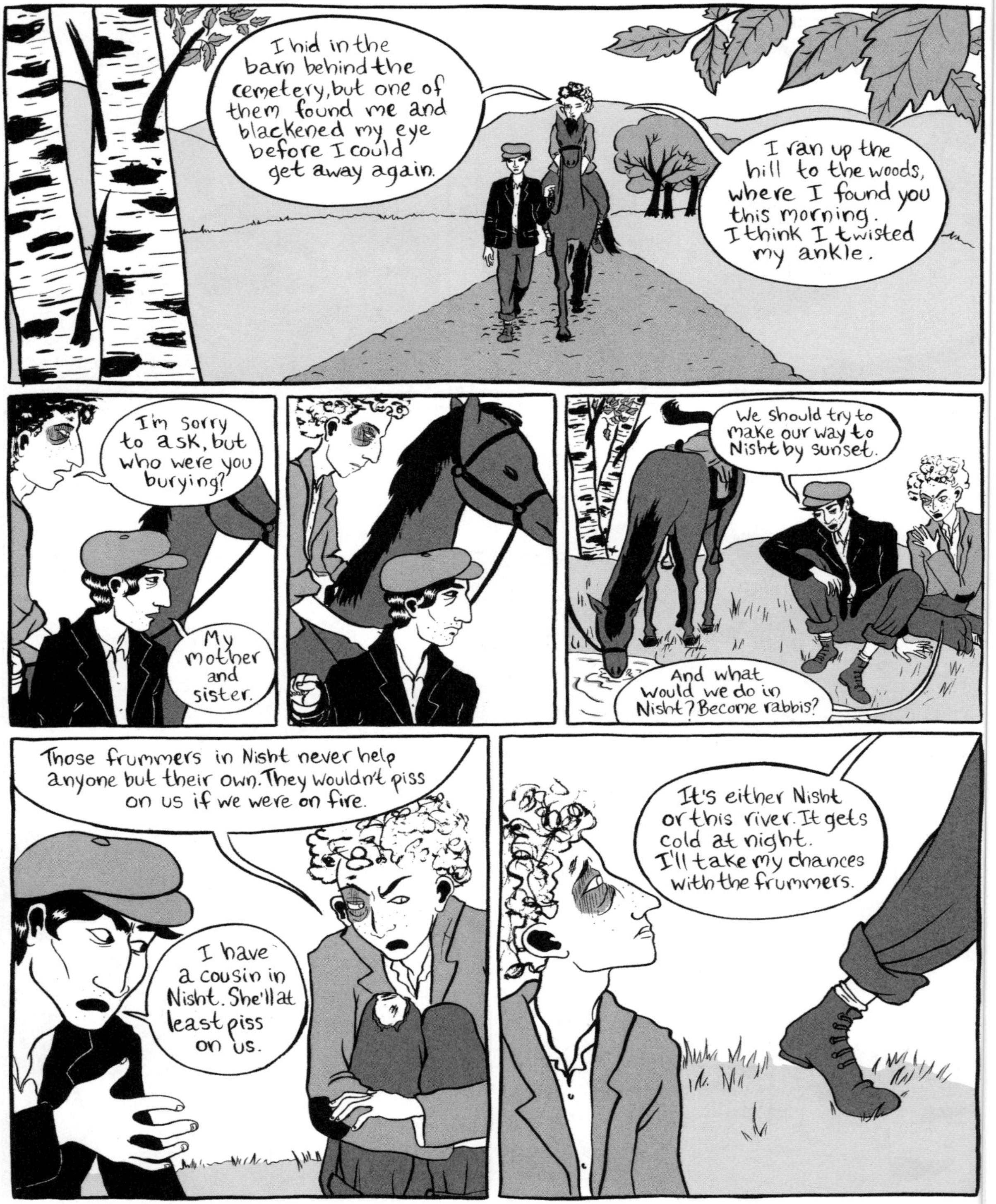
I hid in the barn behind the cemetery, but one of them found me and blackened my eye before I could get away again.
I ran up the hill to the woods, where I found you this morning. I think I twisted my ankle.
I'm sorry to ask, but who were you burying?
My mother and sister.
We should try to make our way to Nisht by sunset.
And what would we do in Nisht? Become rabbis?
Those frummers in Nisht never help anyone but their own. They wouldn't piss on us if we were on fire.
I have a cousin in Nisht. She'll at least piss on us.
It's either Nisht or this river. It gets cold at night. I'll take my chances with the frummers.

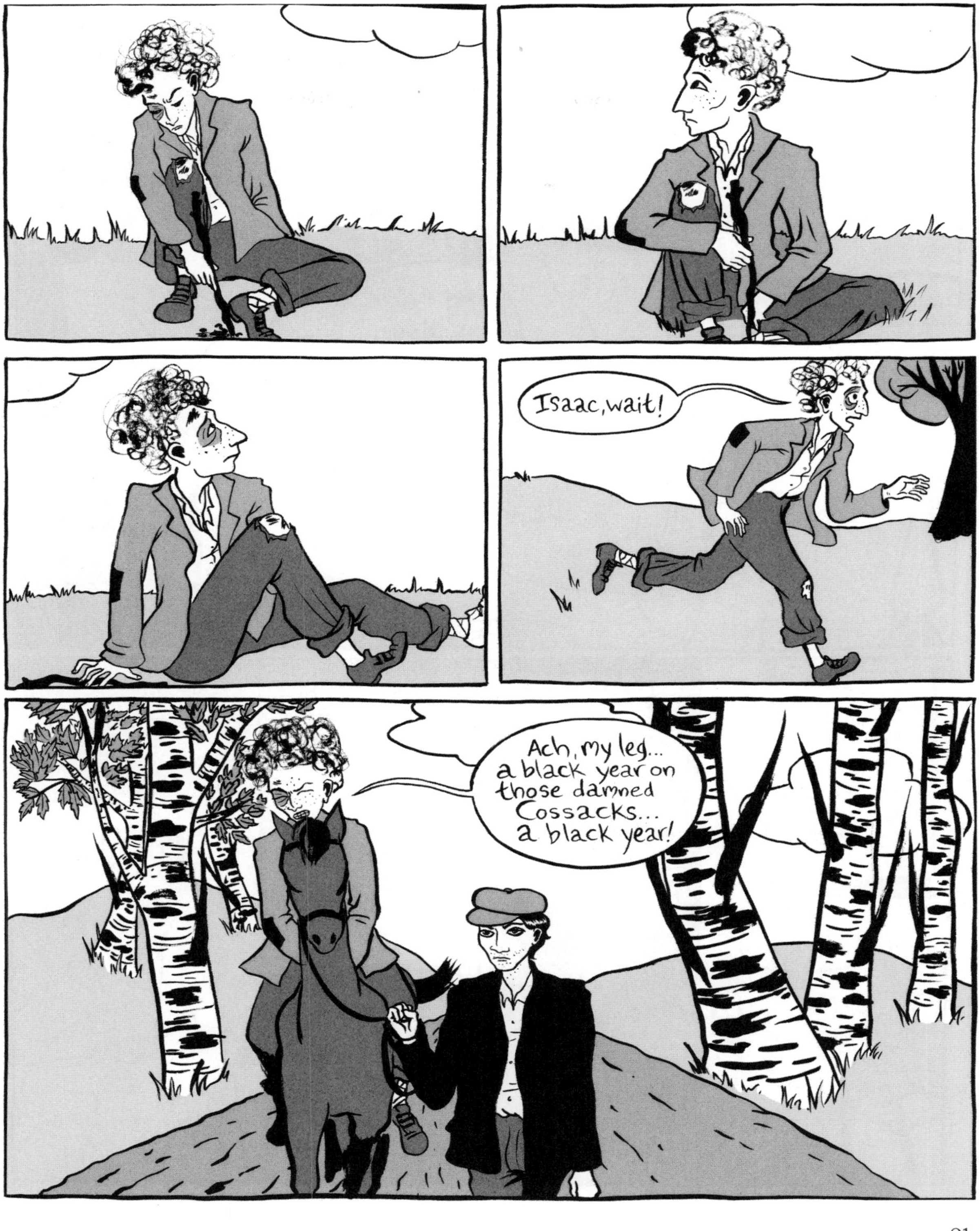
Isaac, wait!
Ach, my leg... a black year on those damned Cossacks... a black year!

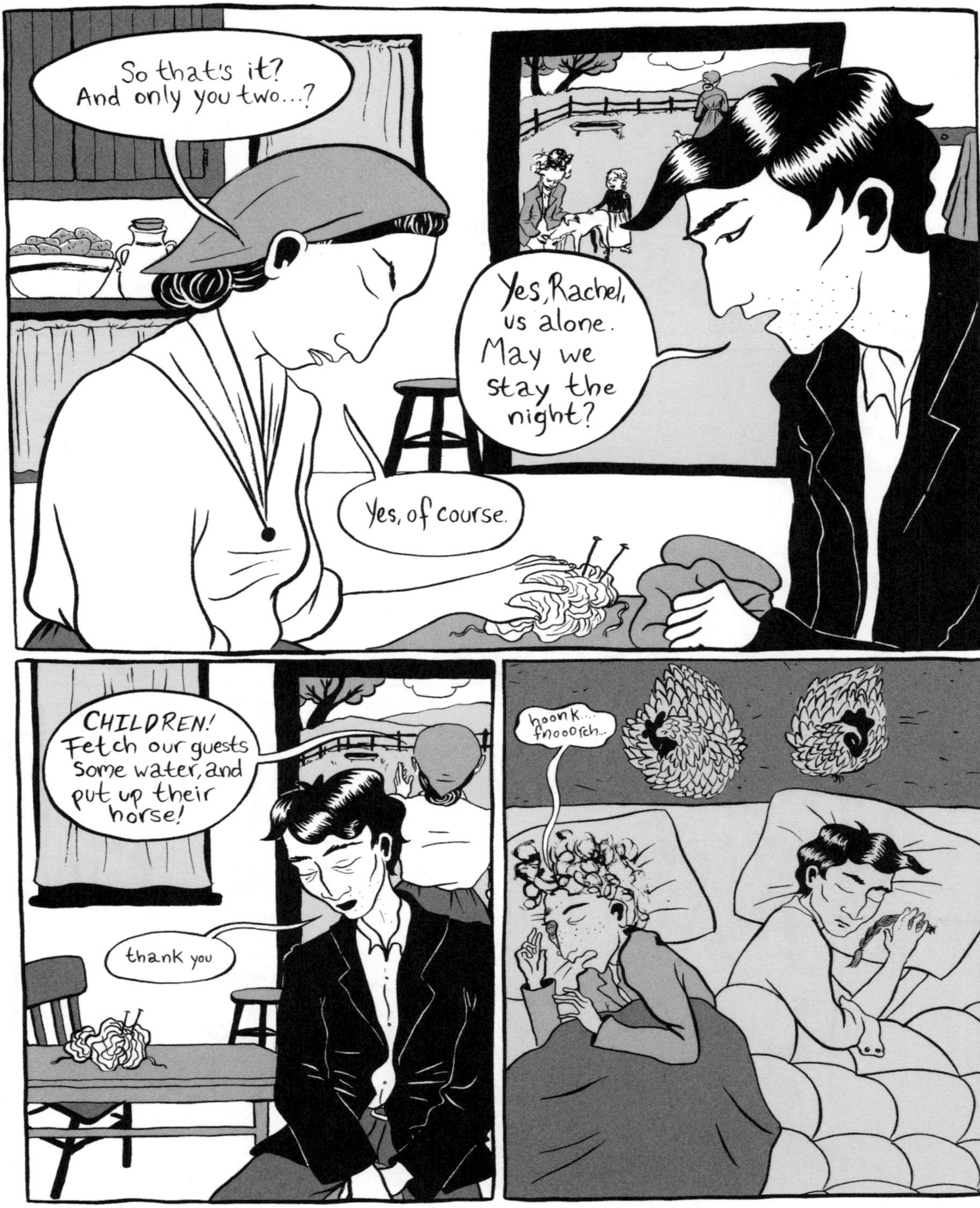
So that's it? And only you two...?
Yes, Rachel, us alone. May we stay the night?
Yes, of course.
CHILDREN! Fetch our guests some water, and put up their horse!
thank you.
hoonk... fnooorch...

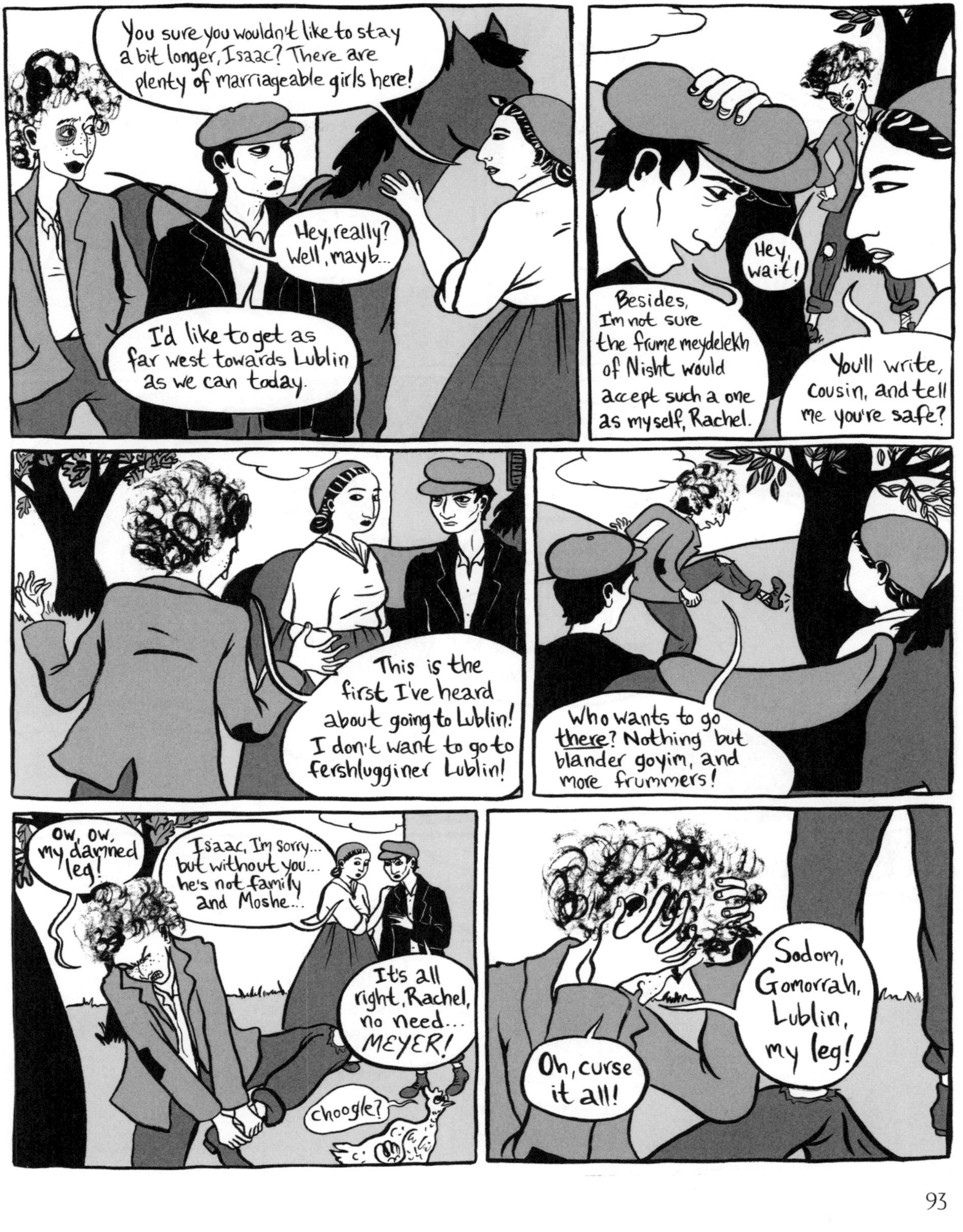
You sure you wouldn't like to stay a bit longer, Isaac? There are plenty of marriageable girls here!
Hey, really? Well, mayb...
I'd like to get as far west towards Lublin as we can today.
Hey, wait!
Besides, I'm not sure the frume meydelekh of Nisht would accept such a one as myself, Rachel.
You'll write, cousin, and tell me you're safe?
This is the first I've heard about going to Lublin! I don't want to go to fershlugginer Lublin!
Who wants to go there? Nothing but blander goyim, and more frummers!
Ow, ow, my damned leg!
Isaac, I'm sorry... but without you... he's not family and Moshe...
It's all right, Rachel, no need... MEYER!
choogle?
Sodom, Gomorrah, Lublin, my leg!
Oh, curse it all!

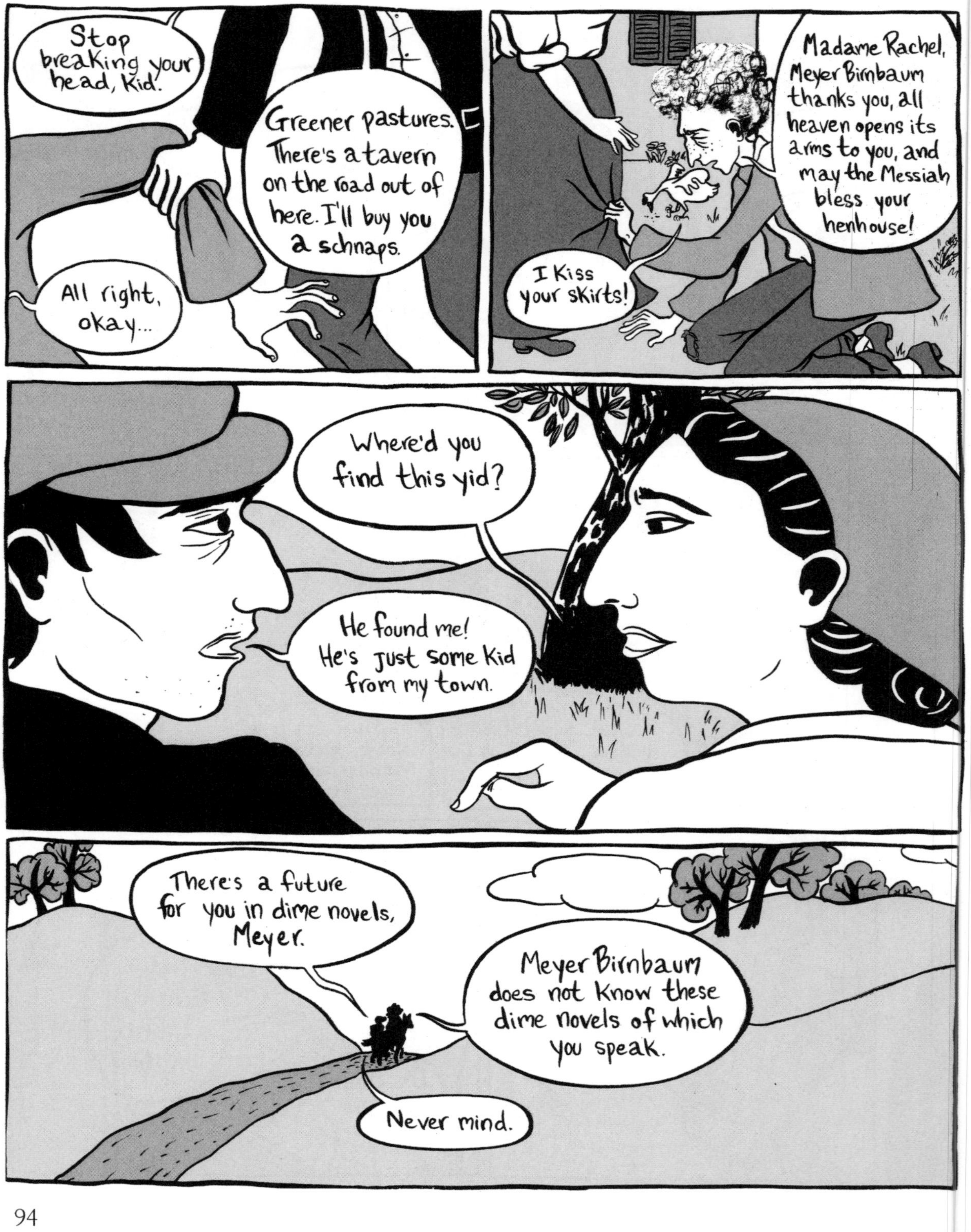

Stop breaking your head, Kid.
Greener pastures. There's a tavern on the road out of here. I'll buy you a schnaps.
All right, okay...
Madame Rachel, Meyer Birnbaum thanks you, all heaven opens its arms to you, and may the Messiah bless your henhouse!
I Kiss your skirts!
Where'd you find this yid?
He found me! He's just some Kid from my town.
There's a future for you in dime novels, Meyer.
Meyer Birnbaum does not Know these dime novels of which you speak.
Never mind.

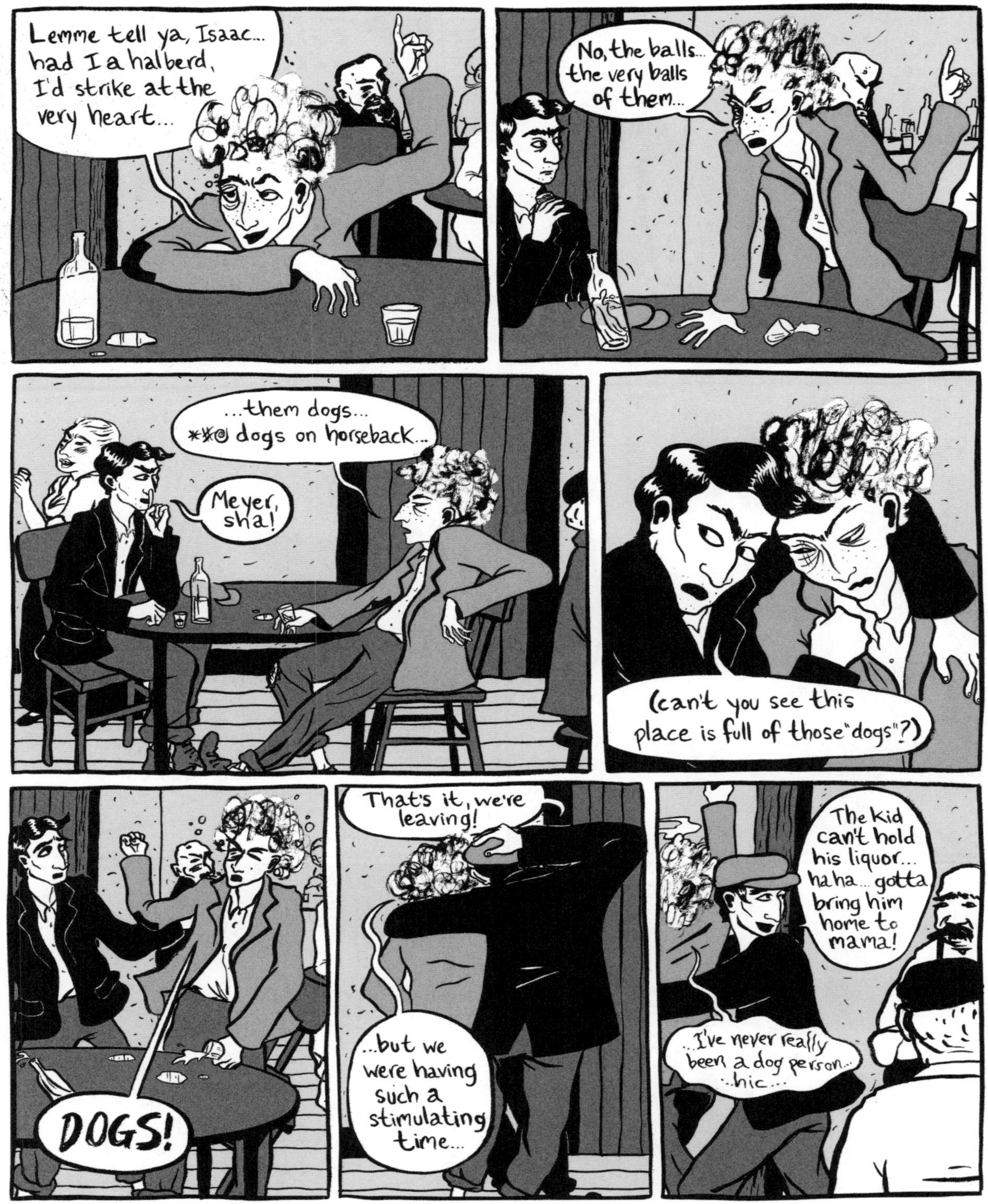

Lemme tell ya, Isaac... had I a halberd, I'd strike at the very heart...
No, the balls... the very balls of them...
...them dogs... *#@ dogs on horseback...
Meyer, sha!
(can't you see this place is full of those "dogs"?)
DOGS!
That's it, we're leaving!
...but we were having such a stimulating time...
The kid can't hold his liquor... ha ha... gotta bring him home to mama!
...I've never really been a dog person... ...hic...

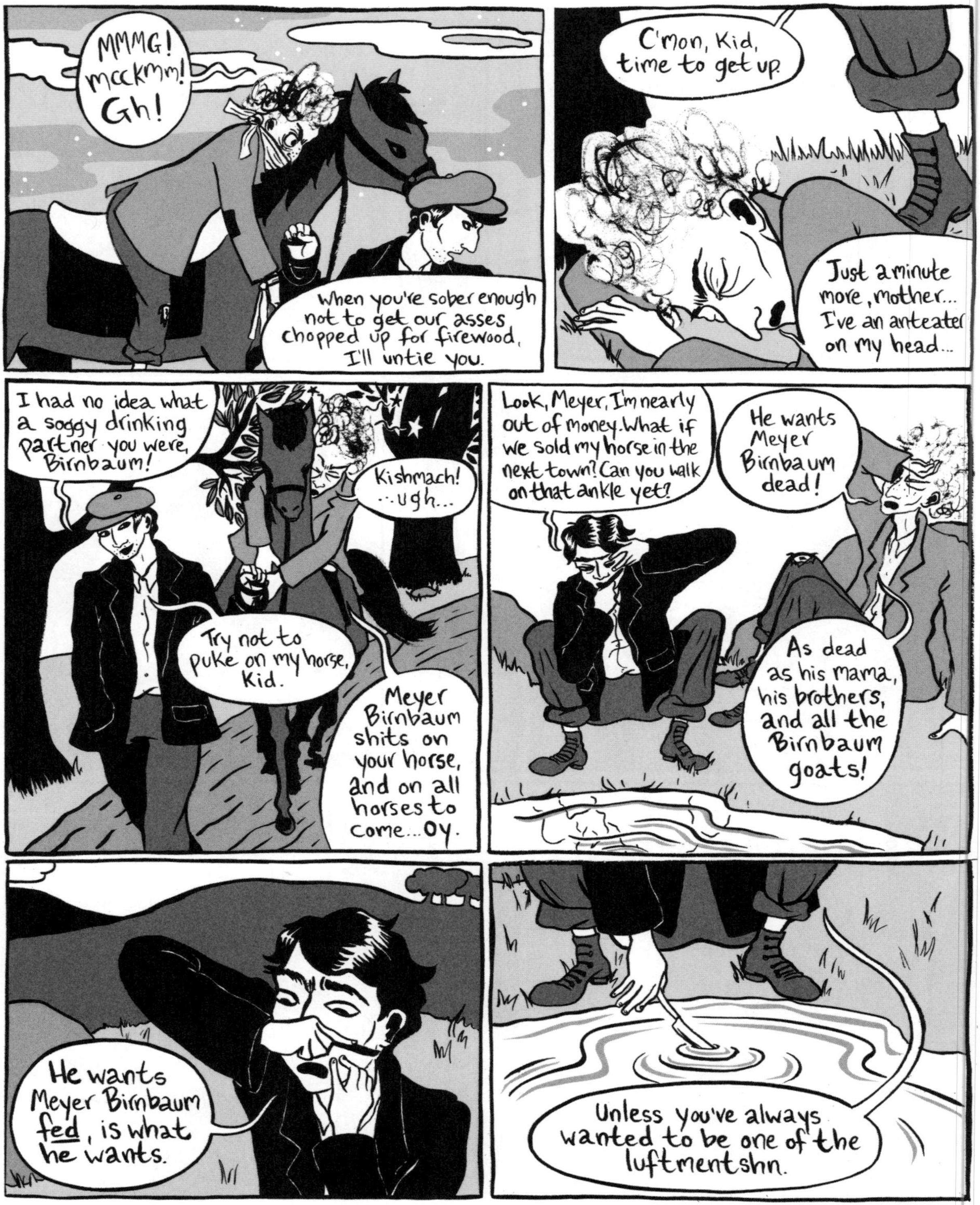
MMMG! mcckmm! Gh!
When you're sober enough not to get our asses chopped up for firewood, I'll untie you.
C'mon, Kid, time to get up.
Just a minute more, mother... I've an anteater on my head...
I had no idea what a soggy drinking partner you were, Birnbaum!
Kishmach! ...ugh...
Try not to puke on my horse, Kid.
Meyer Birnbaum shits on your horse, and on all horses to come... Oy.
Look, Meyer, I'm nearly out of money. What if we sold my horse in the next town? Can you walk on that ankle yet?
He wants Meyer Birnbaum dead!
As dead as his mama, his brothers, and all the Birnbaum goats!
He wants Meyer Birnbaum fed, is what he wants.
Unless you've always wanted to be one of the luftmentshn.

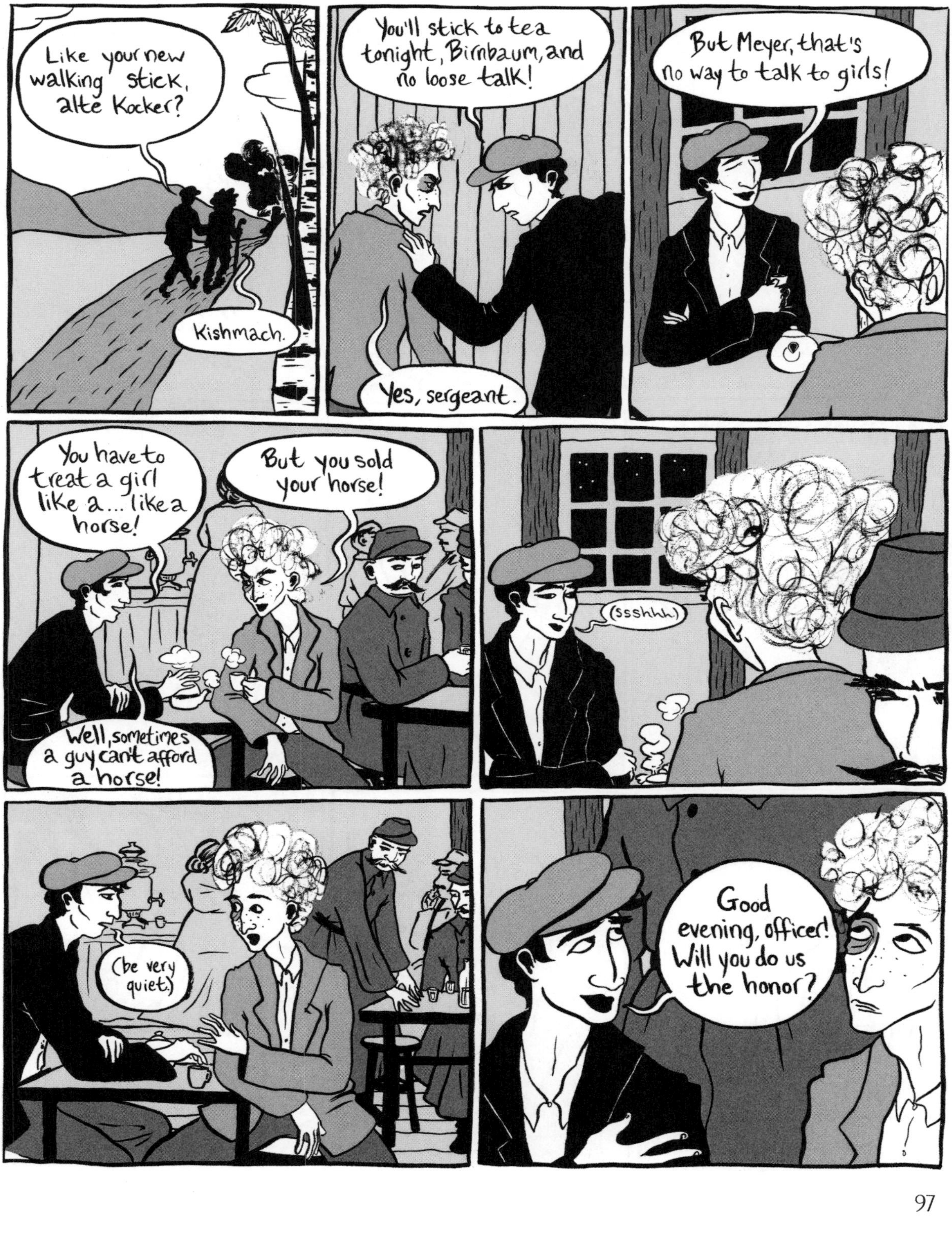
Like your new walking stick, alte Kocker?
Kishmach.
You'll stick to tea tonight, Birnbaum, and no loose talk!
Yes, sergeant.
But Meyer, that's no way to talk to girls!
You have to treat a girl like a... like a horse!
But you sold your horse!
Well, sometimes a guy can't afford a horse!
(ssshhh.)
(be very quiet.)
Good evening, officer! Will you do us the honor?

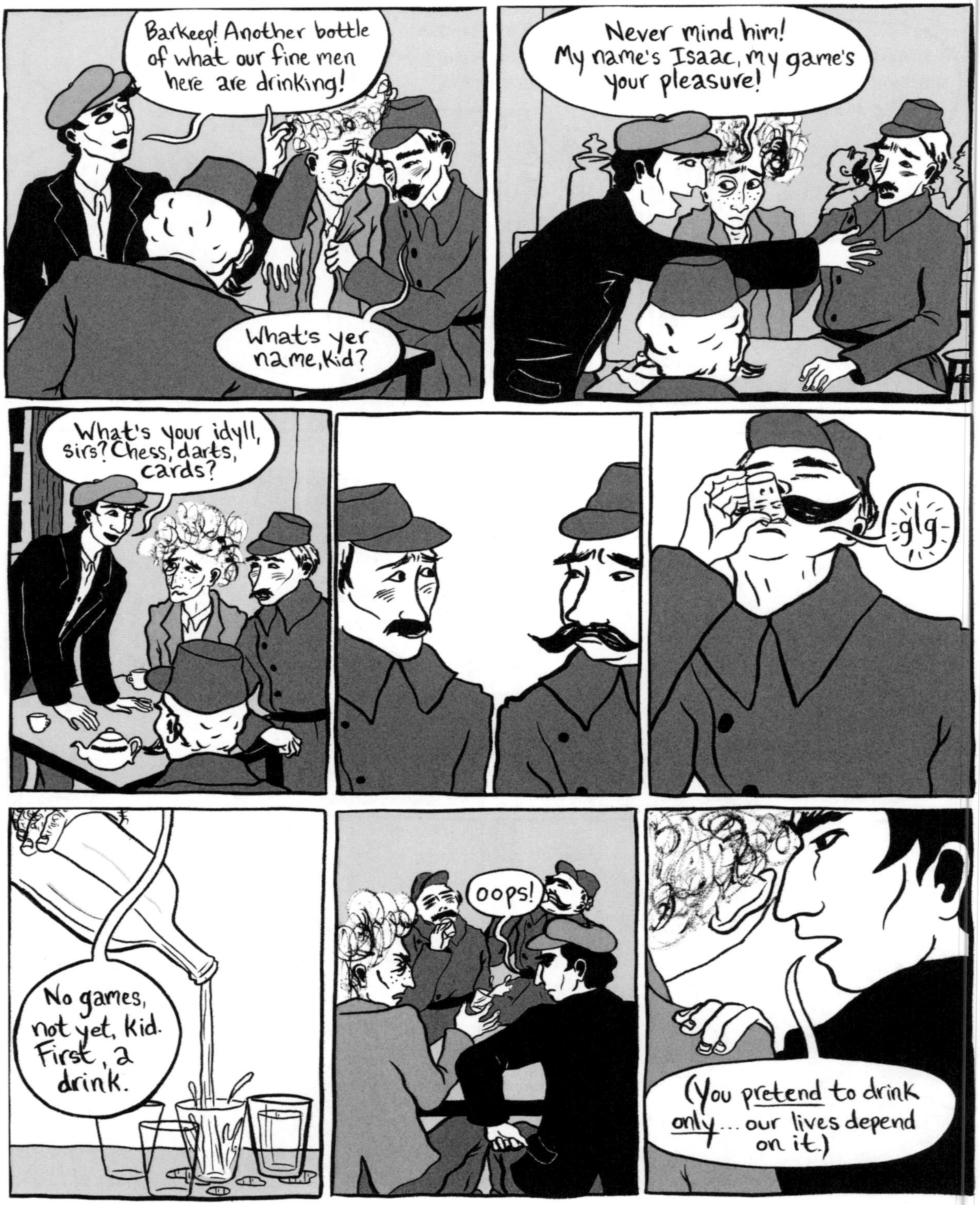
Barkeep! Another bottle of what our fine men here are drinking!
What's yer name, Kid?
Never mind him! My name's Isaac, my game's your pleasure!
What's your idyll, sirs? Chess, darts, cards?
glg
No games, not yet, Kid. First, a drink.
oops!
(You pretend to drink only... our lives depend on it.)

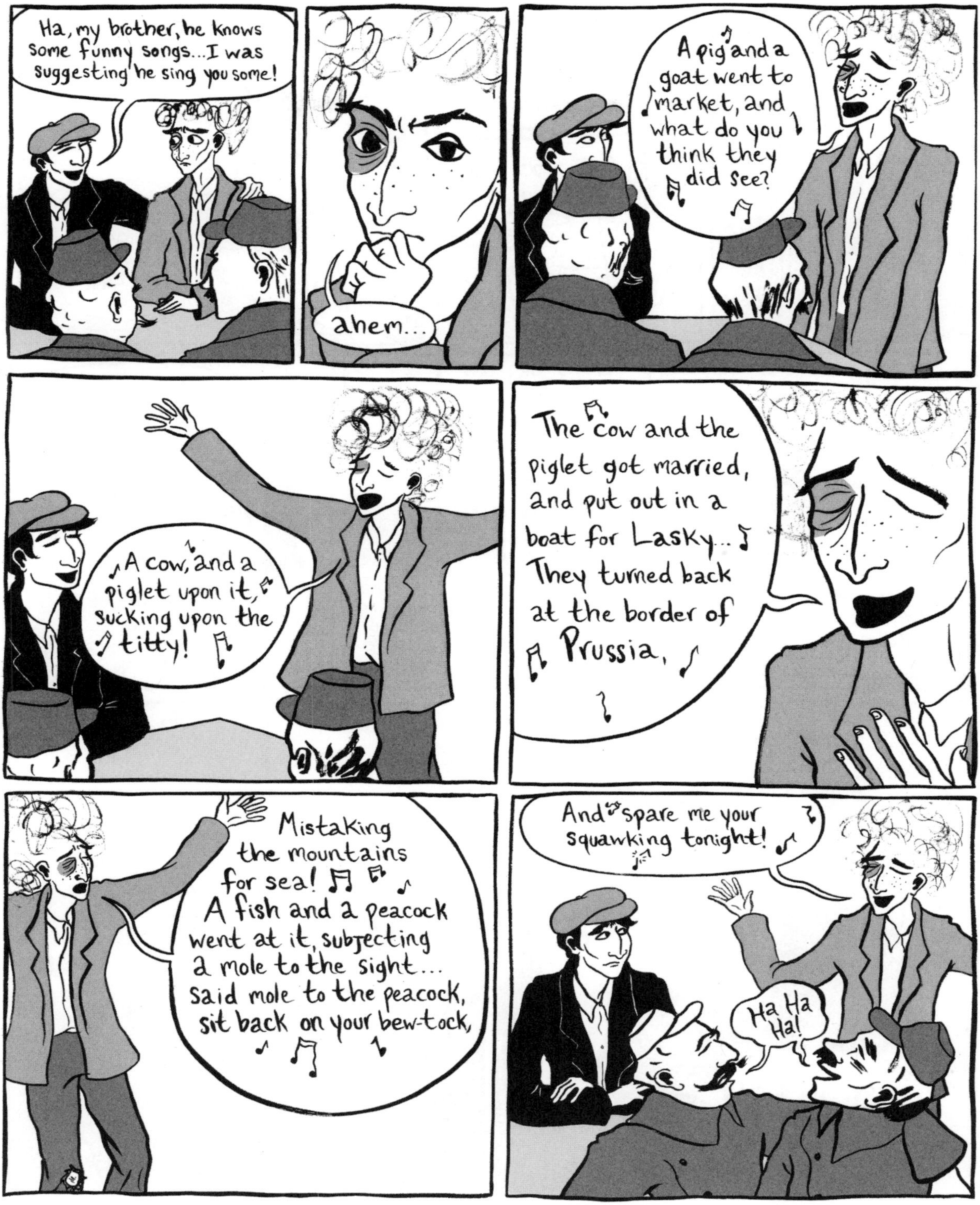
Ha, my brother, he knows some funny songs... I was suggesting he sing you some!
ahem...
A pig and a goat went to market, and what do you think they did see?
A cow, and a piglet upon it, sucking upon the titty!
The cow and the piglet got married, and put out in a boat for Lasky... They turned back at the border of Prussia,
Mistaking the mountains for sea! A fish and a peacock went at it, subjecting a mole to the sight... said mole to the peacock, sit back on your bew-tock,
And spare me your squawking tonight!
Ha Ha Ha!

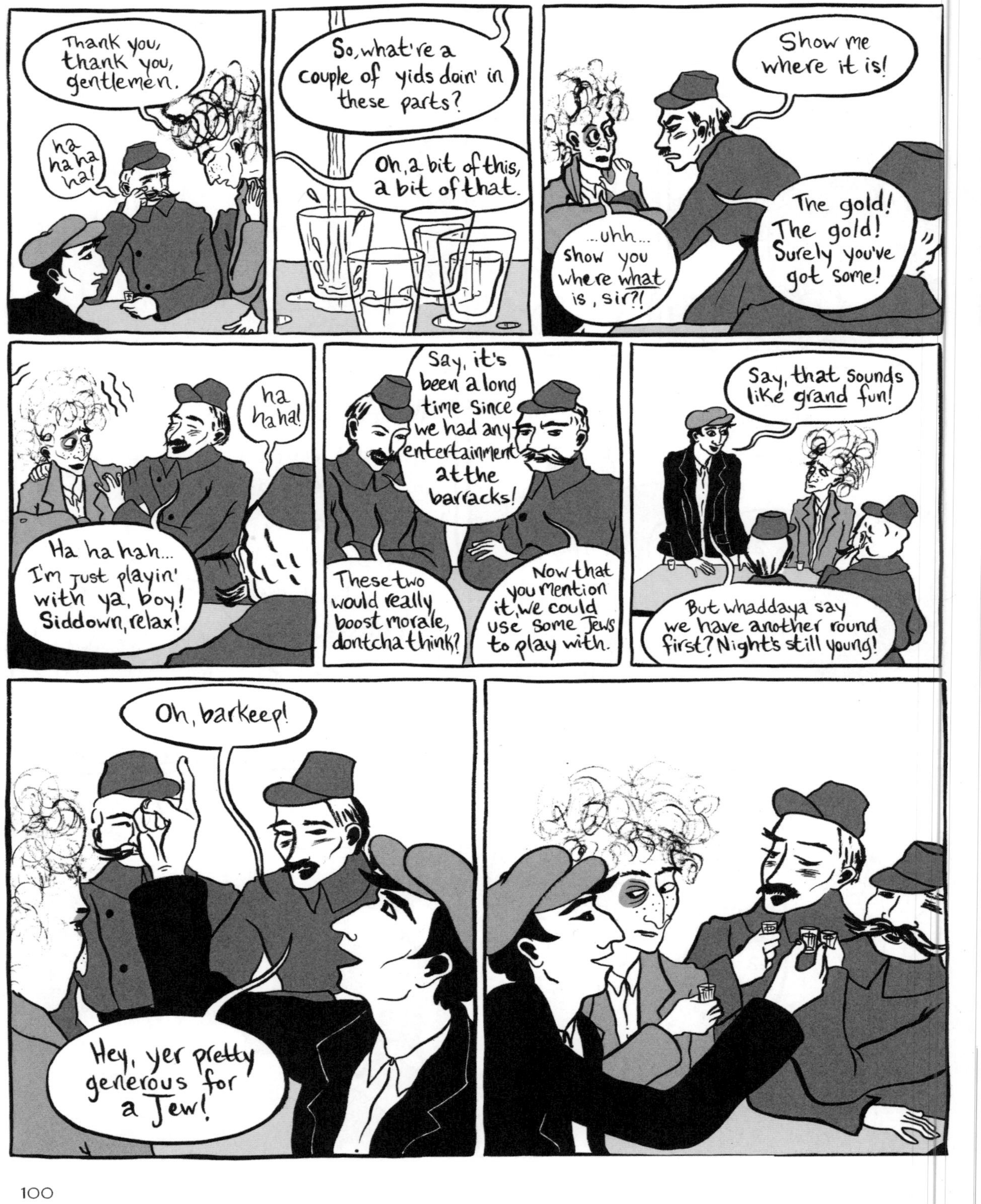

Thank you, thank you, gentlemen.
ha ha ha ha!
So, what're a couple of yids doin' in these parts?
Oh, a bit of this, a bit of that.
Show me where it is!
...uhh... show you where what is, sir?!
The gold! The gold! Surely you've got some!
ha ha ha!
Ha ha hah... I'm just playin' with ya, boy! Siddown, relax!
Say, it's been a long time since we had any entertainment at the barracks!
These two would really boost morale, dontcha think?
Now that you mention it, we could use some Jews to play with.
Say, that sounds like grand fun!
But whaddaya say we have another round first? Night's still young!
Oh, barkeep!
Hey, yer pretty generous for a Jew!

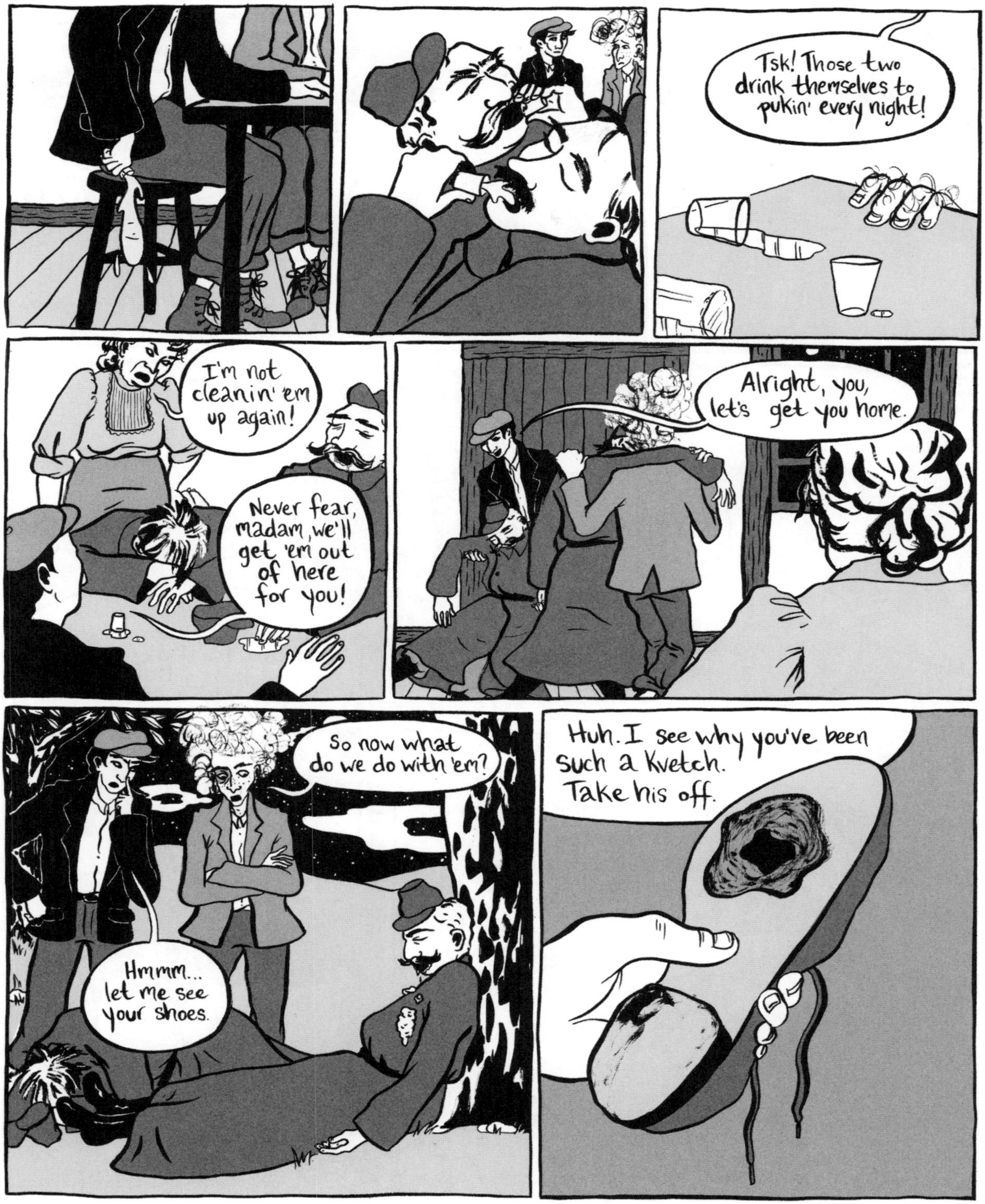
Tsk! Those two drink themselves to pukin' every night!
I'm not cleanin' 'em up again!
Never fear, madam, we'll get 'em out of here for you!
Alright, you, let's get you home.
So now what do we do with 'em?
Hmmm... let me see your shoes.
Huh. I see why you've been such a Kvetch. Take his off.

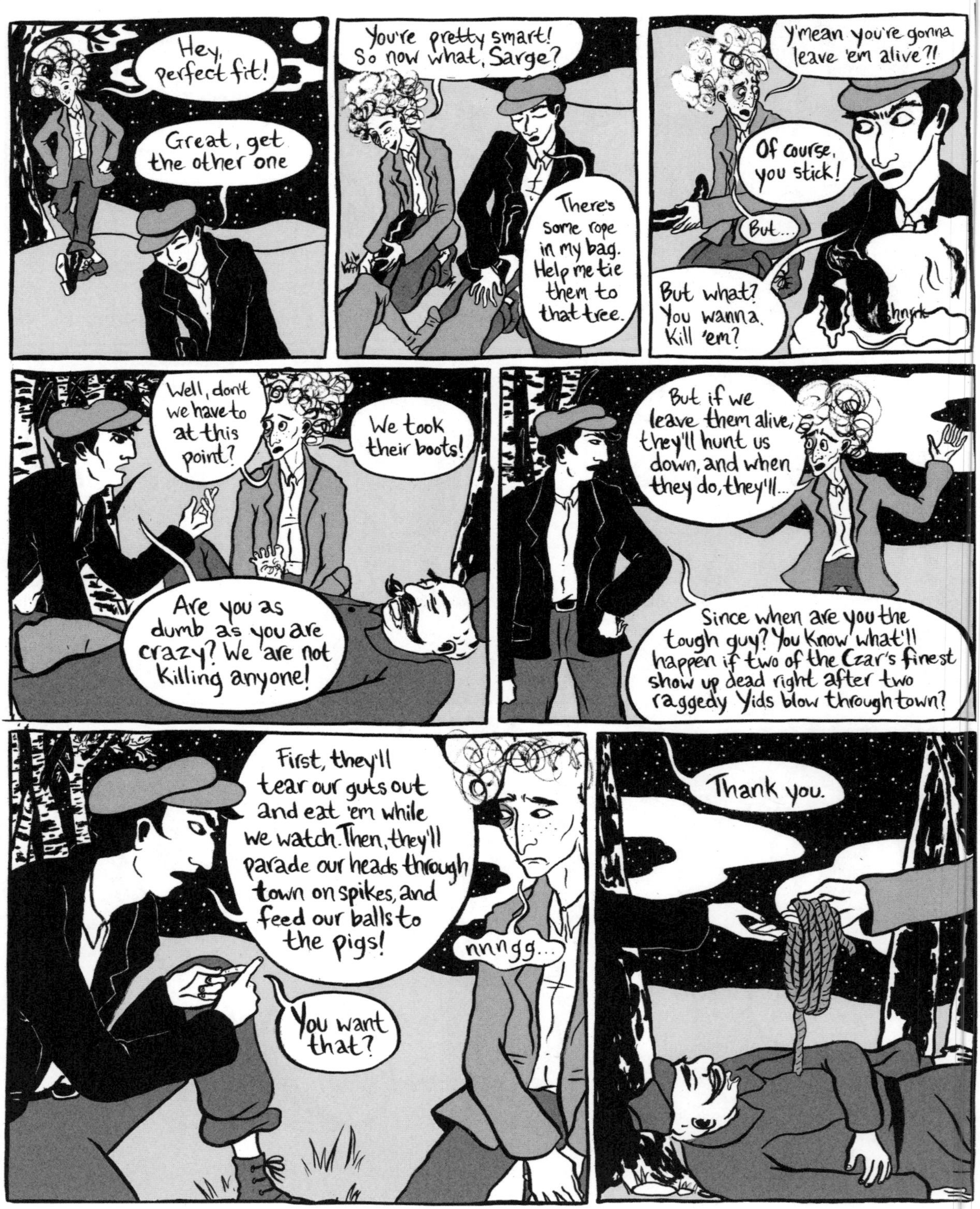
Hey, perfect fit!
Great, get the other one
You're pretty smart! So now what, Sarge?
There's some rope in my bag. Help me tie them to that tree.
Y'mean you're gonna leave 'em alive?!
Of course, you stick!
But...
But what? You wanna kill 'em?
shnrk
Well, don't we have to at this point?
We took their boots!
Are you as dumb as you are crazy? We are not killing anyone!
But if we leave them alive, they'll hunt us down, and when they do, they'll...
Since when are you the tough guy? You know what'll happen if two of the Czar's finest show up dead right after two raggedy Yids blow through town?
First, they'll tear our guts out and eat 'em while we watch. Then, they'll parade our heads through town on spikes, and feed our balls to the pigs!
You want that?
nnngg...
Thank you.

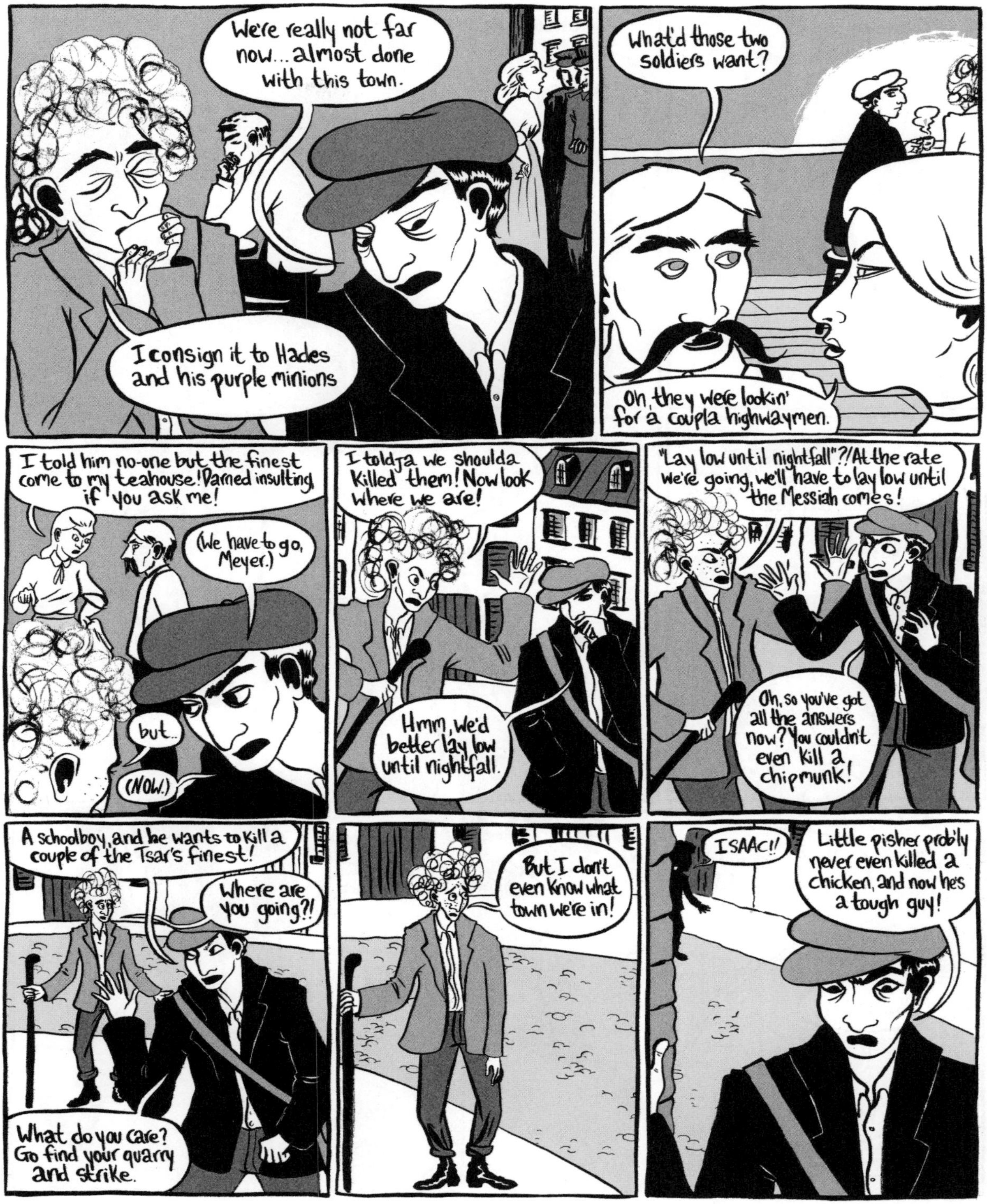
We're really not far now... almost done with this town.
I consign it to Hades and his purple minions
What'd those two soldiers want?
Oh, they were lookin' for a coupla highwaymen.
I told him no-one but the finest come to my teahouse! Darned insulting, if you ask me!
(We have to go, Meyer.)
but...
(NOW.)
I toldja we shoulda killed them! Now look where we are!
Hmm, we'd better lay low until nightfall.
"Lay low until nightfall"?! At the rate we're going, we'll have to lay low until the Messiah comes!
Oh, so you've got all the answers now? You couldn't even kill a chipmunk!
A schoolboy, and he wants to kill a couple of the Tsar's finest!
Where are you going?!
What do you care? Go find your quarry and strike.
But I don't even know what town we're in!
ISAAC!!
Little pisher probly never even killed a chicken, and now he's a tough guy!

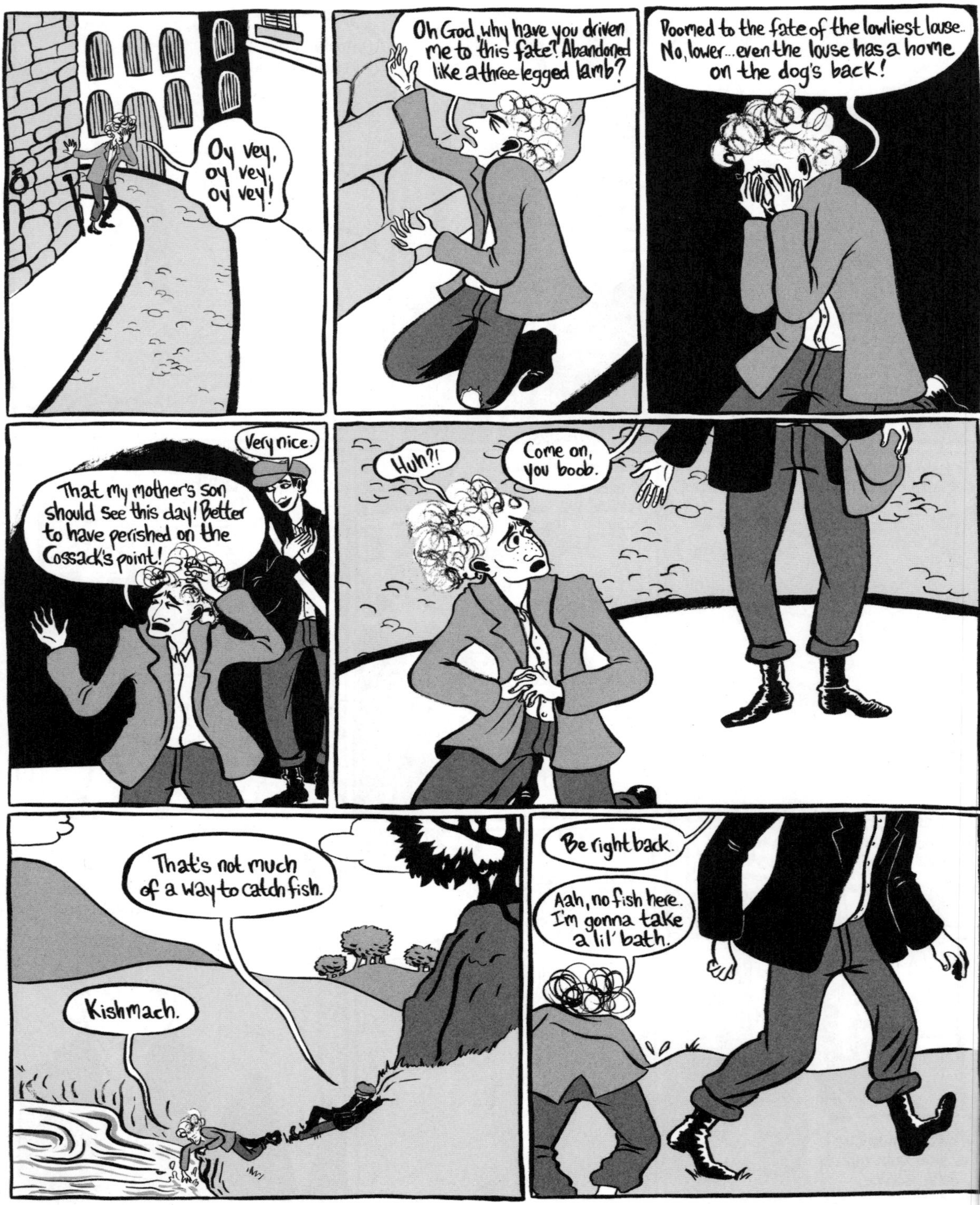
Oy vey, oy vey, oy vey!
Oh God, why have you driven me to this fate? Abandoned like a three-legged lamb?
Doomed to the fate of the lowliest louse.. No, lower... even the louse has a home on the dog's back!
Very nice.
That my mother's son should see this day! Better to have perished on the Cossack's point!
Huh?!
Come on, you boob.
That's not much of a way to catch fish.
Kishmach.
Be right back.
Aah, no fish here. I'm gonna take a lil' bath.

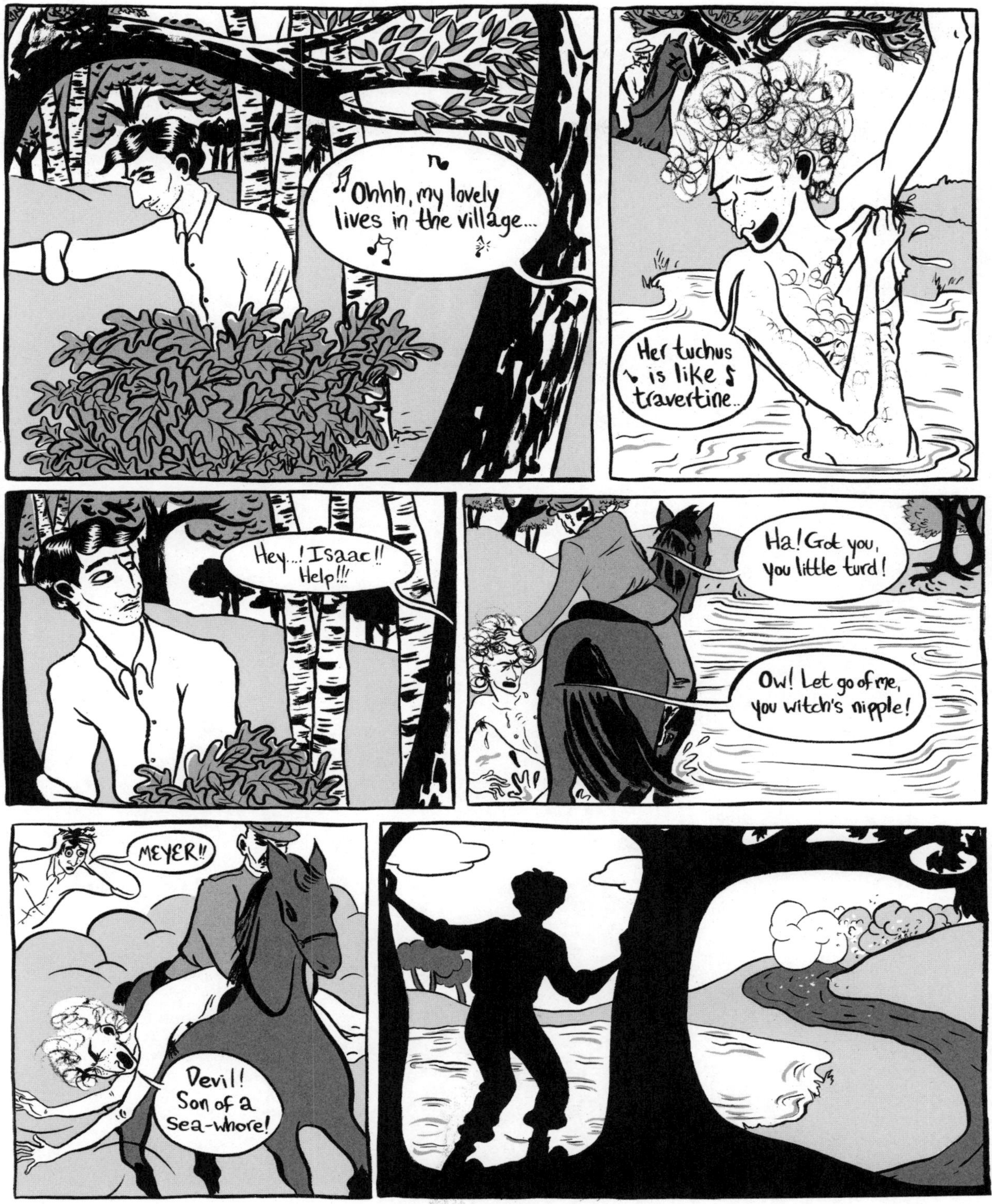
Ohhh, my lovely lives in the village...
Her tuchus is like travertine..
Hey...! Isaac!! Help!!!
Ha! Got you, you little turd!
Ow! Let go of me, you witch's nipple!
MEYER!!
Devil! Son of a sea-whore!

1896

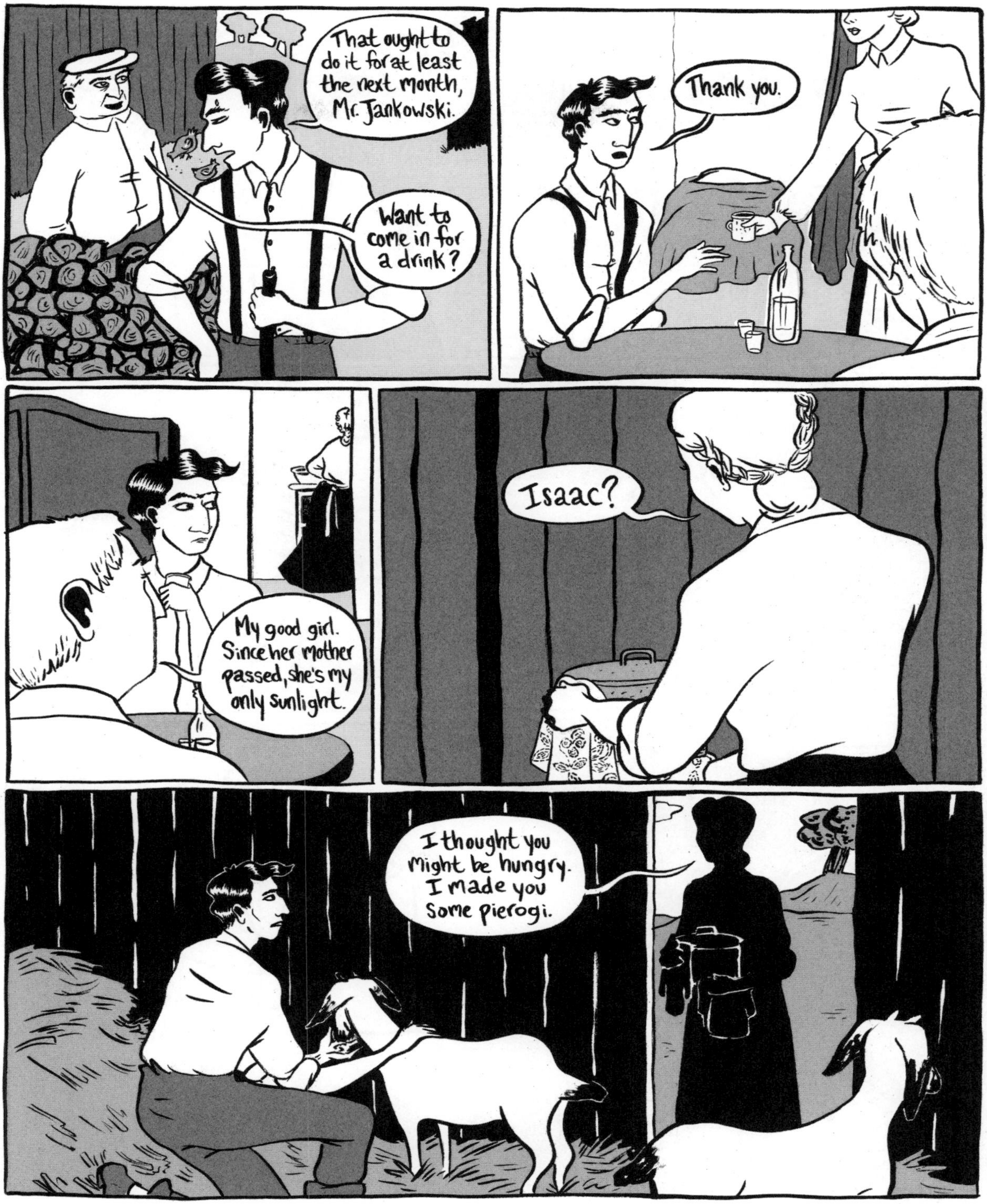
That ought to do it for at least the next month, Mr. Jankowski.
Want to come in for a drink?
Thank you.
My good girl. Since her mother passed, she's my only sunlight.
Isaac?
I thought you might be hungry. I made you some pierogi.

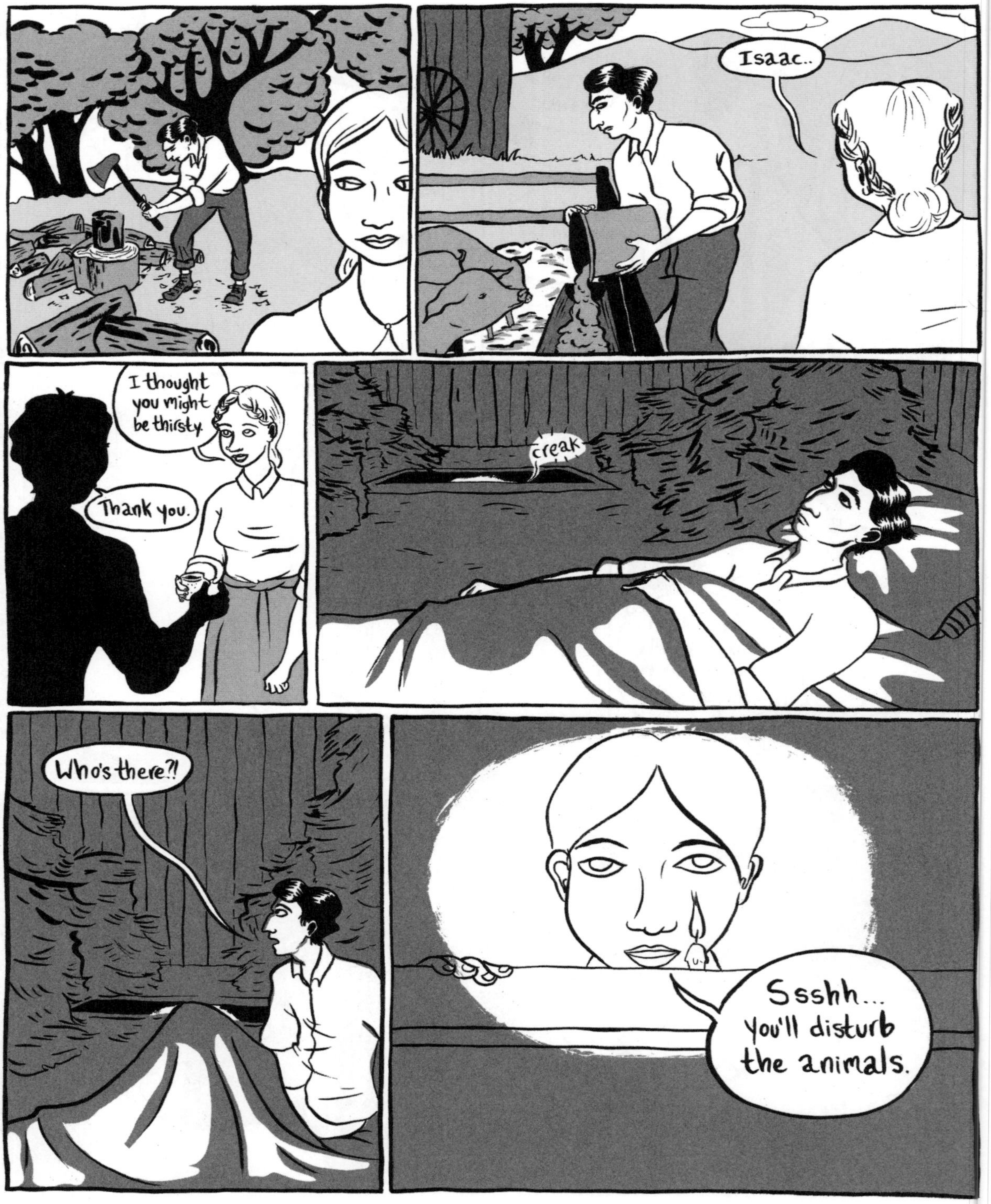
Isaac..
I thought you might be thirsty.
Thank you.
creak
Who's there?!
Ssshh... you'll disturb the animals.

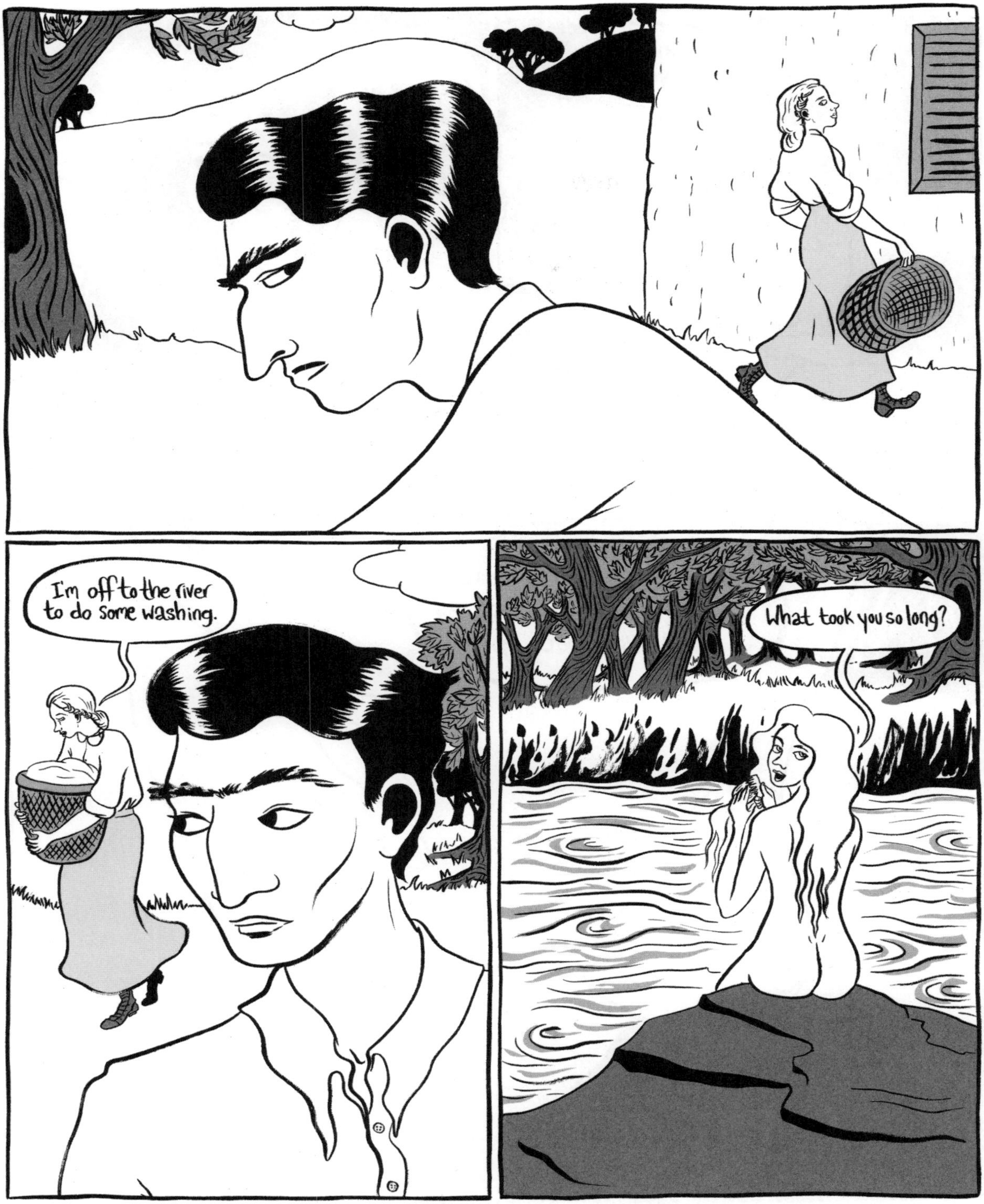
I'm off to the river to do some washing.
What took you so long?

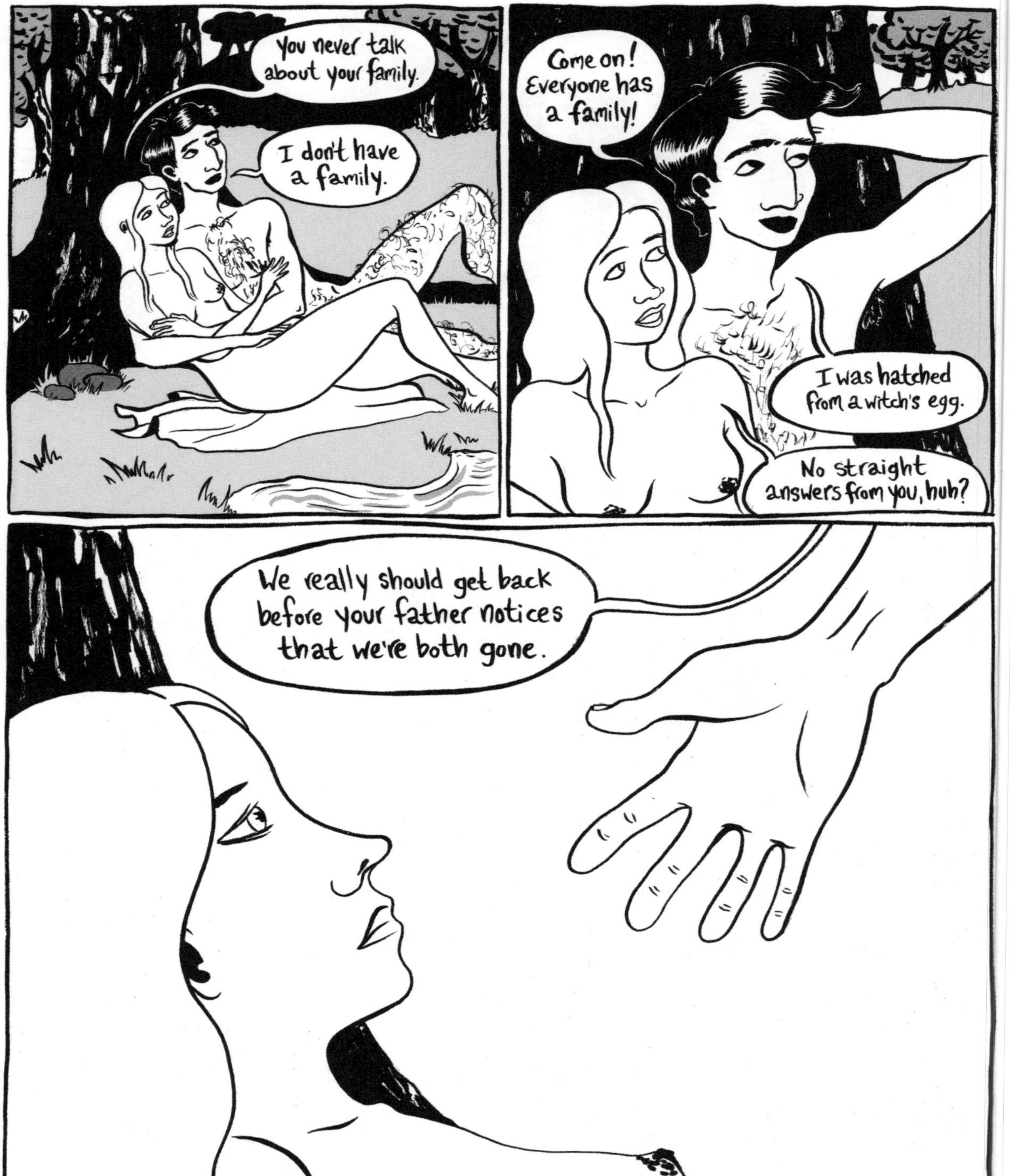
You never talk about your family.
I don't have a family.
Come on! Everyone has a family!
I was hatched from a witch's egg.
No straight answers from you, huh?
We really should get back before your father notices that we're both gone.

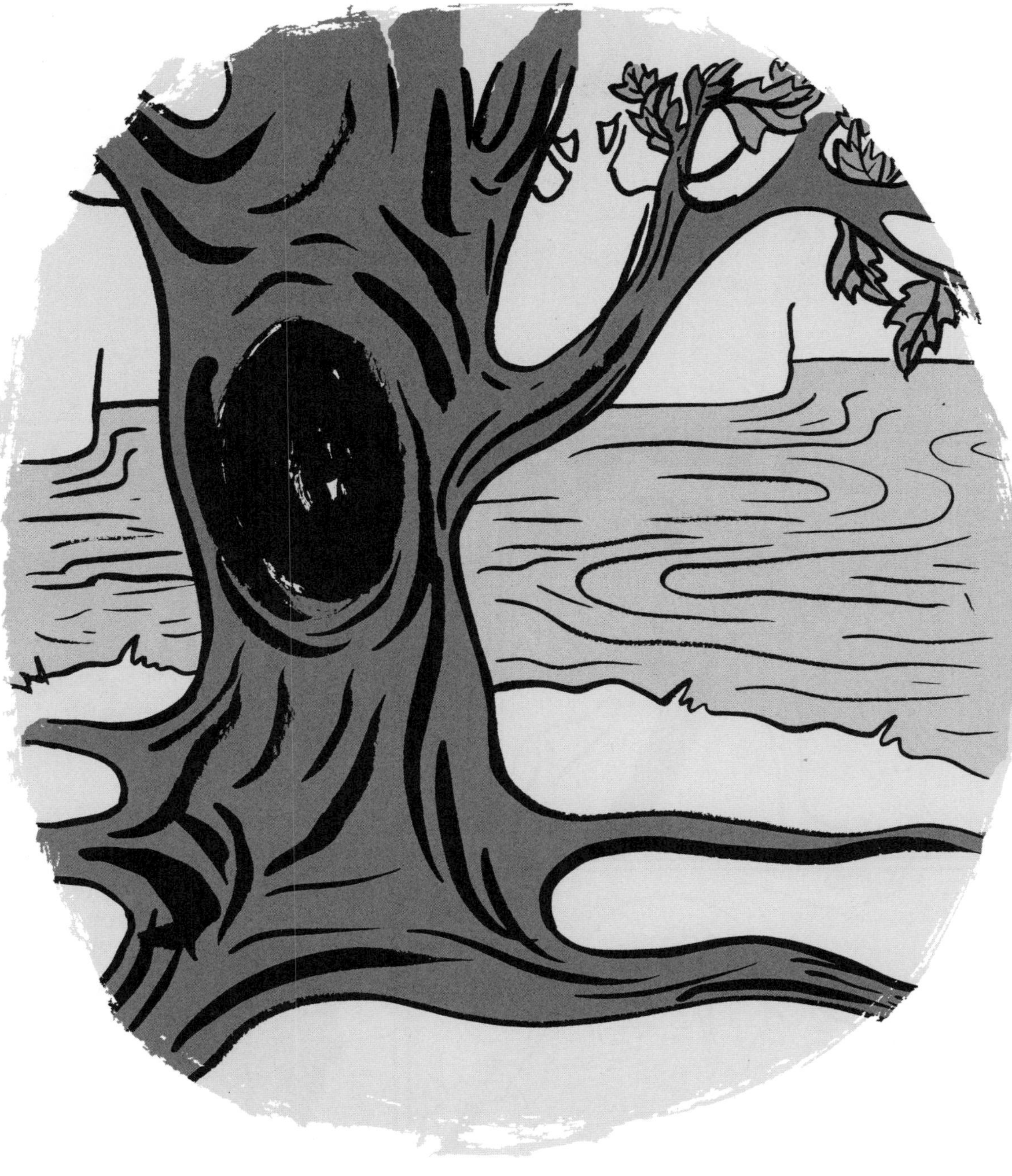

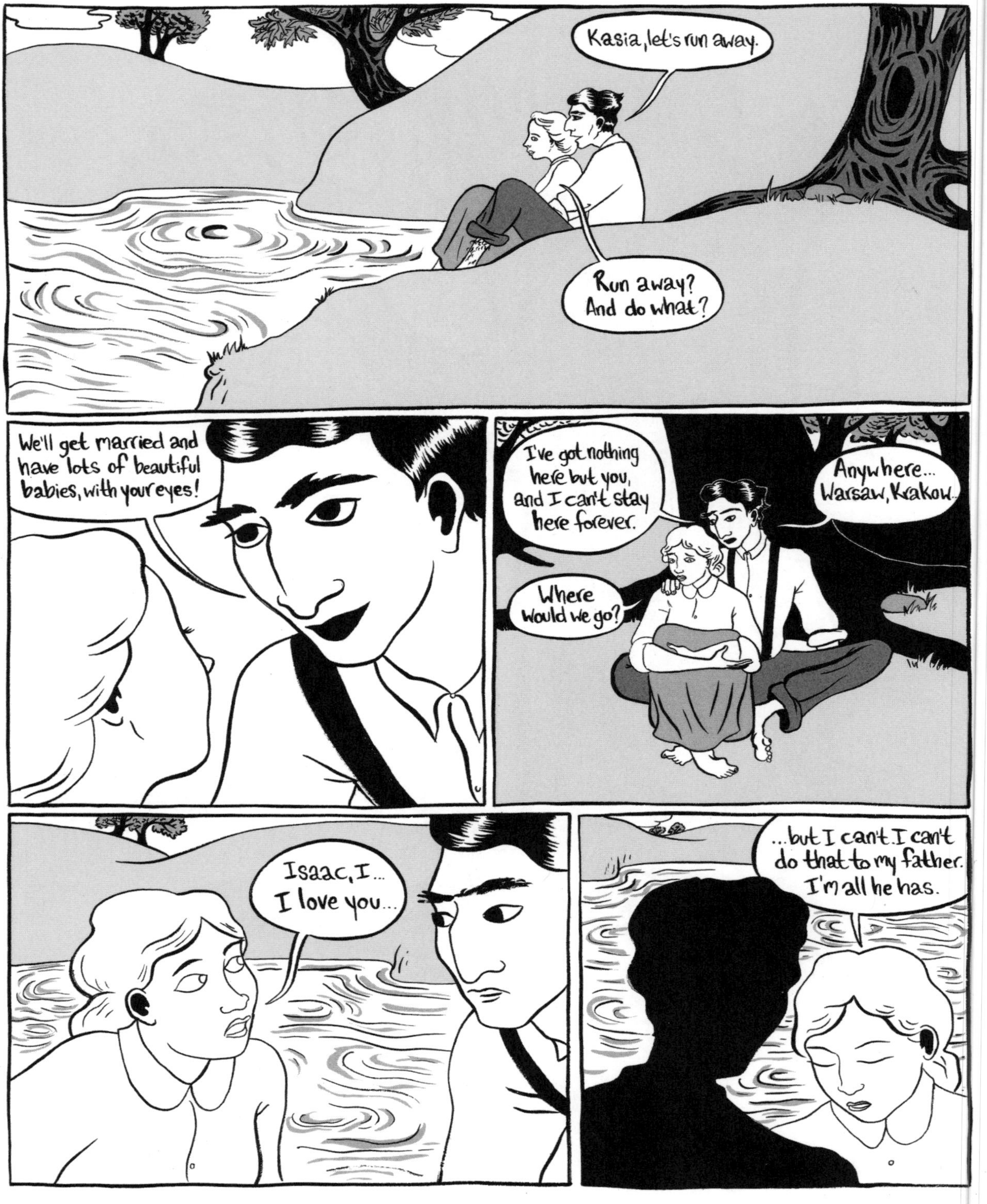
Kasia, let's run away.
Run away? And do what?
We'll get married and have lots of beautiful babies, with your eyes!
I've got nothing here but you, and I can't stay here forever.
Where would we go?
Anywhere... Warsaw, Krakow...
Isaac, I... I love you...
...but I can't. I can't do that to my father. I'm all he has.

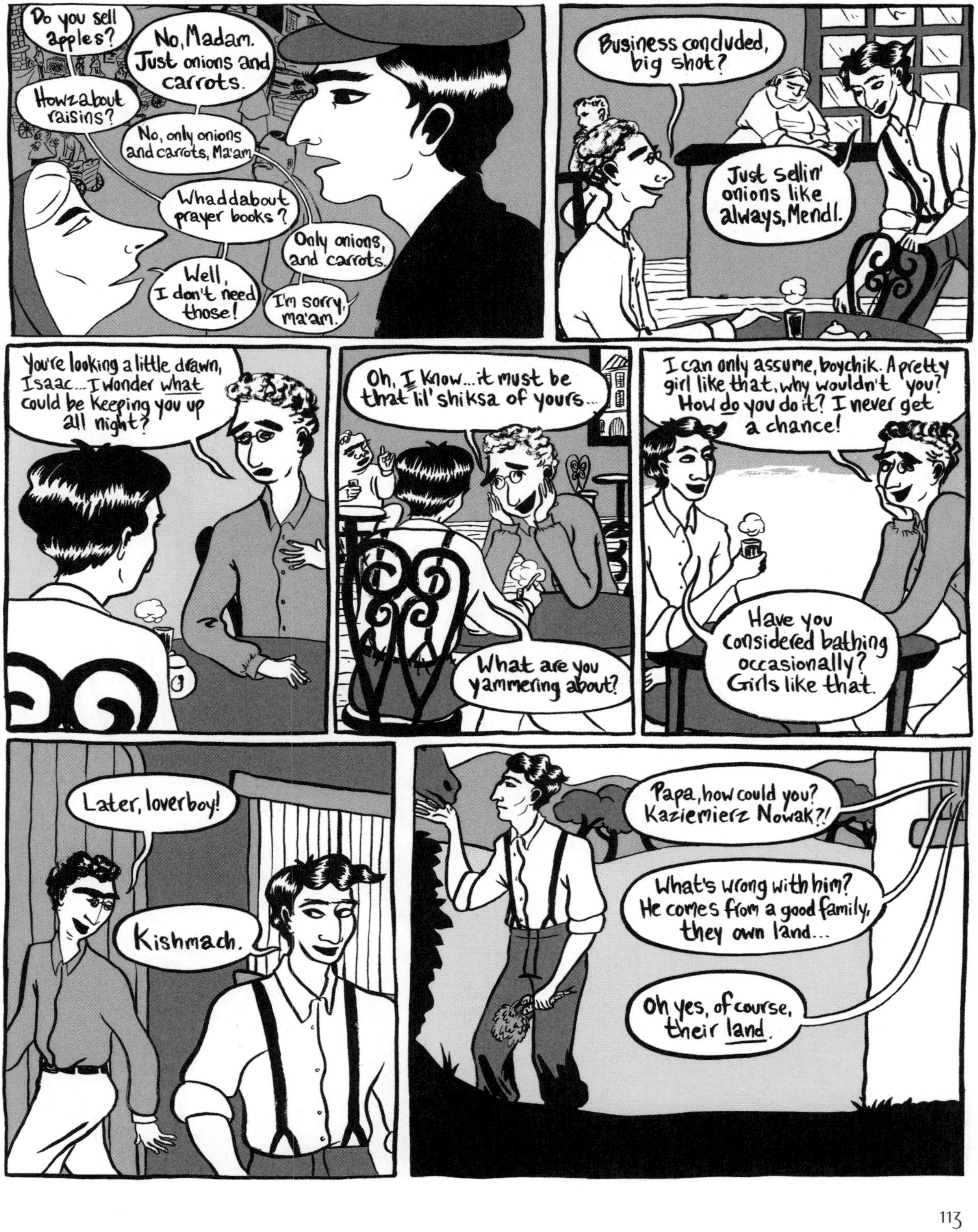
Do you sell apples?
No, Madam. Just onions and carrots.
Howzabout raisins?
No, only onions and carrots, Ma'am.
Whaddabout prayer books?
Only onions, and carrots.
Well, I don't need those!
I'm sorry, ma'am.
Business concluded, big shot?
Just sellin' onions like always, Mendl.
You're looking a little drawn, Isaac... I wonder what could be keeping you up all night?
Oh, I know... it must be that lil' shiksa of yours...
What are you yammering about?
I can only assume, boychik. A pretty girl like that, why wouldn't you? How do you do it? I never get a chance!
Have you considered bathing occasionally? Girls like that.
Later, loverboy!
Kishmach.
Papa, how could you? Kaziemierz Nowak?!
What's wrong with him? He comes from a good family, they own land...
Oh yes, of course, their land.

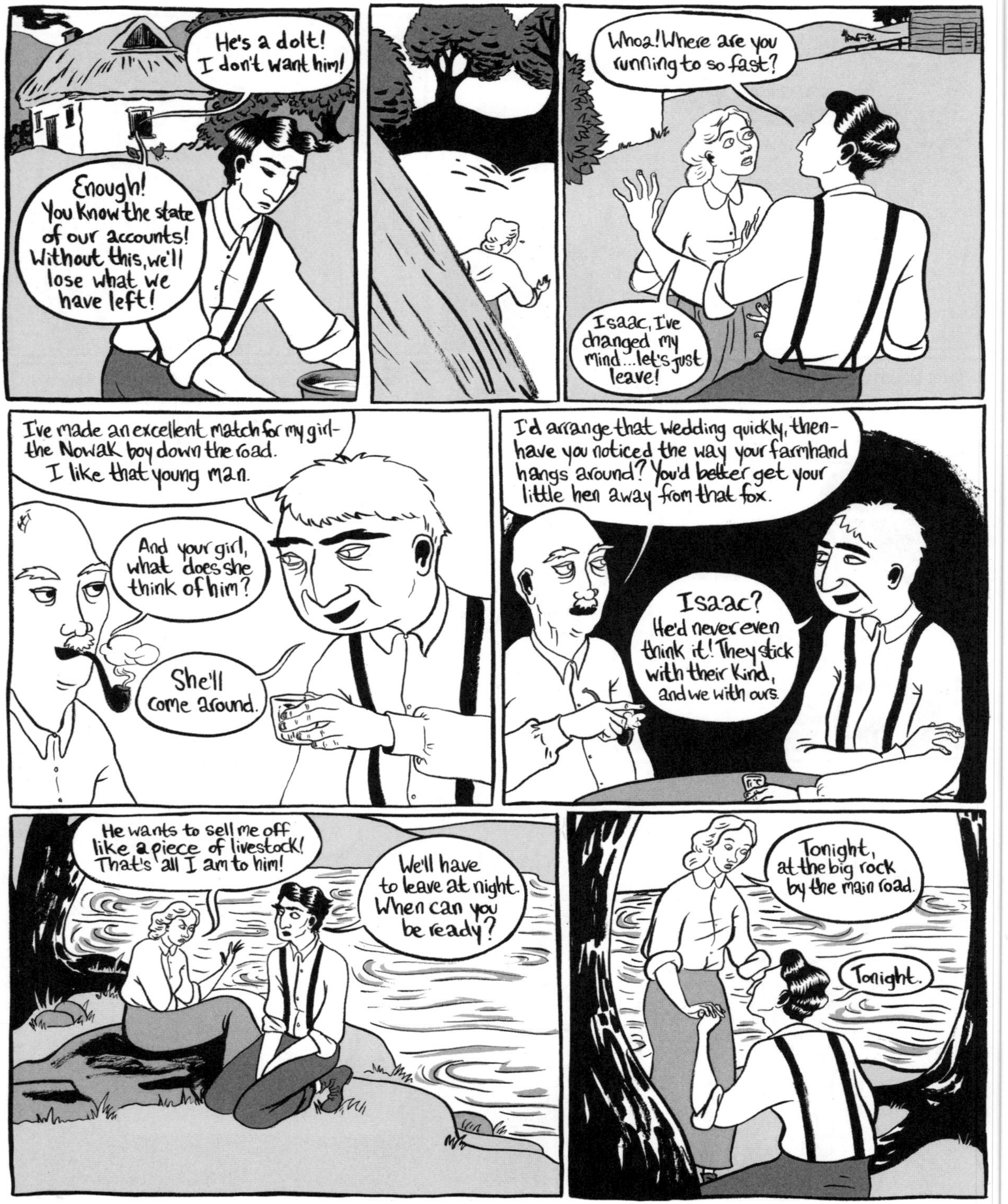
He's a dolt! I don't want him!
Enough! You know the state of our accounts! Without this, we'll lose what we have left!
Whoa! Where are you running to so fast?
Isaac, I've changed my mind... let's just leave!
I've made an excellent match for my girl- the Nowak boy down the road. I like that young man.
And your girl, what does she think of him?
She'll come around.
I'd arrange that wedding quickly, then- have you noticed the way your farmhand hangs around? You'd better get your little hen away from that fox.
Isaac? He'd never even think it! They stick with their kind, and we with ours.
He wants to sell me off like a piece of livestock! That's all I am to him!
We'll have to leave at night. When can you be ready?
Tonight, at the big rock by the main road.
Tonight.

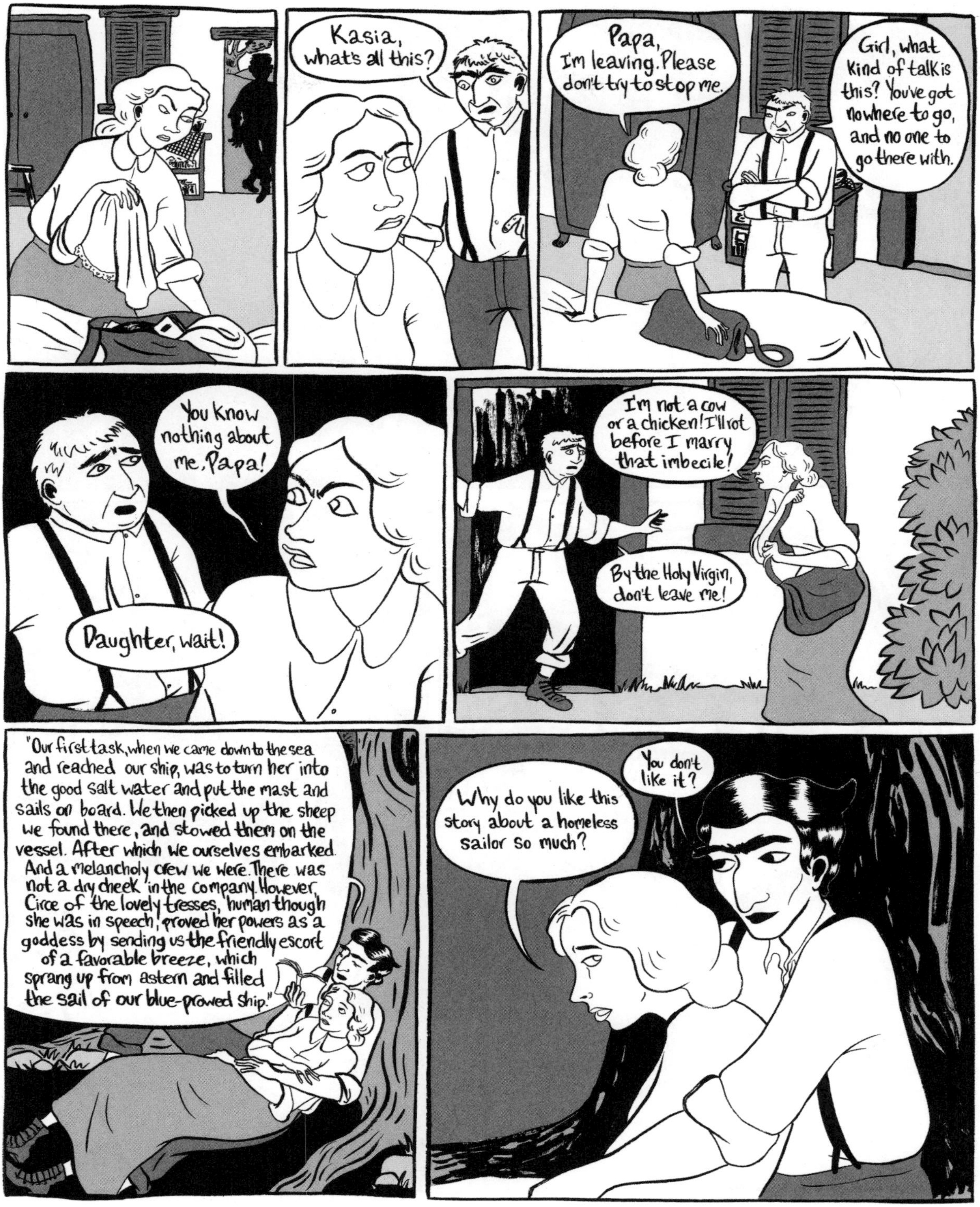
Kasia, what's all this?
Papa, I'm leaving. Please don't try to stop me.
Girl, what kind of talk is this? You've got nowhere to go, and no one to go there with.
You know nothing about me, Papa!
Daughter, wait!
I'm not a cow or a chicken! I'll rot before I marry that imbecile!
By the Holy Virgin, don't leave me!
"Our first task, when we came down to the sea and reached our ship, was to turn her into the good salt water and put the mast and sails on board. We then picked up the sheep we found there, and stowed them on the vessel. After which we ourselves embarked. And a melancholy crew we were. There was not a dry cheek in the company. However, Circe of the lovely tresses, human though she was in speech, proved her powers as a goddess by sending us the friendly escort of a favorable breeze, which sprang up from astern and filled the sail of our blue-prowed ship."
Why do you like this story about a homeless sailor so much?
You don't like it?

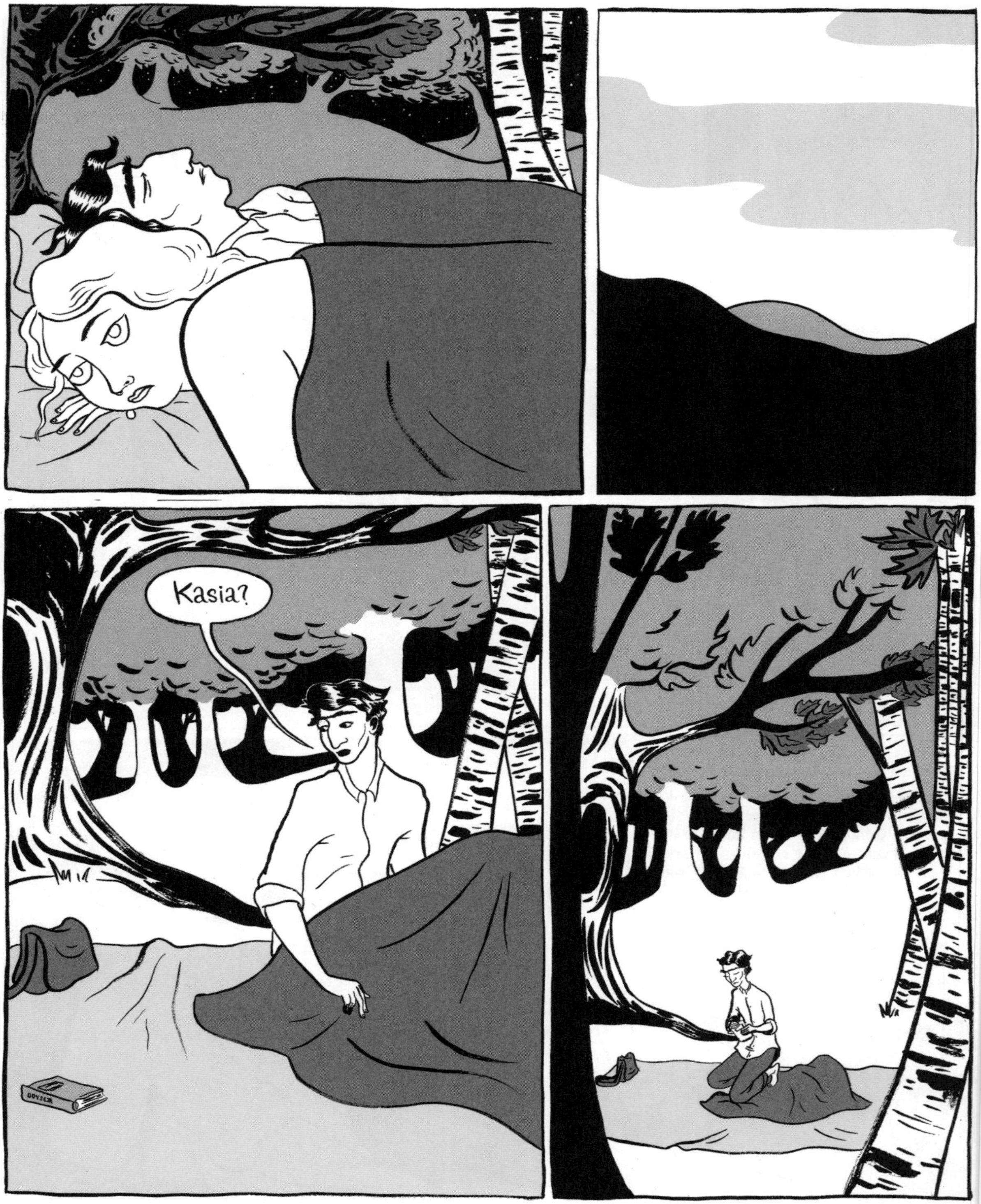
Kasia?

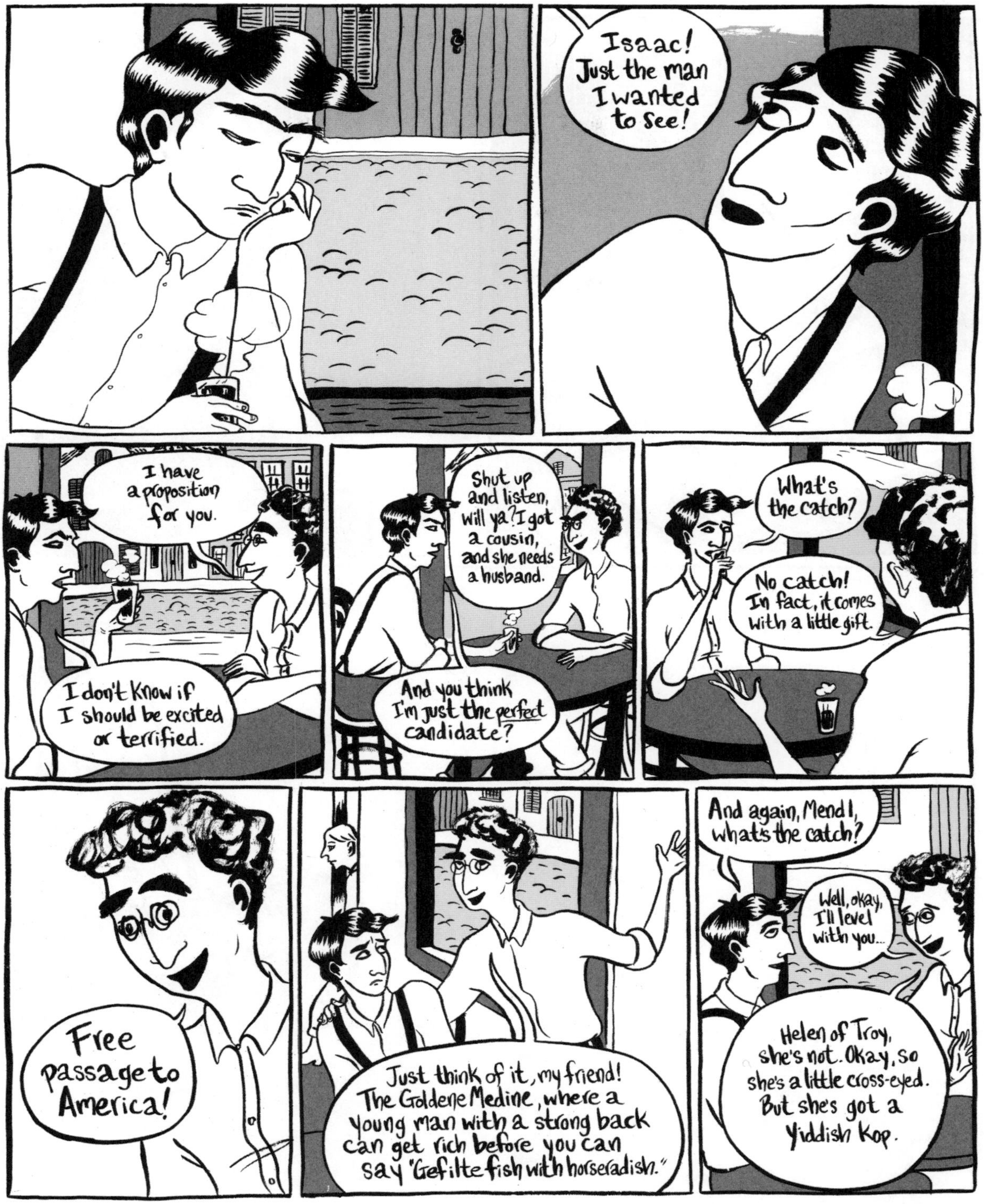
Isaac! Just the man I wanted to see!
I have a proposition for you.
I don't know if I should be excited or terrified.
Shut up and listen, will ya? I got a cousin, and she needs a husband.
And you think I'm just the perfect candidate?
What's the catch?
No catch! In fact, it comes with a little gift.
Free passage to America!
Just think of it, my friend! The Goldene Medine, where a young man with a strong back can get rich before you can say "Gefilte fish with horseradish."
And again, Mendl, what's the catch?
Well, okay, I'll level with you...
Helen of Troy, she's not. Okay, so she's a little cross-eyed. But she's got a Yiddish Kop.

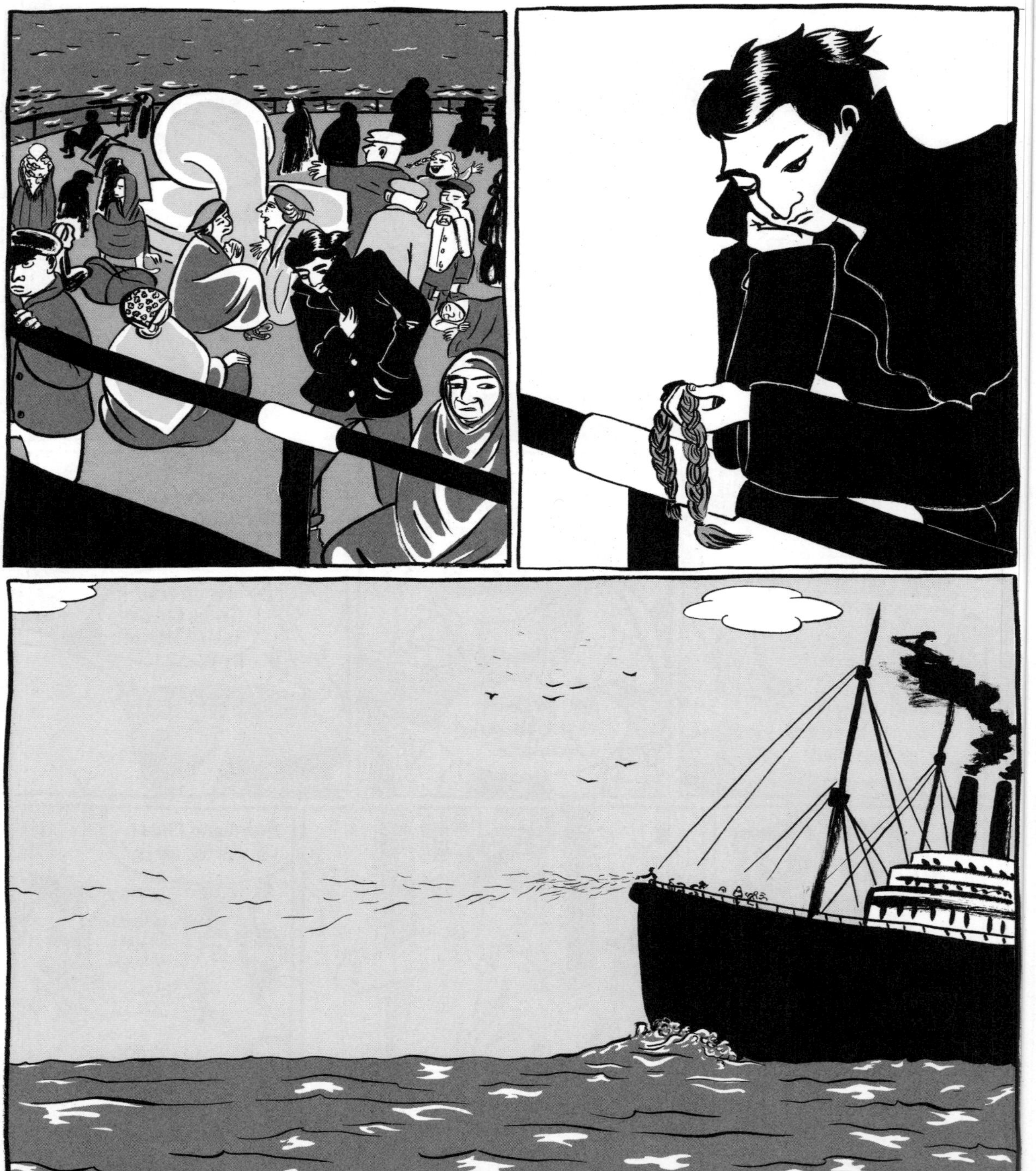

1917

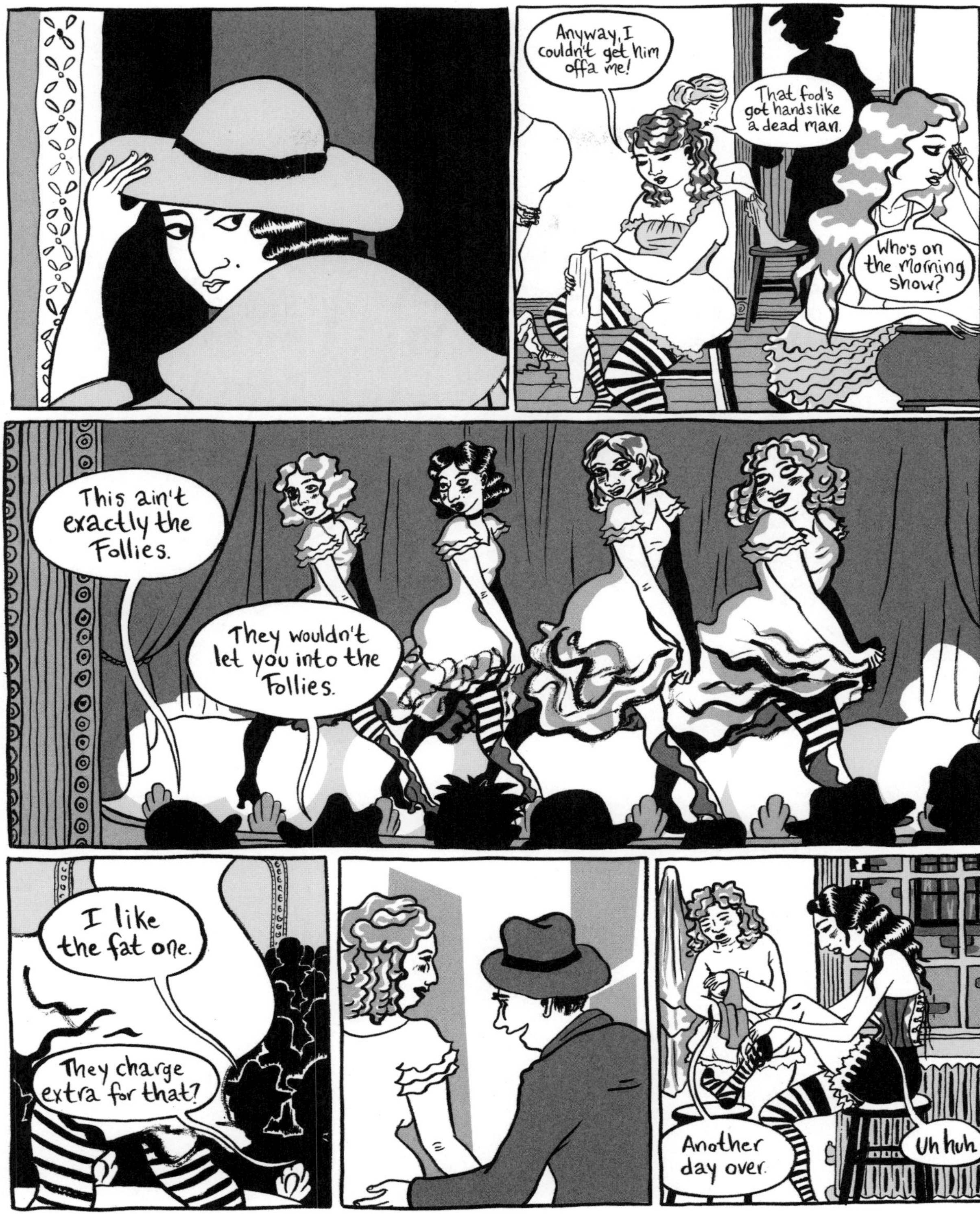
Anyway, I couldn't get him offa me!
That fool's got hands like a dead man.
Who's on the morning show?
This ain't exactly the Follies.
They wouldn't let you into the Follies.
I like the fat one.
They charge extra for that?
Another day over.
Uh huh

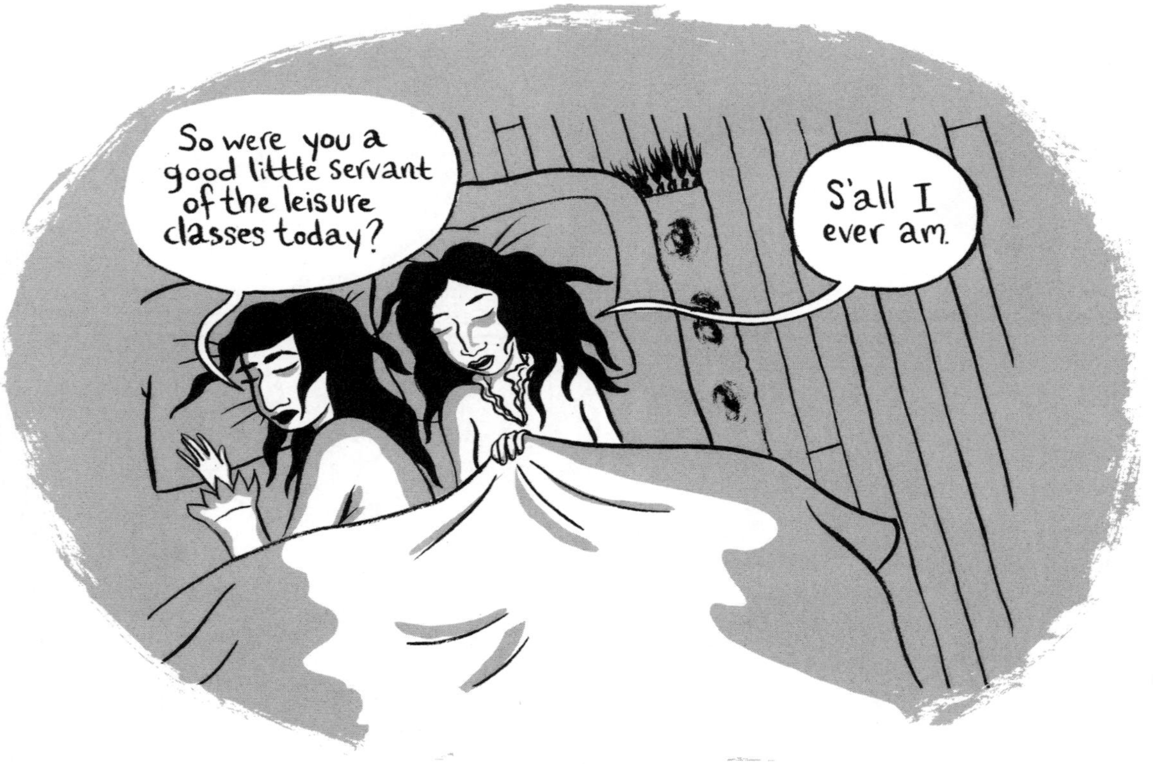
So were you a good little servant of the leisure classes today?
S'all I ever am.

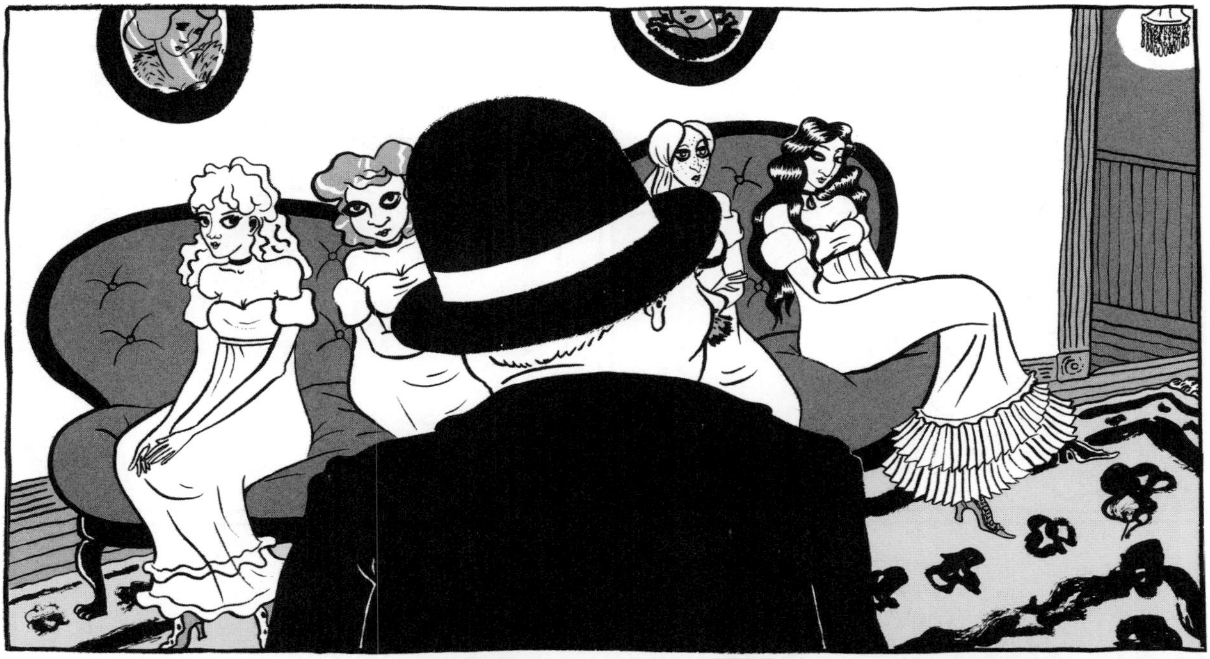

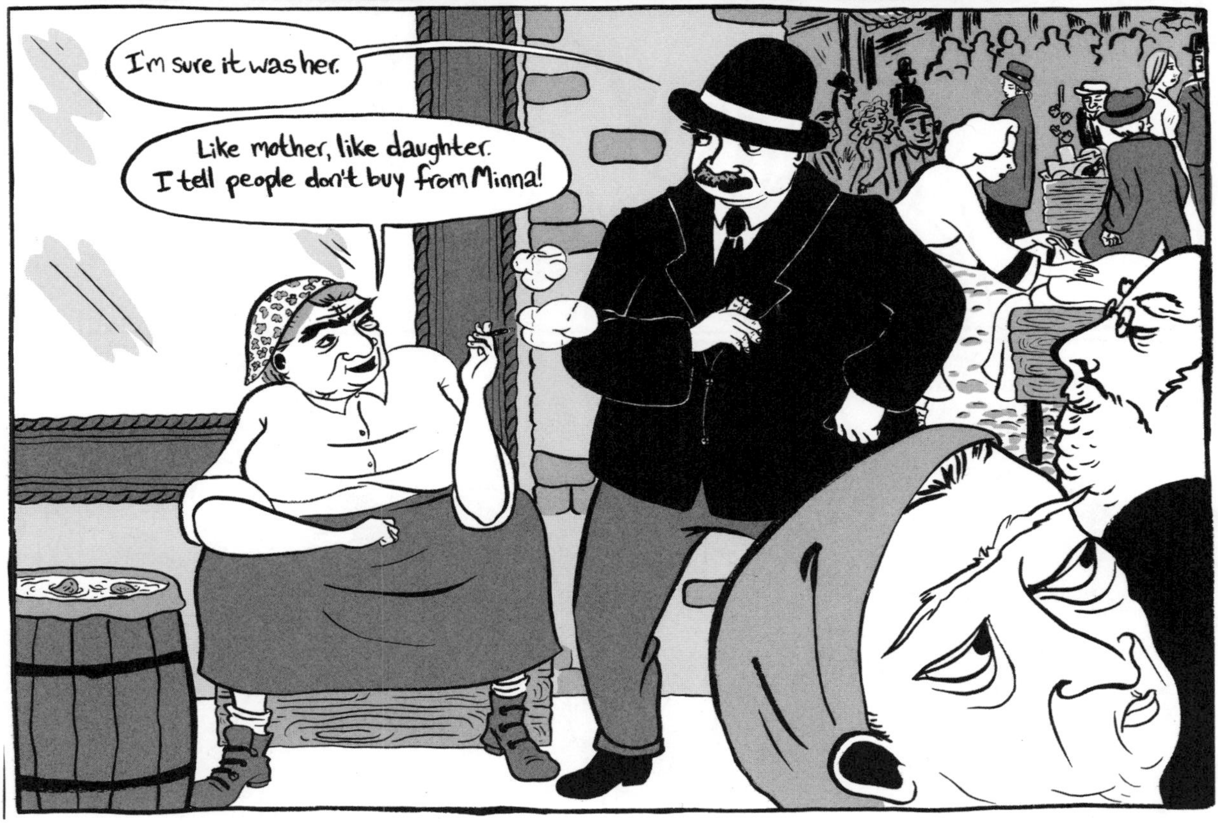
I'm sure it was her.
Like mother, like daughter. I tell people don't buy from Minna!

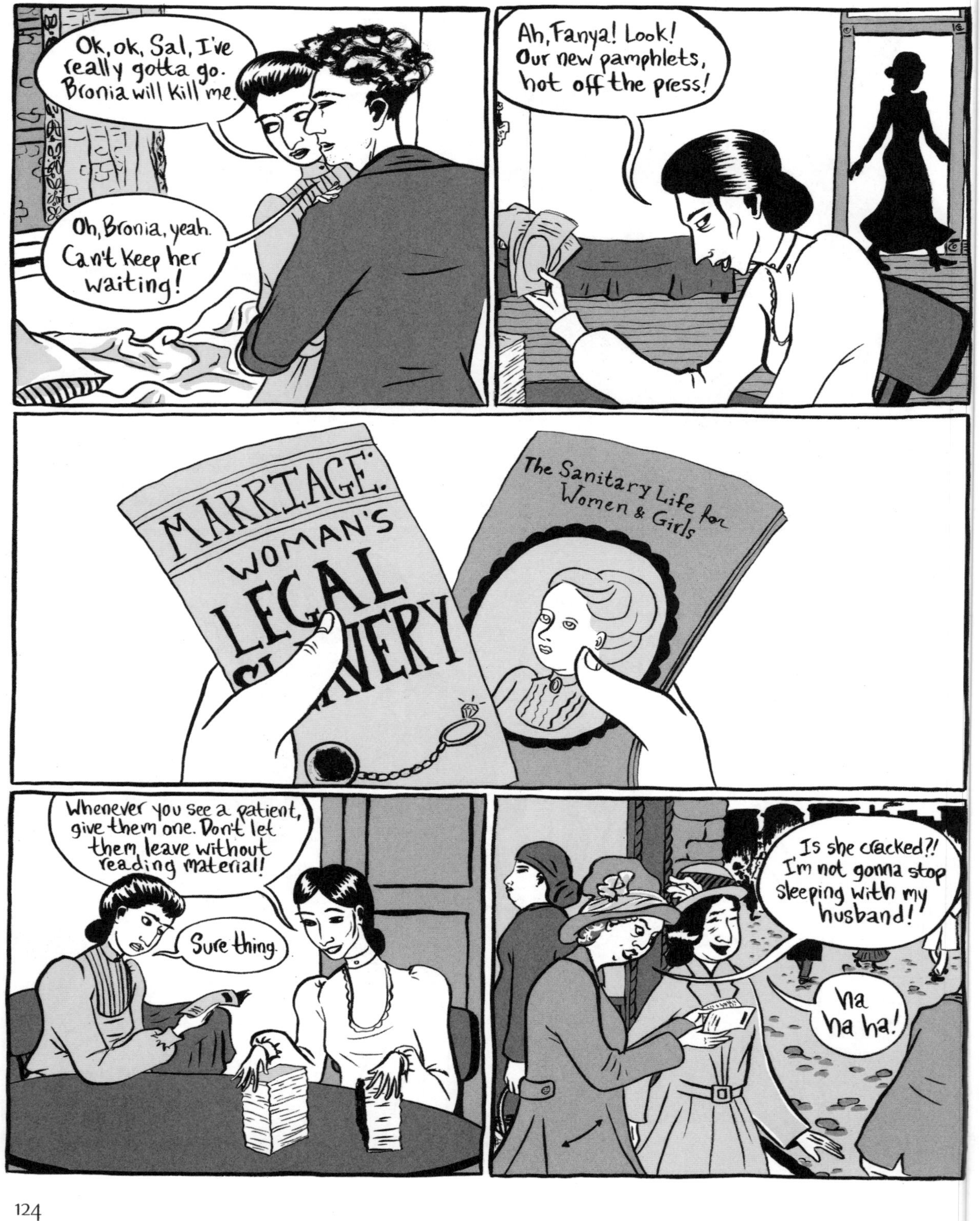
Ok, ok, Sal, I've really gotta go. Bronia will kill me.
Oh, Bronia, yeah. Can't keep her waiting!
Ah, Fanya! Look! Our new pamphlets, hot off the press!
MARRIAGE: WOMAN'S LEGAL
The Sanitary Life for Women & Girls
Whenever you see a patient, give them one. Don't let them leave without reading material!
Sure thing.
Is she cracked?! I'm not gonna stop sleeping with my husband!
ha ha ha!

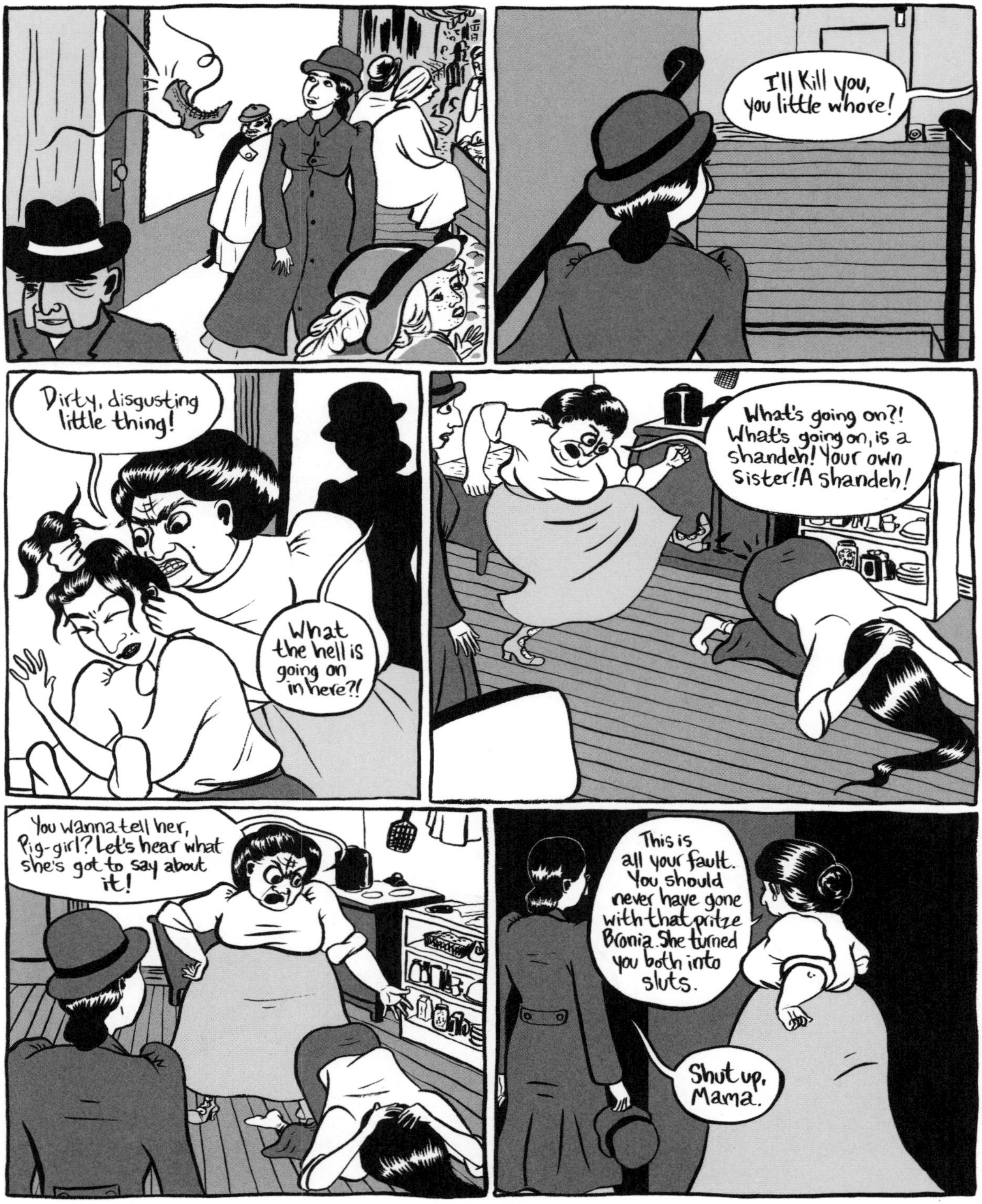
I'll Kill you, you little whore!
Dirty, disgusting little thing!
What the hell is going on in here?!
What's going on?! What's going on, is a shandeh! Your own sister! A shandeh!
You wanna tell her, Pig-girl? Let's hear what she's got to say about it!
This is all your fault. You should never have gone with that pritze Bronia. She turned you both into sluts.
Shut up, Mama.

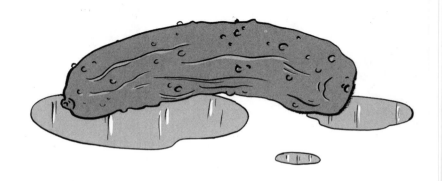

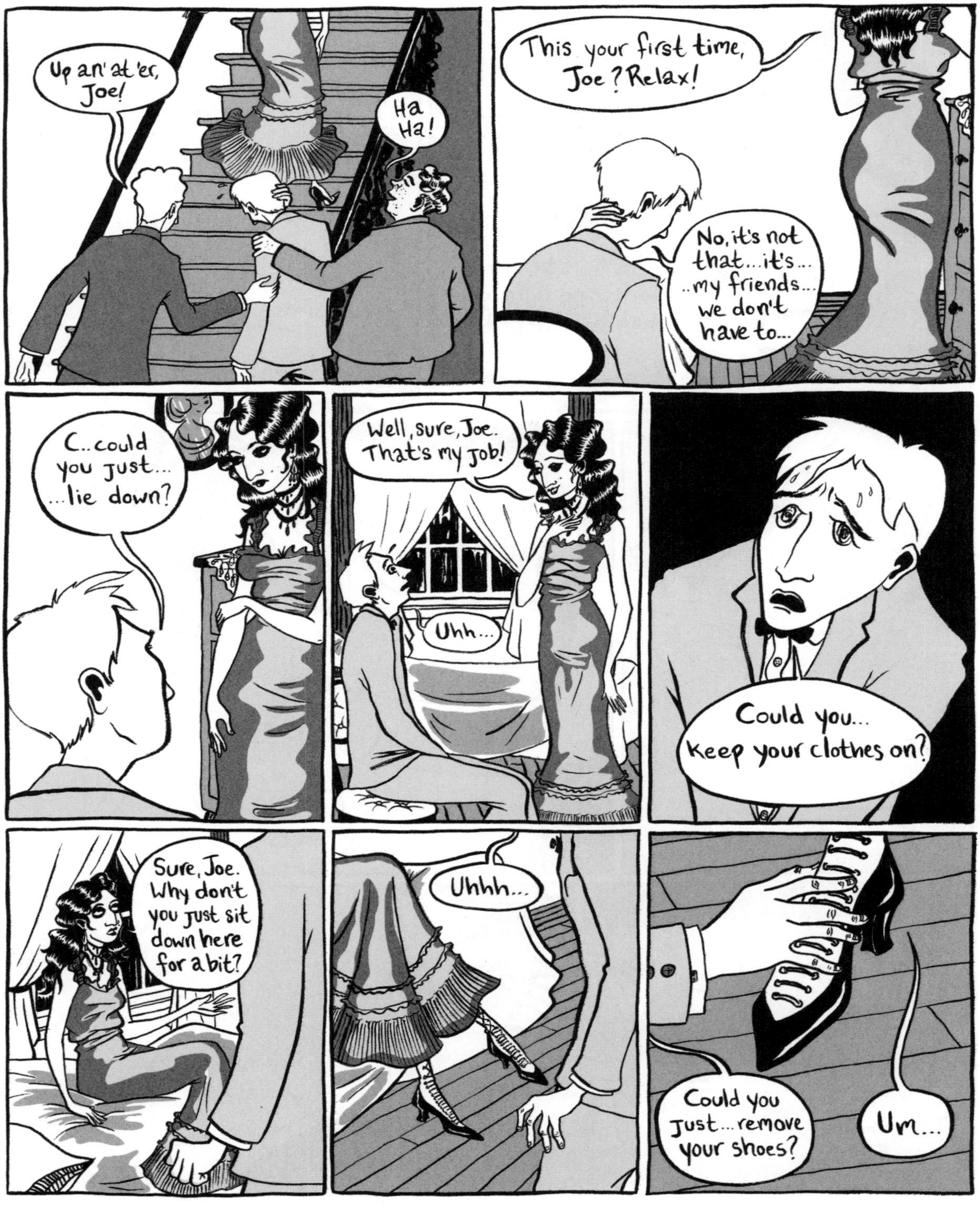
Up an' at 'er, Joe!
Ha Ha!
This your first time, Joe? Relax!
No, it's not that... it's... ..my friends... we don't have to...
C.. could you just... ...lie down?
Well, sure, Joe. That's my job!
Uhh...
Could you... keep your clothes on?
Sure, Joe. Why don't you just sit down here for a bit?
Uhhh...
Could you just... remove your shoes?
Um...

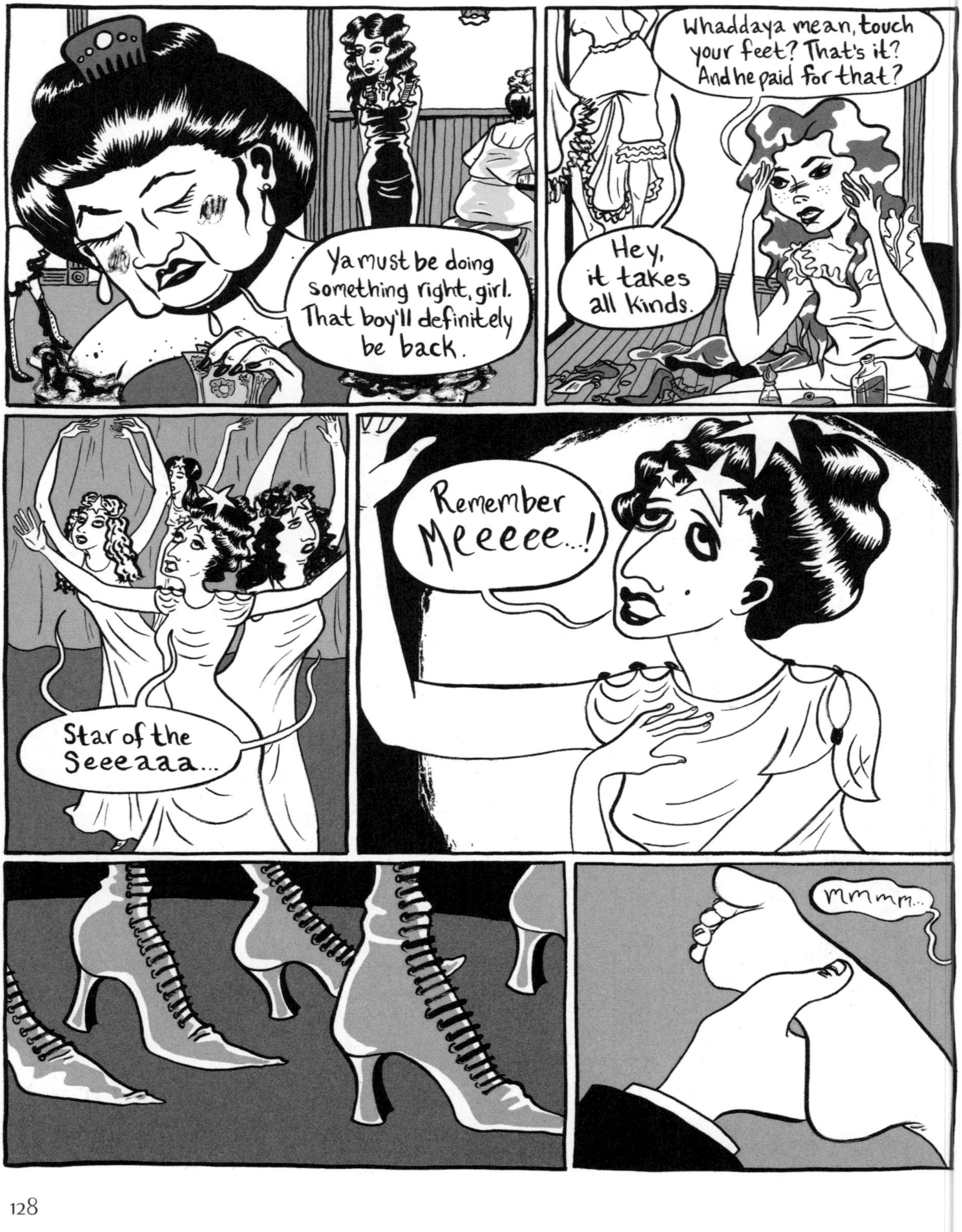
Ya must be doing something right, girl. That boy'll definitely be back.
Whaddaya mean, touch your feet? That's it? And he paid for that?
Hey, it takes all kinds.
Star of the Seeeaaa...
Remember Meeeee...!
Mmmm...

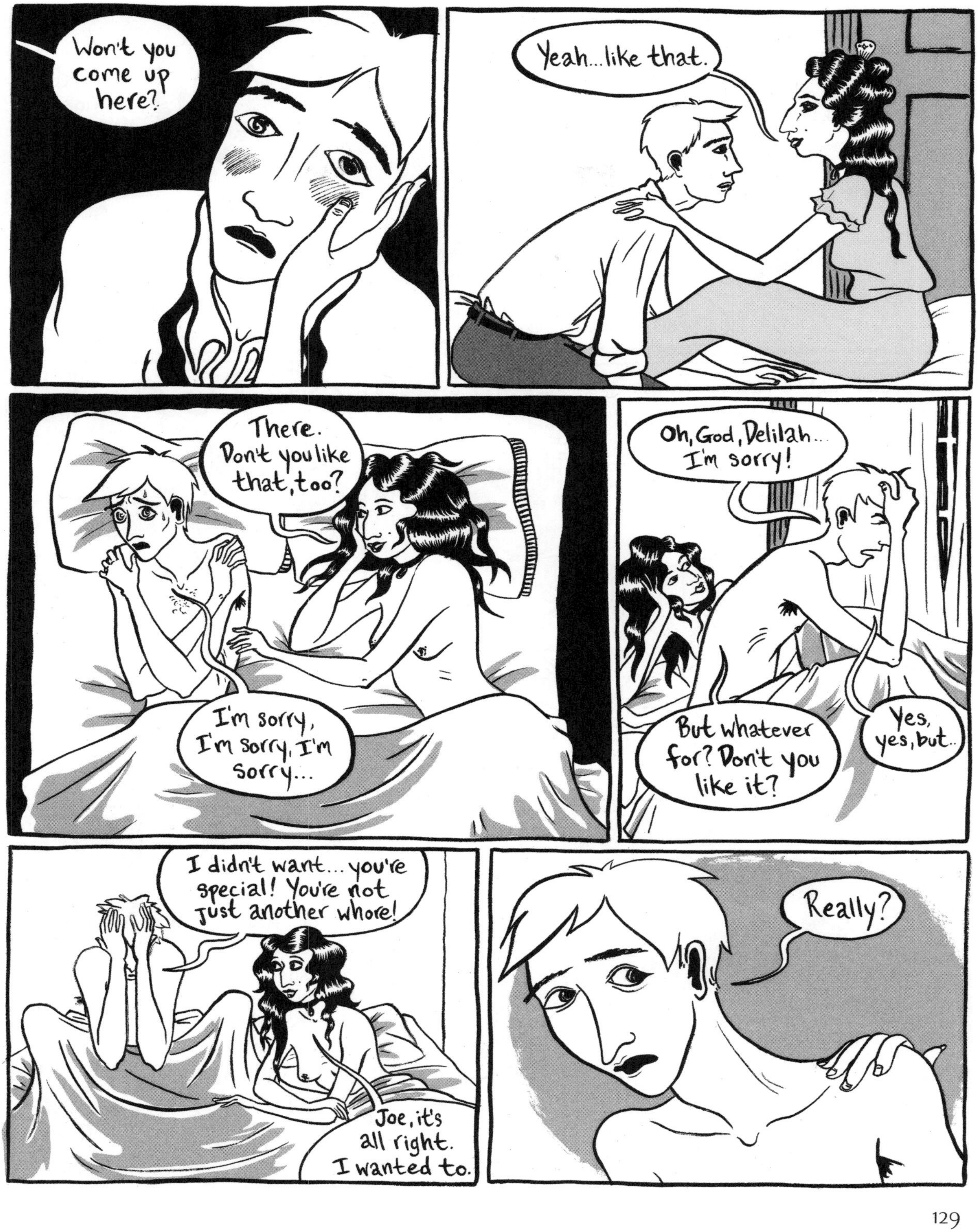
Won't you come up here?
Yeah...like that.
There. Don't you like that, too?
I'm sorry, I'm sorry, I'm sorry...
Oh, God, Delilah... I'm sorry!
But whatever for? Don't you like it?
Yes, yes, but..
I didn't want... you're special! You're not just another whore!
Joe, it's all right. I wanted to.
Really?

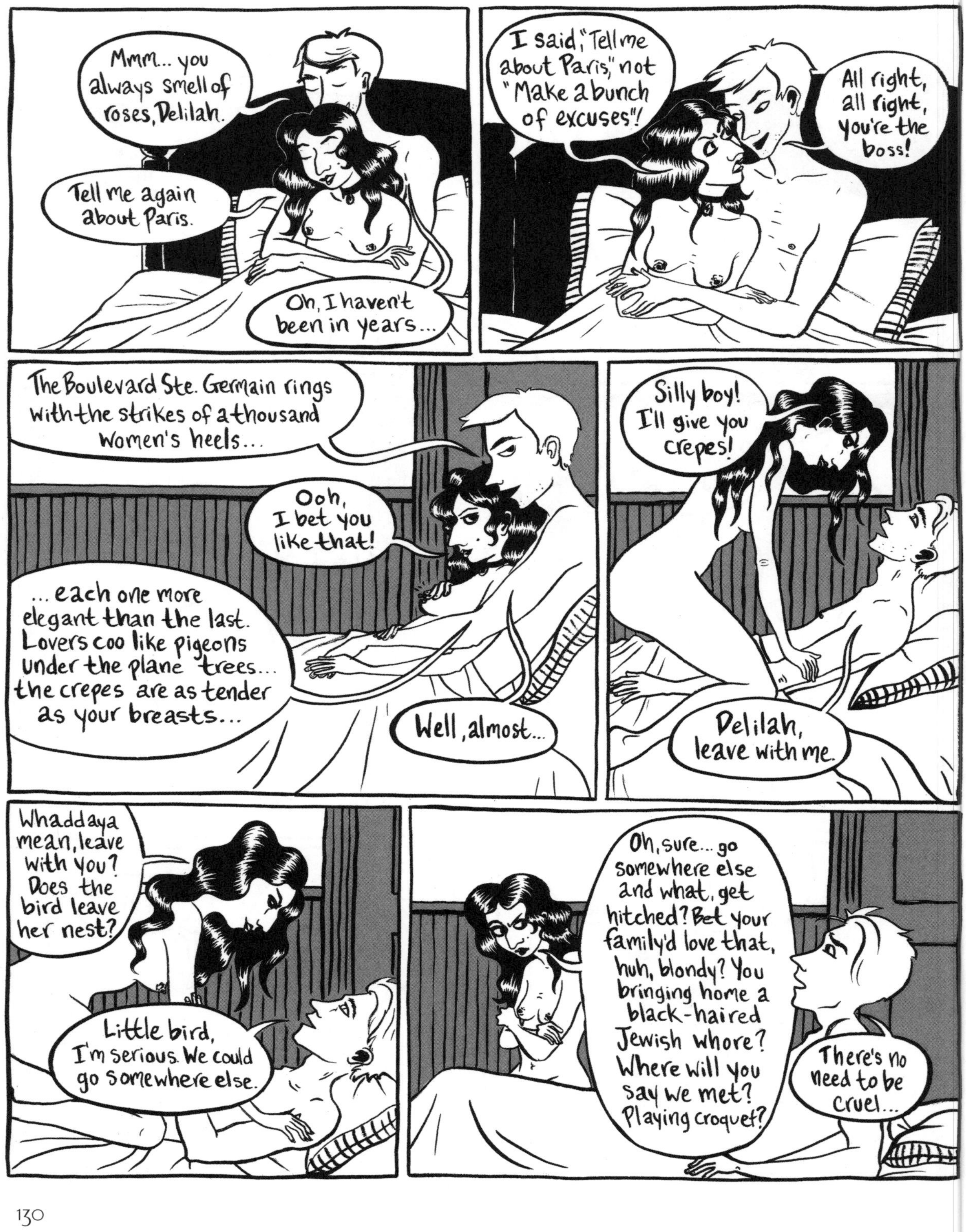
Mmm... you always smell of roses, Delilah.
Tell me again about Paris.
Oh, I haven't been in years...
I said, "Tell me about Paris," not "Make a bunch of excuses"!
All right, all right, you're the boss!
The Boulevard Ste. Germain rings with the strikes of a thousand women's heels...
Ooh, I bet you like that!
... each one more elegant than the last. Lovers coo like pigeons under the plane trees... the crepes are as tender as your breasts...
Well, almost...
Silly boy! I'll give you crepes!
Delilah, leave with me.
Whaddaya mean, leave with you? Does the bird leave her nest?
Little bird, I'm serious. We could go somewhere else.
Oh, sure... go somewhere else and what, get hitched? Bet your family'd love that, huh, blondy? You bringing home a black-haired Jewish whore? Where will you say we met? Playing croquet?
There's no need to be cruel...

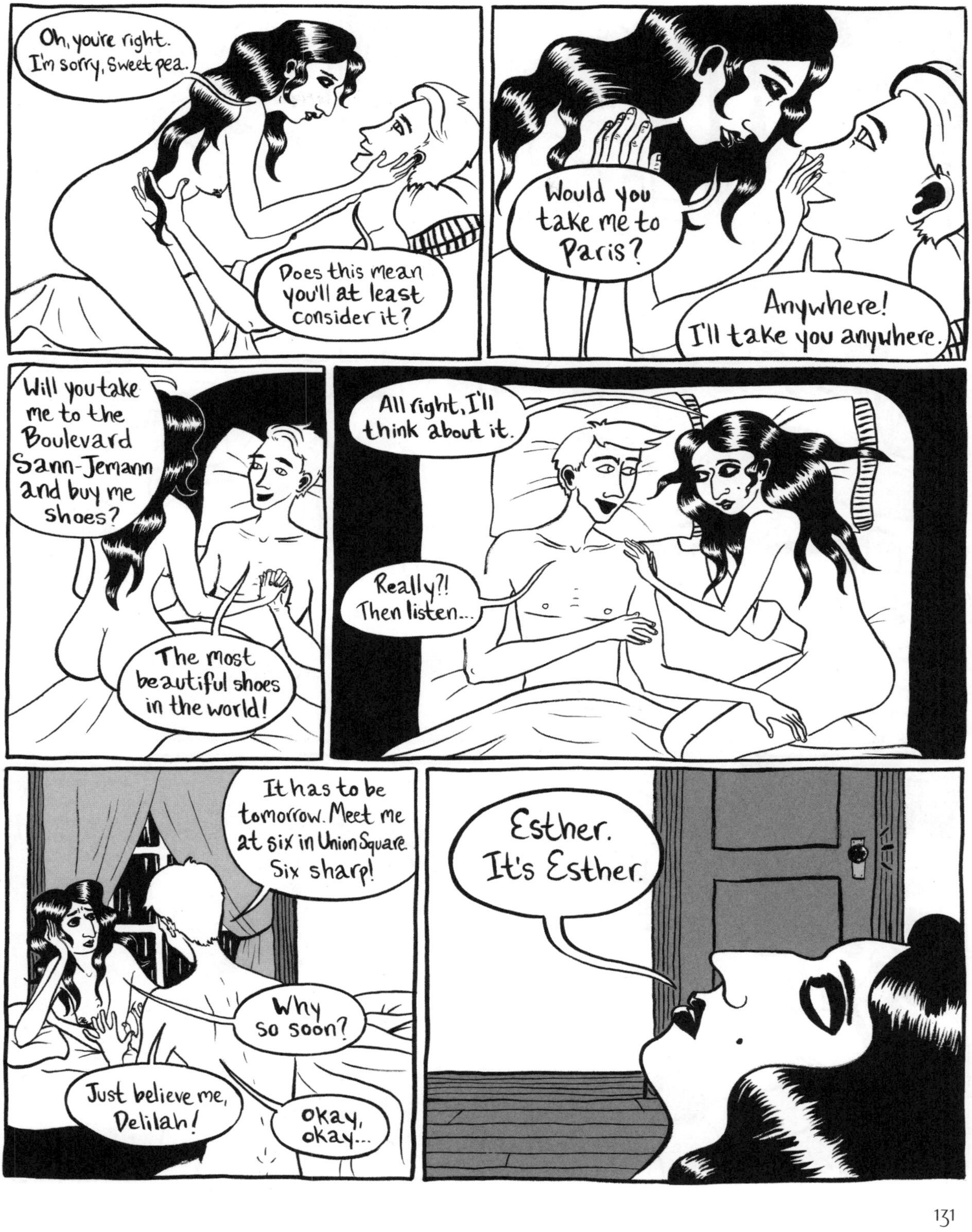
Oh, you're right. I'm sorry, Sweet pea.
Does this mean you'll at least consider it?
Would you take me to Paris?
Anywhere! I'll take you anywhere.
Will you take me to the Boulevard Sann-Jemann and buy me shoes?
The most beautiful shoes in the world!
All right, I'll think about it.
Really?! Then listen...
It has to be tomorrow. Meet me at six in Union Square. Six sharp!
Why so soon?
Just believe me, Delilah!
okay, okay...
Esther. It's Esther.

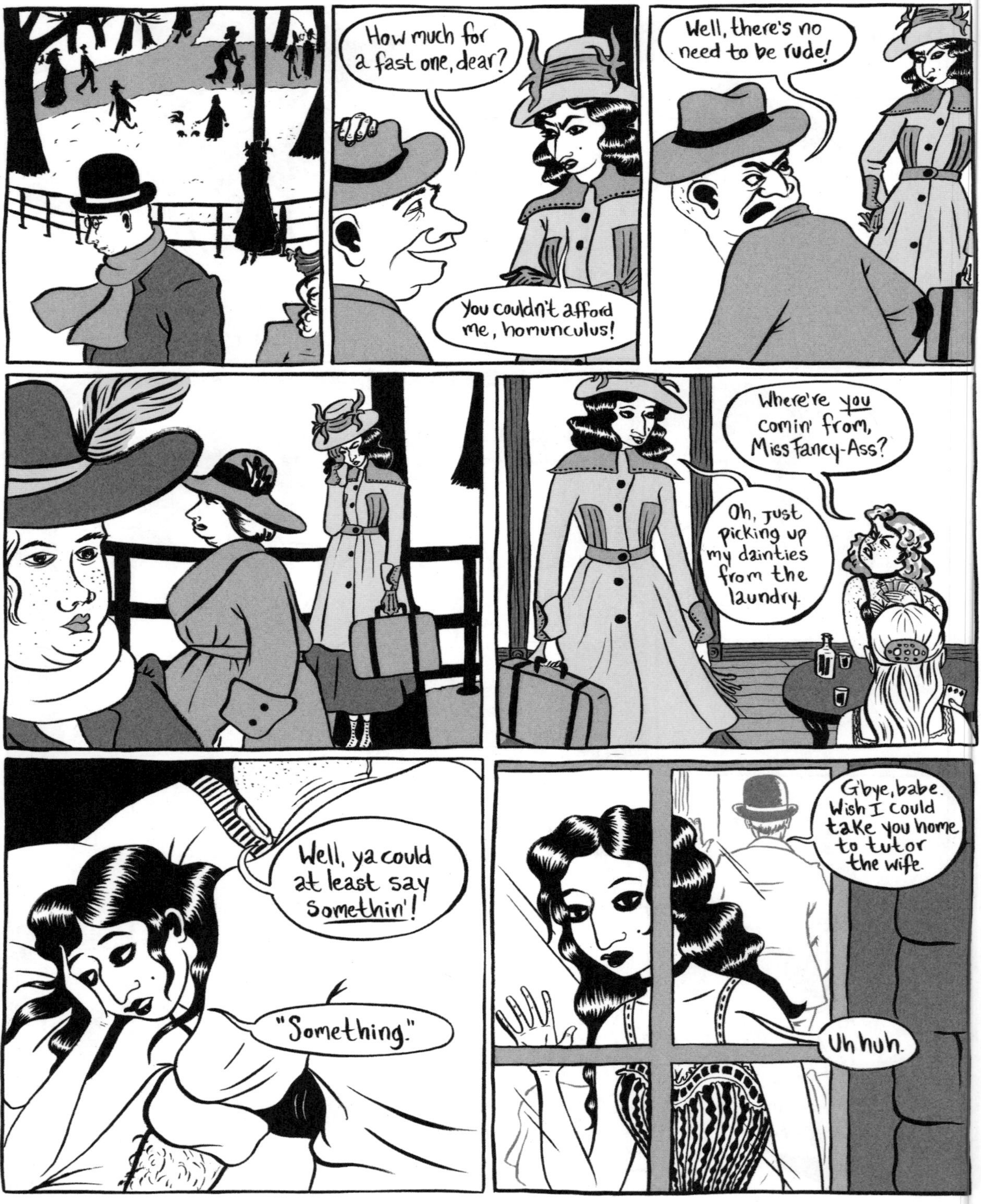

How much for a fast one, dear?
You couldn't afford me, homunculus!
Well, there's no need to be rude!
Where're you comin' from, Miss Fancy-Ass?
Oh, just picking up my dainties from the laundry.
Well, ya could at least say Somethin'!
"Something."
G'bye, babe. Wish I could take you home to tutor the wife.
Uh huh.

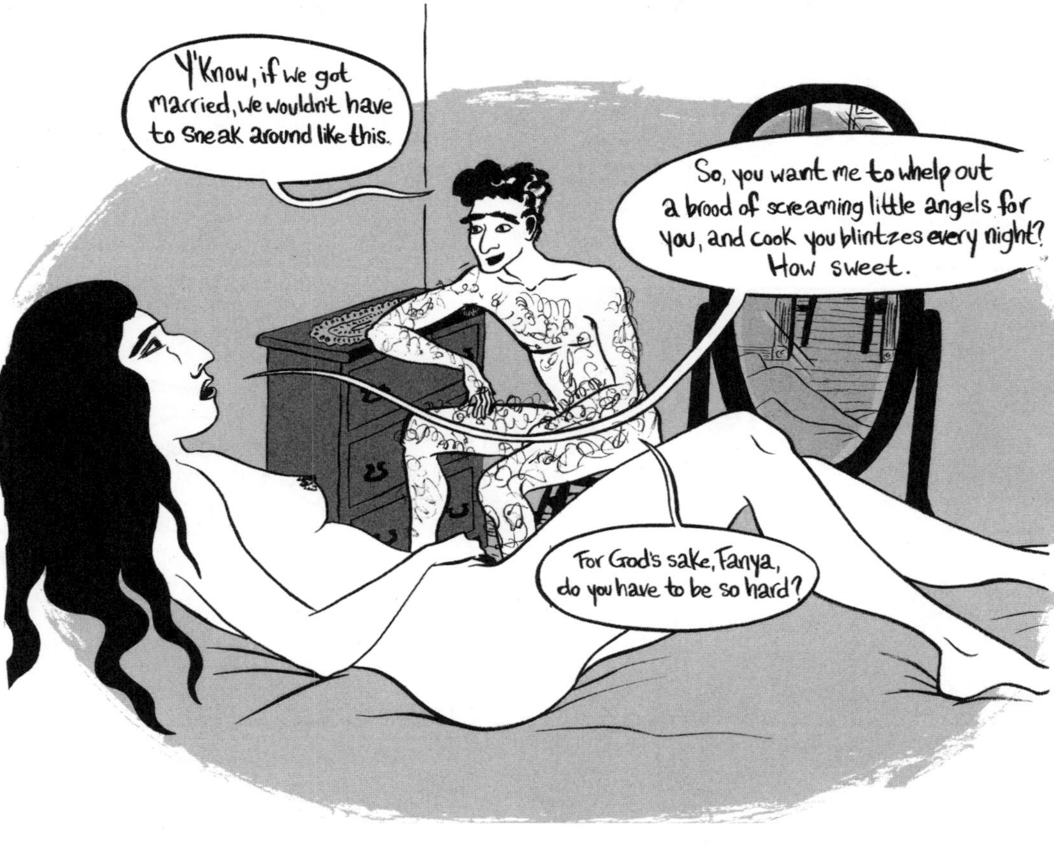
Y'Know, if we got married, we wouldn't have to sneak around like this.
So, you want me to whelp out a brood of screaming little angels for you, and cook you blintzes every night? How sweet.
For God's sake, Fanya, do you have to be so hard?

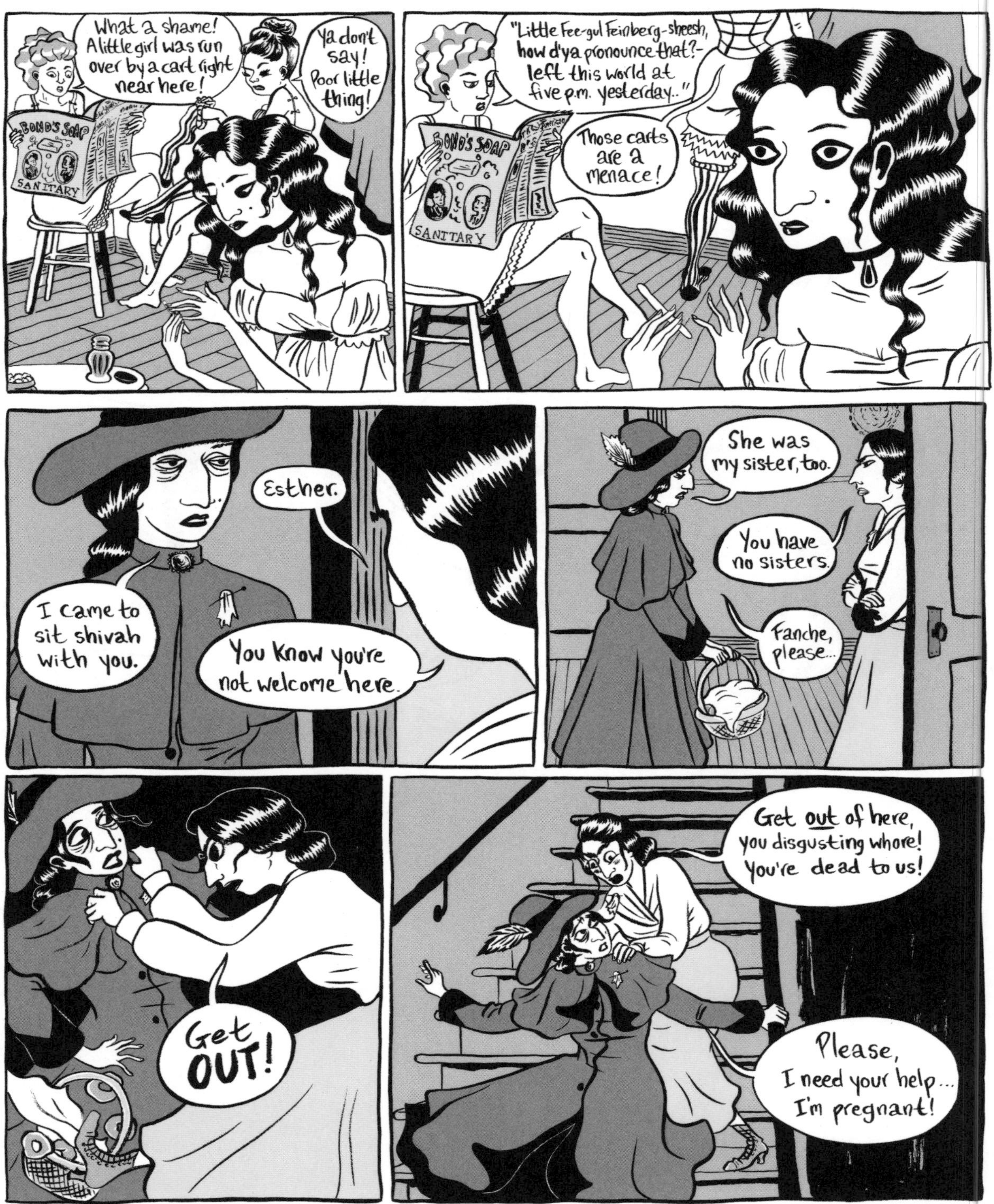
What a shame! A little girl was run over by a cart right near here!
Ya don't say! Poor little thing!
BOND'S SOAP
SANITARY
"Little Fee-gul Feinberg-sheesh, how d'ya pronounce that?- left this world at five p.m. yesterday.."
Those carts are a menace!
BOND'S SOAP
SANITARY
Esther.
I came to sit shivah with you.
You know you're not welcome here.
She was my sister, too.
You have no sisters.
Fanche, please...
Get OUT!
Get out of here, you disgusting whore! You're dead to us!
Please, I need your help... I'm pregnant!

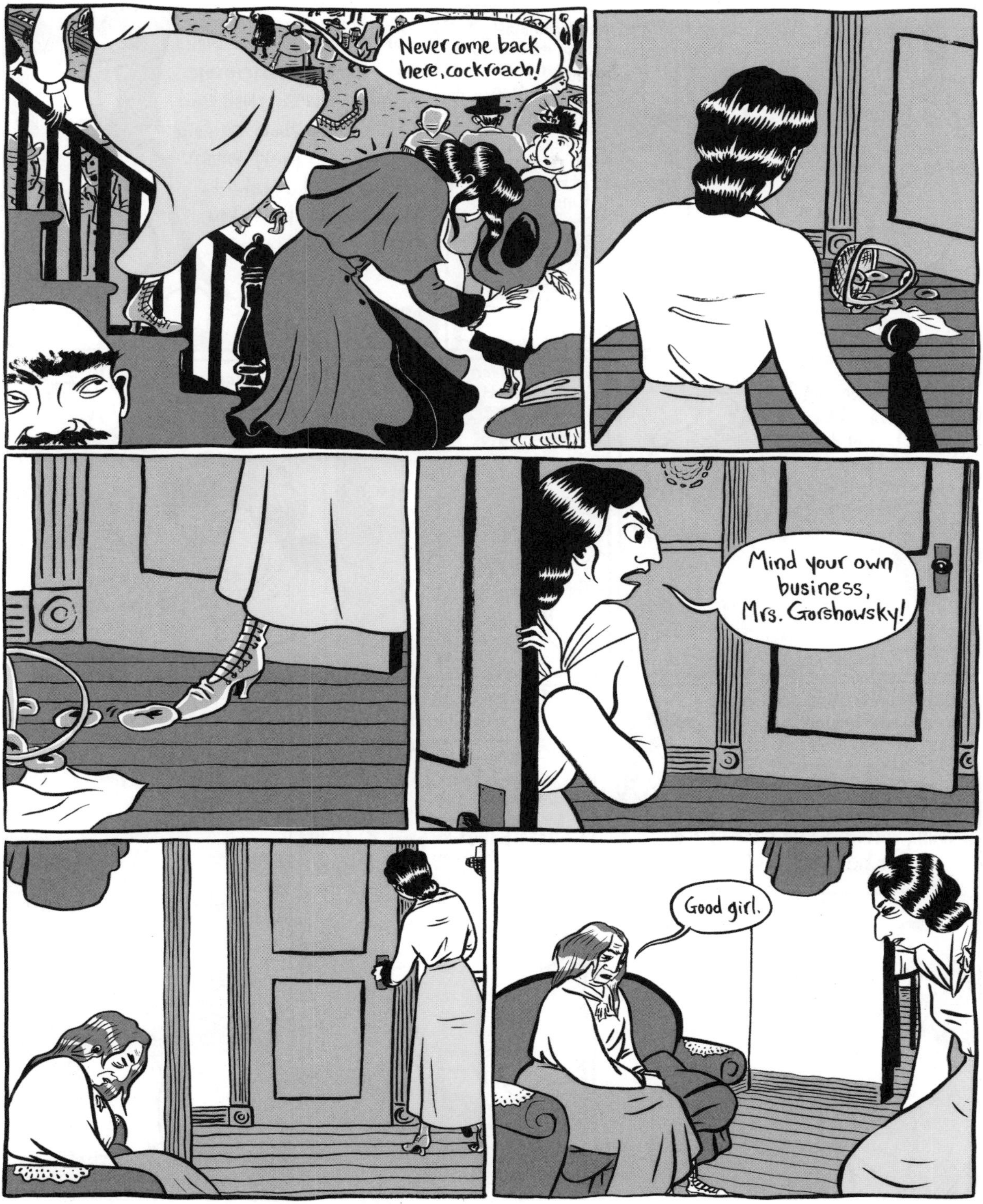
Never come back here, cockroach!
Mind your own business, Mrs. Gorshowsky!
Good girl.

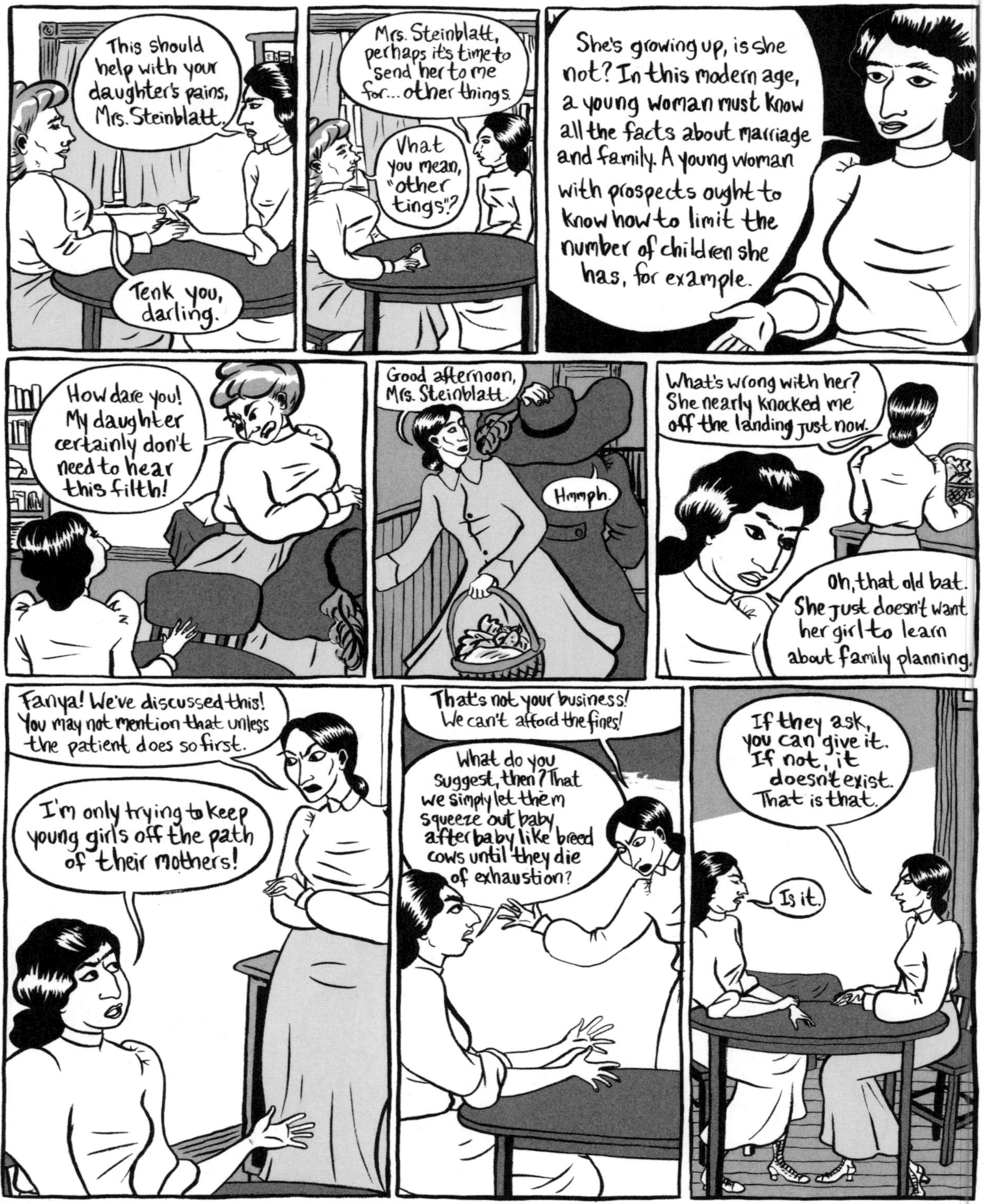
This should help with your daughter's pains, Mrs. Steinblatt.
Tenk you, darling.
Mrs. Steinblatt, perhaps it's time to send her to me for... other things.
Vhat you mean, "other tings"?
She's growing up, is she not? In this modern age, a young woman must know all the facts about marriage and family. A young woman with prospects ought to know how to limit the number of children she has, for example.
How dare you! My daughter certainly don't need to hear this filth!
Good afternoon, Mrs. Steinblatt.
Hmmph.
What's wrong with her? She nearly knocked me off the landing just now.
Oh, that old bat. She just doesn't want her girl to learn about family planning.
Fanya! We've discussed this! You may not mention that unless the patient does so first.
I'm only trying to keep young girls off the path of their mothers!
That's not your business! We can't afford the fines!
What do you suggest, then? That we simply let them squeeze out baby after baby like breed cows until they die of exhaustion?
If they ask, you can give it. If not, it doesn't exist. That is that.
Is it.

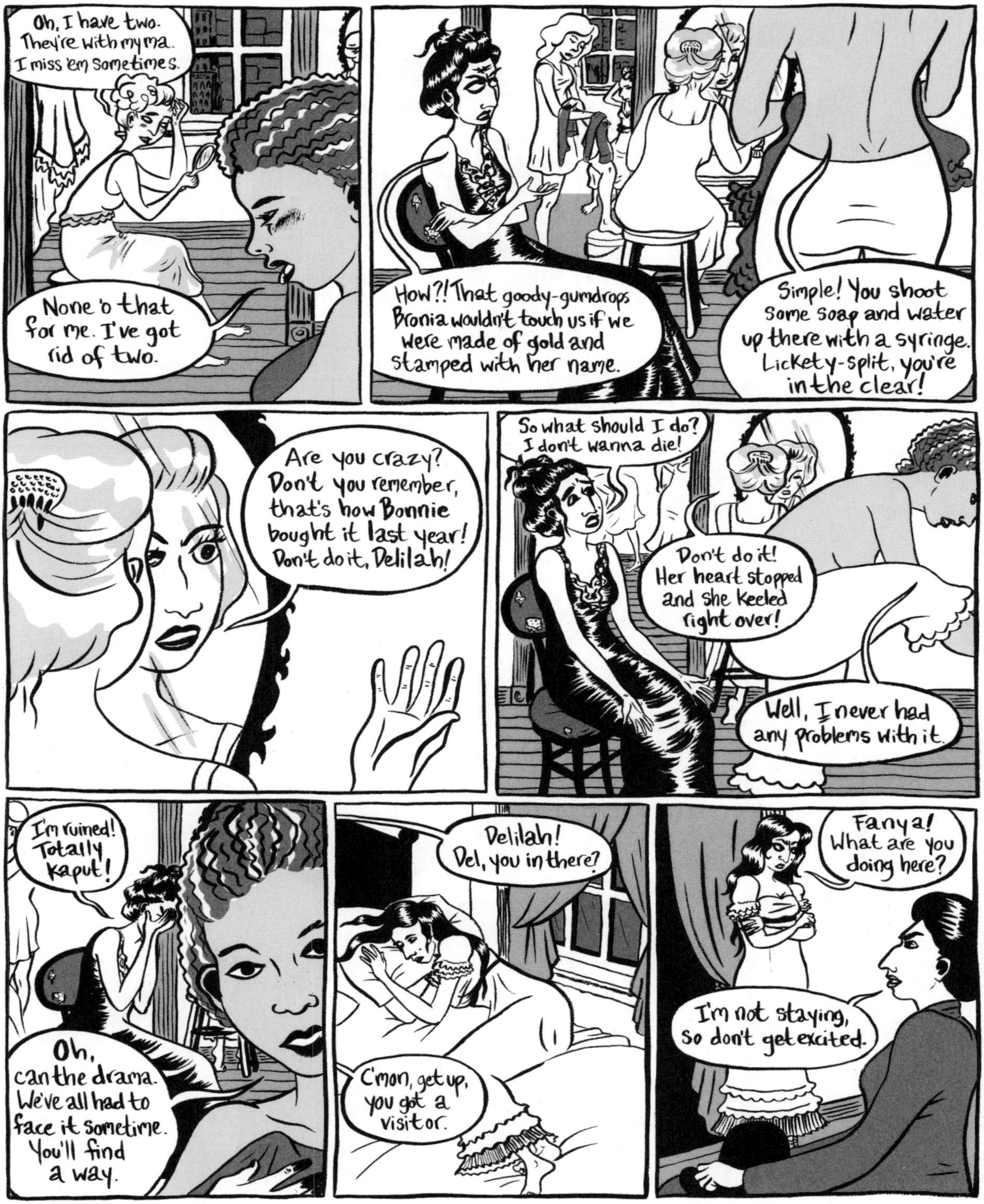
Oh, I have two. They're with my ma. I miss 'em sometimes.
None 'o that for me. I've got rid of two.
How?! That goody-gumdrops Bronia wouldn't touch us if we were made of gold and stamped with her name.
Simple! You shoot some soap and water up there with a syringe. Lickety-split, you're in the clear!
Are you crazy? Don't you remember, that's how Bonnie bought it last year! Don't do it, Delilah!
So what should I do? I don't wanna die!
Don't do it! Her heart stopped and she keeled right over!
Well, I never had any problems with it.
I'm ruined! Totally kaput!
Oh, can the drama. We've all had to face it sometime. You'll find a way.
Delilah! Del, you in there?
C'mon, get up, you got a visitor.
Fanya! What are you doing here?
I'm not staying, so don't get excited.

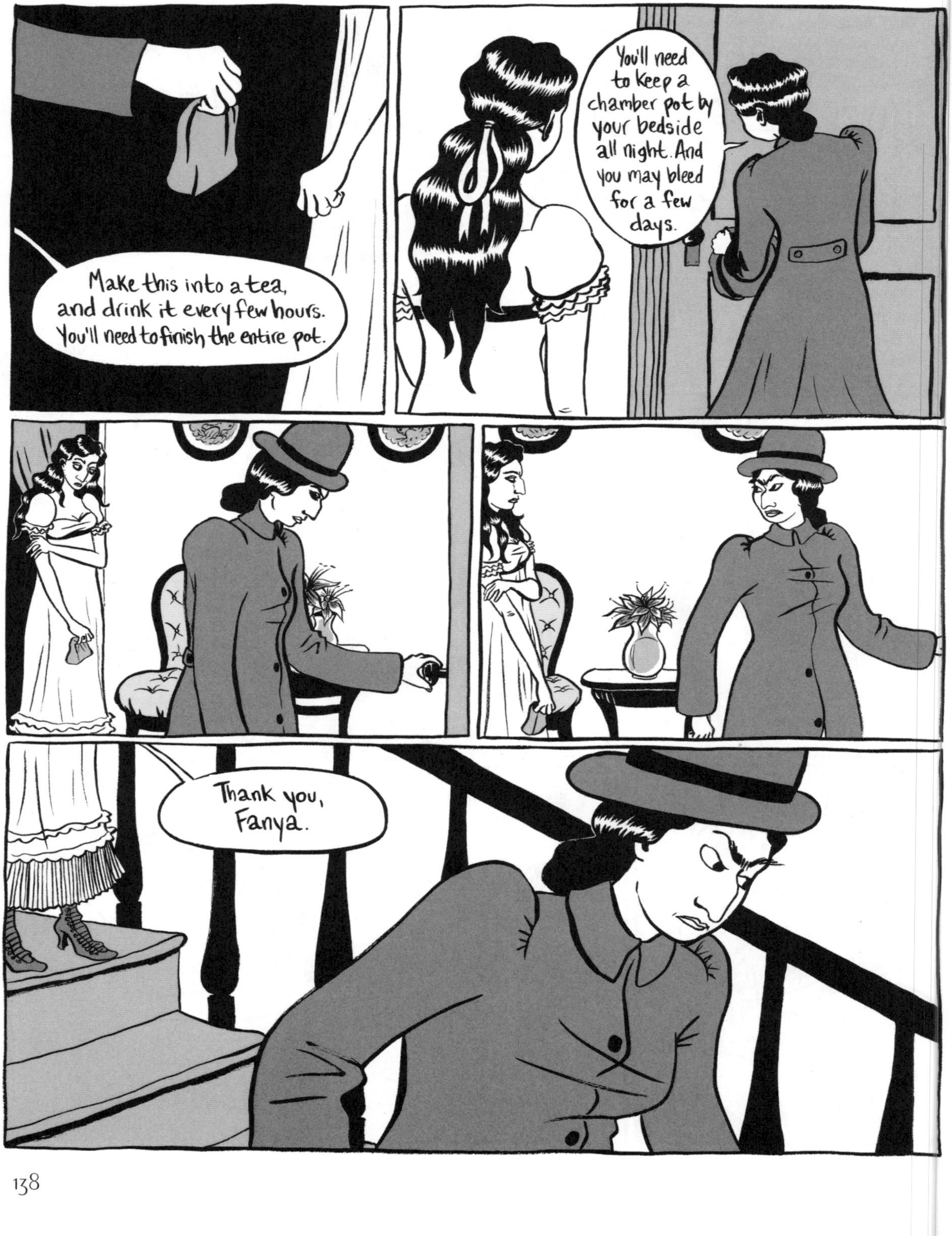
Make this into a tea, and drink it every few hours. You'll need to finish the entire pot.
You'll need to keep a chamber pot by your bedside all night. And you may bleed for a few days.
Thank you, Fanya.

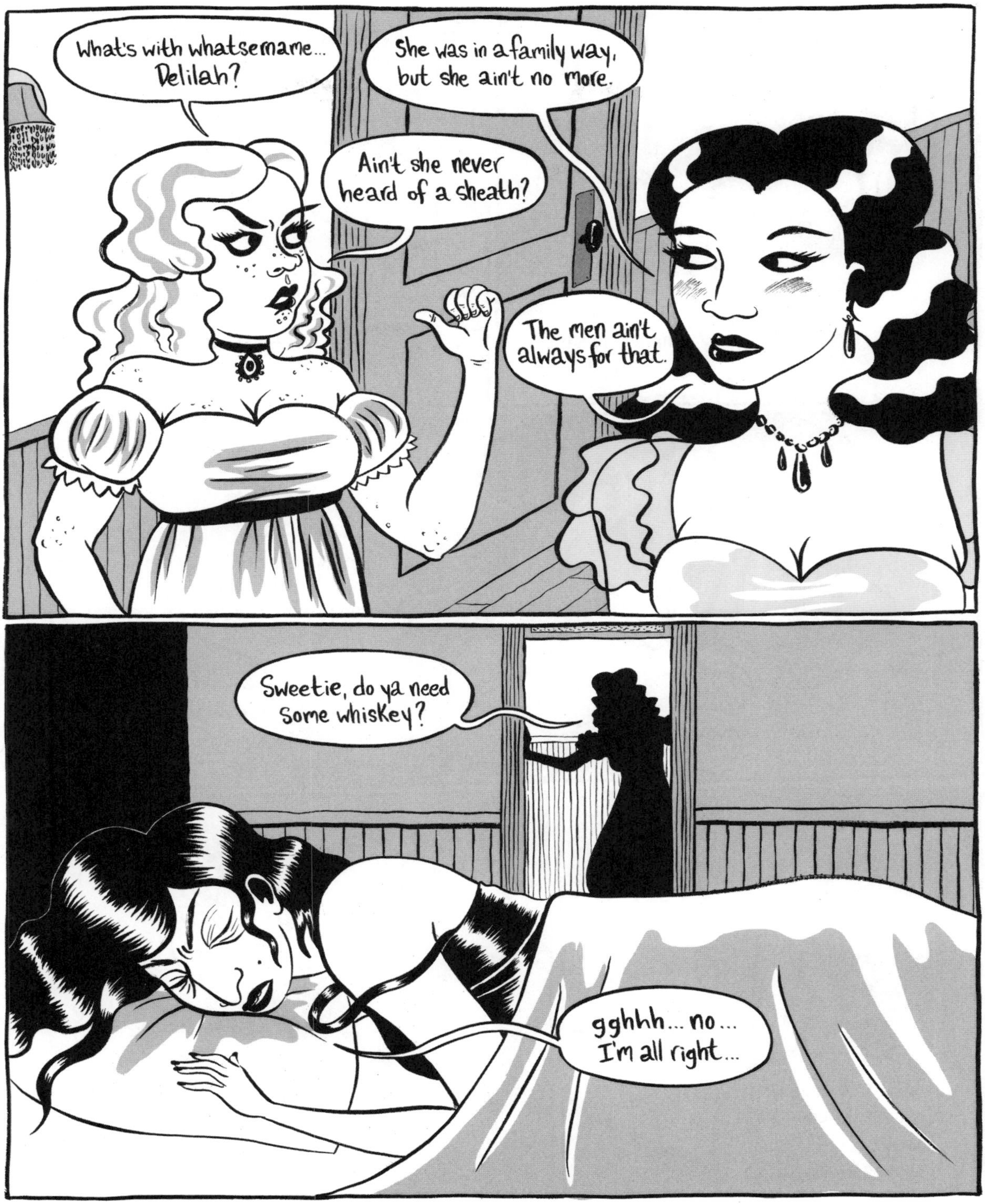
What's with whatsername... Delilah?
She was in a family way, but she ain't no more.
Ain't she never heard of a sheath?
The men ain't always for that.
Sweetie, do ya need some whiskey?
gghhh... no... I'm all right...

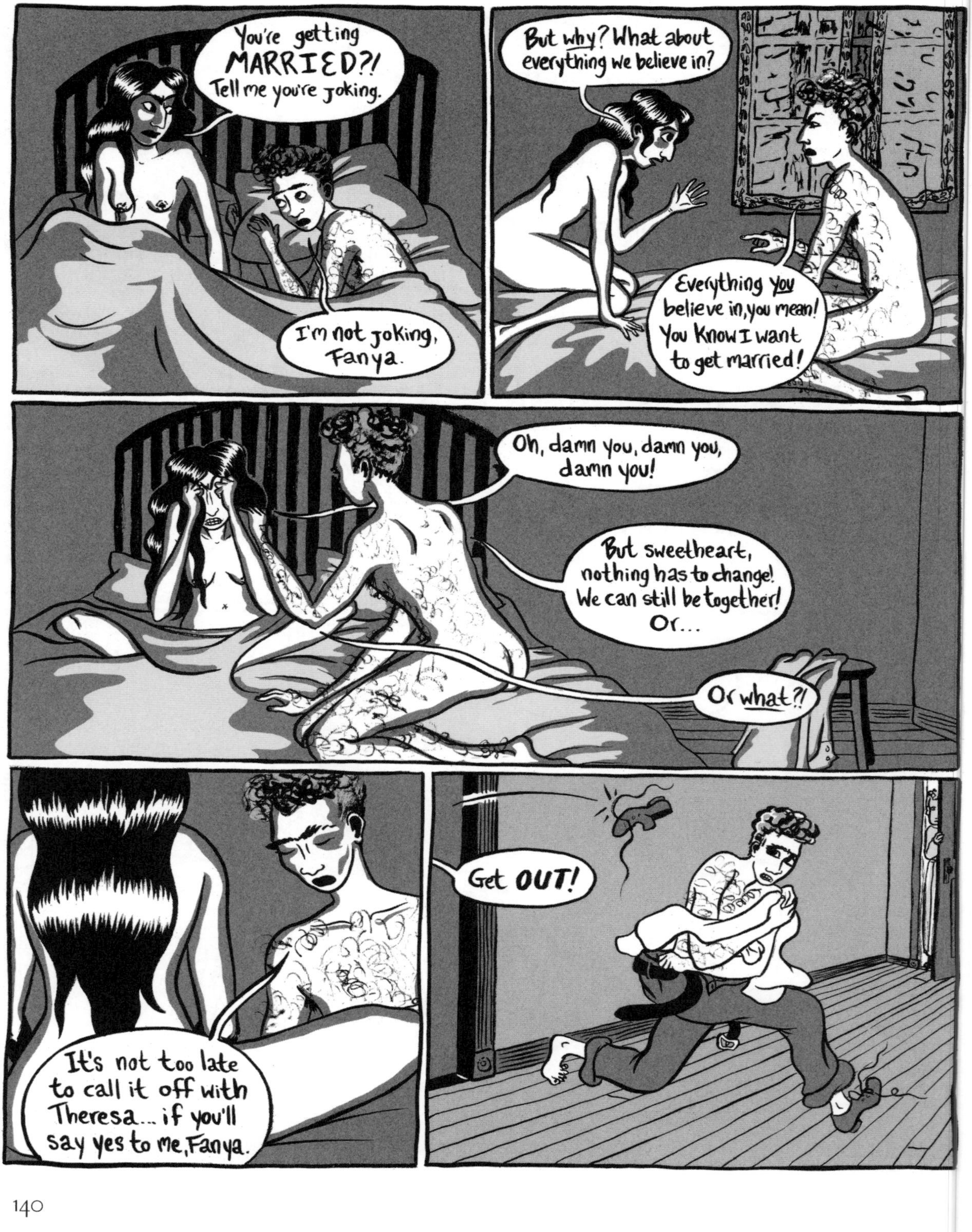
You're getting MARRIED?! Tell me you're joking.
I'm not joking, Fanya.
But why? What about everything we believe in?
Everything you believe in, you mean! You know I want to get married!
Oh, damn you, damn you, damn you!
But sweetheart, nothing has to change! We can still be together! Or...
Or what?!
It's not too late to call it off with Theresa... if you'll say yes to me, Fanya.
Get OUT!

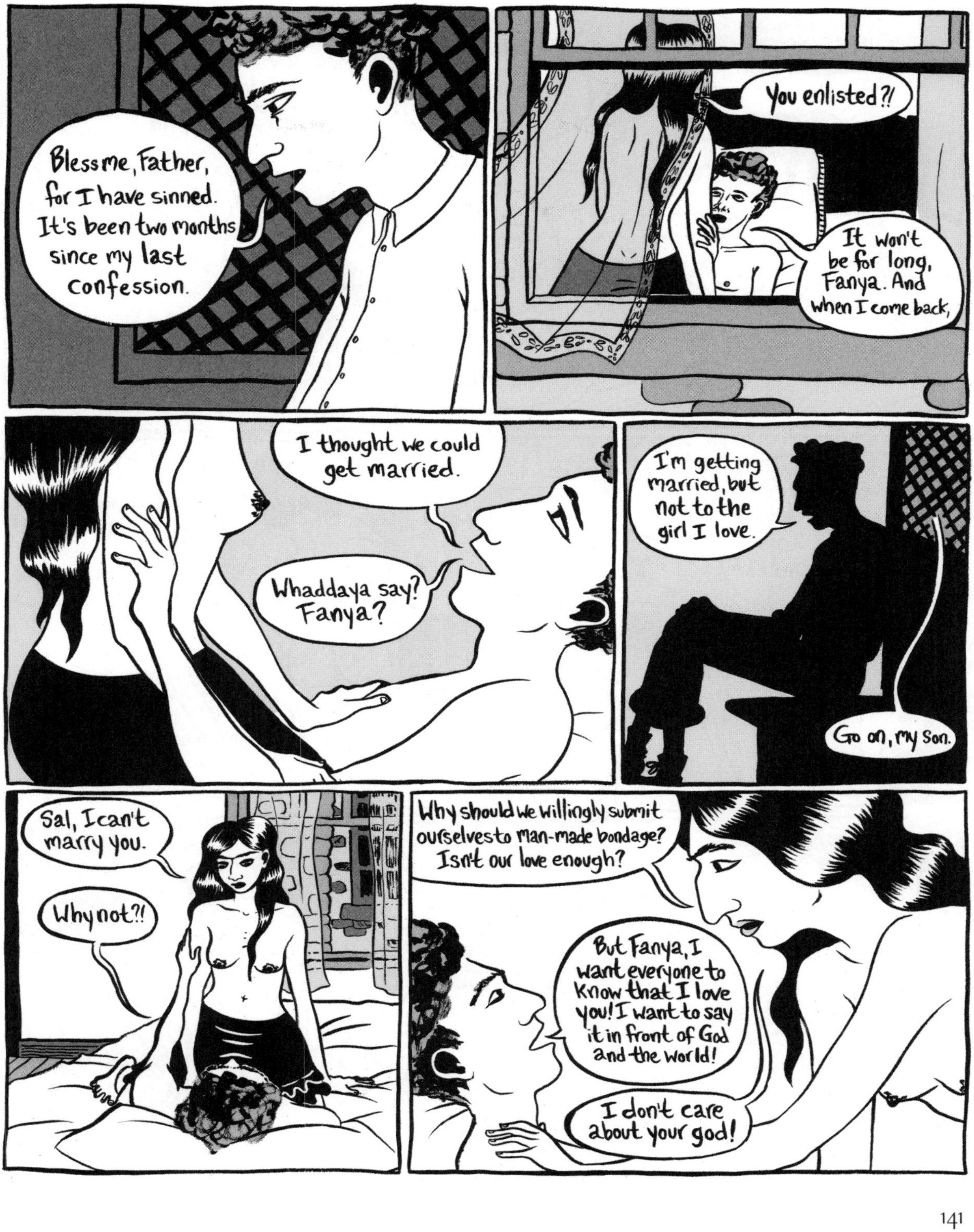
Bless me, Father, for I have sinned. It's been two months since my last confession.
You enlisted?!
It won't be for long, Fanya. And when I come back,
I thought we could get married.
Whaddaya say? Fanya?
I'm getting married, but not to the girl I love.
Go on, my son.
Sal, I can't marry you.
Why not?!
Why should we willingly submit ourselves to man-made bondage? Isn't our love enough?
But Fanya, I want everyone to know that I love you! I want to say it in front of God and the world!
I don't care about your god!

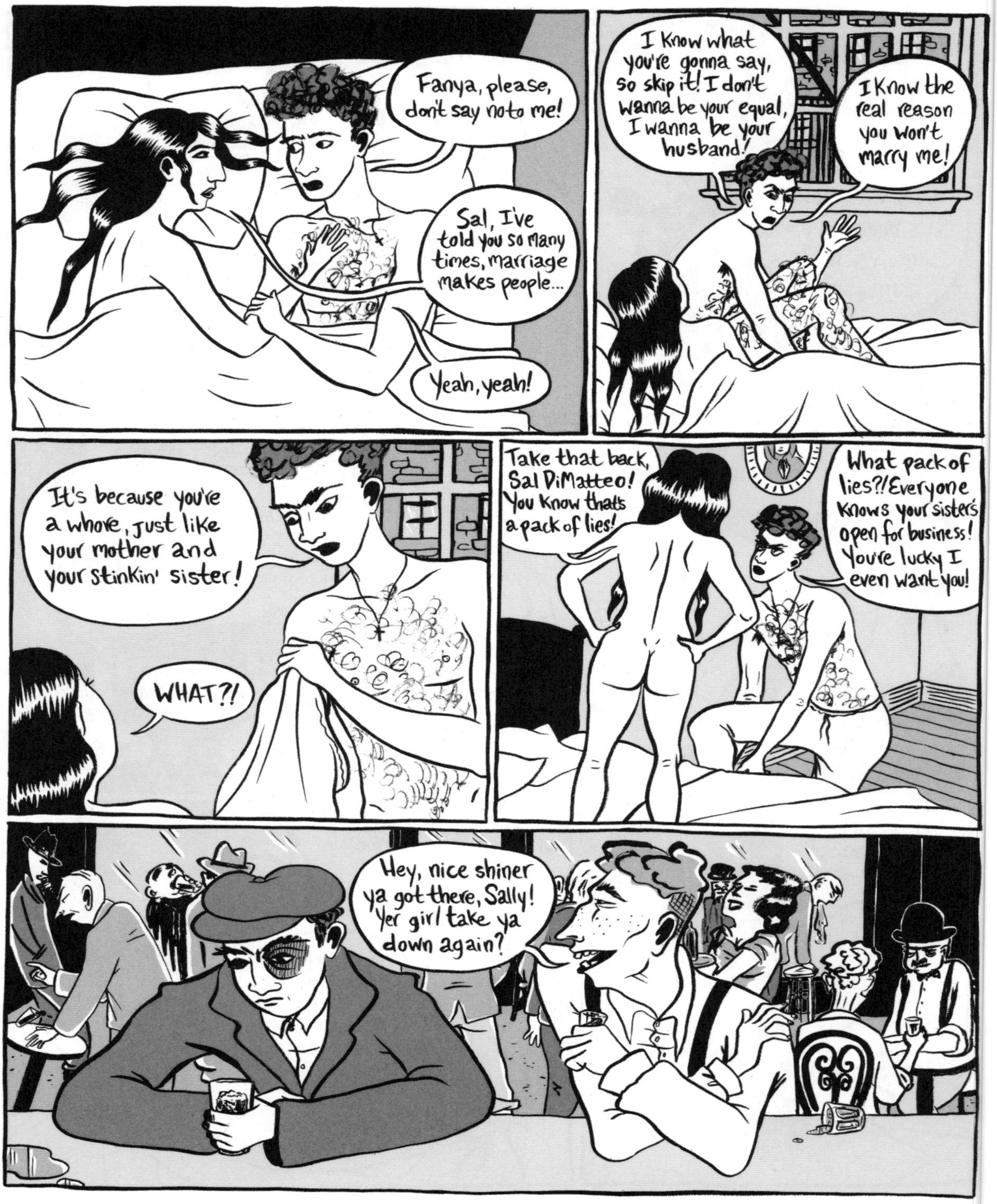

Fanya, please, don't say no to me!
Sal, I've told you so many times, marriage makes people...
Yeah, yeah!
I know what you're gonna say, so skip it! I don't wanna be your equal, I wanna be your husband!
I know the real reason you won't marry me!
It's because you're a whore, just like your mother and your stinkin' sister!
WHAT?!
Take that back, Sal DiMatteo! You know that's a pack of lies!
What pack of lies?! Everyone knows your sister's open for business! You're lucky I even want you!
Hey, nice shiner ya got there, Sally! Yer girl take ya down again?

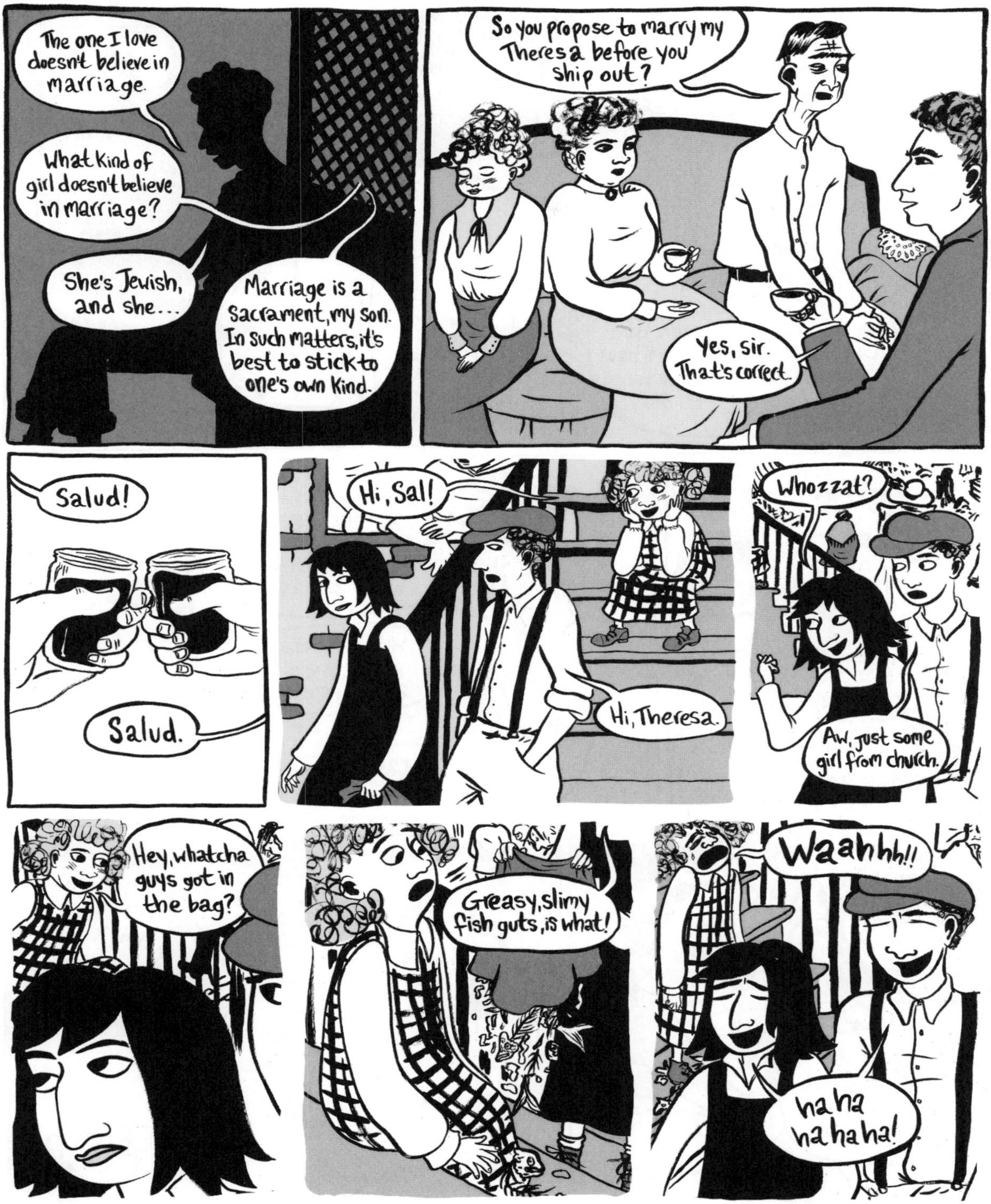

The one I love doesn't believe in marriage.
What kind of girl doesn't believe in marriage?
She's Jewish, and she...
Marriage is a sacrament, my son. In such matters, it's best to stick to one's own kind.
So you propose to marry my Theresa before you ship out?
Yes, sir. That's correct.
Salud!
Salud.
Hi, Sal!
Hi, Theresa.
Whozzat?
Aw, just some girl from church.
Hey, whatcha guys got in the bag?
Greasy, slimy fish guts, is what!
Waahhh!!
ha ha ha ha ha!

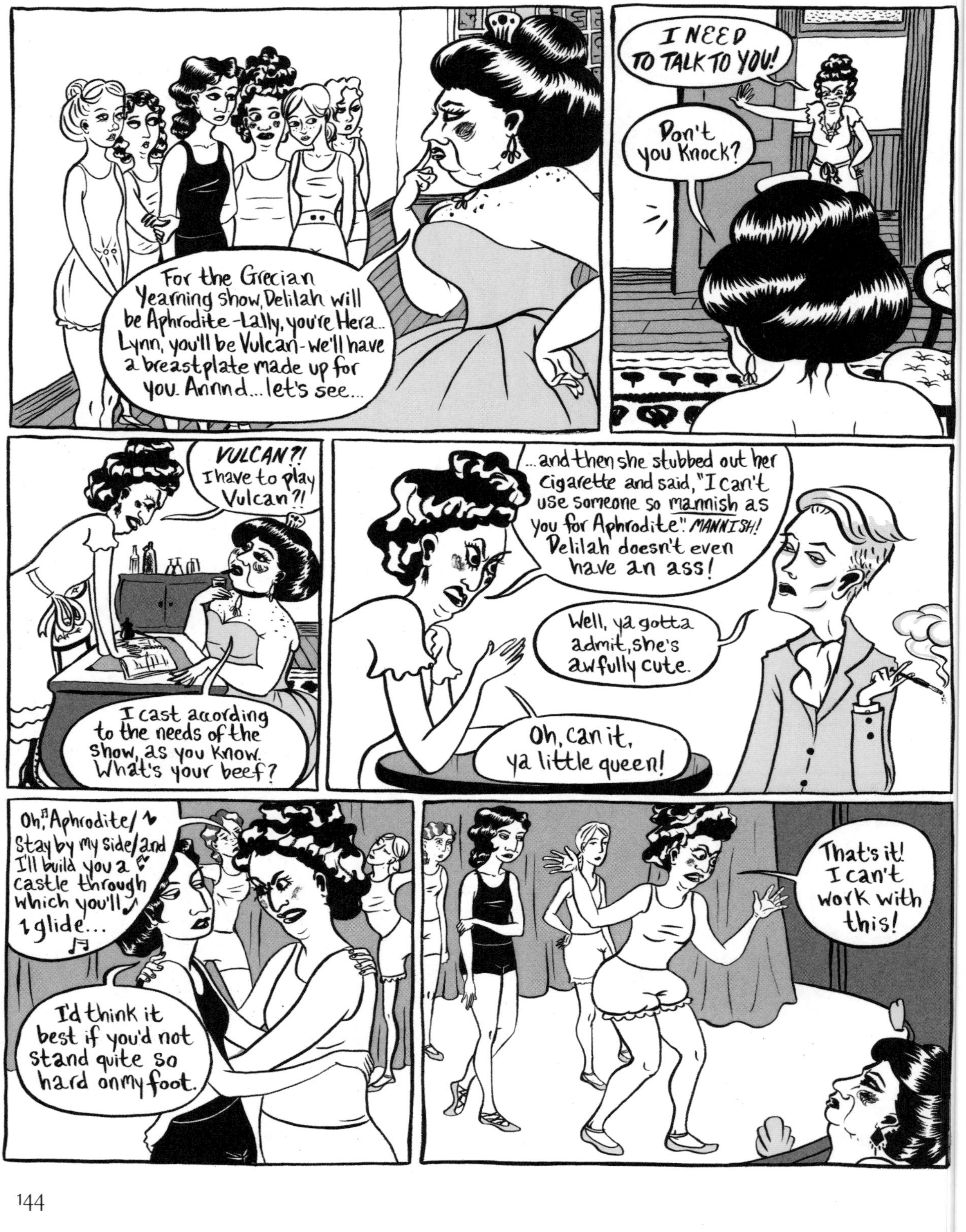
For the Grecian Yearning show, Delilah will be Aphrodite-Lally, you're Hera... Lynn, you'll be Vulcan-we'll have a breastplate made up for you. Annnd... let's see...
I NEED TO TALK TO YOU!
Don't you Knock?
VULCAN?! I have to play Vulcan?!
I cast according to the needs of the show, as you know. What's your beef?
...and then she stubbed out her cigarette and said, "I can't use someone so mannish as you for Aphrodite." MANNISH! Delilah doesn't even have an ass!
Well, ya gotta admit, she's awfully cute.
Oh, can it, ya little queen!
Oh, Aphrodite/ Stay by my side/ and I'll build you a castle through which you'll glide...
I'd think it best if you'd not stand quite so hard on my foot.
That's it! I can't work with this!

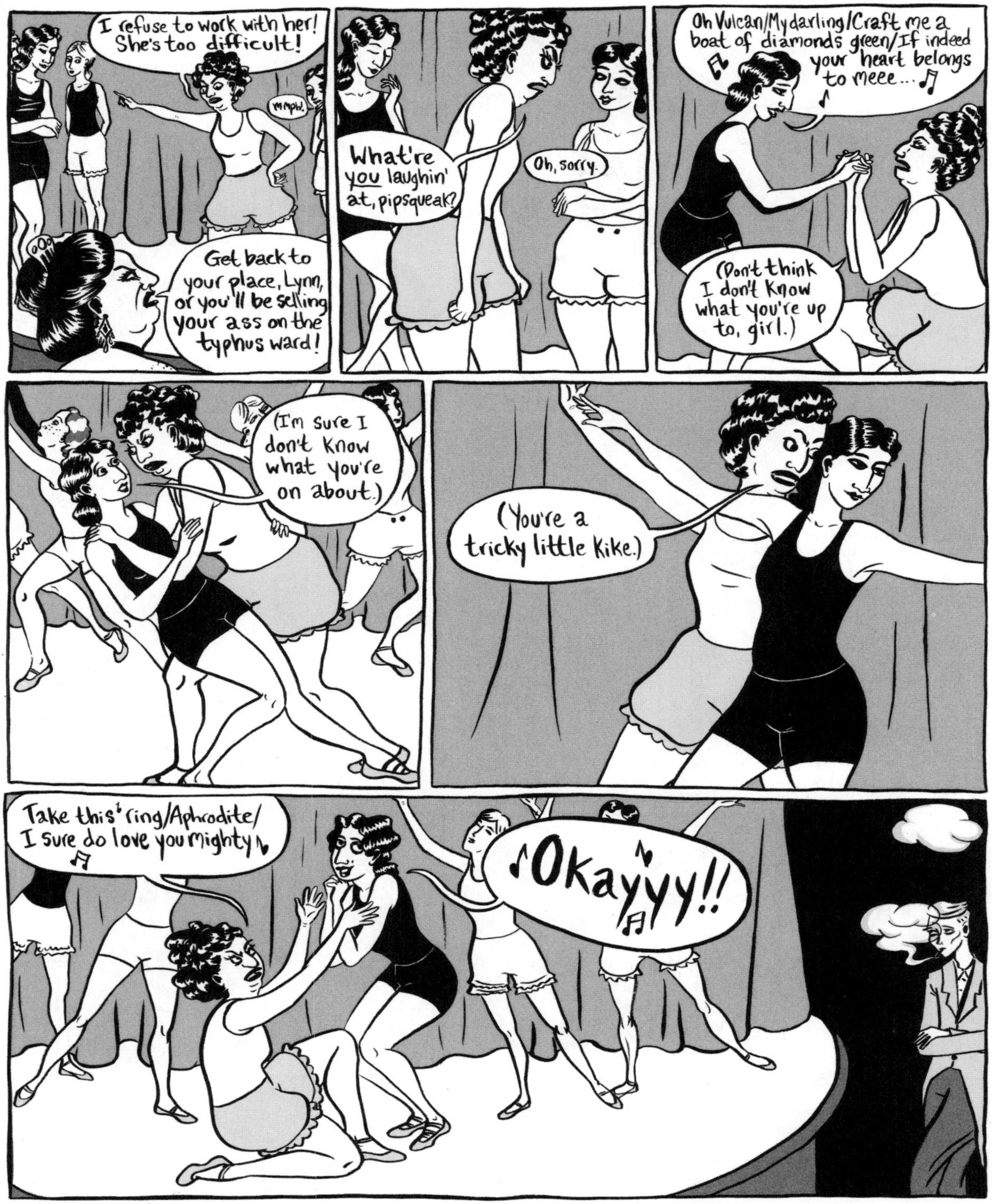
I refuse to work with her! She's too difficult!
Mmph!
Get back to your place, Lynn, or you'll be selling your ass on the typhus ward!
What're you laughin' at, pipsqueak?
Oh, sorry.
Oh Vulcan/My darling/Craft me a boat of diamonds green/If indeed your heart belongs to meee...
(Don't think I don't know what you're up to, girl.)
(I'm sure I don't know what you're on about.)
(You're a tricky little kike.)
Take this ring/Aphrodite/I sure do love you mighty
Okayyy!!

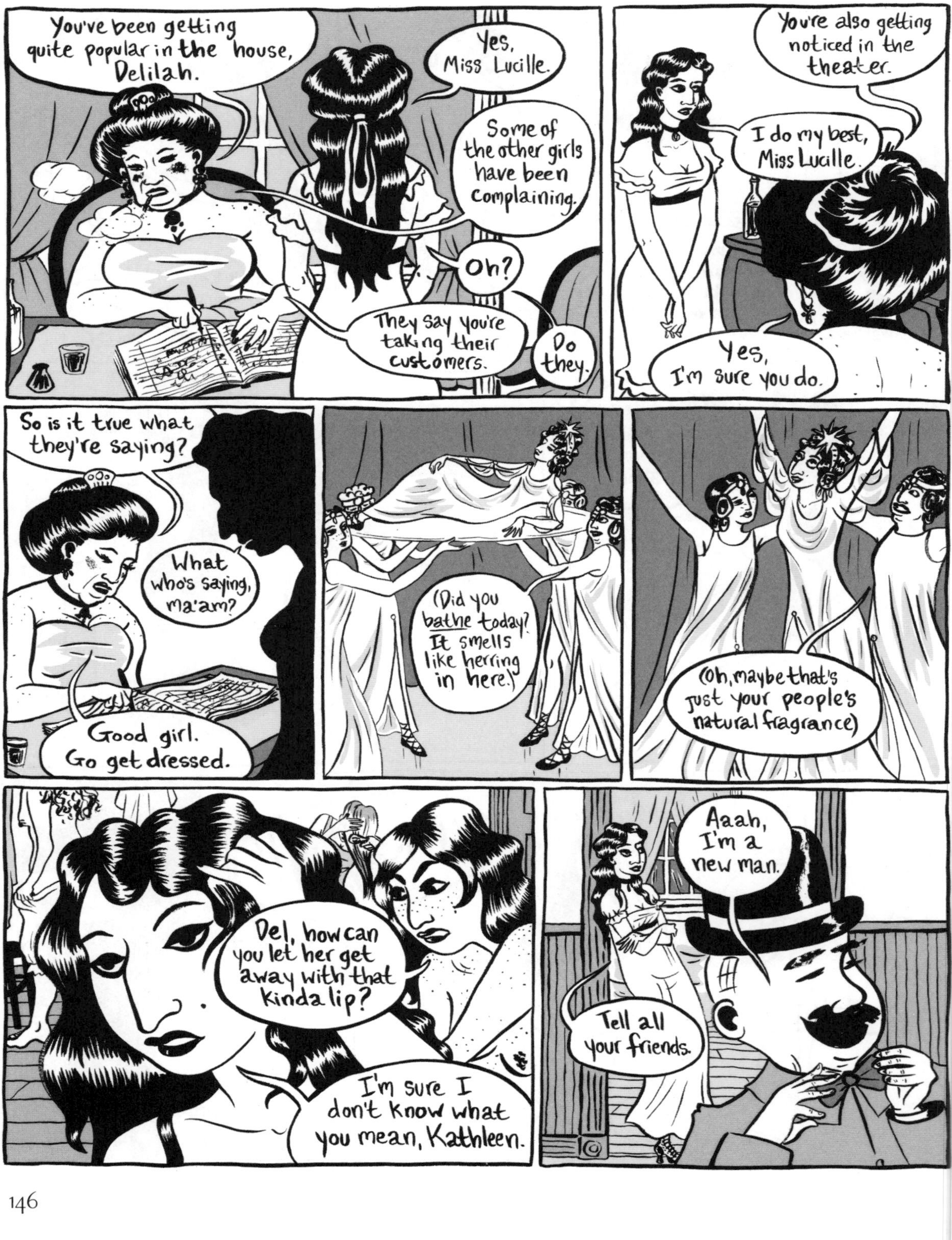
You've been getting quite popular in the house, Delilah.
Yes, Miss Lucille.
Some of the other girls have been complaining.
Oh?
They say you're taking their customers.
Do they.
You're also getting noticed in the theater.
I do my best, Miss Lucille.
Yes, I'm sure you do.
So is it true what they're saying?
What who's saying, ma'am?
Good girl. Go get dressed.
(Did you bathe today? It smells like herring in here.)
(Oh, maybe that's just your people's natural fragrance)
Del, how can you let her get away with that kinda lip?
I'm sure I don't know what you mean, Kathleen.
Aaah, I'm a new man.
Tell all your friends.

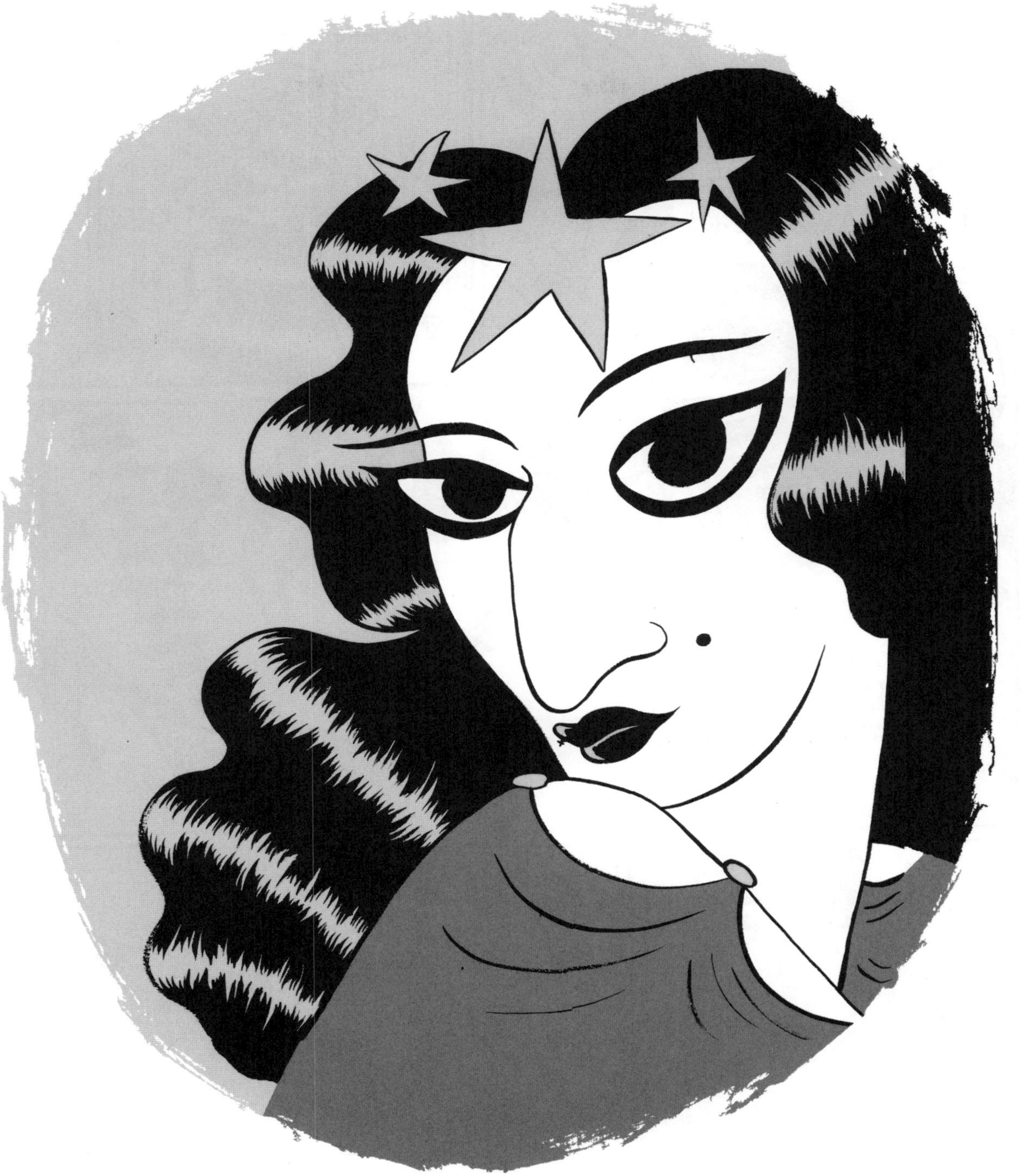

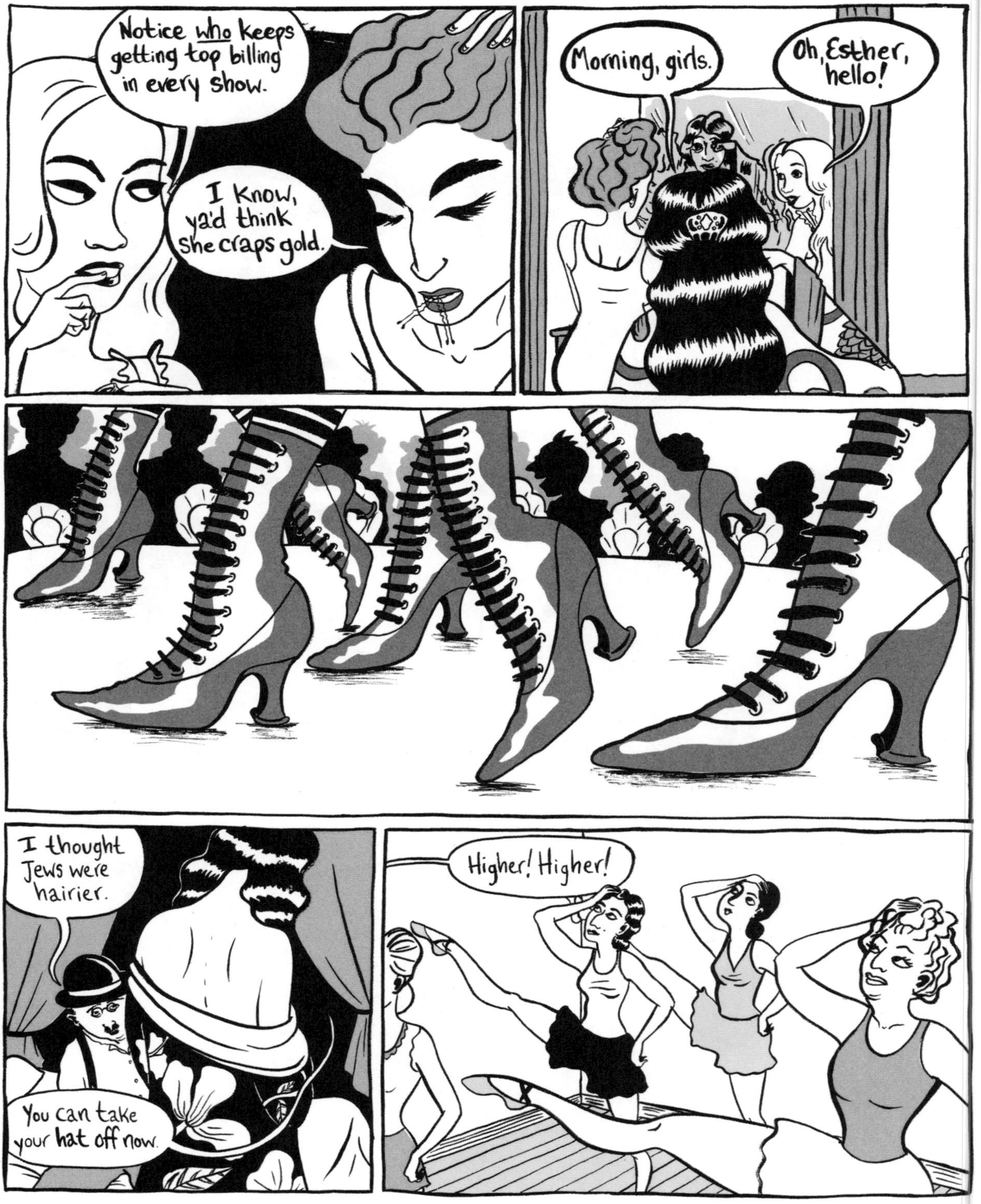
Notice who keeps getting top billing in every show.
I know, ya'd think she craps gold.
Morning, girls.
Oh, Esther, hello!
I thought Jews were hairier.
You can take your hat off now.
Higher! Higher!

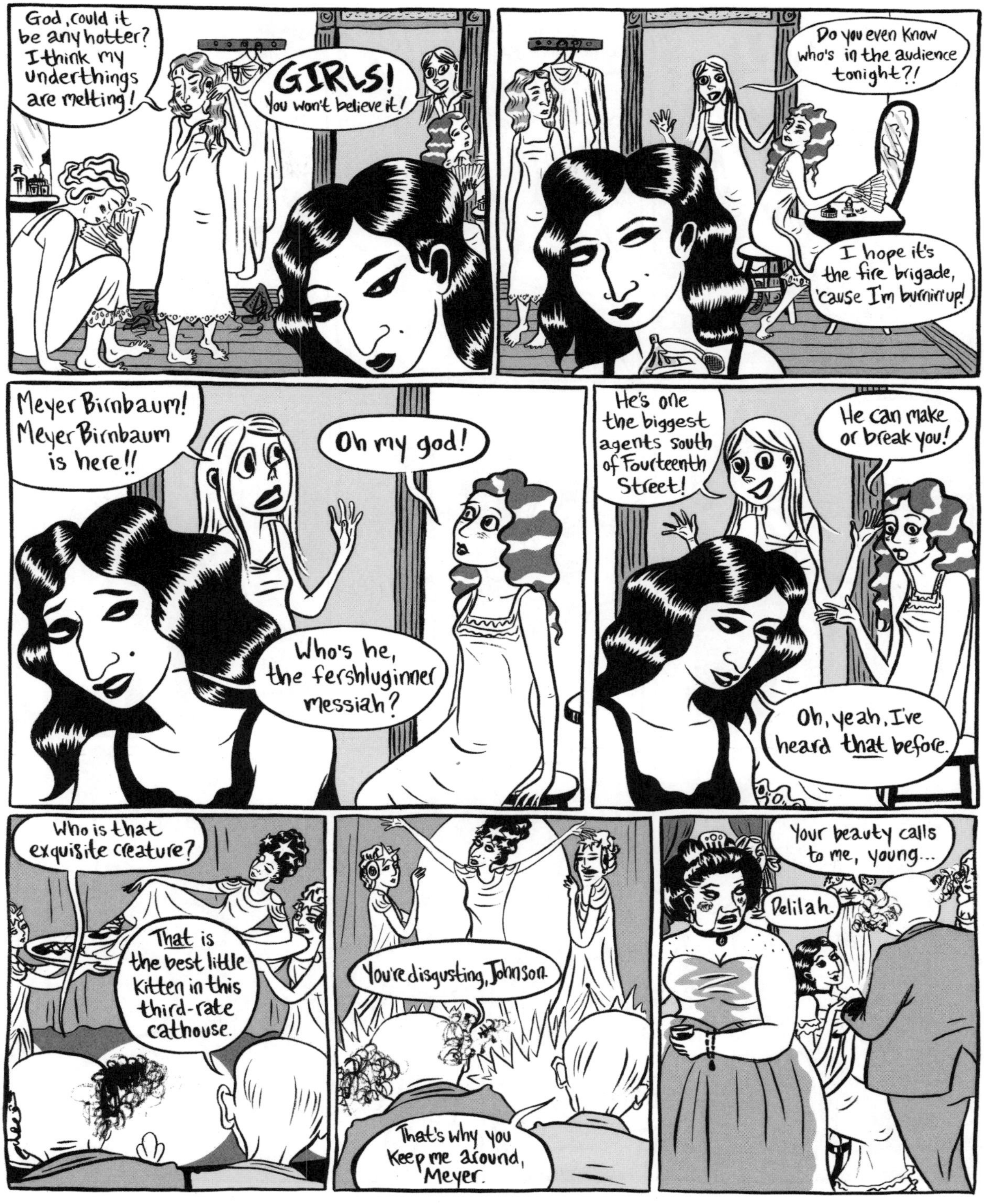
God, could it be any hotter? I think my underthings are melting!
GIRLS! You won't believe it!
Do you even know who's in the audience tonight?!
I hope it's the fire brigade, 'cause I'm burnin' up!
Meyer Birnbaum! Meyer Birnbaum is here!!
Oh my god!
Who's he, the fershluginner messiah?
He's one the biggest agents south of Fourteenth Street!
He can make or break you!
Oh, yeah, I've heard that before.
Who is that exquisite creature?
That is the best little kitten in this third-rate cathouse.
You're disgusting, Johnson.
That's why you keep me around, Meyer.
Your beauty calls to me, young...
Delilah.

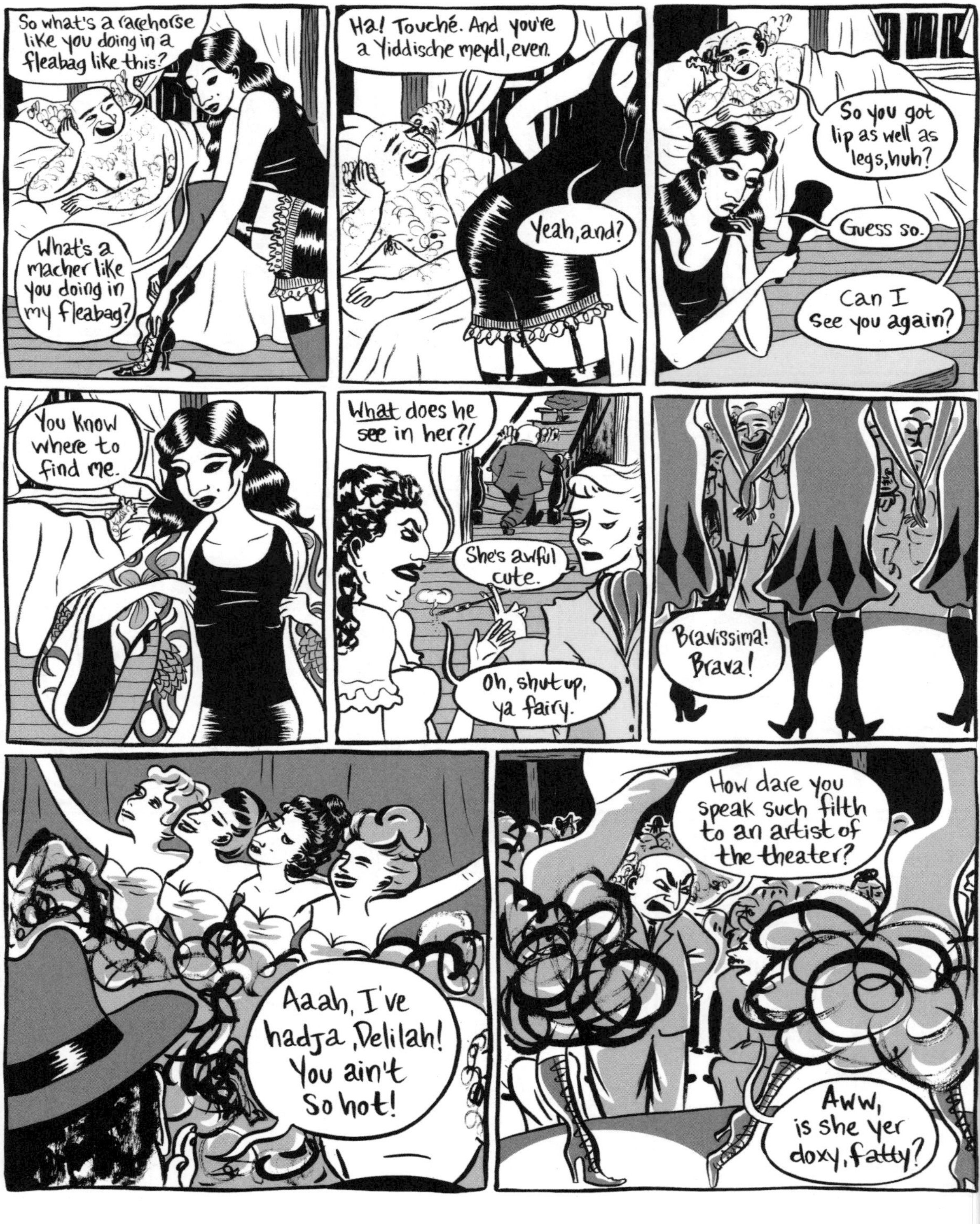
So what's a racehorse like you doing in a fleabag like this?
What's a macher like you doing in my fleabag?
Ha! Touché. And you're a Yiddische meydl, even.
Yeah, and?
So you got lip as well as legs, huh?
Guess so.
Can I see you again?
You know where to find me.
What does he see in her?!
She's awful cute.
Oh, shut up, ya fairy.
Bravissima! Brava!
Aaah, I've hadja, Delilah! You ain't so hot!
How dare you speak such filth to an artist of the theater?
Aww, is she yer doxy, fatty?

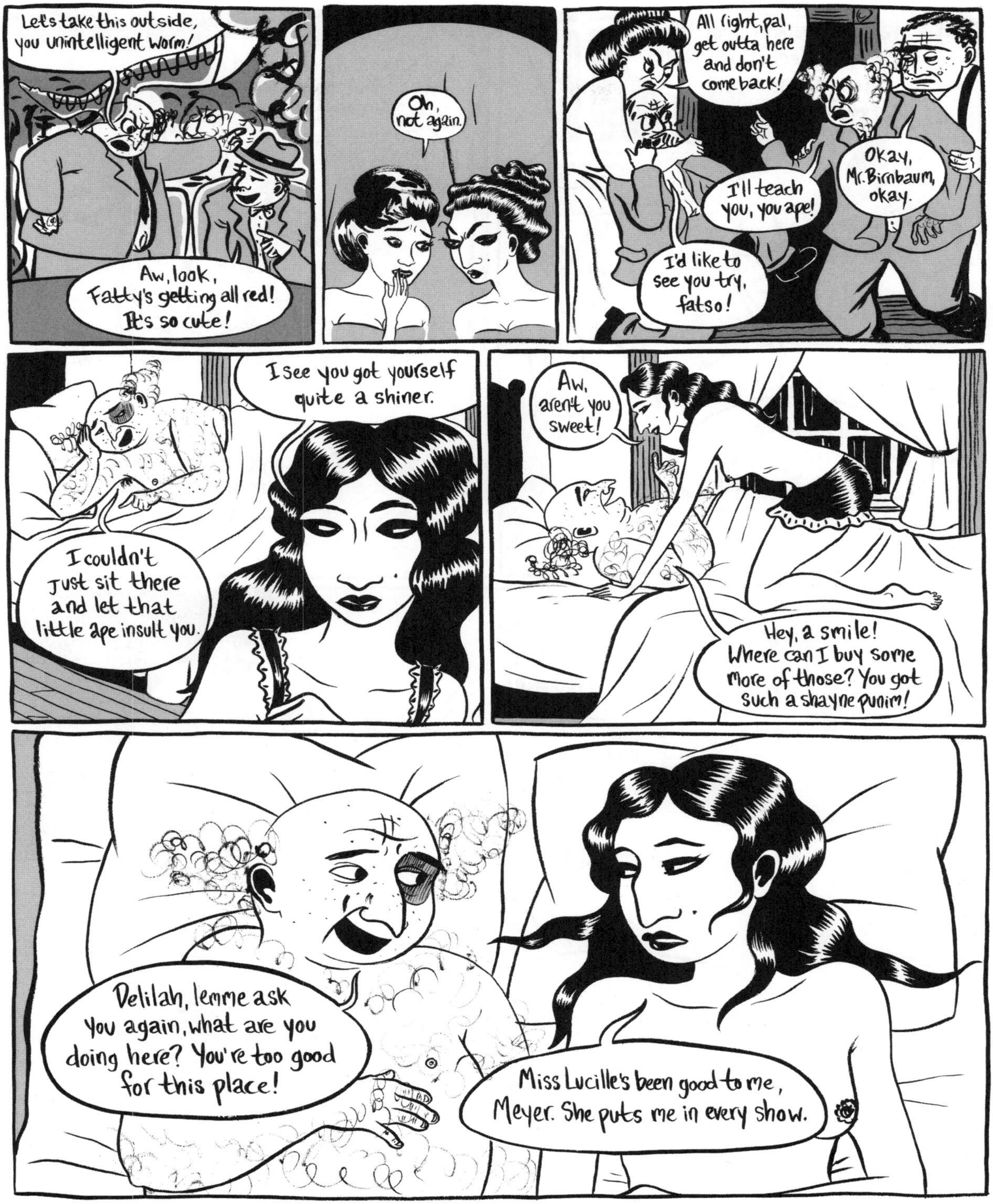
Let's take this outside, you unintelligent worm!
Aw, look, Fatty's getting all red! It's so cute!
Oh, not again.
All right, pal, get outta here and don't come back!
I'll teach you, you ape!
Okay, Mr. Birnbaum, okay.
I'd like to see you try, fatso!
I see you got yourself quite a shiner.
I couldn't just sit there and let that little ape insult you.
Aw, aren't you sweet!
Hey, a smile! Where can I buy some more of those? You got such a shayne punim!
Delilah, lemme ask you again, what are you doing here? You're too good for this place!
Miss Lucille's been good to me, Meyer. She puts me in every show.

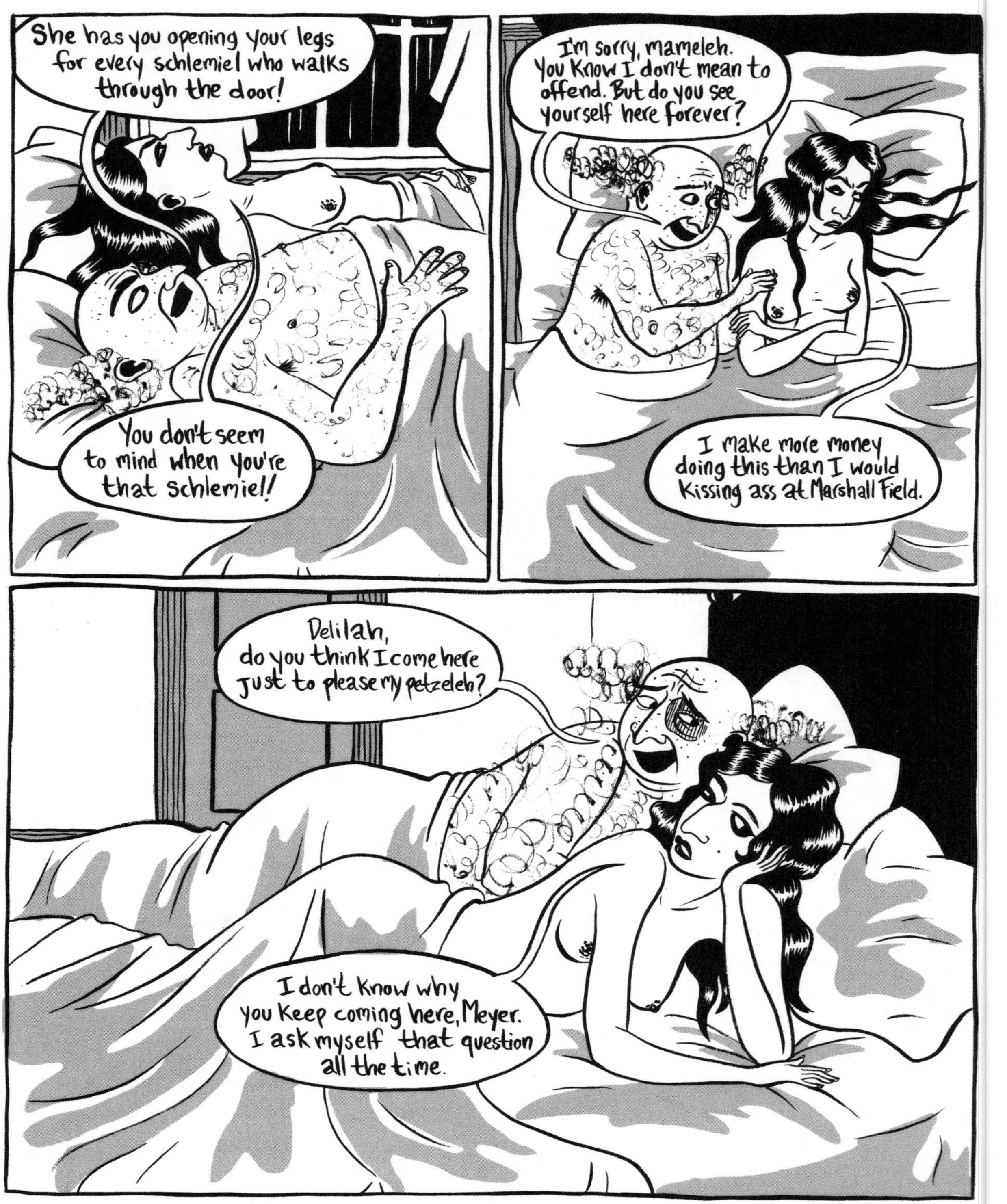
She has you opening your legs for every schlemiel who walks through the door!
You don't seem to mind when you're that schlemiel!
I'm sorry, mameleh. You know I don't mean to offend. But do you see yourself here forever?
I make more money doing this than I would kissing ass at Marshall Field.
Delilah, do you think I come here just to please my petzeleh?
I don't know why you keep coming here, Meyer. I ask myself that question all the time.

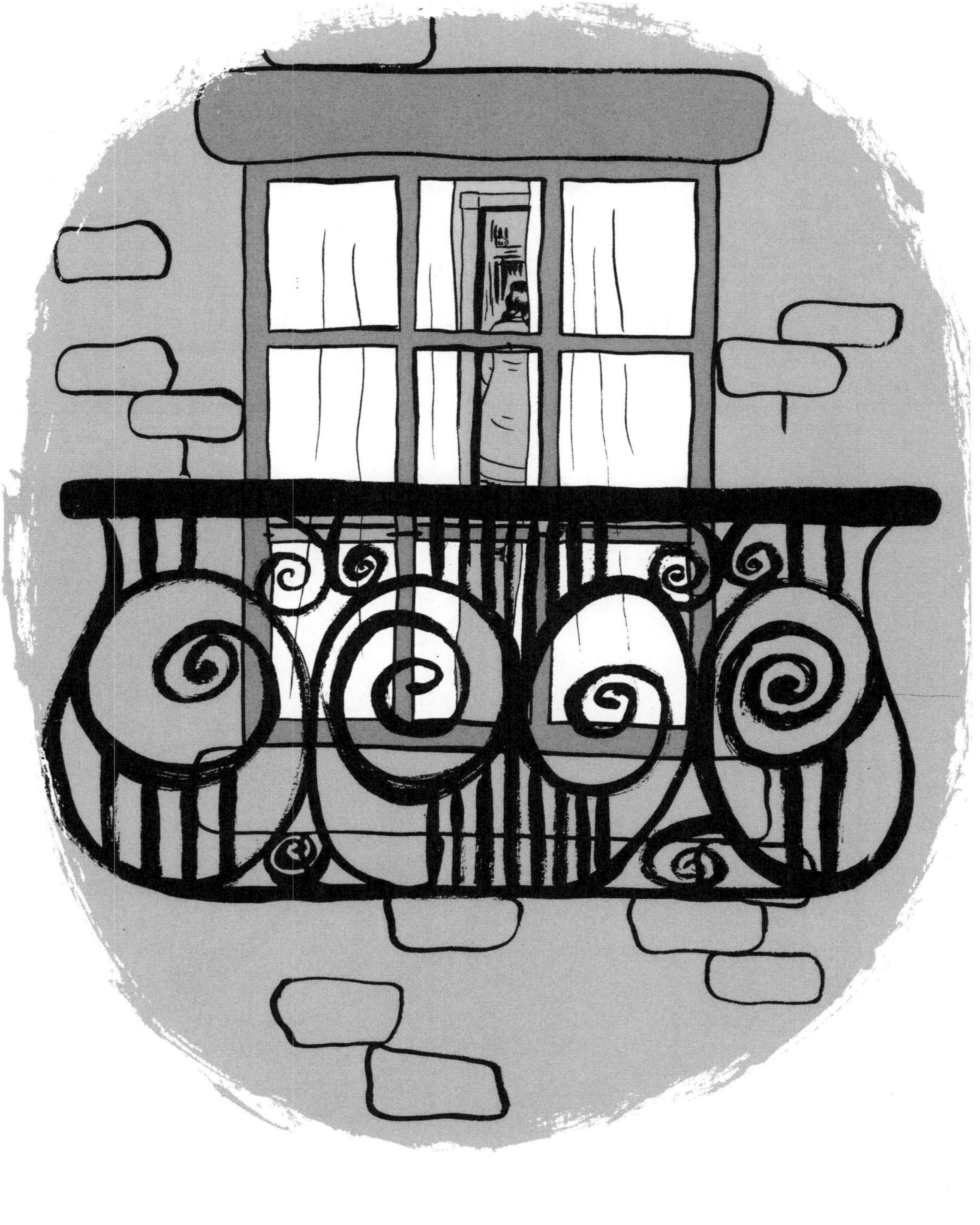

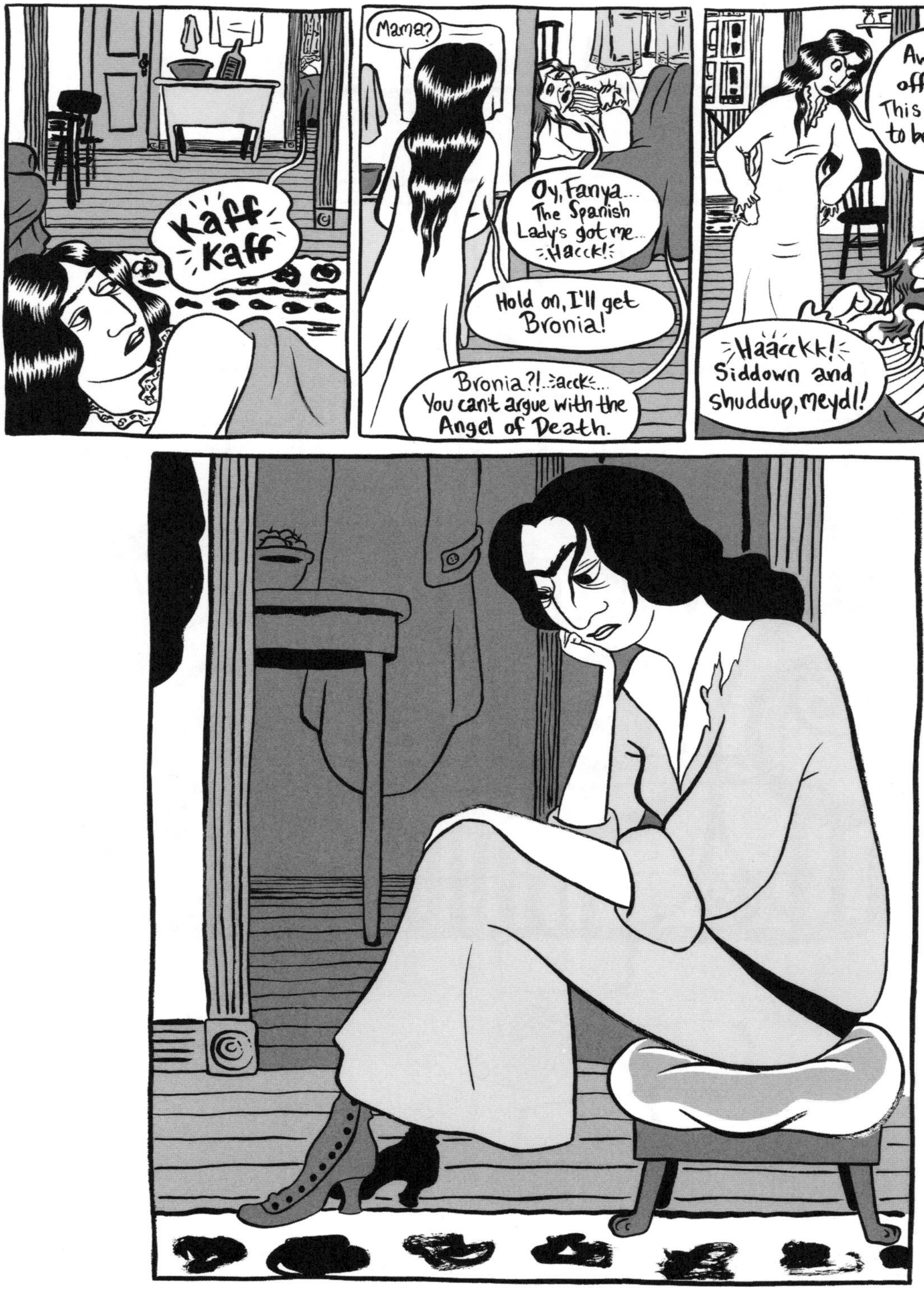
Kaff Kaff
Mama?
Oy, Fanya... The Spanish Lady's got me... Haccck!
Hold on, I'll get Bronia!
Bronia?!...acck... You can't argue with the Angel of Death.
Aww, come off it, Ma! This is no time to be stubborn!
Haaacckk! Siddown and shuddup, meydl!

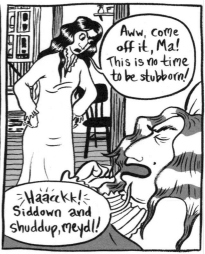

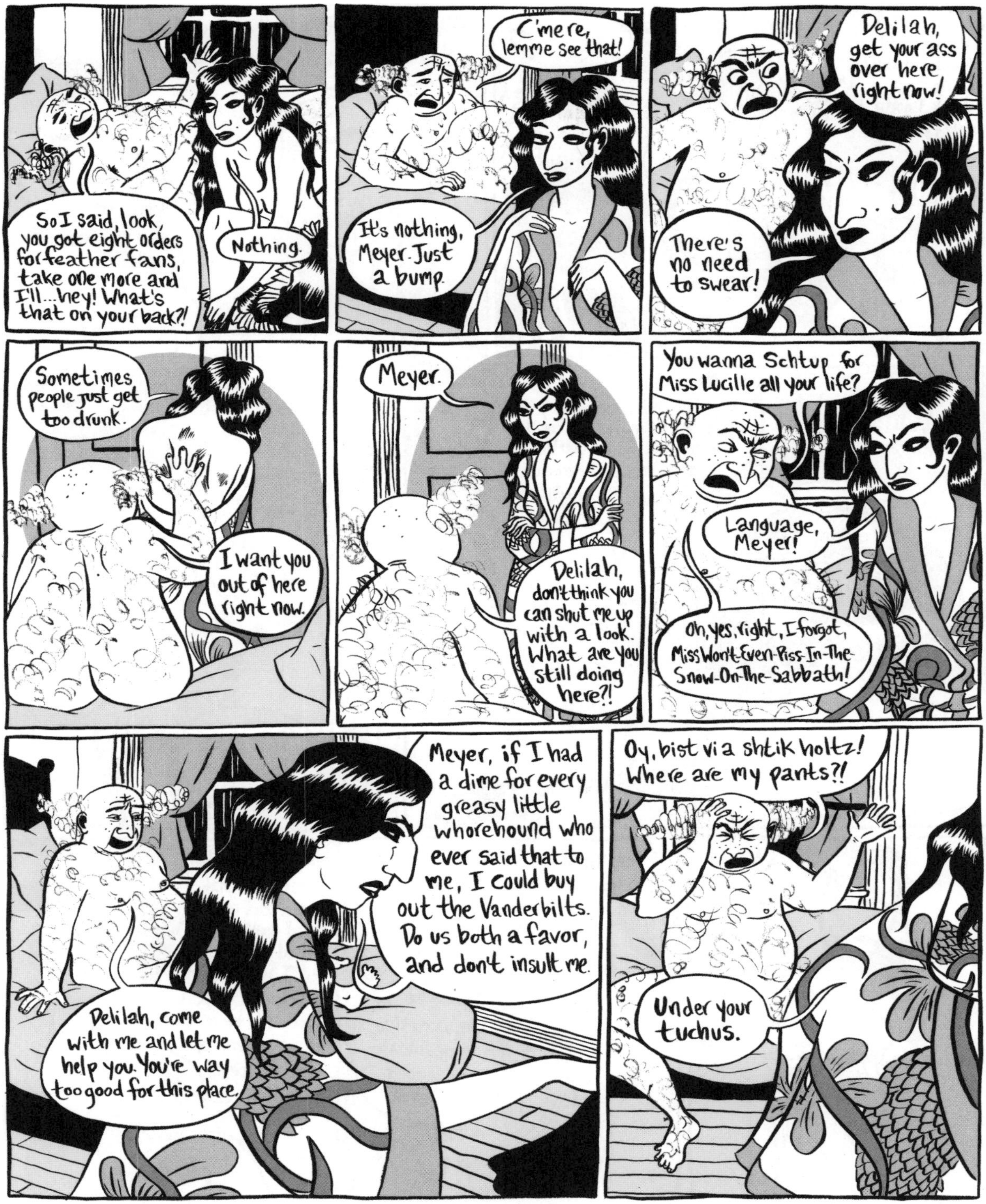
So I said, look, you got eight orders for feather fans, take one more and I'll...hey! What's that on your back?!
Nothing.
C'mere, lemme see that!
It's nothing, Meyer. Just a bump.
Delilah, get your ass over here right now!
There's no need to swear!
Sometimes people just get too drunk.
I want you out of here right now.
Meyer.
Delilah, don't think you can shut me up with a look. What are you still doing here?!
You wanna Schtup for Miss Lucille all your life?
Language, Meyer!
Oh, yes, right, I forgot, Miss-Won't-Even-Piss-In-The-Snow-On-The-Sabbath!
Meyer, if I had a dime for every greasy little whorehound who ever said that to me, I could buy out the Vanderbilts. Do us both a favor, and don't insult me.
Delilah, come with me and let me help you. You're way too good for this place.
Oy, bist via shtik holtz! Where are my pants?!
Under your tuchus.

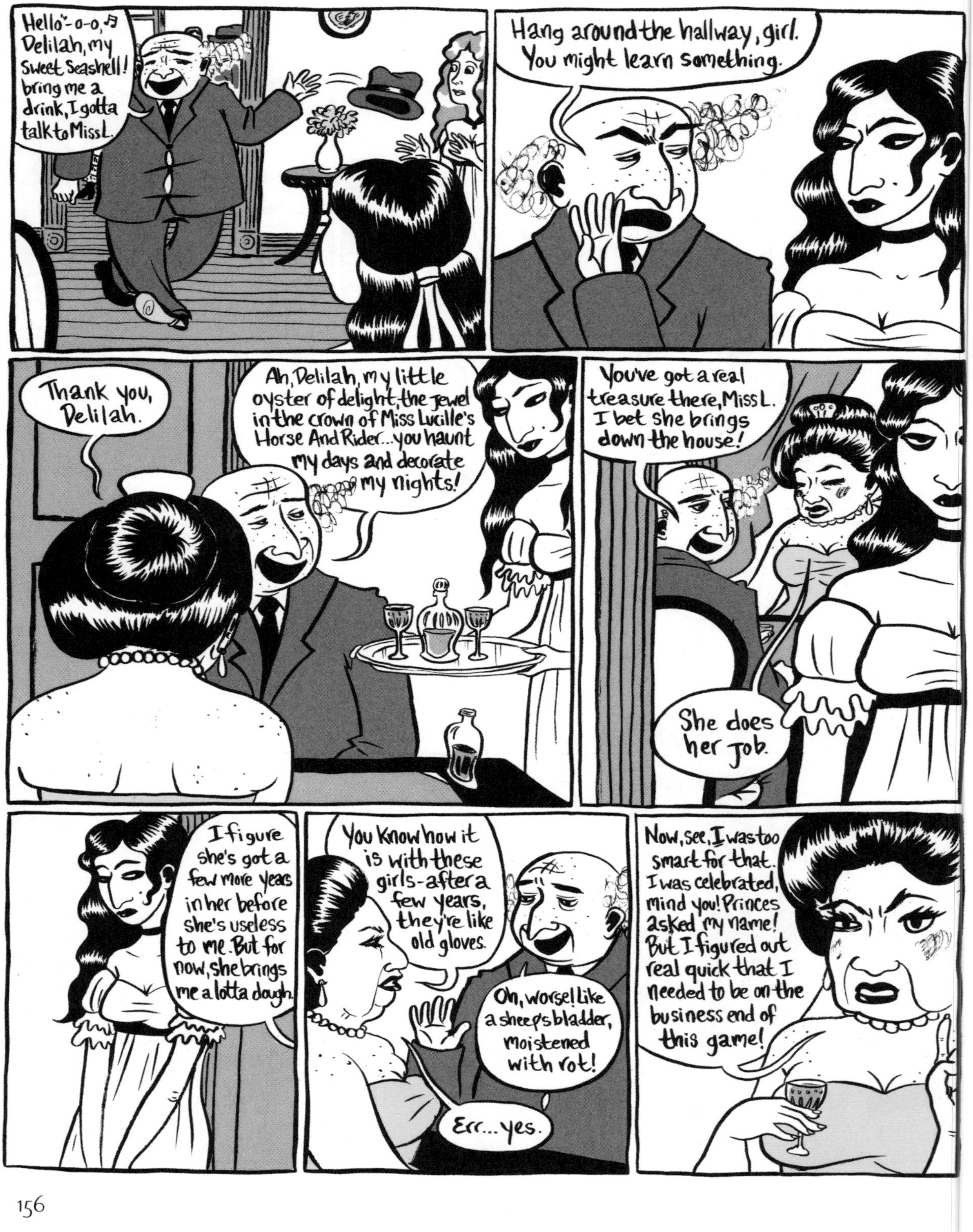
Hello-o-o, Delilah, my sweet Seashell! bring me a drink, I gotta talk to Miss L.
Hang around the hallway, girl. You might learn something.
Thank you, Delilah.
Ah, Delilah, my little oyster of delight, the jewel in the crown of Miss Lucille's Horse And Rider... you haunt my days and decorate my nights!
You've got a real treasure there, Miss L. I bet she brings down the house!
She does her job.
I figure she's got a few more years in her before she's useless to me. But for now, she brings me a lotta dough.
You know how it is with these girls - after a few years, they're like old gloves.
Oh, worse! Like a sheep's bladder, moistened with rot!
Err... yes.
Now, see, I was too smart for that. I was celebrated, mind you! Princes asked my name! But I figured out real quick that I needed to be on the business end of this game!

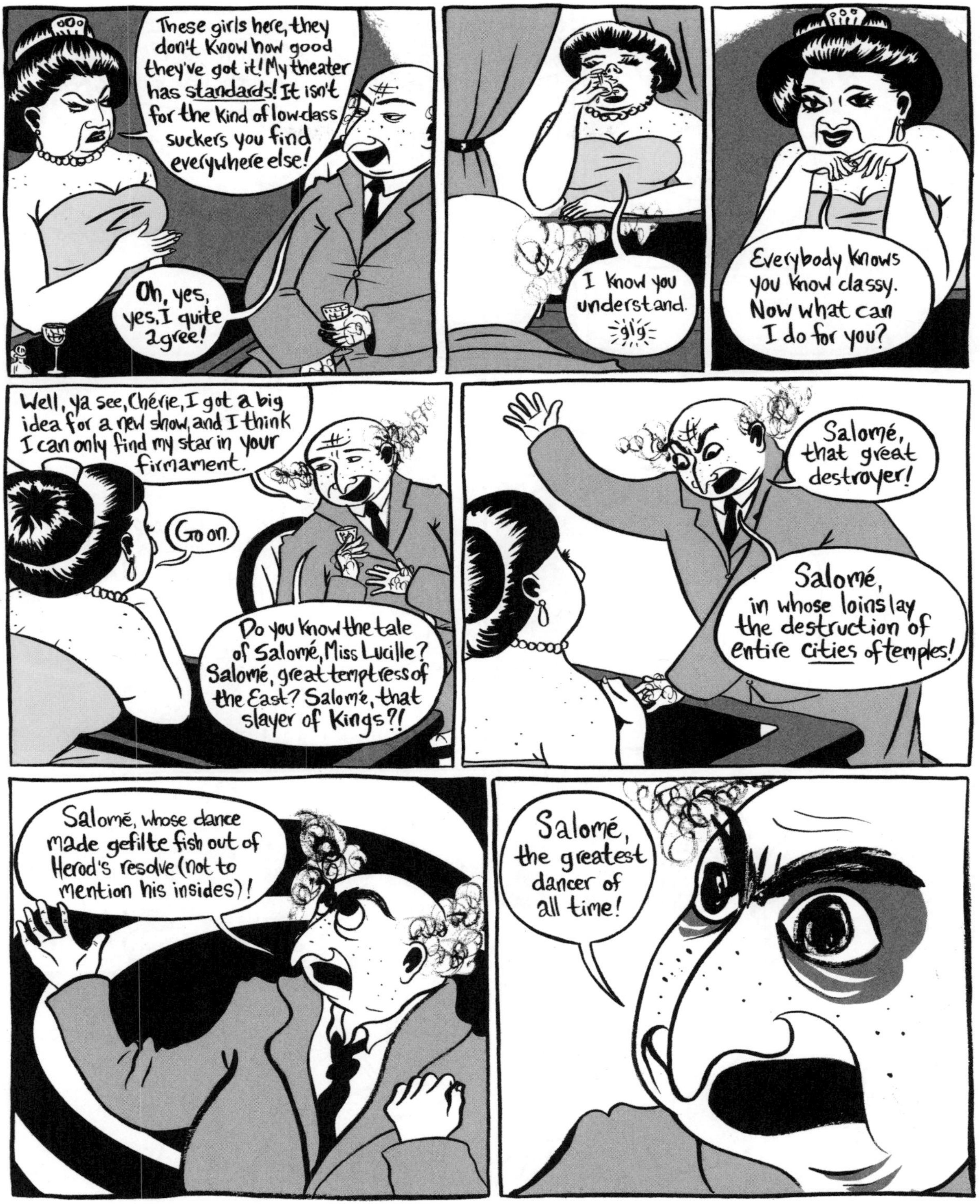
These girls here, they don't know how good they've got it! My theater has standards! It isn't for the kind of low-class suckers you find everywhere else!
Oh, yes, yes, I quite agree!
I know you understand.
gig
Everybody knows you know classy. Now what can I do for you?
Well, ya see, Chérie, I got a big idea for a new show, and I think I can only find my star in your firmament.
Go on.
Do you know the tale of Salomé, Miss Lucille? Salomé, great temptress of the East? Salomé, that slayer of Kings?!
Salomé, that great destroyer!
Salomé, in whose loins lay the destruction of entire cities of temples!
Salomé, whose dance made gefilte fish out of Herod's resolve (not to mention his insides)!
Salomé, the greatest dancer of all time!

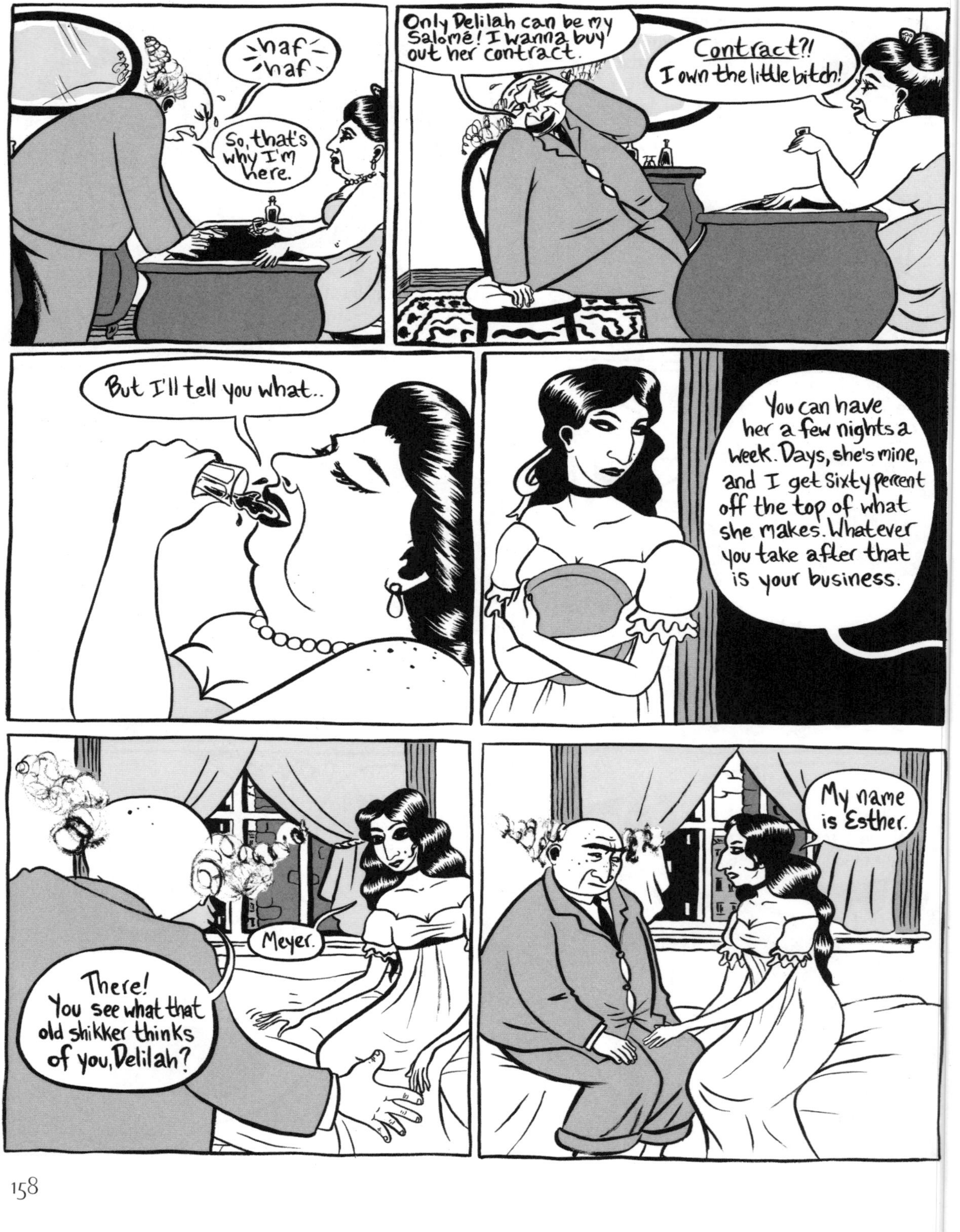
haf haf
So, that's why I'm here.
Only Delilah can be my Salomé! I wanna buy out her contract.
Contract?! I own the little bitch!
But I'll tell you what..
You can have her a few nights a week. Days, she's mine, and I get sixty percent off the top of what she makes. Whatever you take after that is your business.
Meyer.
There! You see what that old shikker thinks of you, Delilah?
My name is Esther.

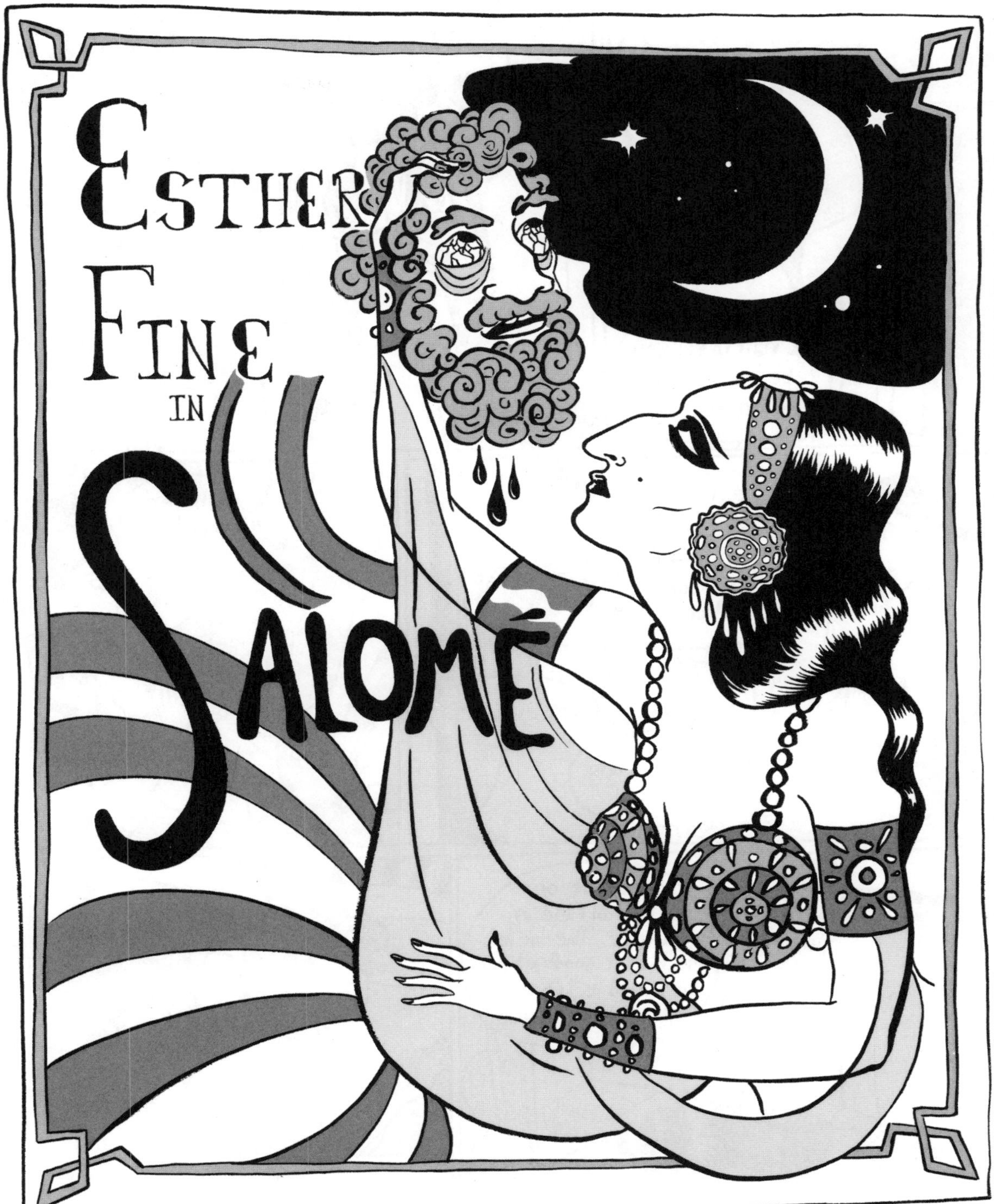
ESTHER
FINE
IN
SALOMÉ

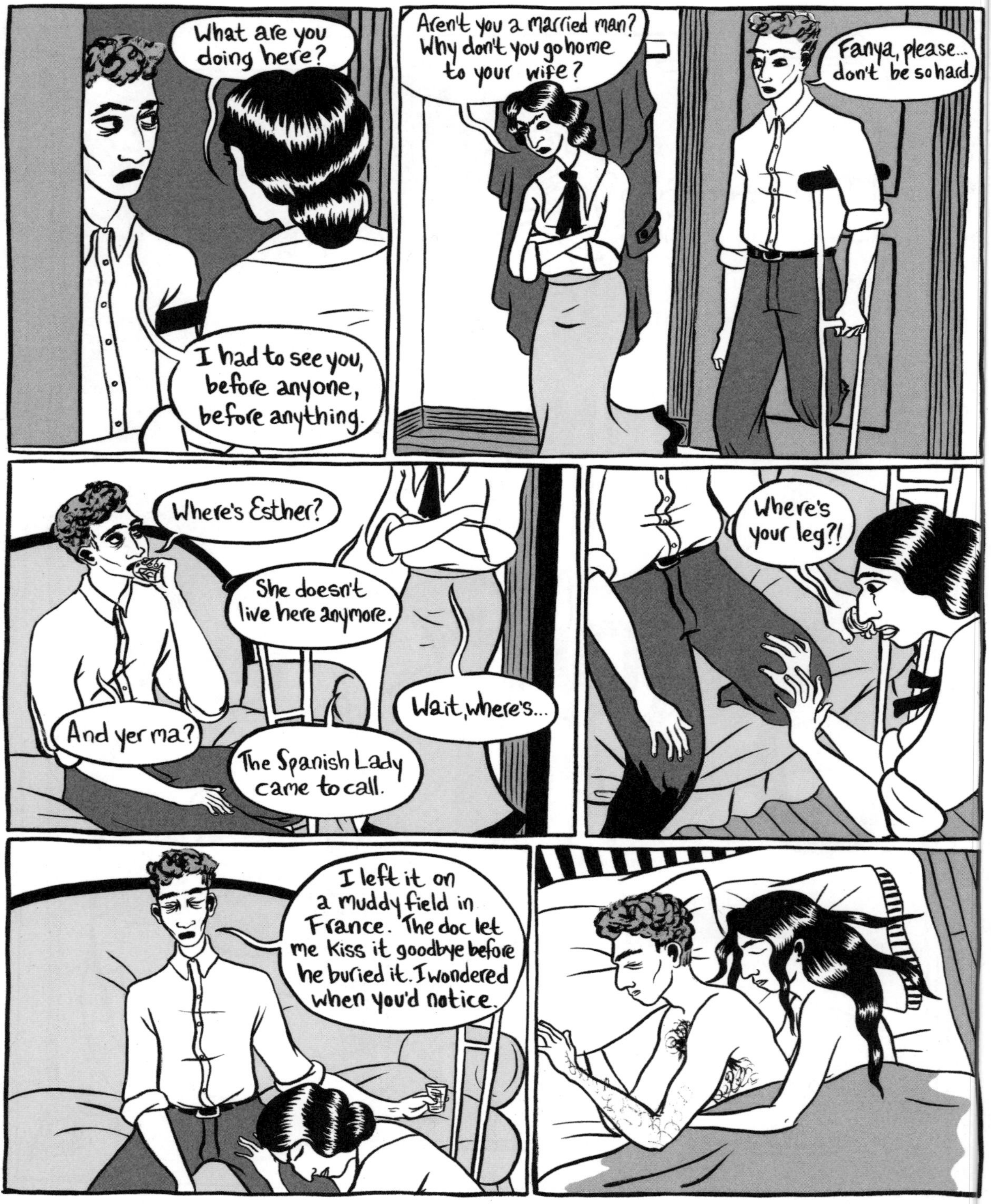
What are you doing here?
I had to see you, before anyone, before anything.
Aren't you a married man? Why don't you go home to your wife?
Fanya, please... don't be so hard.
Where's Esther?
She doesn't live here anymore.
And yer ma?
The Spanish Lady came to call.
Wait, where's...
Where's your leg?!
I left it on a muddy field in France. The doc let me kiss it goodbye before he buried it. I wondered when you'd notice.

1923

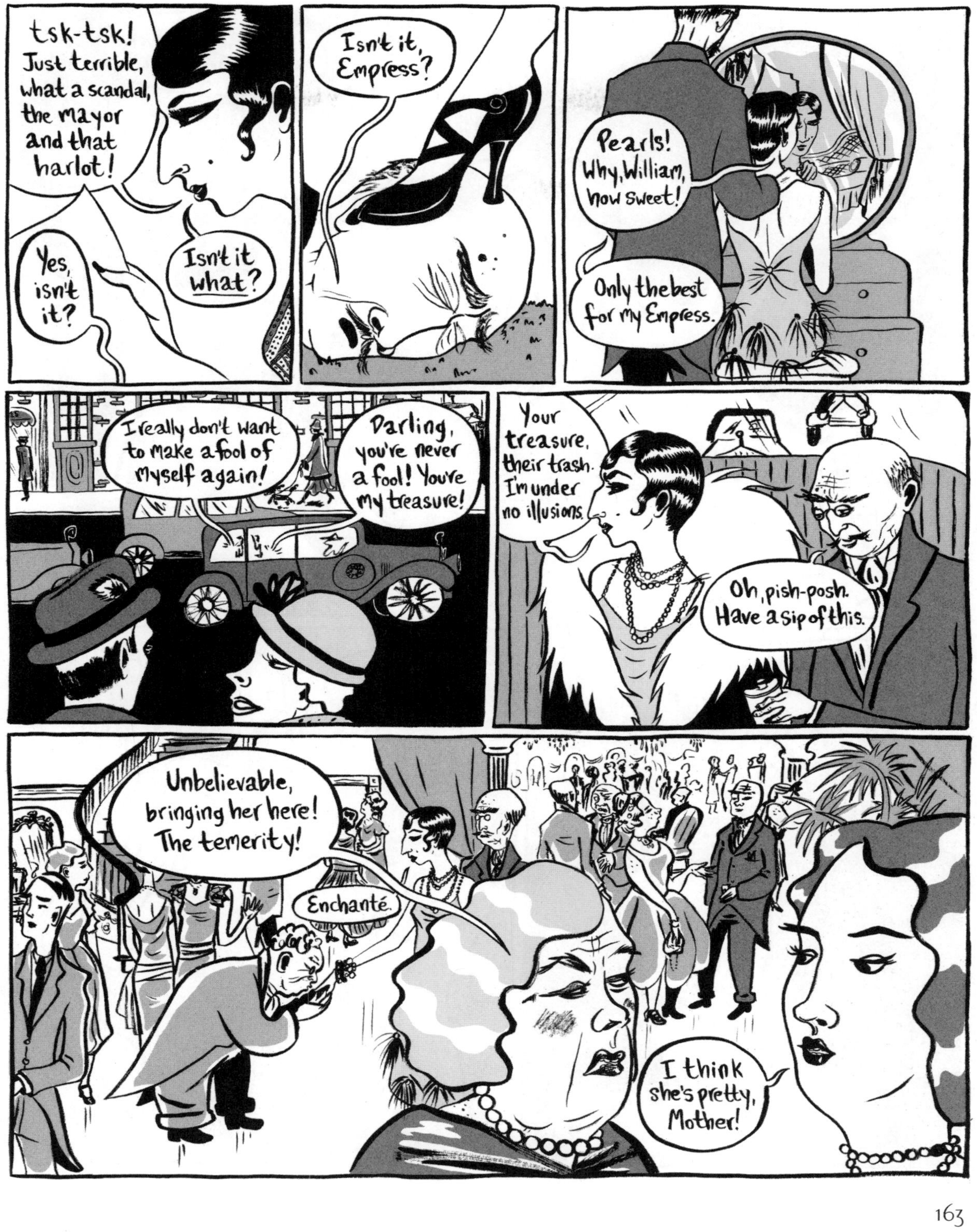
tsk-tsk! Just terrible, what a scandal, the mayor and that harlot!
Yes, isn't it?
Isn't it what?
Isn't it, Empress?
Pearls! Why, William, how sweet!
Only the best for my Empress.
I really don't want to make a fool of myself again!
Darling, you're never a fool! You're my treasure!
Your treasure, their trash. I'm under no illusions.
Oh, pish-posh. Have a sip of this.
Unbelievable, bringing her here! The temerity!
Enchanté.
I think she's pretty, Mother!

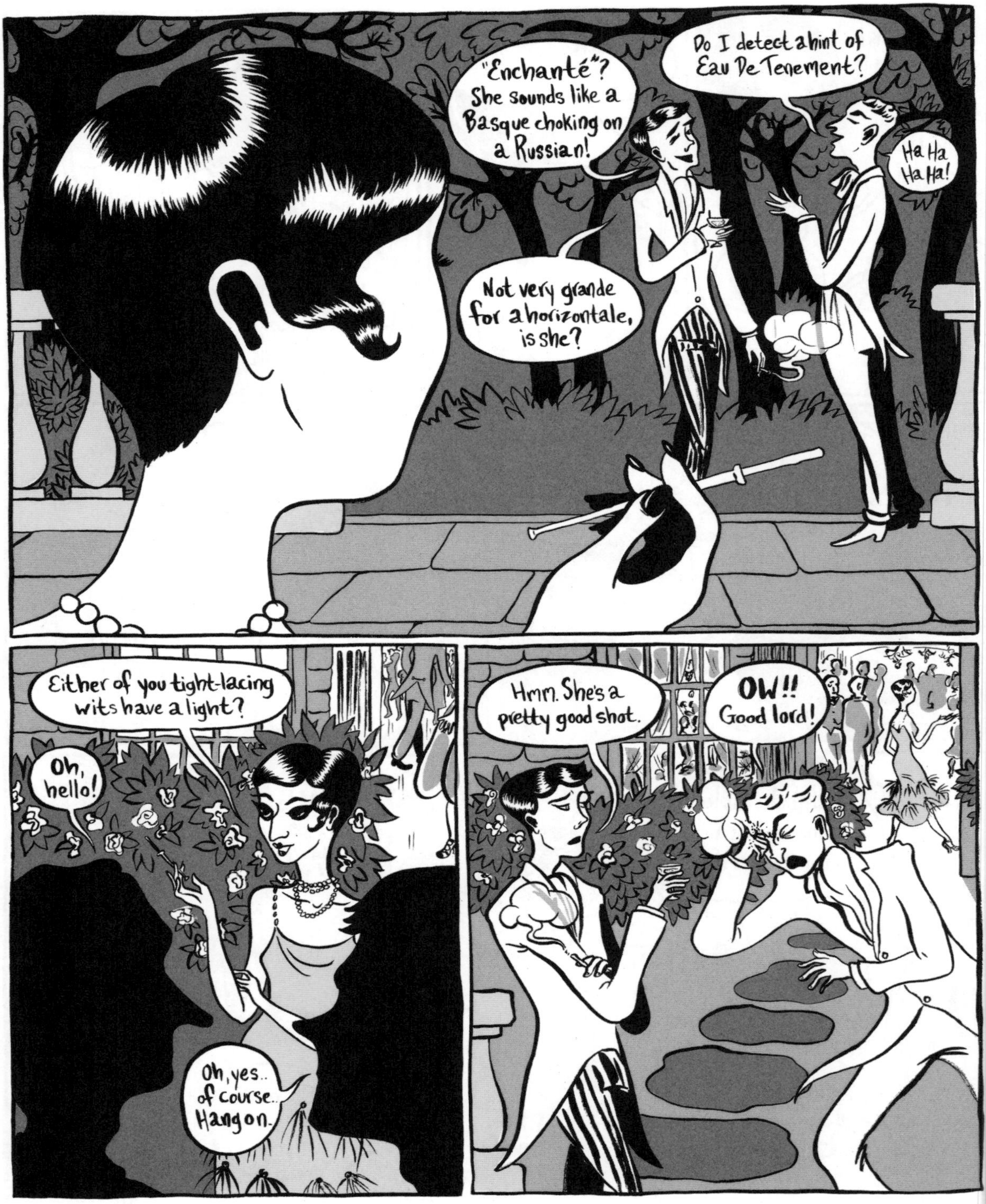
"Enchanté"? She sounds like a Basque choking on a Russian!
Do I detect a hint of Eau De Tenement?
Ha Ha Ha Ha!
Not very grande for a horizontale, is she?
Either of you tight-lacing wits have a light?
Oh, hello!
Oh, yes.. of course.. Hang on..
Hmm. She's a pretty good shot.
OW!! Good lord!

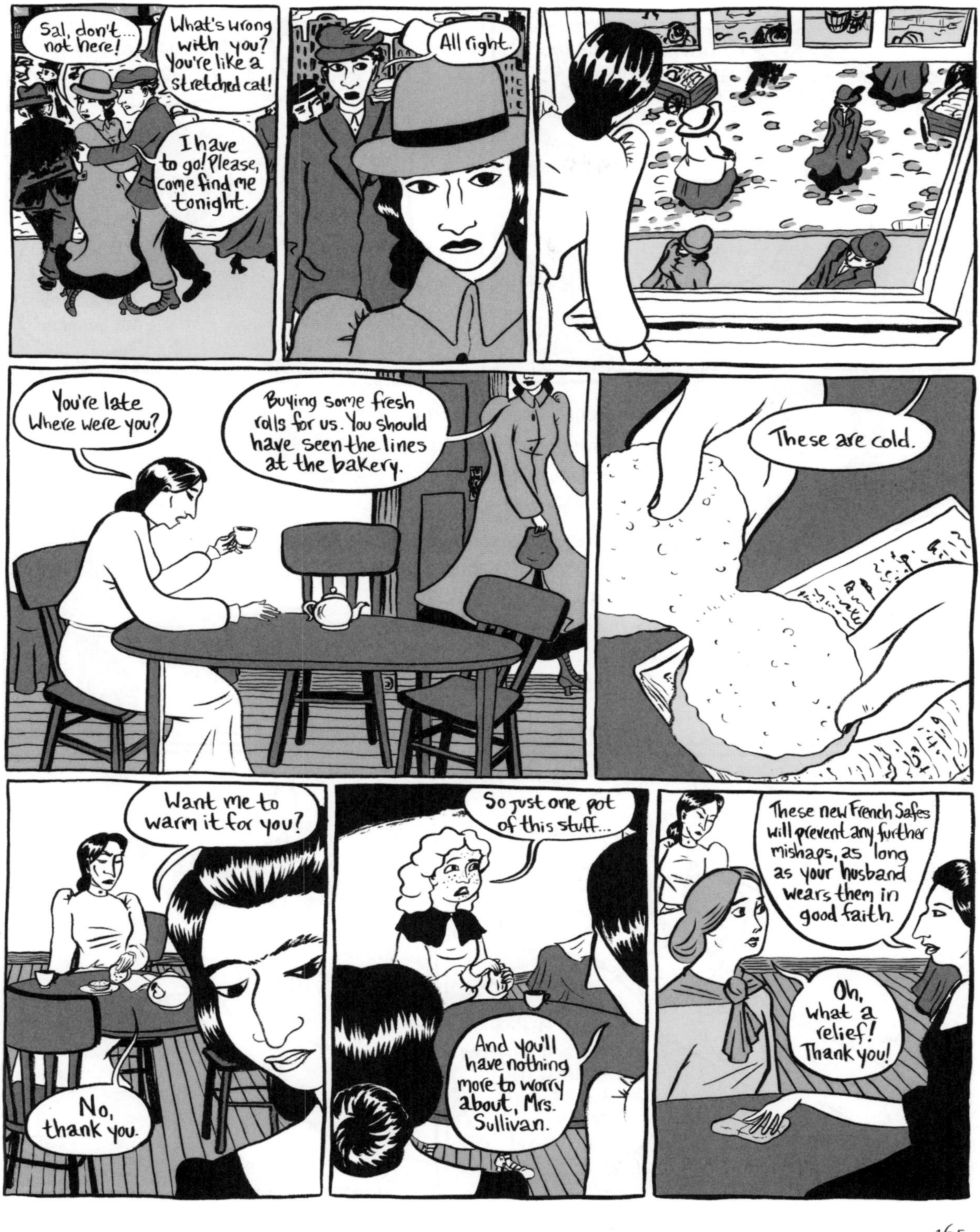
Sal, don't... not here!
What's wrong with you? You're like a stretched cat!
I have to go! Please, come find me tonight.
All right.
You're late Where were you?
Buying some fresh rolls for us. You should have seen the lines at the bakery.
These are cold.
Want me to warm it for you?
No, thank you.
So just one pot of this stuff...
And you'll have nothing more to worry about, Mrs. Sullivan.
These new French Safes will prevent any further mishaps, as long as your husband wears them in good faith.
Oh, what a relief! Thank you!

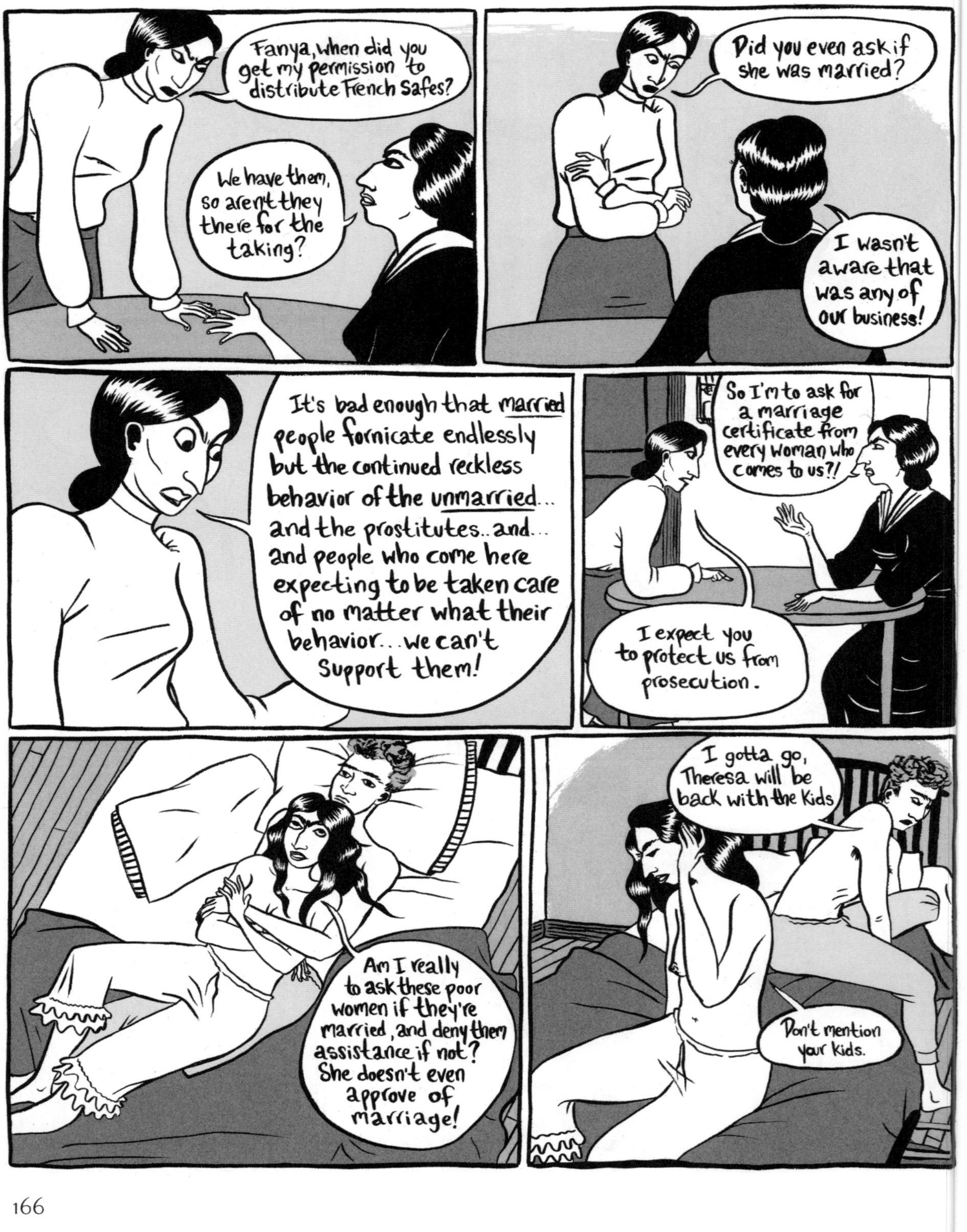
Fanya, when did you get my permission to distribute French Safes?
We have them, so aren't they there for the taking?
Did you even ask if she was married?
I wasn't aware that was any of our business!
It's bad enough that married people fornicate endlessly but the continued reckless behavior of the unmarried... and the prostitutes.. and... and people who come here expecting to be taken care of no matter what their behavior... we can't support them!
So I'm to ask for a marriage certificate from every woman who comes to us?!
I expect you to protect us from prosecution.
Am I really to ask these poor women if they're married, and deny them assistance if not? She doesn't even approve of marriage!
I gotta go, Theresa will be back with the kids
Don't mention your kids.

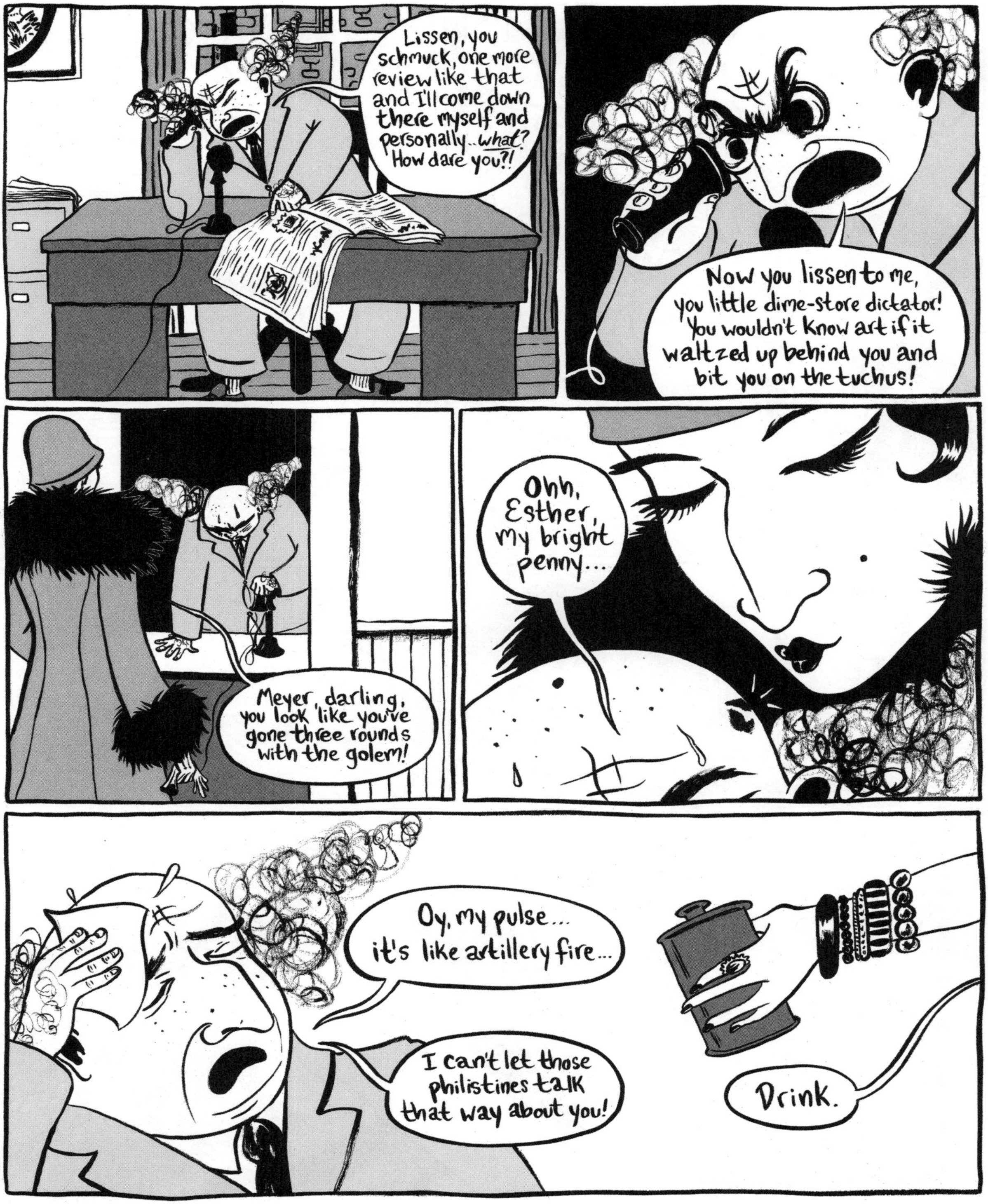
Lissen, you schmuck, one more review like that and I'll come down there myself and personally... what? How dare you?!
Now you lissen to me, you little dime-store dictator! You wouldn't know art if it waltzed up behind you and bit you on the tuchus!
Meyer, darling, you look like you've gone three rounds with the golem!
Ohh, Esther, my bright penny...
Oy, my pulse... it's like artillery fire...
I can't let those philistines talk that way about you!
Drink.

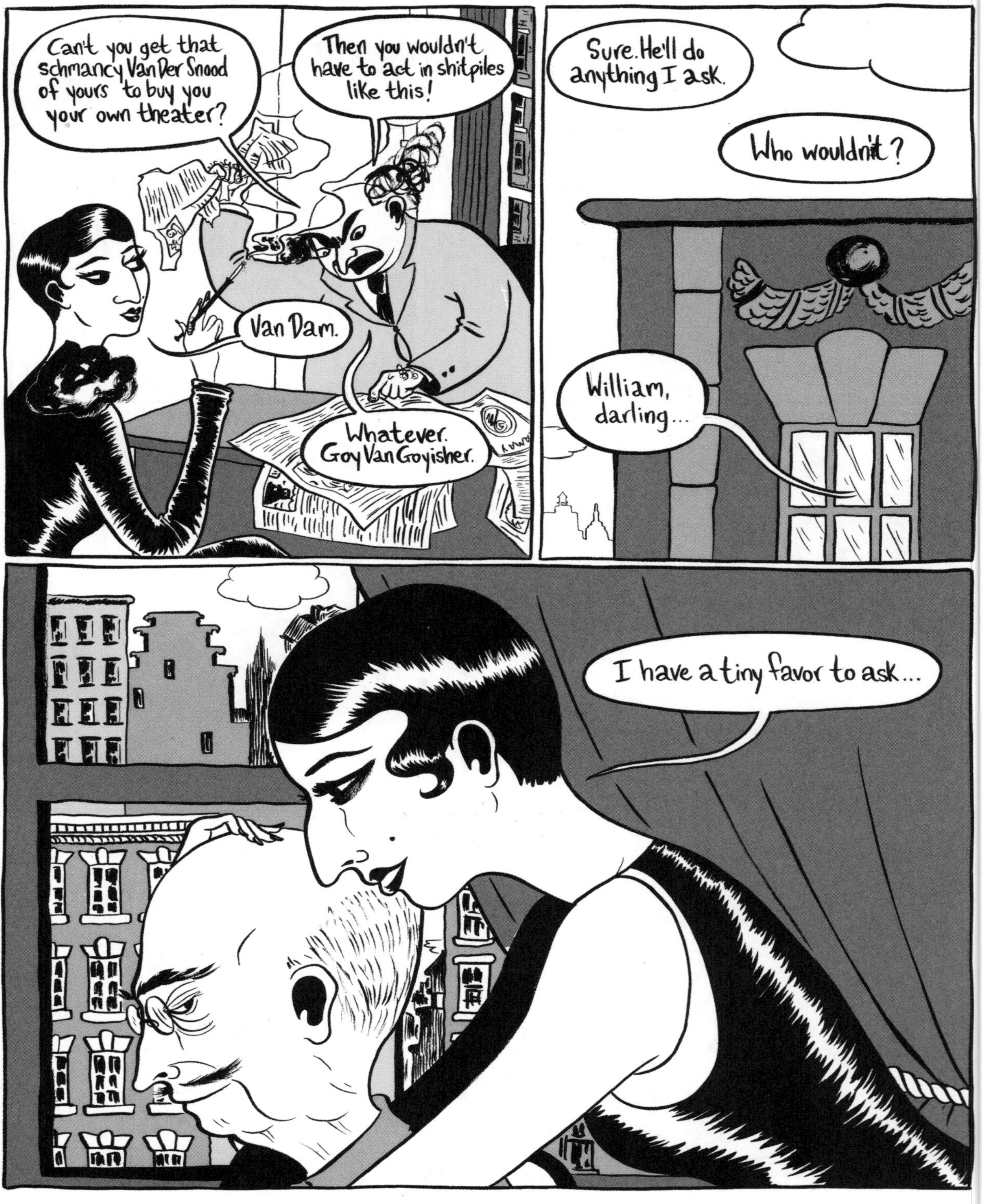
Can't you get that schmancy Van Der Snood of yours to buy you your own theater?
Then you wouldn't have to act in shitpiles like this!
Van Dam.
Whatever. Goy Van Goyisher.
Sure. He'll do anything I ask.
Who wouldn't?
William, darling...
I have a tiny favor to ask...

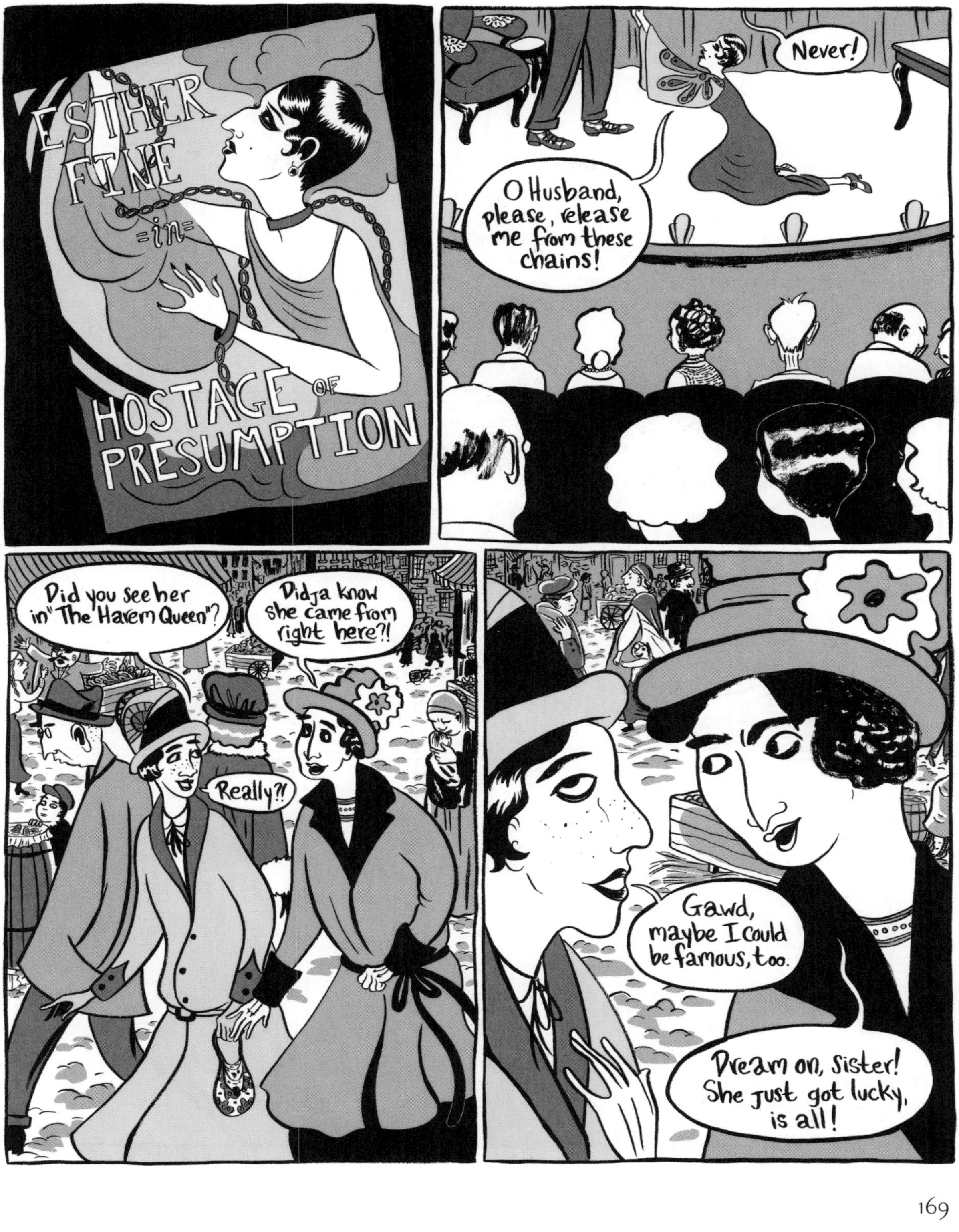
ESTHER FINE
=in=
HOSTAGE OF PRESUMPTION
Never!
O Husband, please, release me from these chains!
Did you see her in "The Harem Queen"?
Didja know she came from right here?!
Really?!
Gawd, maybe I could be famous, too.
Dream on, sister! She just got lucky, is all!

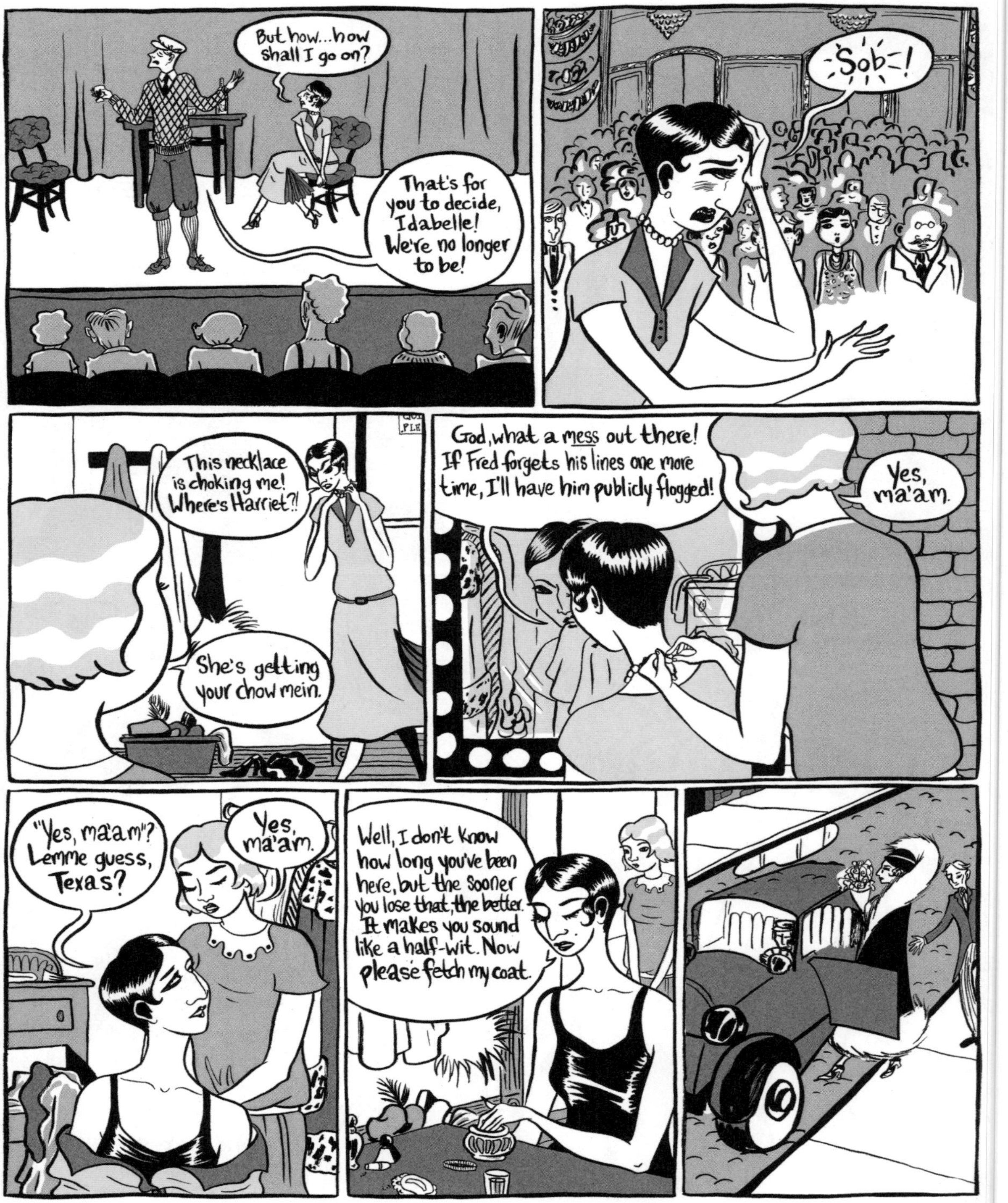

But how... how shall I go on?
That's for you to decide, Idabelle! We're no longer to be!
Sob!
This necklace is choking me! Where's Harriet?!
She's getting your chow mein.
God, what a mess out there! If Fred forgets his lines one more time, I'll have him publicly flogged!
Yes, ma'am.
"Yes, ma'am"? Lemme guess, Texas?
Yes, ma'am.
Well, I don't know how long you've been here, but the sooner you lose that, the better. It makes you sound like a half-wit. Now please fetch my coat.

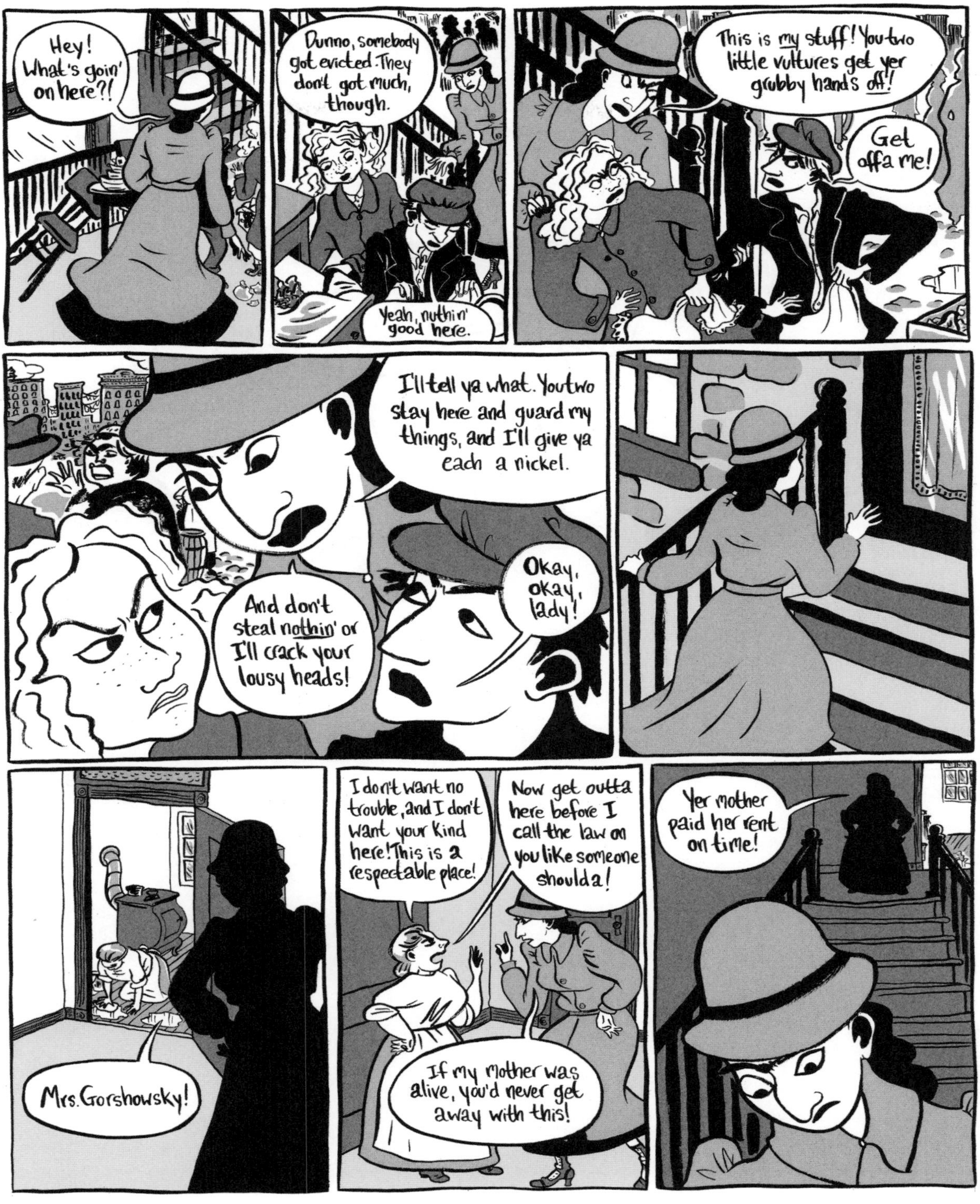

Hey! What's goin' on here?!
Dunno, somebody got evicted. They don't got much, though.
Yeah, nuthin' good here.
This is my stuff! You two little vultures get yer grubby hands off!
Get offa me!
I'll tell ya what. You two stay here and guard my things, and I'll give ya each a nickel.
And don't steal nothin' or I'll crack your lousy heads!
Okay, okay, lady!
Mrs. Gorshowsky!
I don't want no trouble, and I don't want your kind here! This is a respectable place!
Now get outta here before I call the law on you like someone shoulda!
If my mother was alive, you'd never get away with this!
Yer mother paid her rent on time!

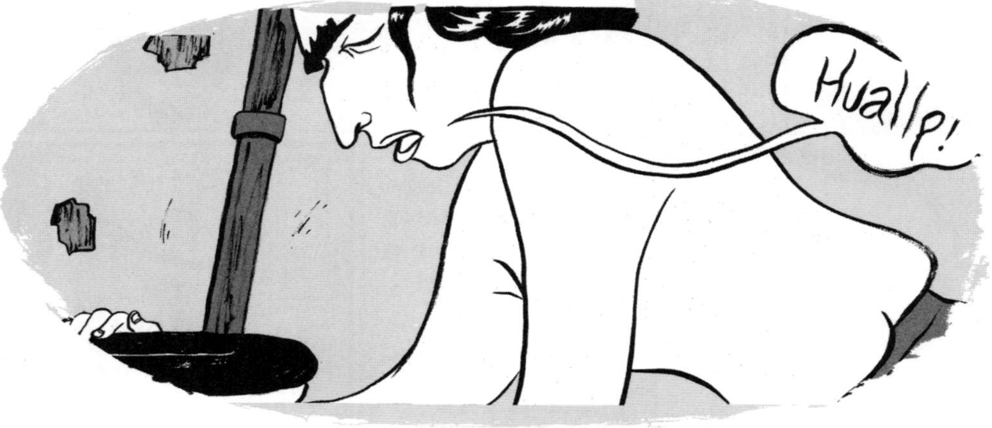
Huallp!

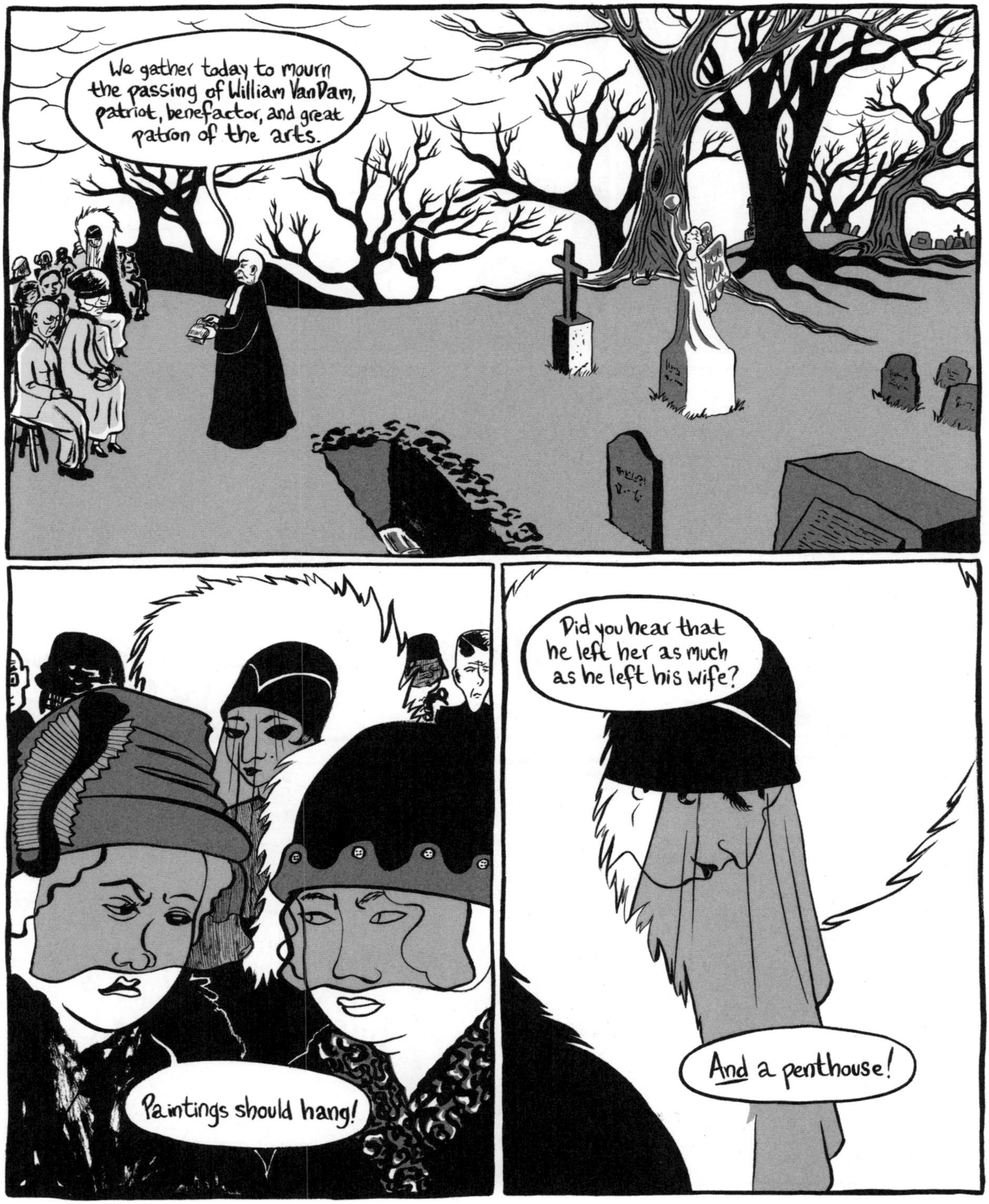
We gather today to mourn the passing of William VanDam, patriot, benefactor, and great patron of the arts.
Paintings should hang!
Did you hear that he left her as much as he left his wife?
And a penthouse!

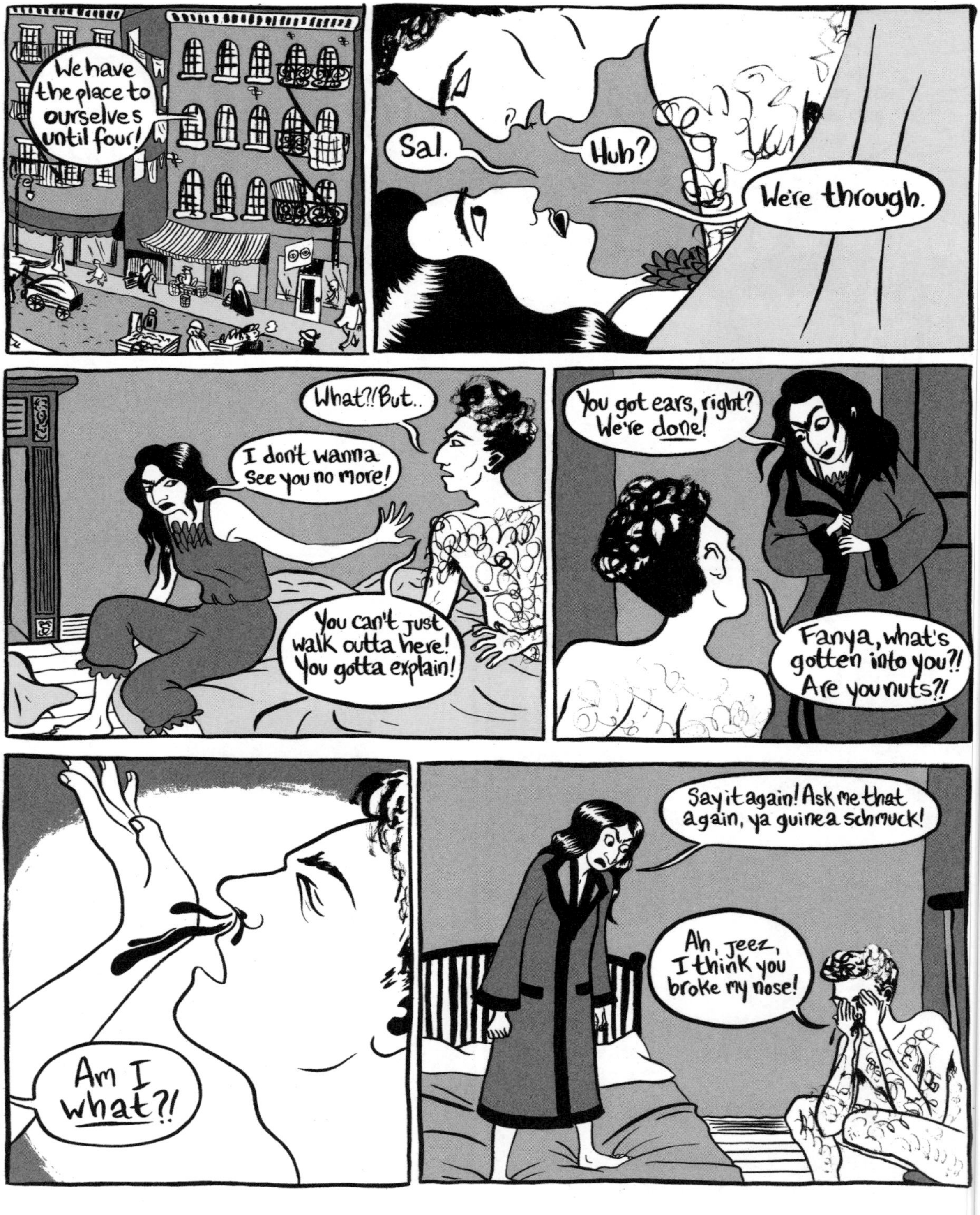
We have the place to ourselves until four!
Sal.
Huh?
We're through.
What?! But..
I don't wanna see you no more!
You can't just walk outta here! You gotta explain!
You got ears, right? We're done!
Fanya, what's gotten into you?! Are you nuts?!
Am I what?!
Say it again! Ask me that again, ya guinea schmuck!
Ah, jeez, I think you broke my nose!

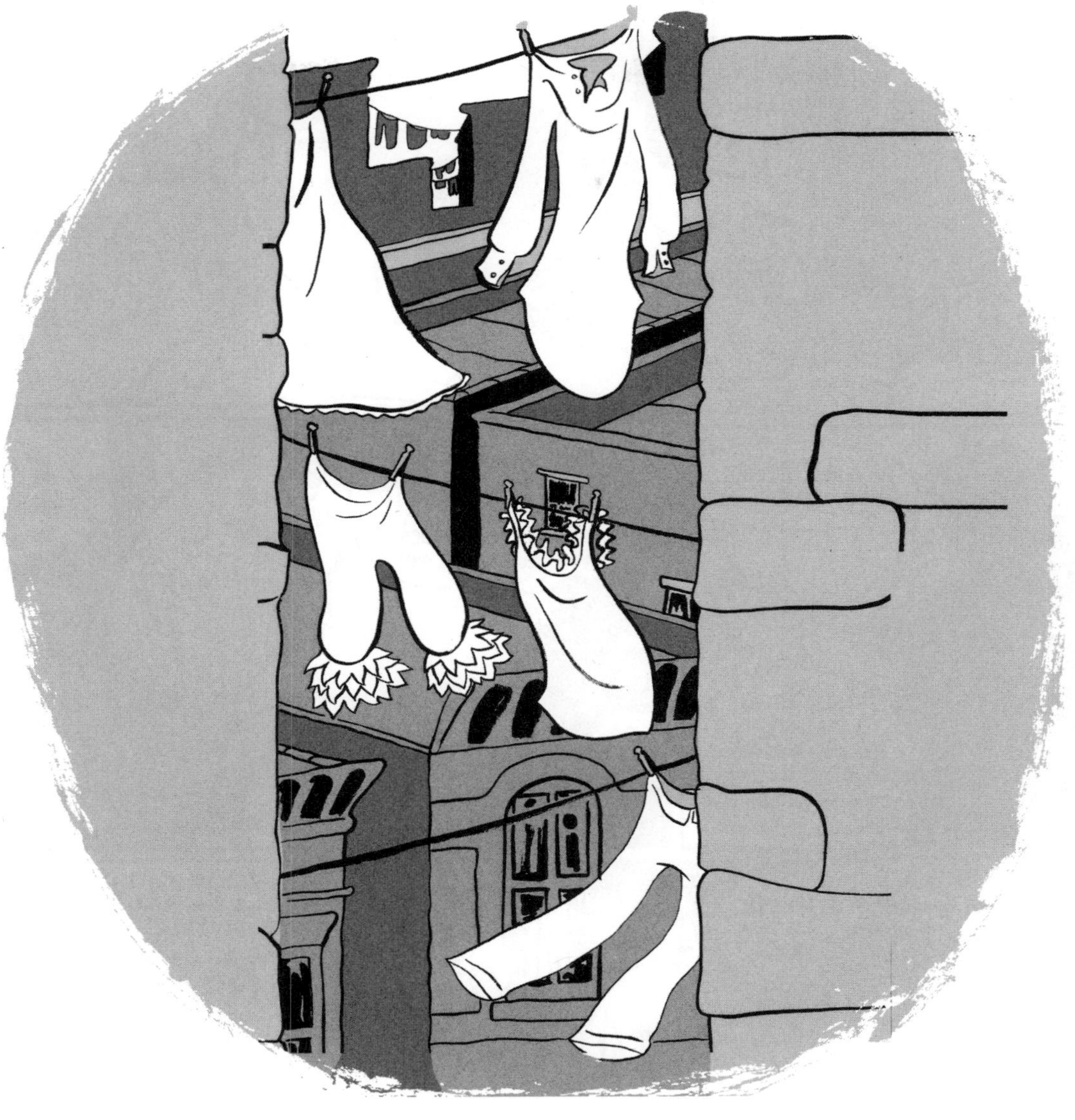

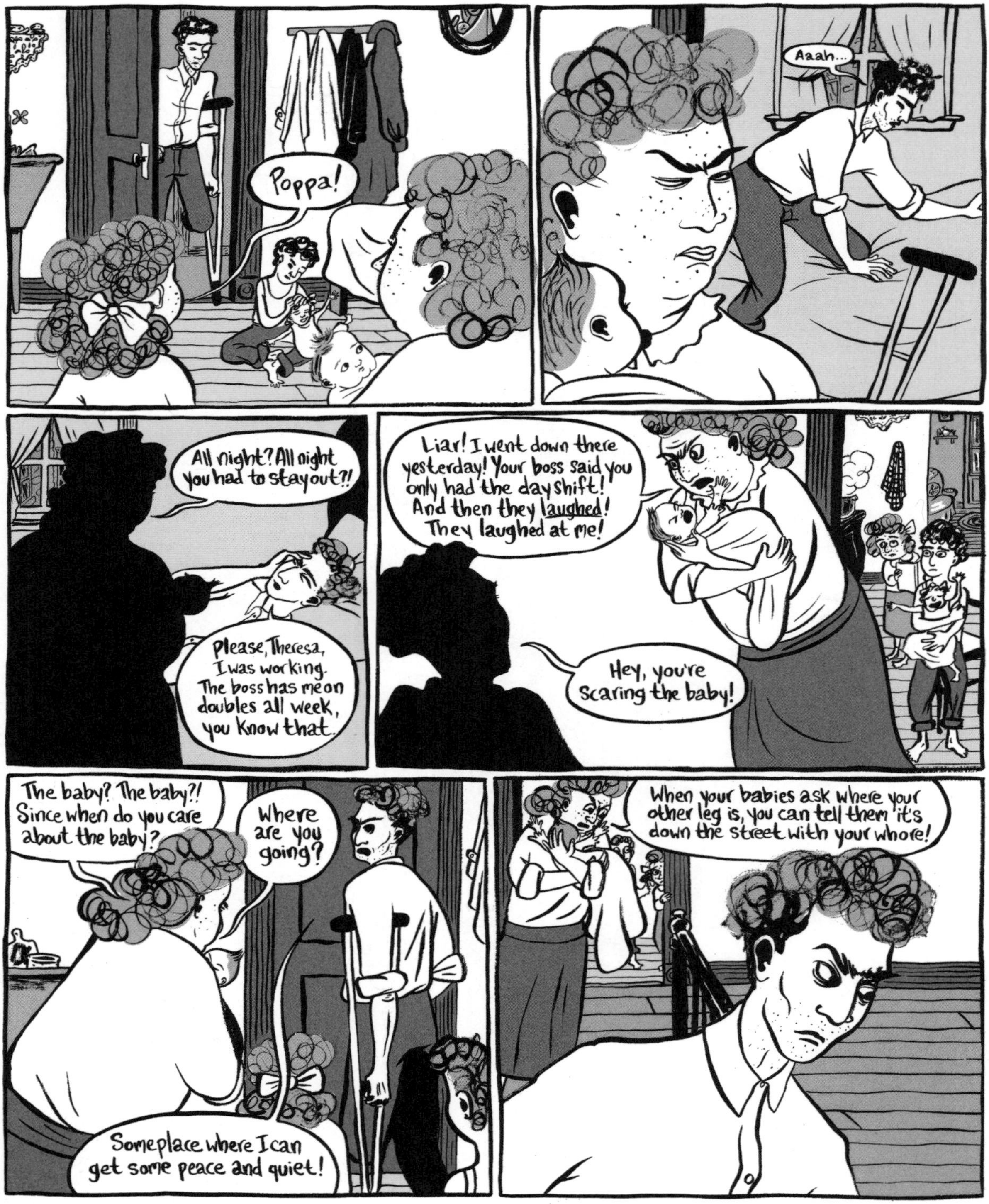
Poppa!
Aaah...
All night? All night you had to stay out?!
Please, Theresa, I was working. The boss has me on doubles all week, you know that.
Liar! I went down there yesterday! Your boss said you only had the day shift! And then they laughed! They laughed at me!
Hey, you're scaring the baby!
The baby? The baby?! Since when do you care about the baby?
Where are you going?
Someplace where I can get some peace and quiet!
When your babies ask where your other leg is, you can tell them it's down the street with your whore!

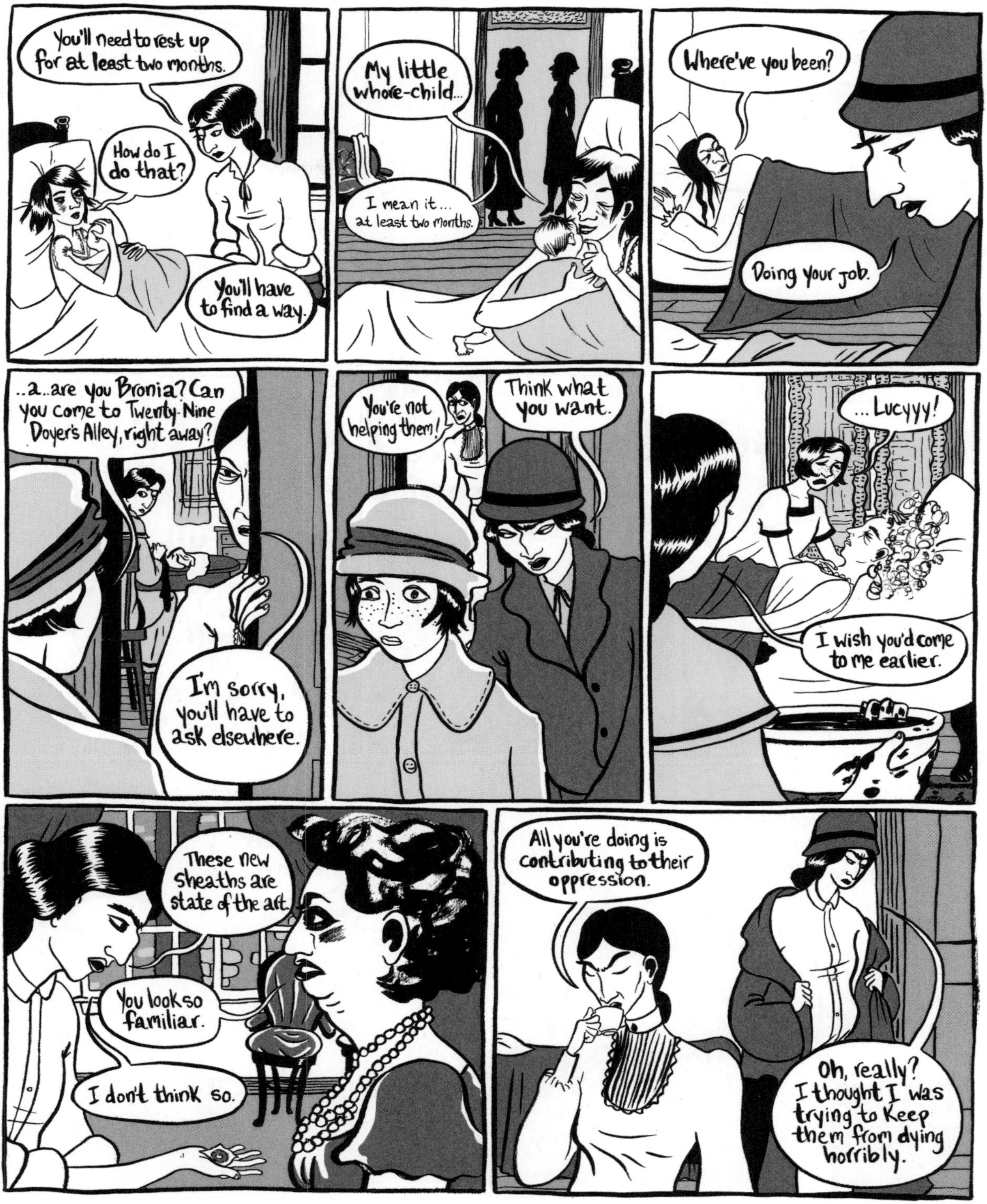
You'll need to rest up for at least two months.
How do I do that?
You'll have to find a way.
My little whore-child...
I mean it... at least two months.
Where've you been?
Doing your job.
..a..are you Bronia? Can you come to Twenty-Nine Doyer's Alley, right away?
I'm sorry, you'll have to ask elsewhere.
You're not helping them!
Think what you want.
...Lucyyy!
I wish you'd come to me earlier.
These new sheaths are state of the art.
You look so familiar.
I don't think so.
All you're doing is contributing to their oppression.
Oh, really? I thought I was trying to keep them from dying horribly.

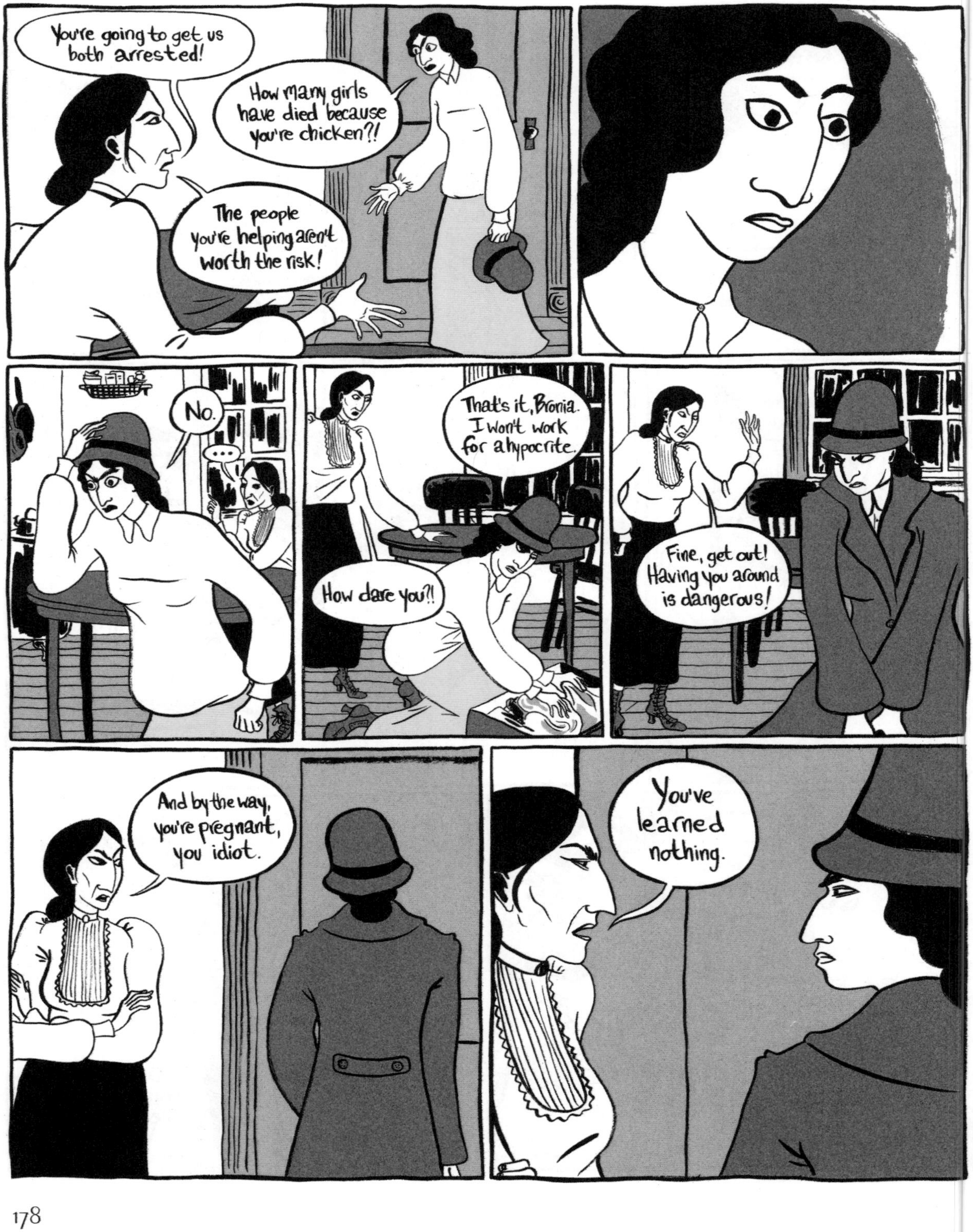
You're going to get us both arrested!
How many girls have died because you're chicken?!
The people you're helping aren't worth the risk!
No.
...
That's it, Bronia. I won't work for a hypocrite.
How dare you?!
Fine, get out! Having you around is dangerous!
And by the way, you're pregnant, you idiot.
You've learned nothing.

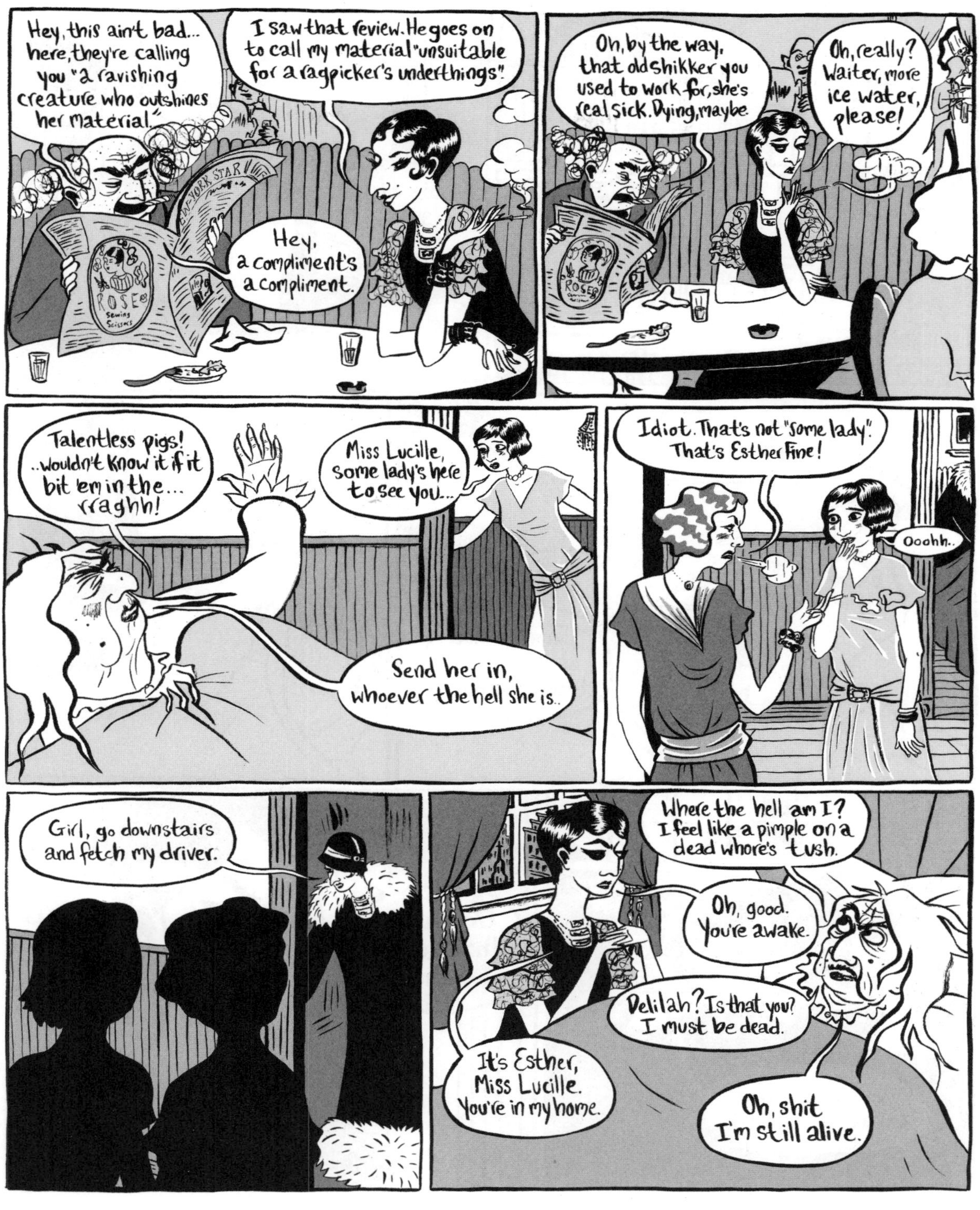
Hey, this ain't bad... here, they're calling you "a ravishing creature who outshines her material."
I saw that review. He goes on to call my material "unsuitable for a ragpicker's underthings".
NEW YORK STAR
ROSE
Sewing Scissors
Hey, a compliment's a compliment.
Oh, by the way, that old shikker you used to work for, she's real sick. Dying, maybe.
Oh, really? Waiter, more ice water, please!
Talentless pigs! ..wouldn't know it if it bit 'em in the... rraghh!
Miss Lucille, some lady's here to see you...
Send her in, whoever the hell she is..
Idiot. That's not "some lady". That's Esther Fine!
Ooohh..
Girl, go downstairs and fetch my driver.
Where the hell am I? I feel like a pimple on a dead whore's tush.
Oh, good. You're awake.
Delilah? Is that you? I must be dead.
It's Esther, Miss Lucille. You're in my home.
Oh, shit I'm still alive.

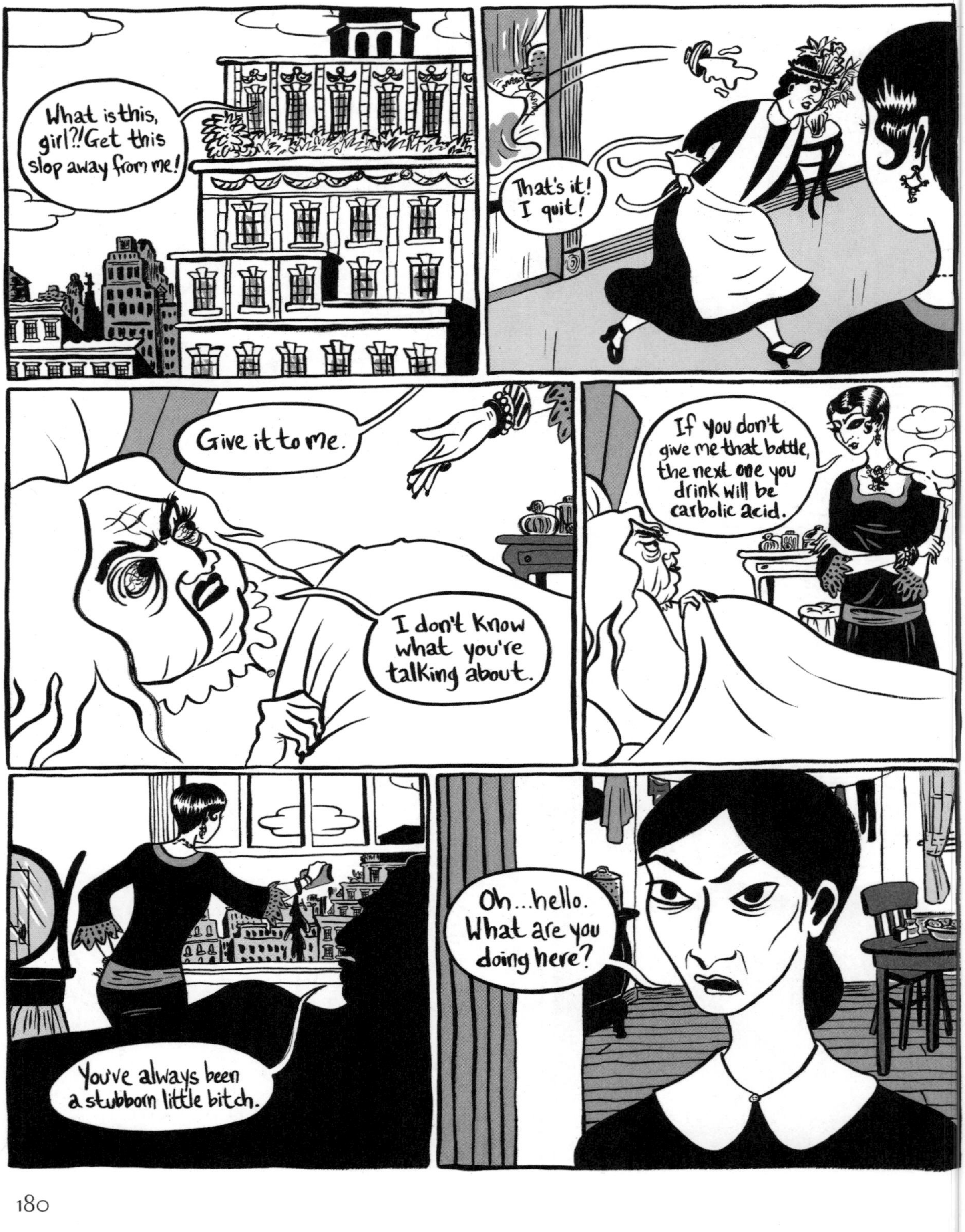
What is this, girl?!/Get this slop away from me!
That's it! I quit!
Give it to me.
I don't know what you're talking about.
If you don't give me that bottle, the next one you drink will be carbolic acid.
You've always been a stubborn little bitch.
Oh...hello. What are you doing here?

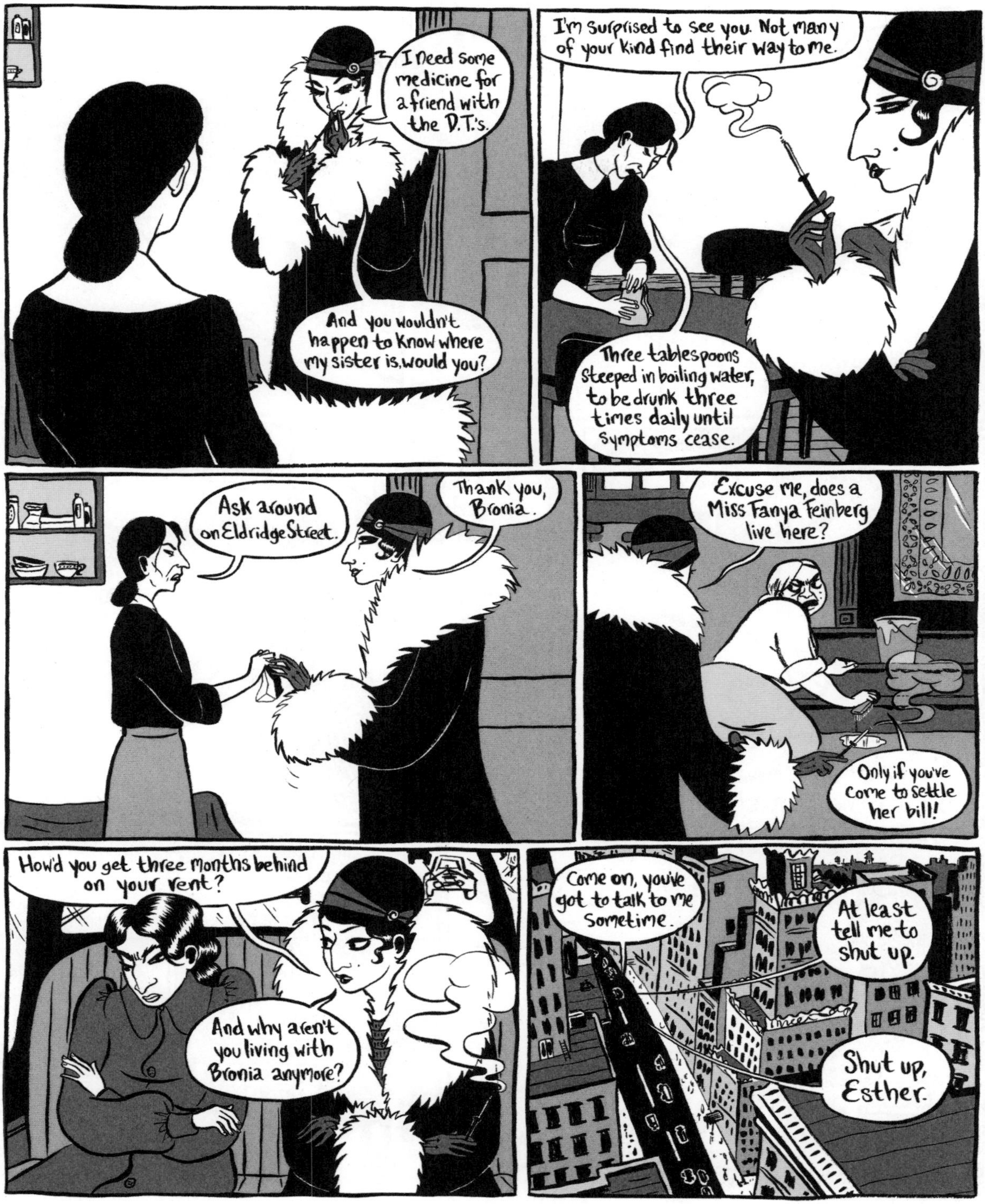
I need some medicine for a friend with the D.T.'s.
And you wouldn't happen to know where my sister is, would you?
I'm surprised to see you. Not many of your kind find their way to me.
Three tablespoons steeped in boiling water, to be drunk three times daily until symptoms cease.
Ask around on Eldridge Street.
Thank you, Bronia.
Excuse me, does a Miss Fanya Feinberg live here?
Only if you've come to settle her bill!
How'd you get three months behind on your rent?
And why aren't you living with Bronia anymore?
Come on, you've got to talk to me sometime.
At least tell me to shut up.
Shut up, Esther.

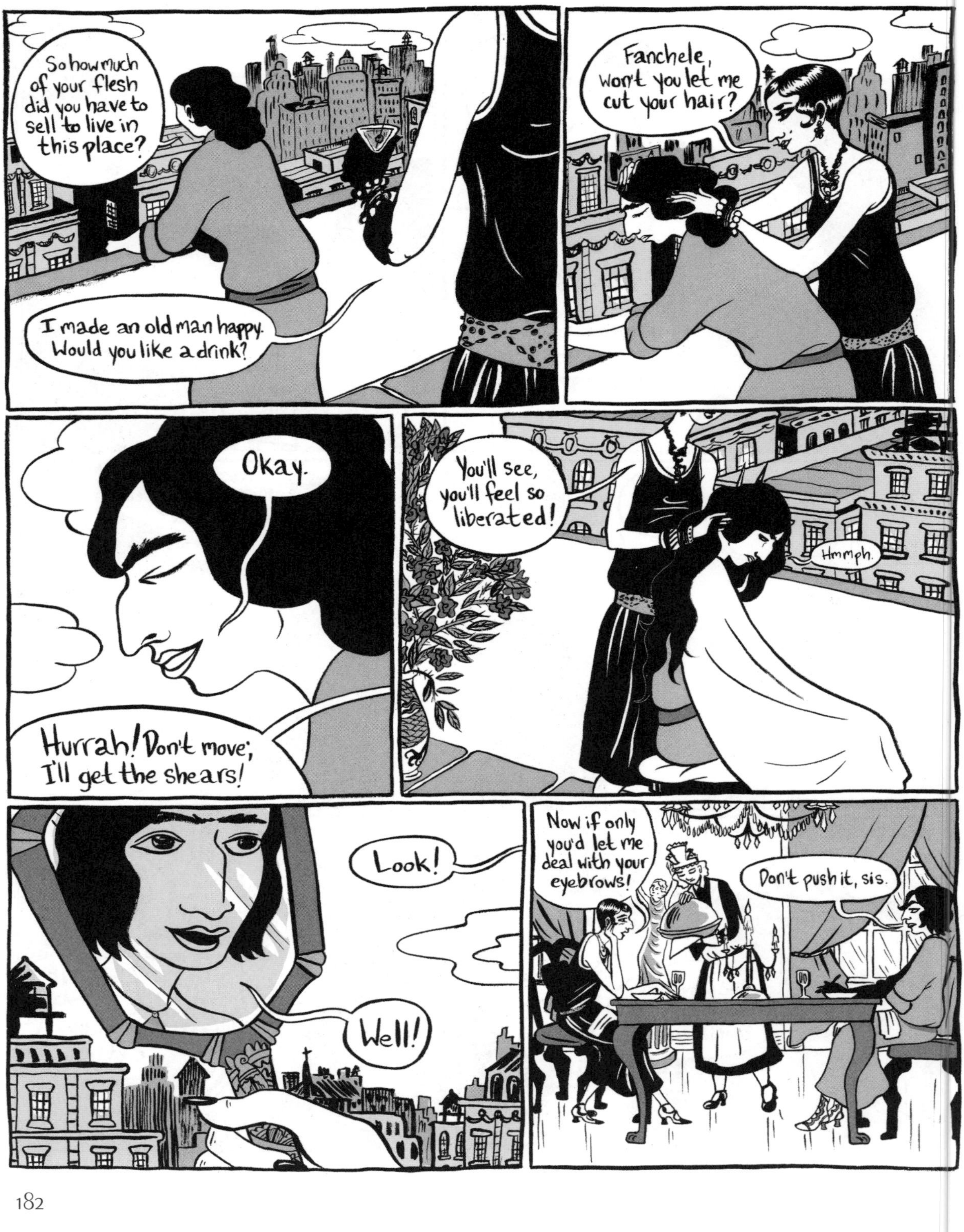
So how much of your flesh did you have to sell to live in this place?
I made an old man happy. Would you like a drink?
Fanchele, won't you let me cut your hair?
Okay.
Hurrah! Don't move; I'll get the shears!
You'll see, you'll feel so liberated!
Hmmph.
Look!
Well!
Now if only you'd let me deal with your eyebrows!
Don't push it, sis.

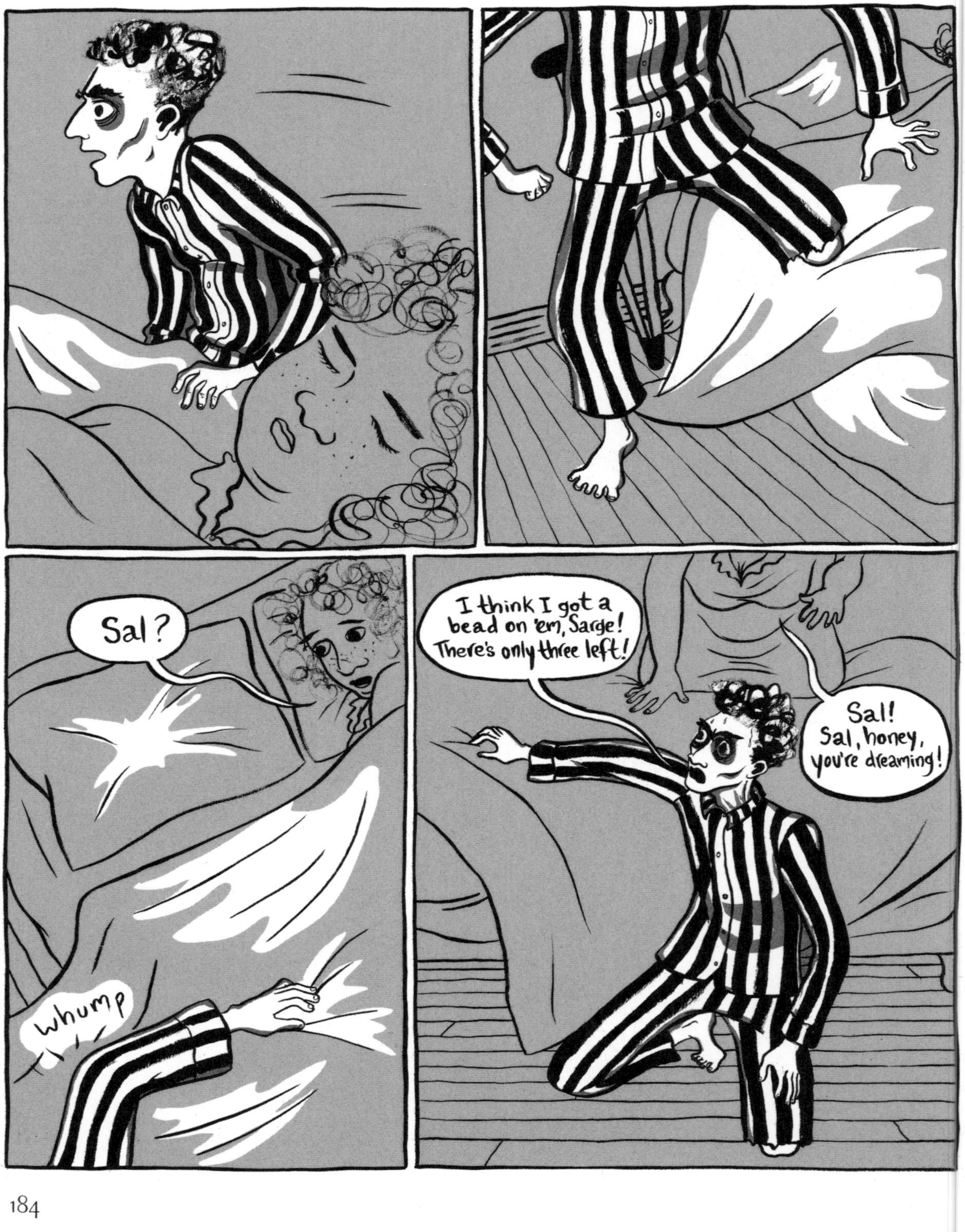

Sal?
whump
I think I got a bead on 'em, Sarge! There's only three left!
Sal! Sal, honey, you're dreaming!

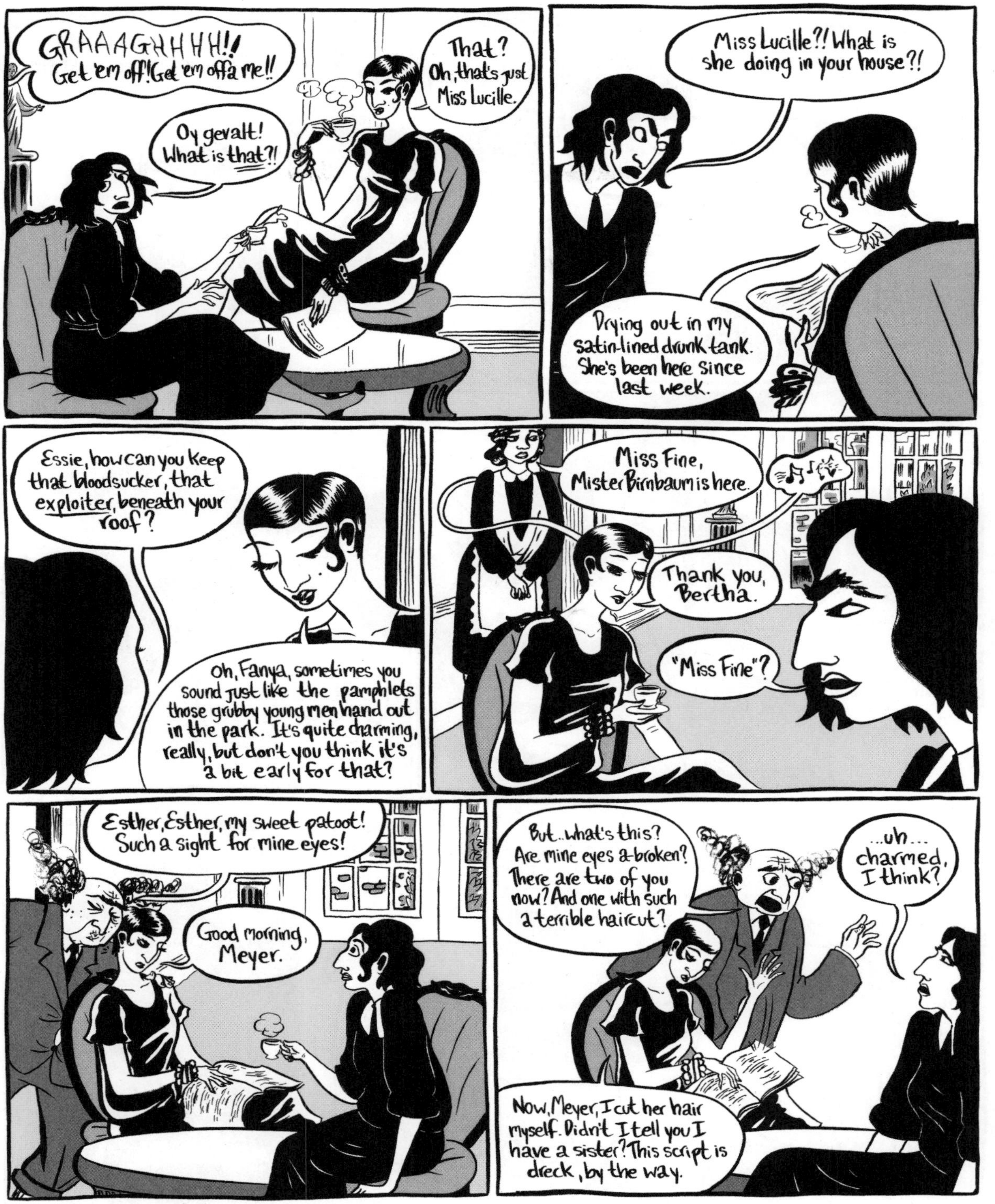
GRAAAGHHHH!!
Get 'em off! Get 'em offa me!!
That? Oh, that's just Miss Lucille.
Oy gevalt! What is that?!
Miss Lucille?! What is she doing in your house?!
Drying out in my satin-lined drunk tank. She's been here since last week.
Essie, how can you keep that bloodsucker, that exploiter, beneath your roof?
Oh, Fanya, sometimes you sound just like the pamphlets those grubby young men hand out in the park. It's quite charming, really, but don't you think it's a bit early for that?
Miss Fine, Mister Birnbaum is here.
Thank you, Bertha.
"Miss Fine"?
Esther, Esther, my sweet patoot! Such a sight for mine eyes!
Good morning, Meyer.
But... what's this? Are mine eyes a-broken? There are two of you now? And one with such a terrible haircut?
...uh... charmed, I think?
Now, Meyer, I cut her hair myself. Didn't I tell you I have a sister? This script is dreck, by the way.

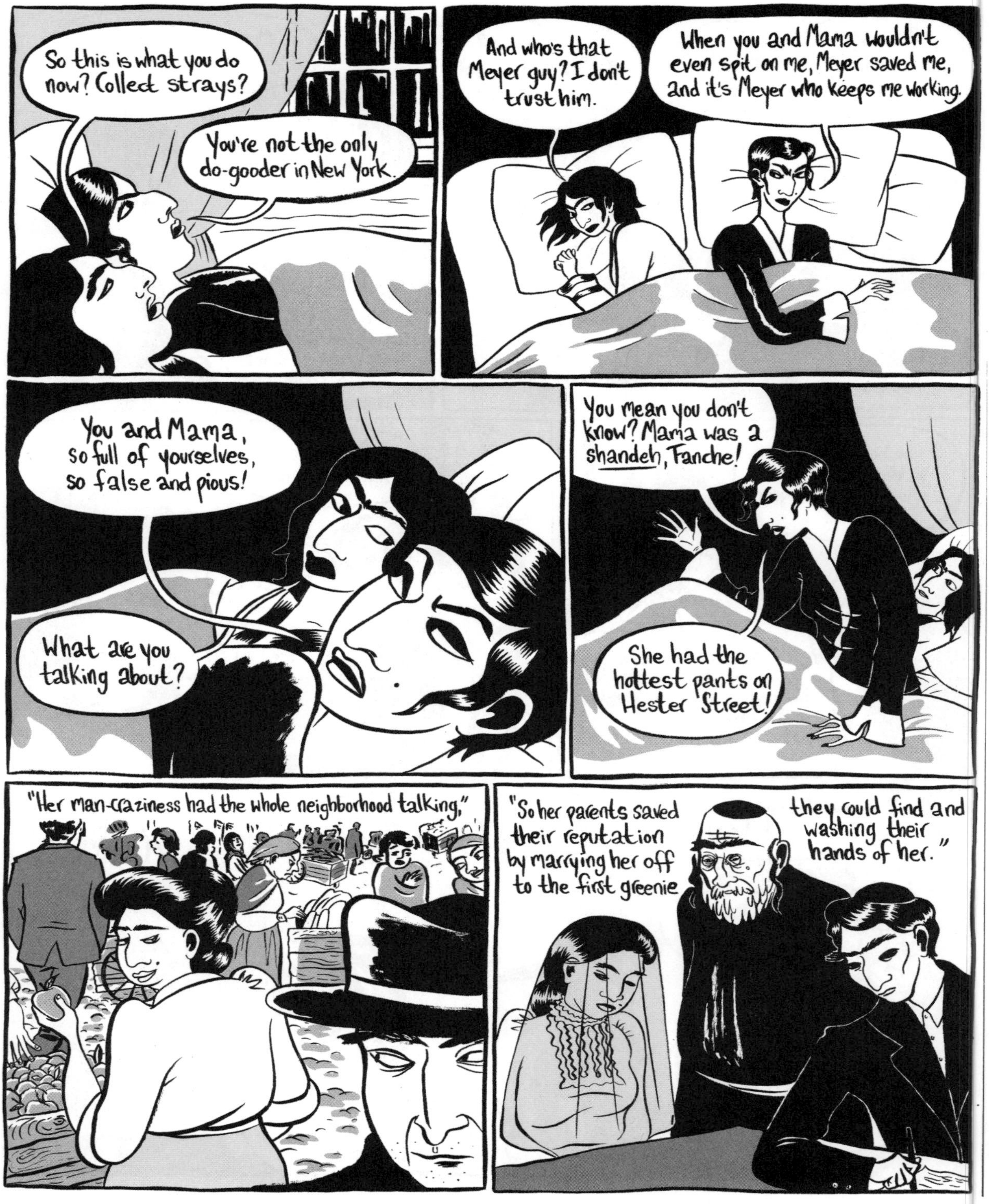
So this is what you do now? Collect strays?
You're not the only do-gooder in New York.
And who's that Meyer guy? I don't trust him.
When you and Mama wouldn't even spit on me, Meyer saved me, and it's Meyer who keeps me working.
You and Mama, so full of yourselves, so false and pious!
What are you talking about?
You mean you don't know? Mama was a shandeh, Fanche!
She had the hottest pants on Hester Street!
"Her man-craziness had the whole neighborhood talking."
"So her parents saved their reputation by marrying her off to the first greenie
they could find and washing their hands of her."

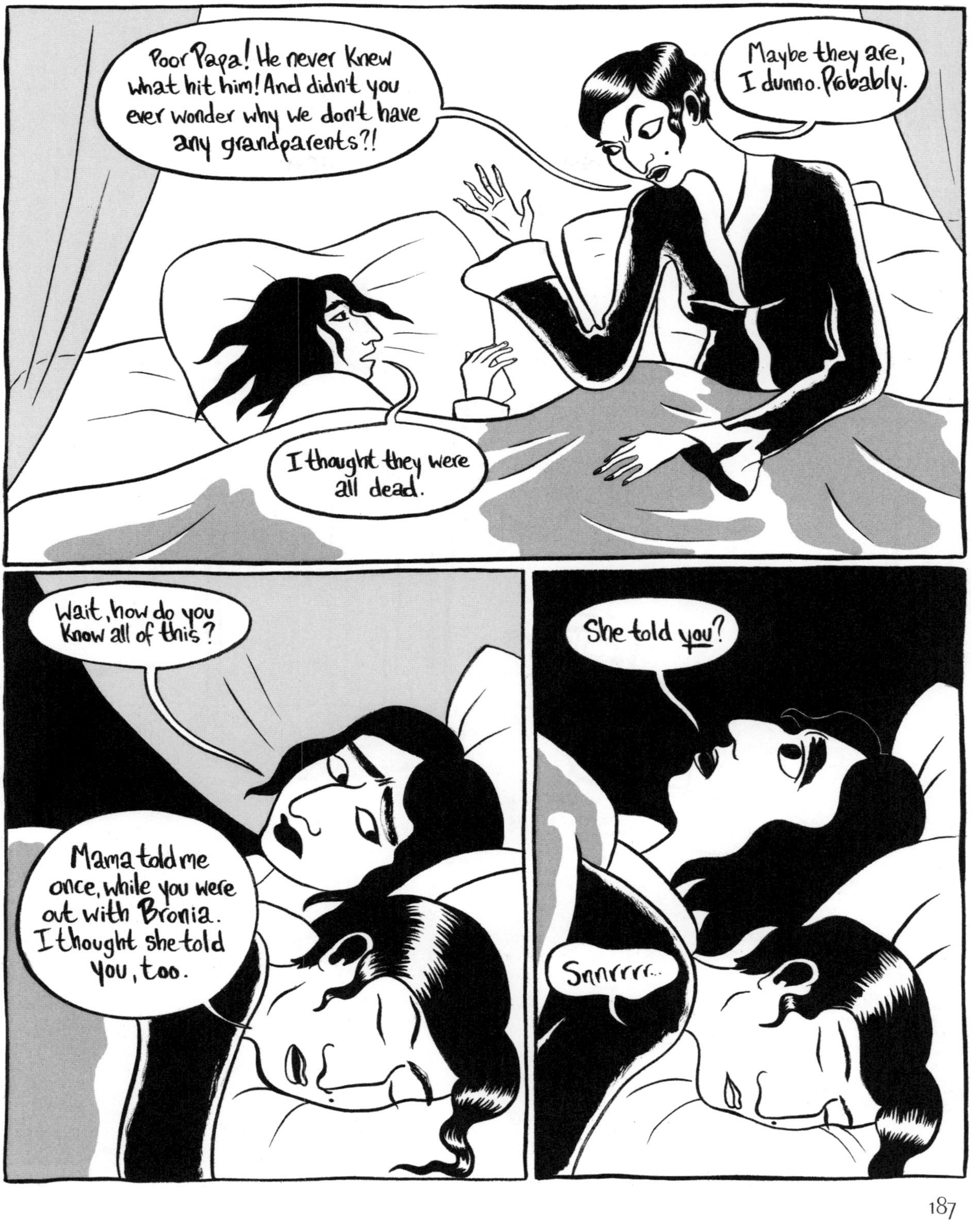
Poor Papa! He never Knew what hit him! And didn't you ever wonder why we don't have any grandparents?!
Maybe they are, I dunno. Probably.
I thought they were all dead.
Wait, how do you Know all of this?
Mama told me once, while you were out with Bronia. I thought she told you, too.
She told you?
Snnrrrr...

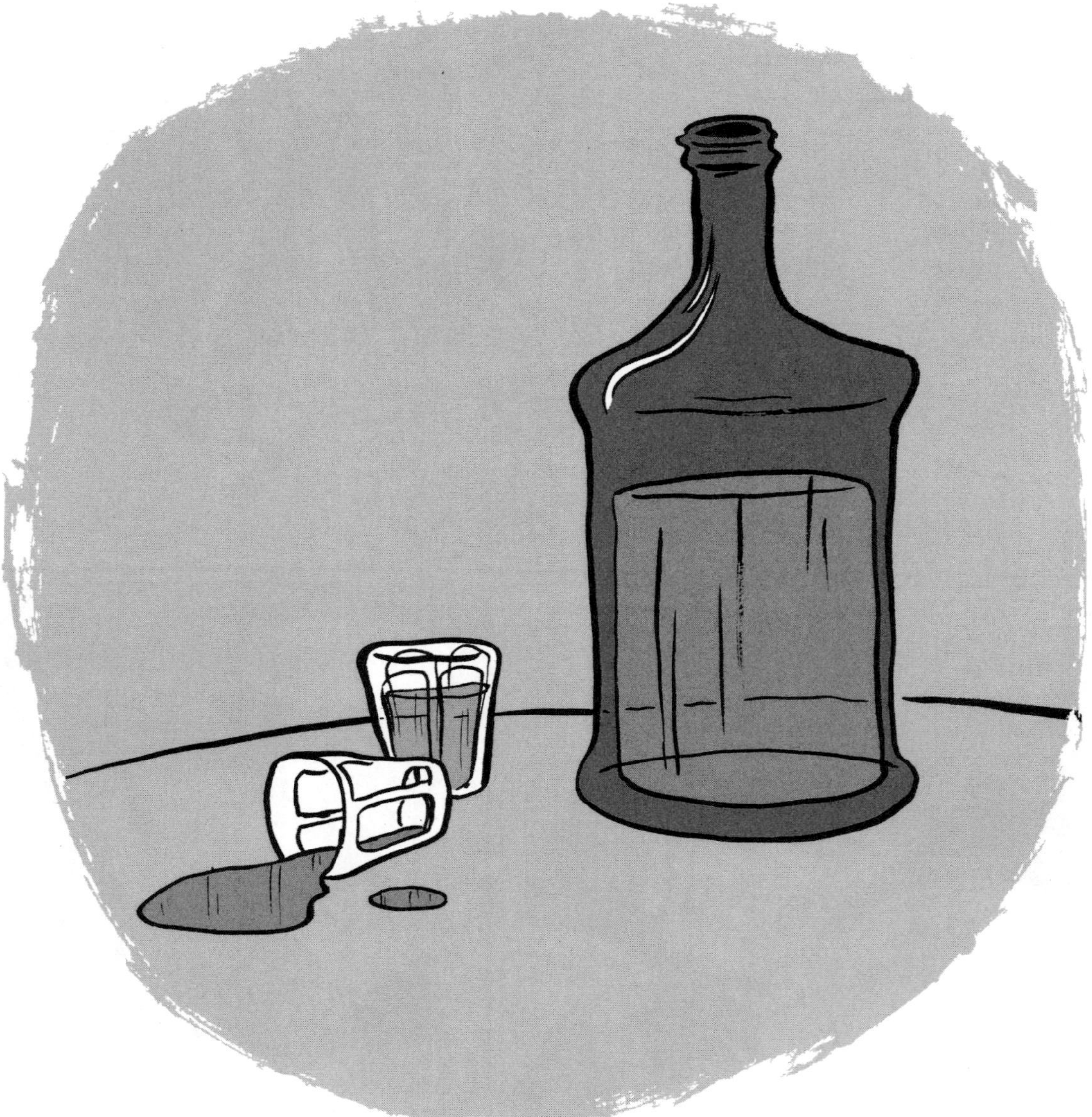

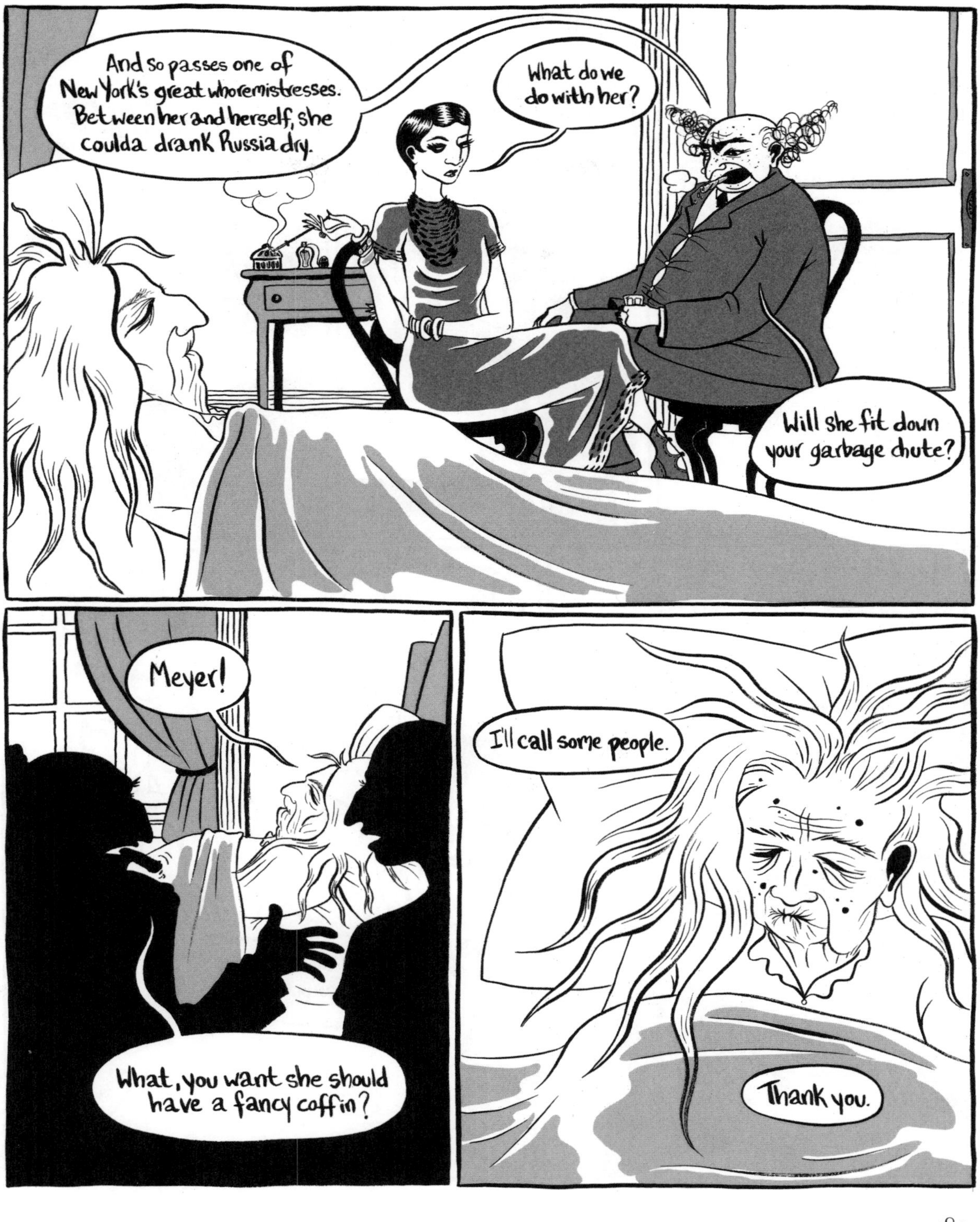
And so passes one of New York's great whoremistresses. Between her and herself, she coulda drank Russia dry.
What do we do with her?
Will she fit down your garbage chute?
Meyer!
What, you want she should have a fancy coffin?
I'll call some people.
Thank you.

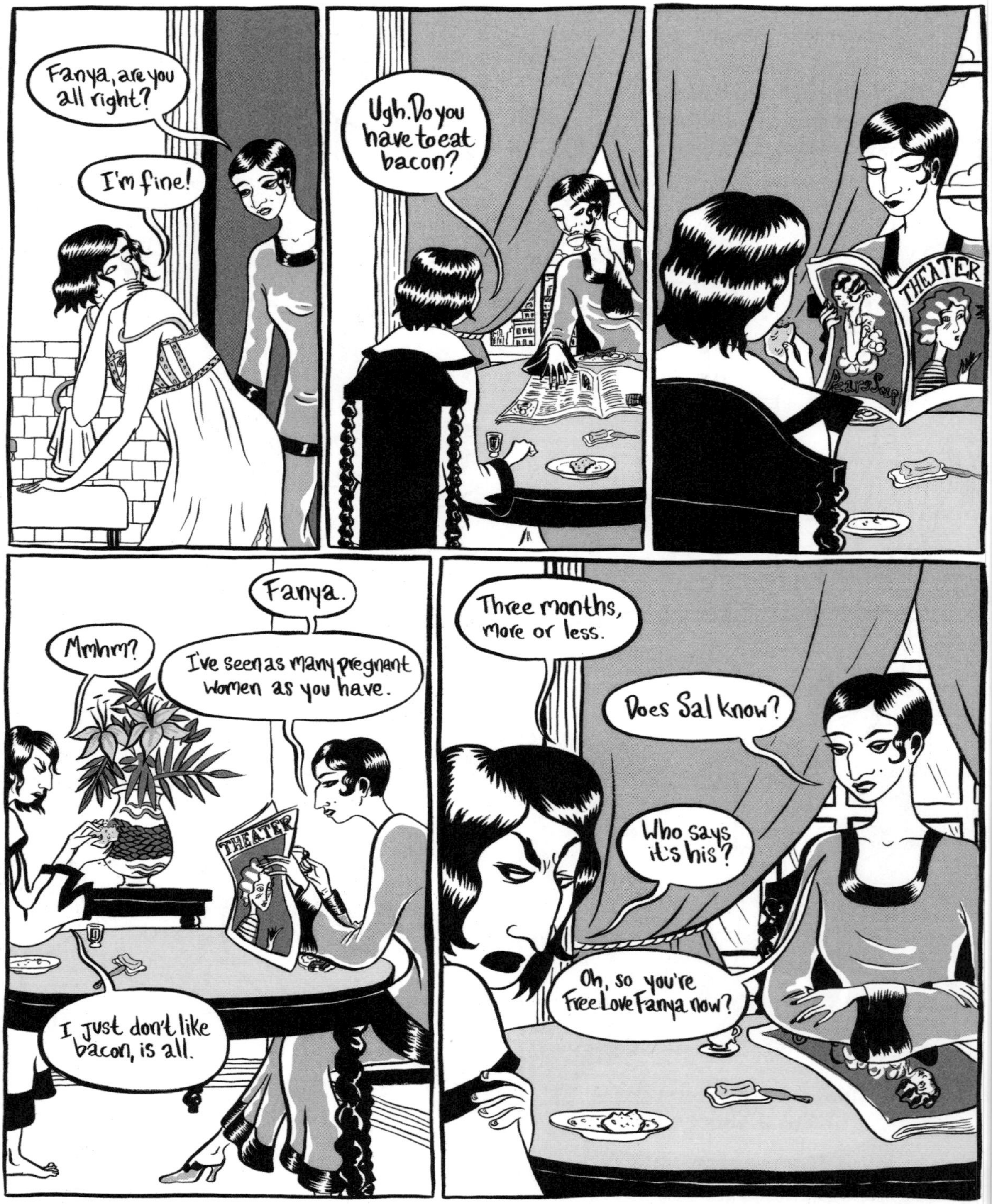

Fanya, are you all right?
I'm fine!
Ugh. Do you have to eat bacon?
THEATER
Pears Soap
Fanya.
Mmhm?
I've seen as many pregnant women as you have.
THEATER
I just don't like bacon, is all.
Three months, more or less.
Does Sal know?
Who says it's his?
Oh, so you're Free Love Fanya now?

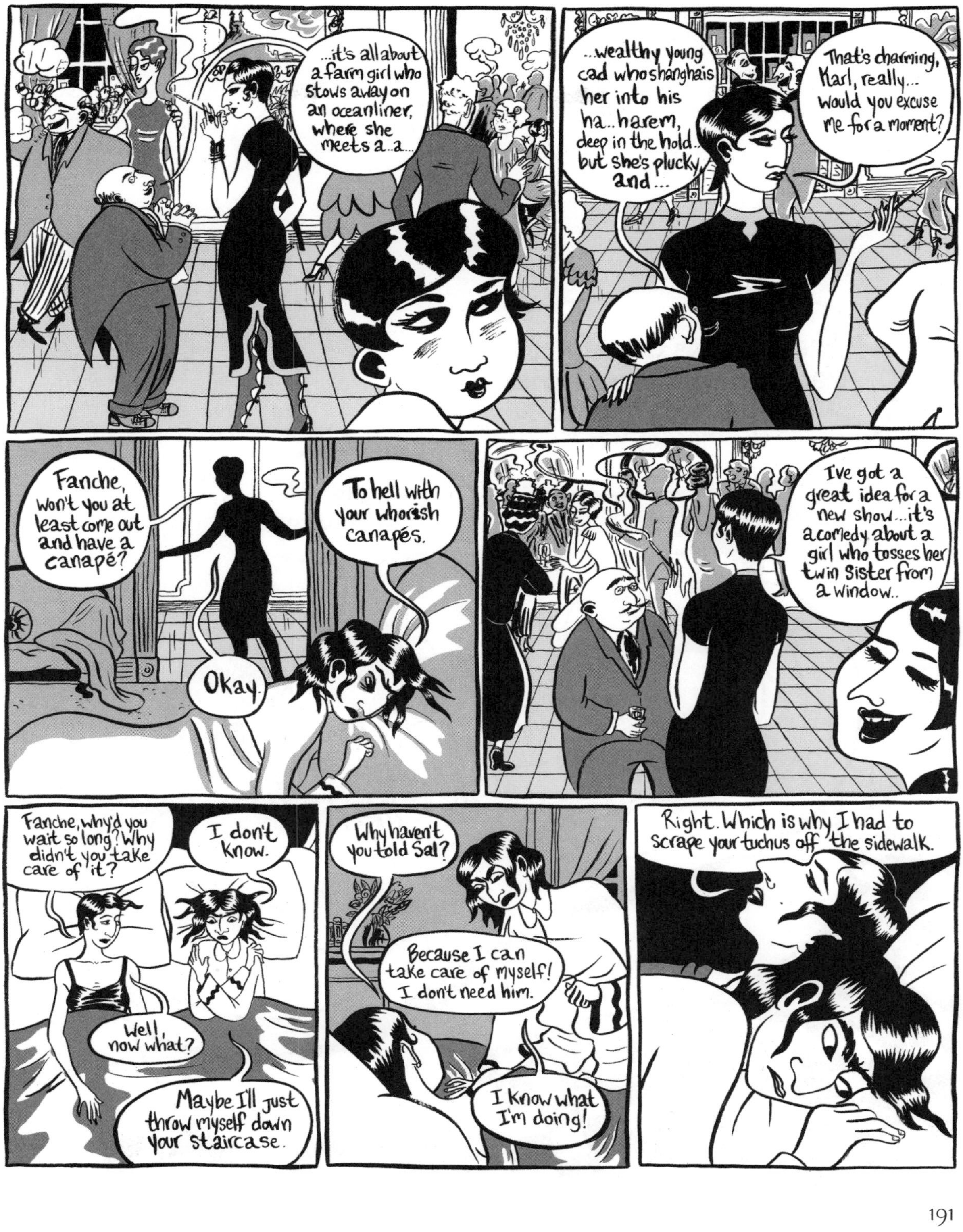
...it's all about a farm girl who stows away on an oceanliner, where she meets a...a...
...wealthy young cad who shanghais her into his ha...harem, deep in the hold... but she's plucky, and...
That's charming, Karl, really... would you excuse me for a moment?
Fanche, won't you at least come out and have a canapé?
To hell with your whorish canapés.
Okay.
I've got a great idea for a new show...it's a comedy about a girl who tosses her twin sister from a window..
Fanche, why'd you wait so long? Why didn't you take care of it?
I don't know.
Well, now what?
Maybe I'll just throw myself down your staircase.
Why haven't you told Sal?
Because I can take care of myself! I don't need him.
I know what I'm doing!
Right. Which is why I had to scrape your tuchus off the sidewalk.

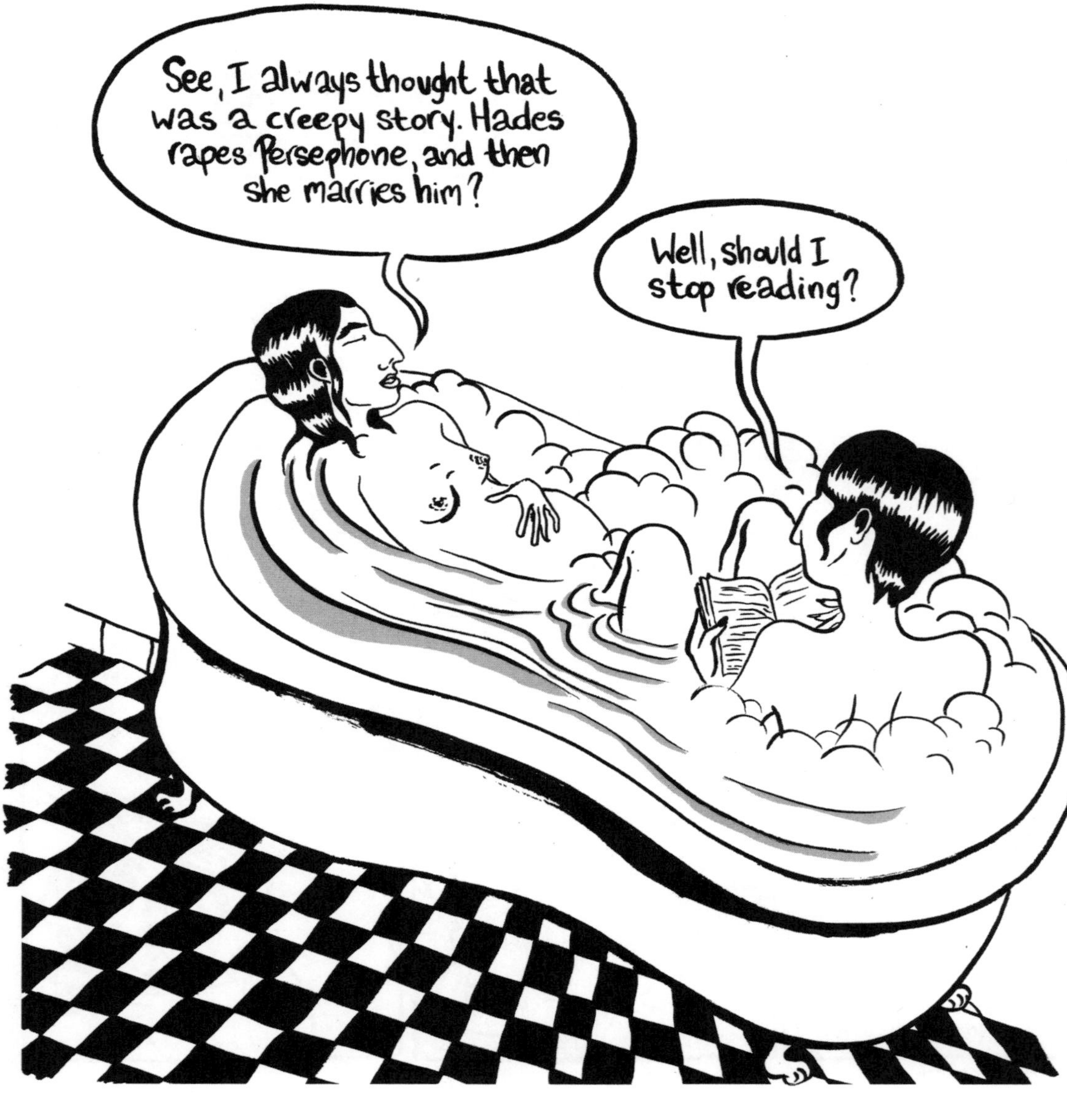
See, I always thought that was a creepy story. Hades rapes Persephone, and then she marries him?
Well, should I stop reading?

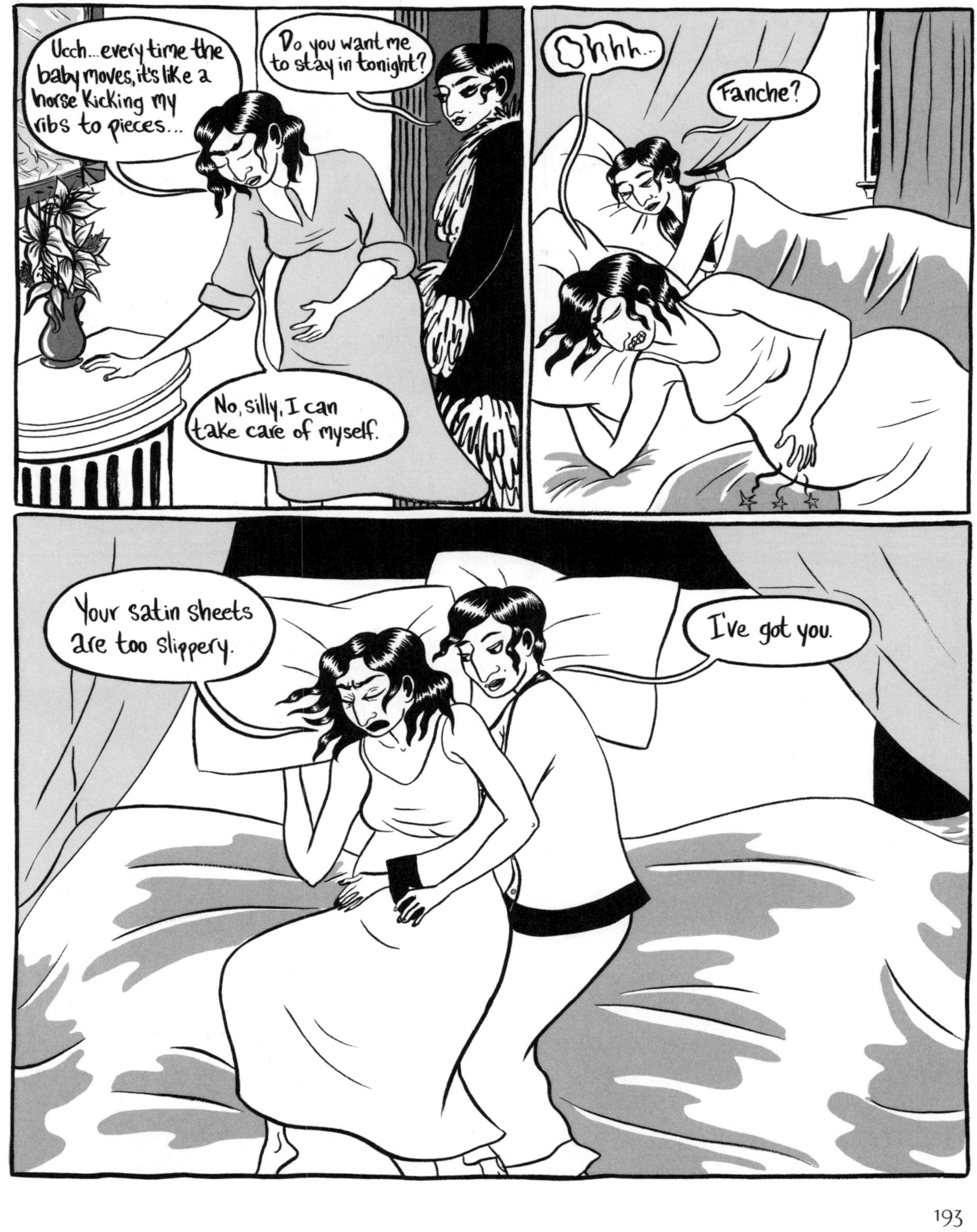
Ucch...every time the baby moves, it's like a horse kicking my ribs to pieces...
Do you want me to stay in tonight?
No, silly, I can take care of myself.
Ohhh...
Fanche?
Your satin sheets are too slippery.
I've got you.

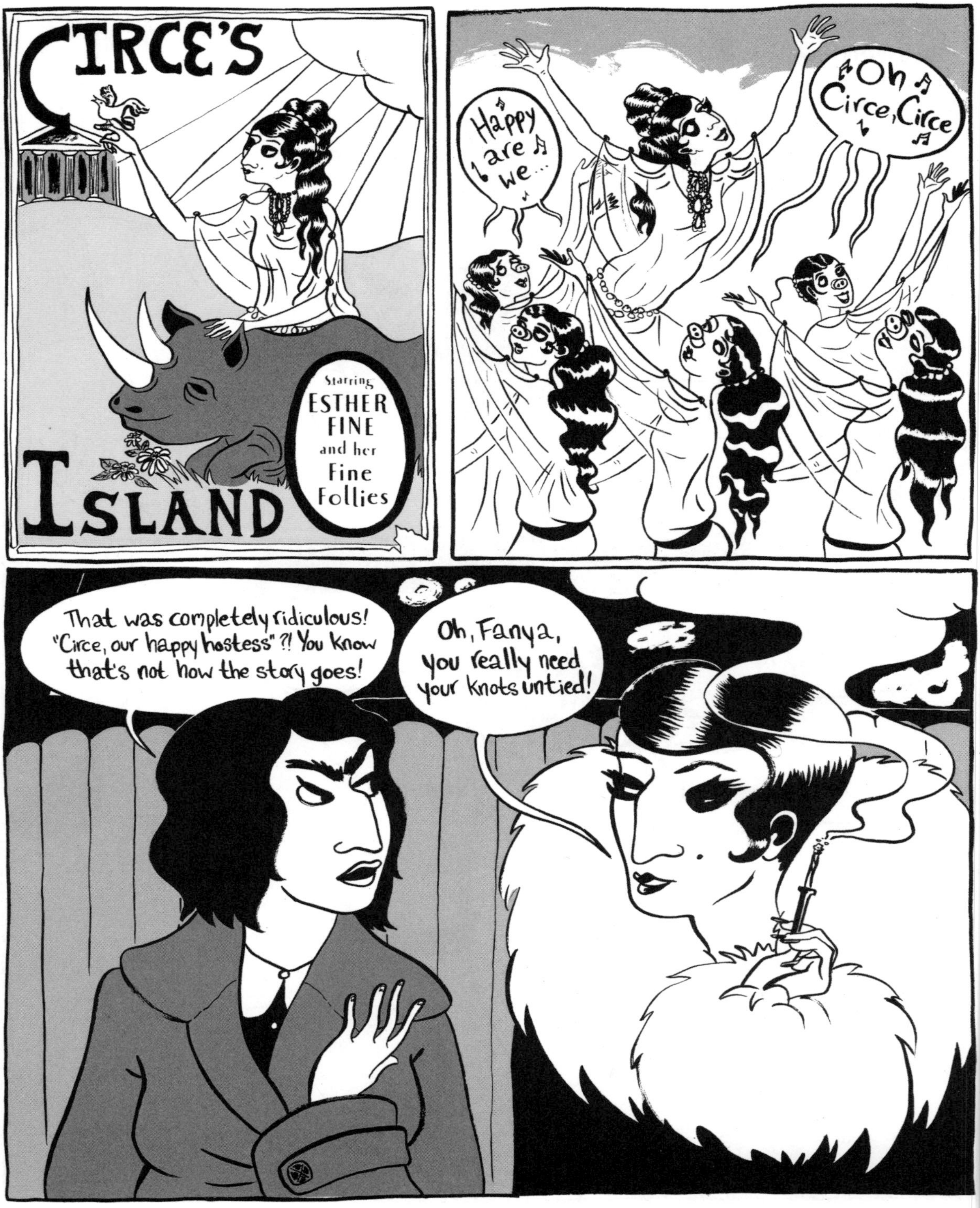
CIRCE'S ISLAND
Starring ESTHER FINE and her Fine Follies
Happy are we...
Oh Circe, Circe
That was completely ridiculous! "Circe, our happy hostess"?! You know that's not how the story goes!
Oh, Fanya, you really need your knots untied!

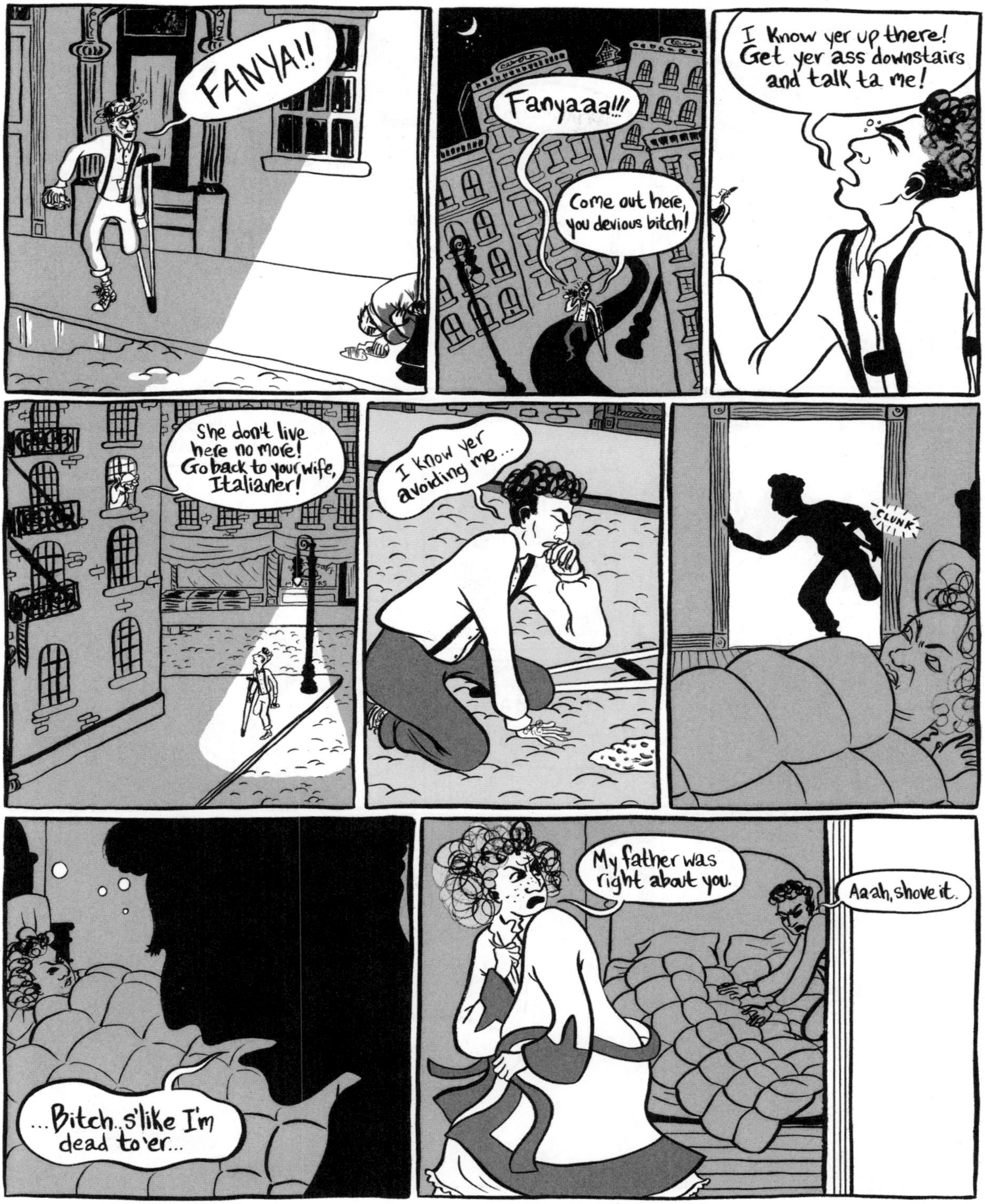
FANYA!!
Fanyaaa!!!
Come out here, you devious bitch!
I know yer up there! Get yer ass downstairs and talk ta me!
She don't live here no more! Go back to your wife, Italianer!
I know yer avoiding me...
CLUNK
...Bitch..s'like I'm dead to'er...
My father was right about you.
Aaah, shove it.

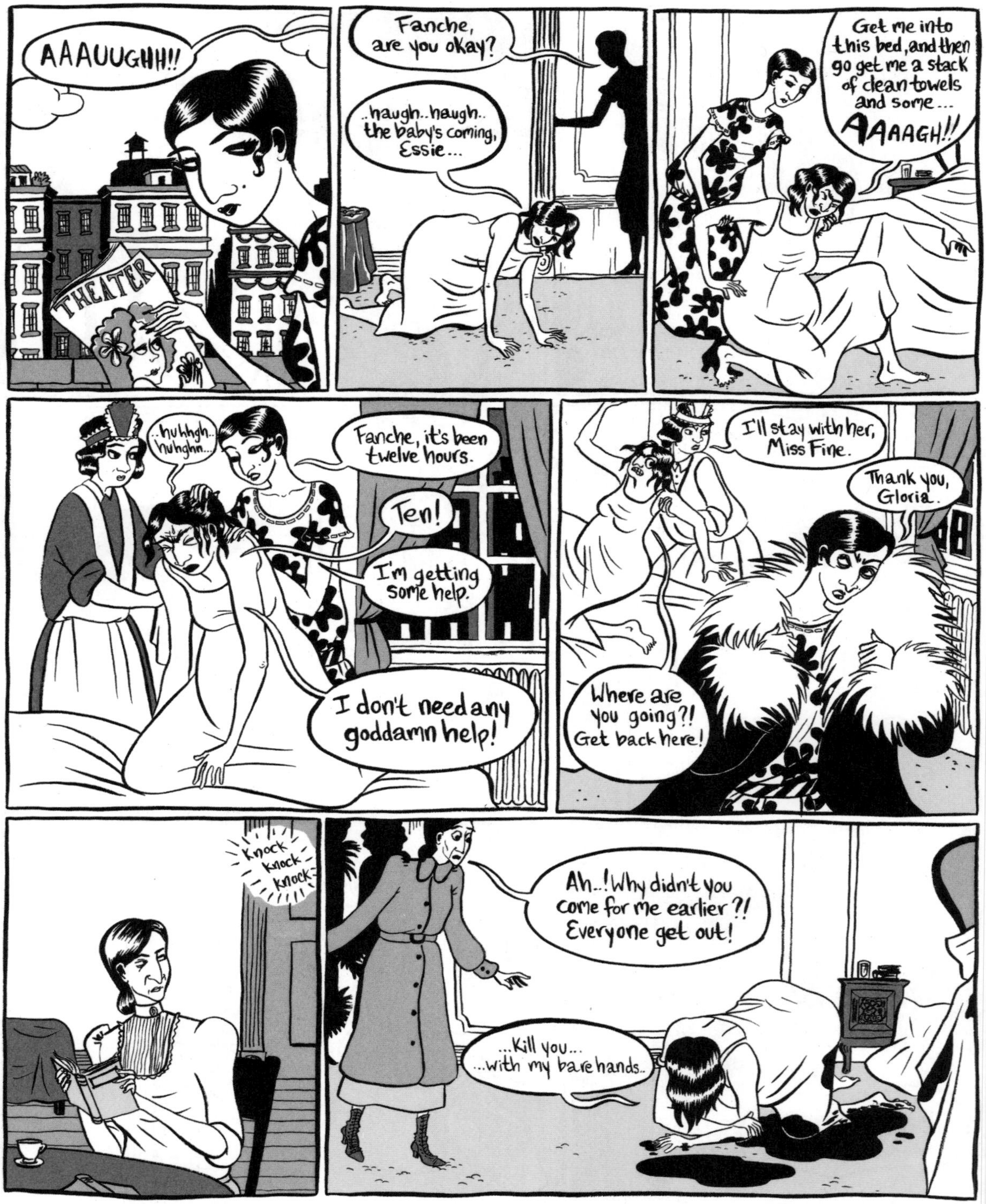
AAAUUGHH!!
THEATER
Fanche, are you okay?
..haugh..haugh.. the baby's coming, Essie...
Get me into this bed, and then go get me a stack of clean towels and some... AAAAGH!!
..huhhgh.. huhghn...
Fanche, it's been twelve hours.
Ten!
I'm getting some help.
I don't need any goddamn help!
I'll stay with her, Miss Fine.
Thank you, Gloria.
Where are you going?! Get back here!
Knock knock knock
Ah..! Why didn't you come for me earlier?! Everyone get out!
...Kill you... ...with my bare hands..

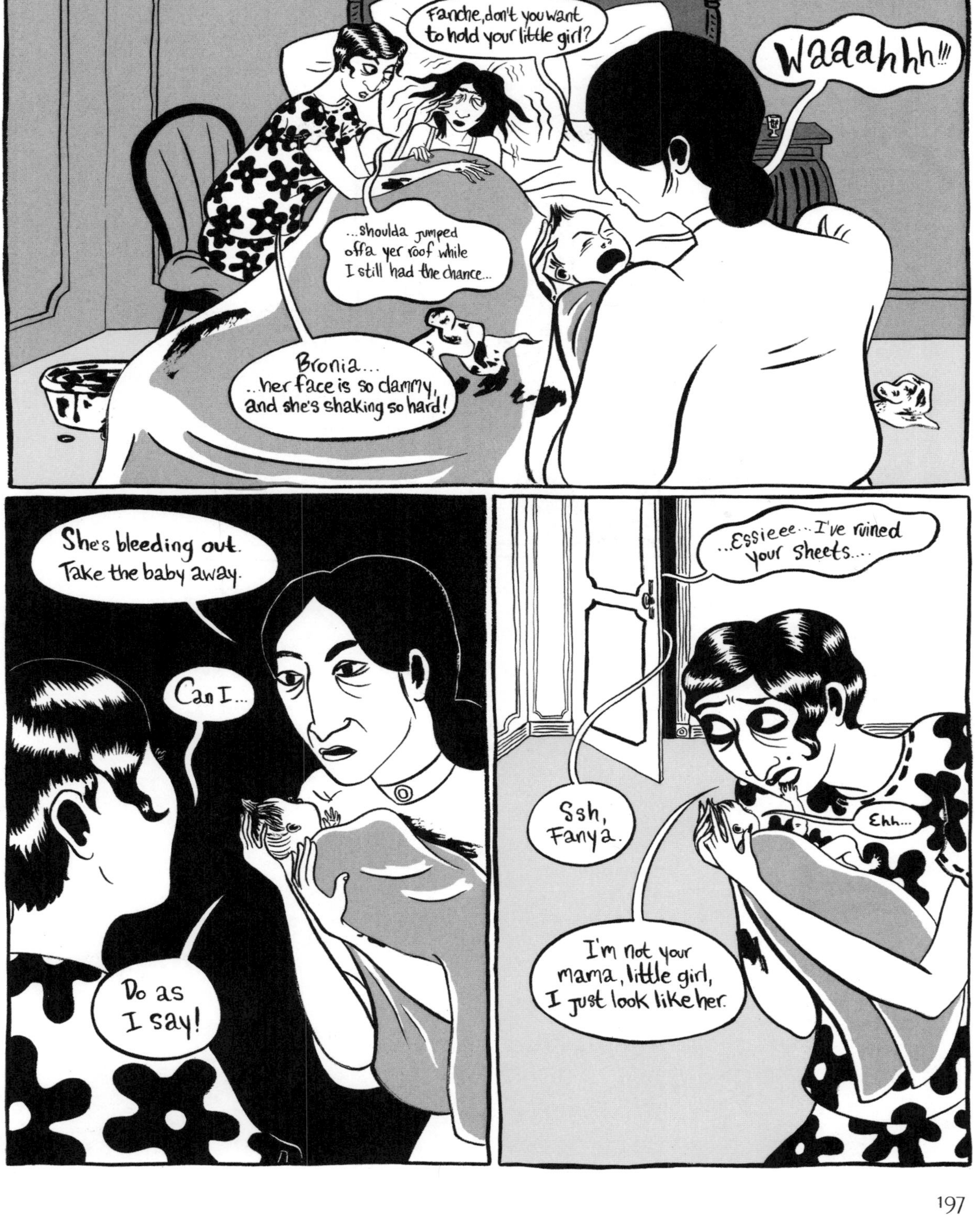
Fanche, don't you want to hold your little girl?
Waaahhh!!!
...shoulda jumped offa yer roof while I still had the chance...
Bronia... ...her face is so clammy, and she's shaking so hard!
She's bleeding out. Take the baby away.
Can I...
Do as I say!
...Essieee... I've ruined your sheets....
Ssh, Fanya.
Ehh...
I'm not your mama, little girl, I just look like her.

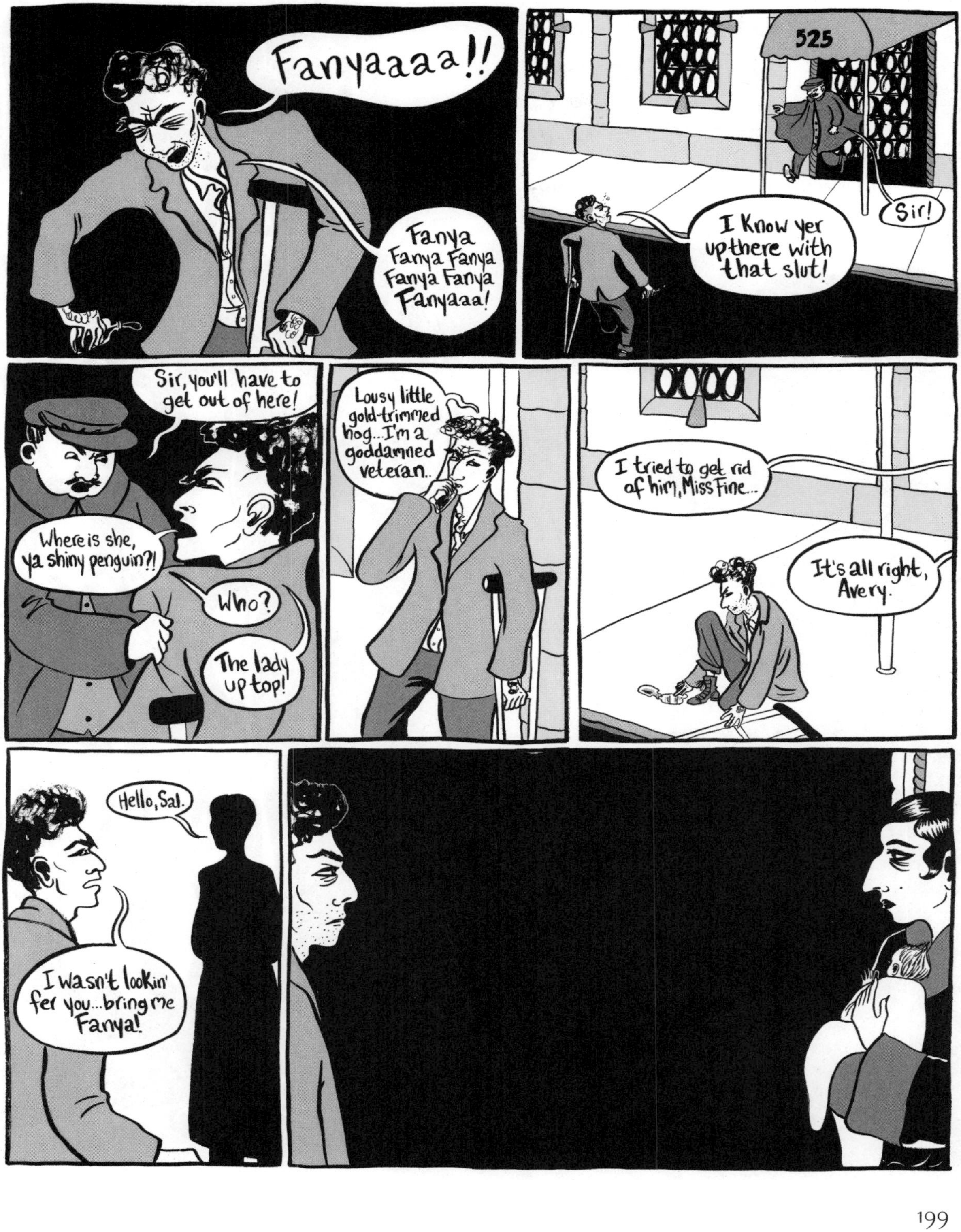
Fanyaaaa!!
Fanya Fanya Fanya Fanya Fanya Fanyaaa!
Sir!
I Know yer up there with that slut!
Sir, you'll have to get out of here!
Where is she, ya shiny penguin?!
Who?
The lady up top!
Lousy little gold-trimmed hog...I'm a goddamned veteran..
I tried to get rid of him, Miss Fine...
It's all right, Avery.
Hello, Sal.
I wasn't lookin' fer you...bring me Fanya!

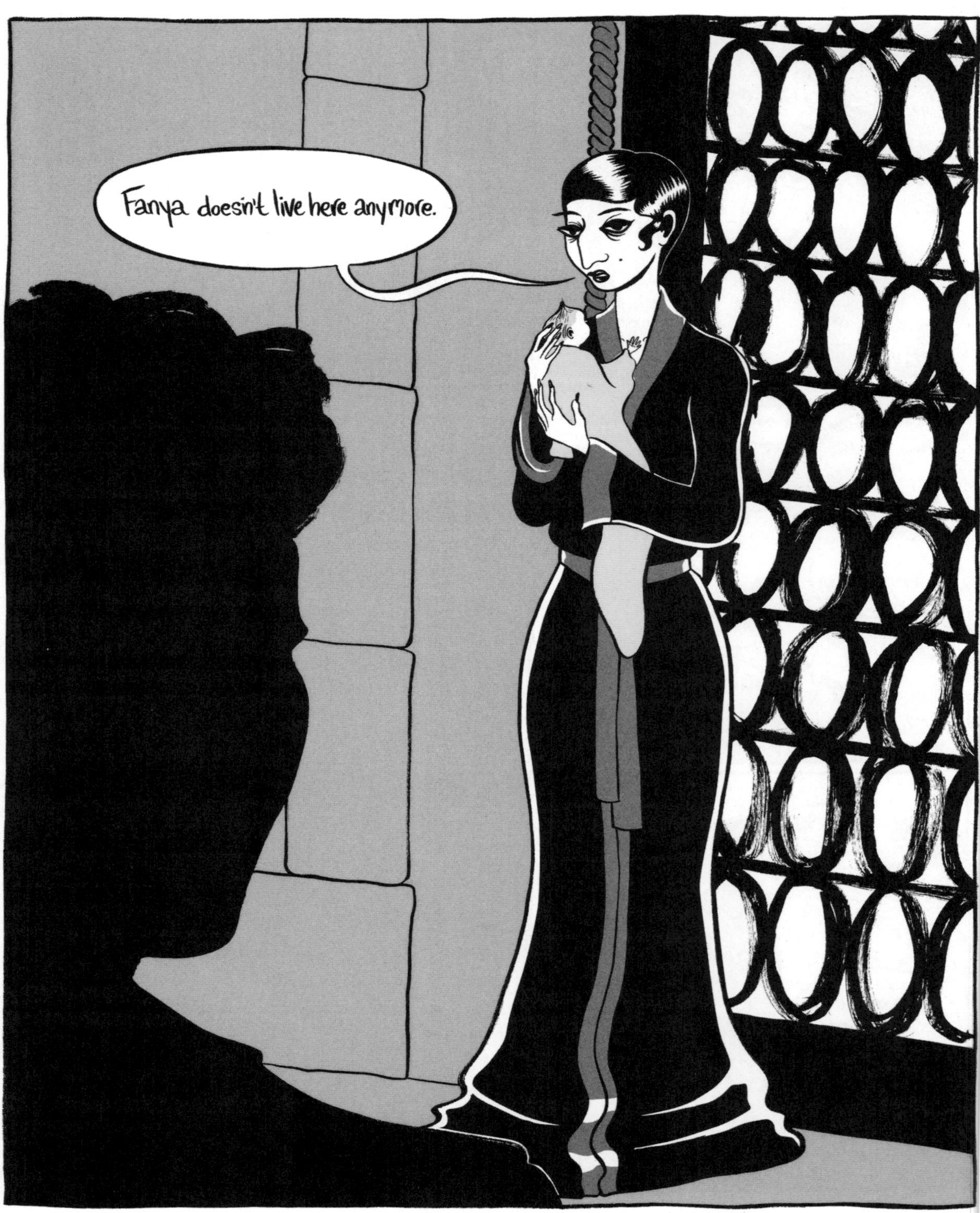
Fanya doesn't live here anymore.

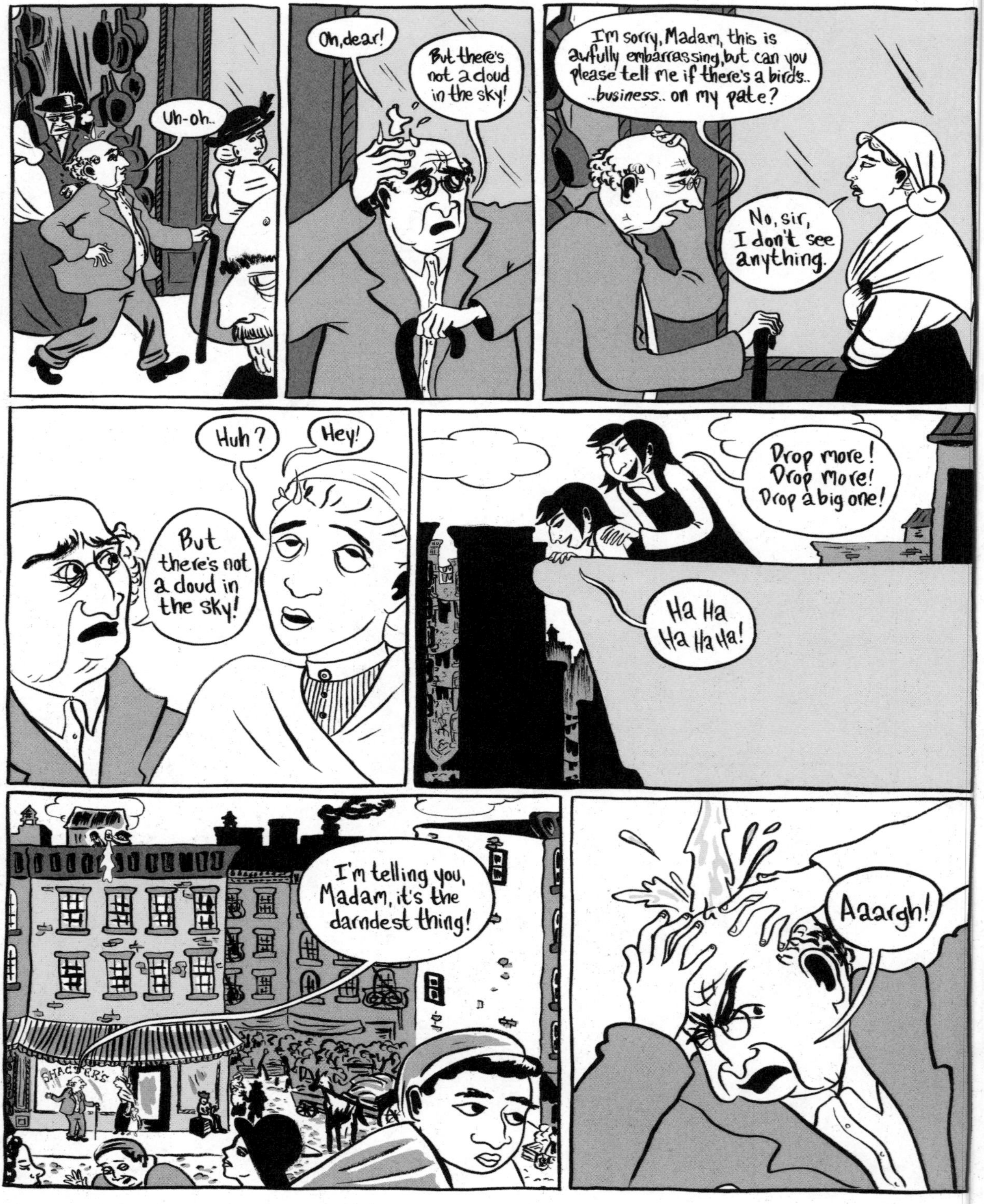
Uh-oh..
Oh, dear!
But there's not a cloud in the sky!
I'm sorry, Madam, this is awfully embarrassing, but can you please tell me if there's a bird's.. ..business.. on my pate?
No, sir, I don't see anything.
Huh?
Hey!
But there's not a cloud in the sky!
Drop more! Drop more! Drop a big one!
Ha Ha Ha Ha Ha!
I'm telling you, Madam, it's the darndest thing!
Aaargh!

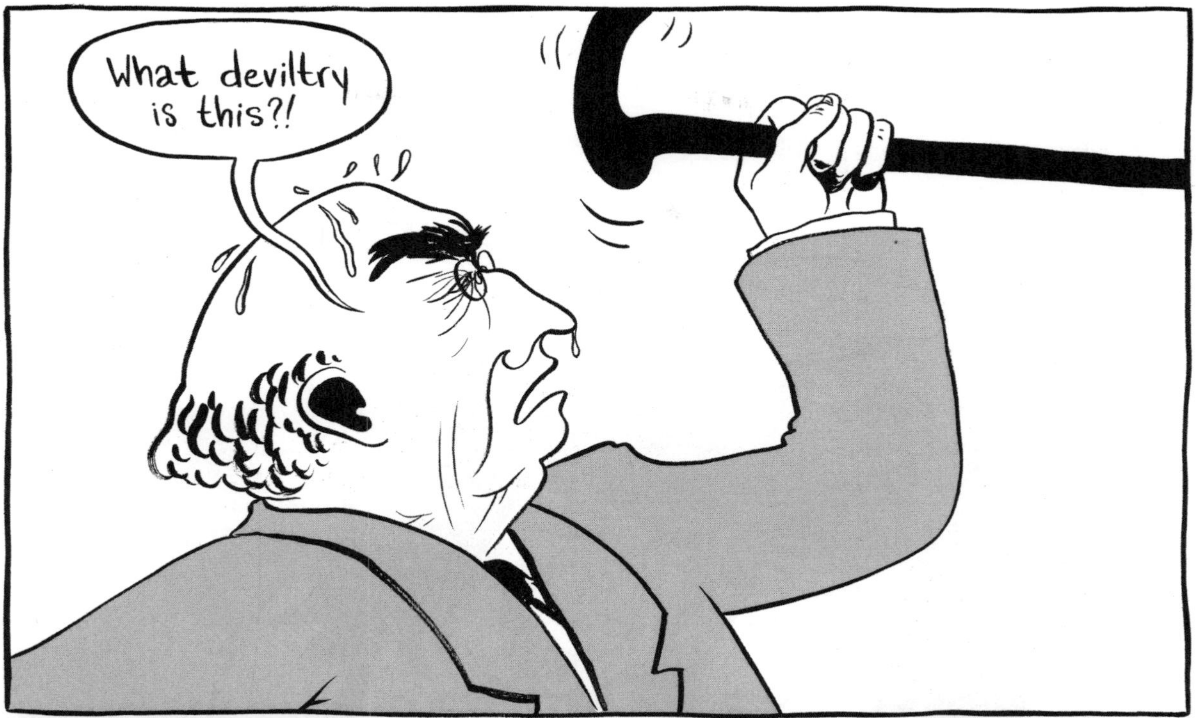
What deviltry is this?!

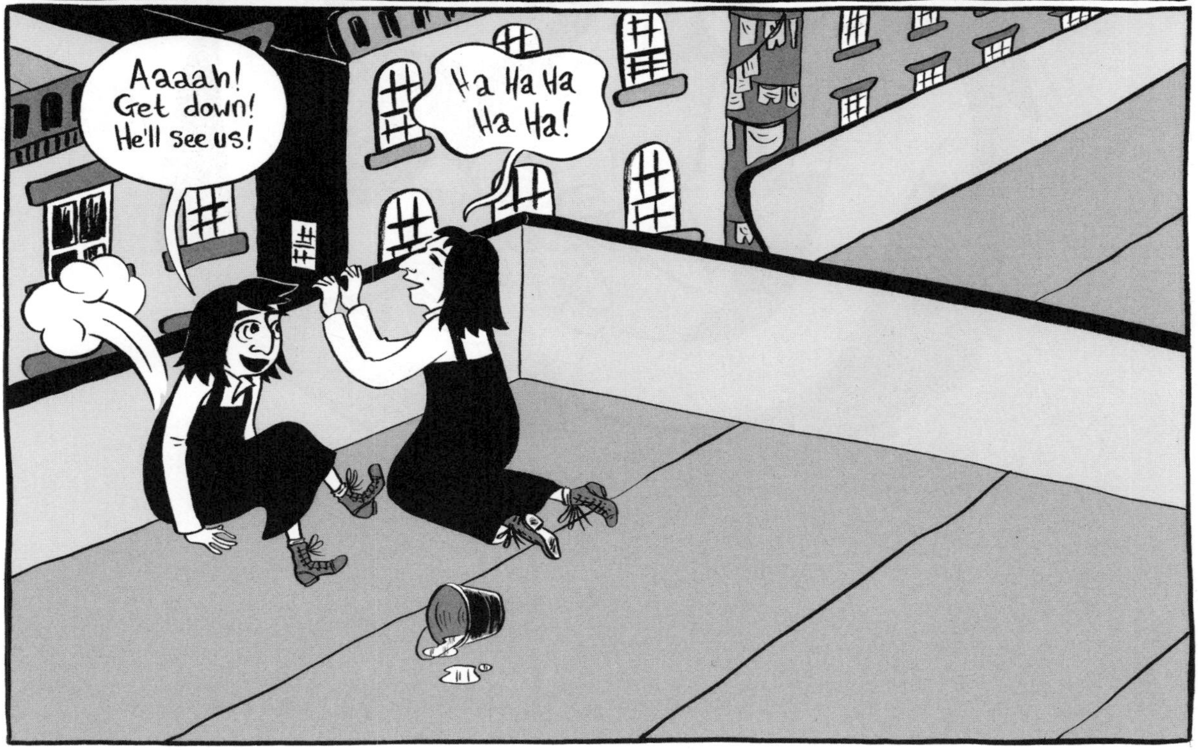
Aaaah! Get down! He'll see us!
Ha Ha Ha Ha Ha!

Acknowledgments

This book would not have been possible without the help of many people. I hope I'm not forgetting any of them here. They are, in no particular order: Riva Danzig, Tante Mimi Lerner, Uncle Marty Lerner, Lucie Weissbard, Laurenn McCubbin, The Center for Cartoon Studies, SVA, Keith Mayerson, David Hirmes, Marguerite Dabaie, Terry Brodner, Sally Cantirino, Michelle Mozes, Stephanie Mannheim, Kate Drwecka, Lauren Redniss, Alana Newhouse, Jeff Mason, Julia Arenson, Douglas Wolk, Nick Bertozzi, Jason Little, Lauren Weinstein, Vanessa Davis, Diana Schutz, Montserrat Terrones, Serge Ewenczyk, Jean-Paul Jennequin, Craig Thompson, Megan Kelso (who gave Fanya her debut), Lilith magazine, Travis Fristoe and the Alachua County Library District, Bob Sikoryak, the Museum at Eldridge Street, the Lower East Side Tenement Museum, Cora "Cupcake" Higgins for teaching me the circus music, Heeb magazine, the late, lamented 2nd St. Bakery, where half this book was written, Jeff Newelt, Josefine Kals, my fantastic editor Altie Karper, my amazing agent Elizabeth Wales, uber-designer Peter Mendelsund, Gene, Lizette, and David Corman, and my husband Tom Hart, the most efficient and excellent support system a person could ask for. And finally, thanks beyond words to the countless ghosts of the disappeared past, the world before this one, among whom dwell my grandmother Ann, who taught me how to swear in Yiddish and made the best pierogn, and my grandfather Mendl, the original (and far more successful) Isaac Feinberg.

Leela Corman is a native New Yorker, cartoonist, illustrator, and performer and instructor of Middle Eastern dance. She lives in Gainesville, Florida, with her husband, cartoonist and educator Tom Hart.

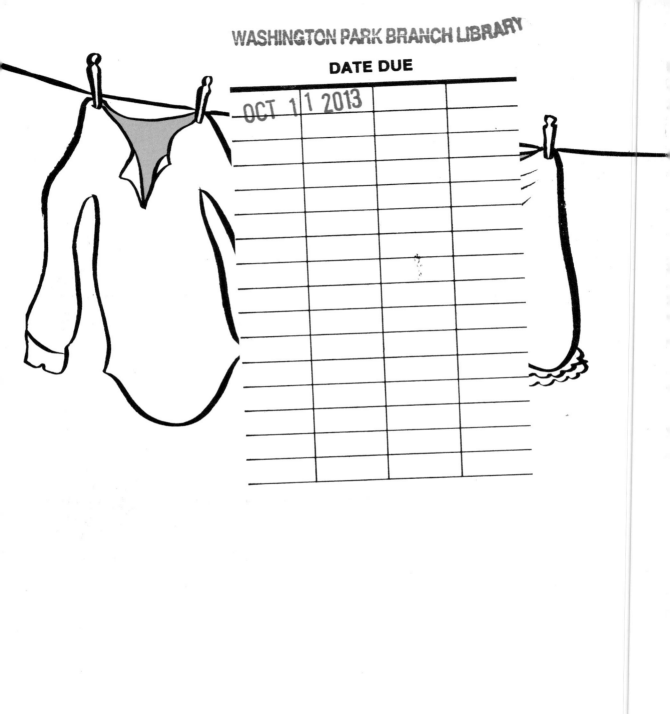

DATE DUE

OCT 11 2013			